WA 1206794 6

Accounting for Hospitality, Touris _ e _ re

second edition

Gareth Owen

Longman

D0543352

Pearson Education Limited
Edinburgh Gate
Harlow,
Essex CM20 2JE
United Kingdom
and Associated Companies throughout the world

© Gareth Owen 1994, 1998

The right of Gareth Owen to be identified
as author of this Work has been asserted by
him in accordance with the Copyright,
Designs and Patents Act 1988.

All rights reserved; no part of this publication may be
reproduced, stored in a retrieval system, or transmitted
in any form or by any means, electronic, mechanical,
photocopying, recording, or otherwise without either
the prior written permission of the Publishers or a
licence permitting restricted copying in the United
Kingdom issued by the Copyright Licensing Agency
Ltd., 90 Tottenham Court Road, London W1P 9HE.

First published 1994
Second impression 1995
Third impression 1996
This edition 1998
Second impression 1999

ISBN   0 582 31295 7

Visit Addison Wesley Longman on the world-wide web at
http://www.awl-he.com

British Library Cataloguing-in-Publication Data

A catalogue record for this book is available from the British Library

Set by 35 in 10/12pt Sabon
Printed in Malaysia, VVP

Learning Resources
Centre

1206794 6

CONTENTS

PREFACE

A modern and effectively working economy should afford opportunities for as many people as possible to meaningfully contribute to the wealth created in a variety of ways, and must not rely too heavily on one group of people while underutilizing or excluding others.

As far as possible, all those involved should be adequately and fairly rewarded for their efforts. The form of the reward should be an optimal combination of financial compensation and adequate leisure time. All too often, national and regional economies develop through becoming overdependent on a core of full-time middle-aged professionals who are overworked and arguably overpaid, supported by a large periphery of part-time and temporary workers made up to a great extent by women, ethnic minorities, significant groups of young people, and even by some people who have already retired from a full-time job.

The danger of this type of demography in the labour market is that those who contribute most have the means but not the time to benefit from leisure opportunities, whereas those who are underutilized may have the time but not the economic means to benefit from the leisure opportunities available to them.

Particularly worrying for the well-being of the leisure industry is the 'double whammy' effect of young people having their leisure time significantly eroded through having to work for low rates of pay to supplement both their personal living expenses and to meet the cost of higher education, the financial burden of which is being put ever more heavily on their shoulders. At the same time, many find that they do not do justice to their educational aspirations, and may not properly benefit from the process for which they have been making these sacrifices.

It is important that the demographic balance in the labour market is altered to some extent, ensuring that those contributing to the economy share the burden more evenly in terms of hours and effort required at the workplace, the levels of remuneration received, and in the amount of leisure time given. If all those factors move into closer harmony, all members of society will have the time and means to enjoy their leisure activities, both as individuals and as families. This provides the sustaining benefits which will be reflected in increased levels of productivity at work and which should then lead to further improvements in the working and leisure conditions of those involved, to the benefit of all in society.

ABOUT THE BOOK

The second edition of this book is aimed at those students who are following or intending to follow programmes of study in any part of the hospitality, tourism and leisure (HTL) sector, and who will be taught accountancy as part of their studies. The book assumes no prior knowledge of accounting, and builds up ideas and principles accordingly.

The book is aimed primarily at BTEC–HND/HNC programmes, HCIMA professional qualifications (Module D4), and at all degree students studying in this area.

Its content recognizes that many programmes in HTL include financial modules which cover both financial accounting, and cost and management accounting. As teaching resources and student incomes get ever tighter, institutions need to become more efficient at providing their programmes and students need to make the best use of their limited funds for study materials. This book is intended to make a contribution in this regard. Firstly, from the student's point of view, this book can be used on most foundation-level accounting modules, whether they cover financial, cost or management accounting. From the teaching institution's perspective, the book is structured to cover financial or cost and management accounting in one single module or semester, or to cover the whole foundation accounting syllabus over a double module in one academic session. In addition, as teaching institutions modularize more extensively, delivering mass lectures in the core business subjects, the need increases for specialist books to provide the additional learning support in those areas, for students studying within vocational courses.

Introduction

The introduction explains the motivation for exchange originating from a hierarchy of human needs. It introduces the types of economic unit within a private enterprise or mixed economy, and the nature of financial transactions that take place between them, describing briefly the relationship between demand and supply within the context of a product or service life cycle. The importance of the service sector to an economy, particularly the tourism, leisure and hospitality industries is highlighted, and finally the role of the accountancy function is explained as it applies to the tourism, leisure and hospitality industries, and within the overall requirements of financial record keeping and decision taking within business as a whole.

Part 1: Financial accounting and external reporting

Part 1 of the book concentrates on the recording and reporting of financial transactions, both for internal records, but also for external financial reporting. This part includes all the main areas of record keeping for financial accounting, and how to prepare the reports of a variety of business organizations, from the sole trader, to leisure and recreational clubs, through to organizations in multiple ownership, such as partnerships and limited companies. This second edition has also incorporated chapters on VAT, PAYE and NI, recognizing the need for people in all types of business to deal with these practical aspects of record keeping.

Part 2: Management accounting and internal reporting

Part 2 of the book examines the ways in which internally generated information is recorded and reported for management decision making, and how these records and reports can be used to improve or maximize the profitability of organizations for their shareholders. The second part of the text is therefore about providing the information to efficiently manage the future activities of the firm in financial terms.

Part 3: Financial assessment and analysis

The final part of the book instructs the student in the assessment and analysis of financial performance and status. This assessment is measured in terms of the profitability, efficiency, stability, vulnerability and productivity of businesses, using a wide range of relevant techniques, and considers their strengths and weaknesses. The second edition has a new chapter on spreadsheet modelling as a tool for analysing and assessing business problems and opportunities within the context of the HTL sector.

OVERALL AIM

My aim is to provide a clearly written and logically structured basic accounting textbook for the financial units of all types of hospitality, tourism and leisure (HTL) programmes offered at the National/Higher National Diploma/Certificate level, and for the first level of a degree in the HTL area.

The text describes the fundamental principles of financial and cost and management accounting that would be relevant and useful to the types of organization which HTL graduates could join or form. Additionally the text aims to instruct students, where relevant, in the specific techniques and systems pertinent to the HTL industry.

LEARNING OBJECTIVES

1 To understand the fundamental purposes of financial and cost and management accounting.
2 To formally record transactions and report on financial performance and position adhering to the fundamental concepts of accounting.
3 To be able to plan, prepare and use financial information to assist in effective business management and decision making.
4 To be able to assess and analyse business profitability, liquidity, productivity and vulnerability in a variety of ways.
5 To be able to use spreadsheet models within business situations with a view to solving problems and making the most of opportunities, using sensitivity analysis.

DISTINCTIVE FEATURES

Comprehensive coverage of accounting

Increasingly, as higher education establishments face pressure on resources, accountancy taught on non-accounting programmes is being taught as one single subject, and weekly teaching hours are being curtailed. This has created the need for a textbook to cover the whole HTL sector, both financial and cost and management accounting, and which can be used as a basis for two single modules or one double module.

Principles and concepts explained simply

The style and content of the text emphasizes the fundamentals of accounting, both financial accounting and cost and management accounting. Technicalities are avoided where basic principles can be successfully explained without them.

The teaching of double-entry bookkeeping in the financial accounting part of the book is carried out using the positive/negative notation, in order to make the system easier to learn, but also to lend it more easily to computer spreadsheet modelling, which is covered in the final chapter. However, the method adopted is in no way a departure from Pacioli's original and enduring system, and is simply an alternative way of presenting the same logic. This method tends to avoid the problems that many students have with the traditional double-entry system in the early stages, with its old-fashioned terminology. It is more effective with students that have no experience of the traditional method, which is likely to be the case for students using this book.

During the early stages of a course, it is important that lecturers should adopt the method used in the book; this minimizes confusion between their method of explanation and the book's method. Lecturers should explain clearly to their students that alternative methods are possible within the double-entry system, but the principles involved are essentially the same. In this way it is possible for students to read other books adopting the traditional methodology, recognizing the approach taken as simply another way of presenting the identical system.

Many examples

Although finance is a largely theoretical subject which applies broadly to a range of business sectors, this text allows the student to understand concepts, principles and techniques applied in an HTL context through the use of appropriately selected examples. Each chapter follows through the theory in a specific HTL situation, so the students see the relevance of what they are learning, in relation to their chosen specialisms.

Service sector context

The emphasis of the text is on the service sector as far as possible, so areas such as manufacturing accounts and complex product and process costing techniques are not included. But areas often ignored by traditional texts, such as accounting for VAT and employee remuneration, are explained and demonstrated. Also included are techniques for cash handling such as ticket systems, currency exchange systems and petty cash systems.

Chapters signposted and highlighted

Each chapter begins with its stated objectives and ends with a summary of the concepts that were covered.

Formative and summative assessment

There are in total 179 questions and suggested answers, devised and adapted from the author's own teaching material. At the end of each chapter are two assessment sections. A selection of five multiple-choice questions covers the breadth of material in the chapter. And four comprehensive exercises, set around HTL business situations, assess the understanding of key concepts and principles introduced in the chapter. Chapter 19 contains ten multiple-choice questions and five exercises. Answers (which include full explanations and workings) to the multiple-choice questions are situated at the back of the text.

At the end of Parts 1 and 2, the students can be assessed summatively through two integrative case studies. The case studies incorporate most of the main learning areas in each of the first two parts of the book, and will help the lecturer to assess the students' understanding of that work in an integrated and holistic context. The case studies include case notes, indicating the learning areas covered and a suggested approach. Fully worked suggested answers are given at the back of the text.

This second edition contains a new chapter of summative workshop exercises using spreadsheet models. The objective is to allow the students to build their own spreadsheet models within the context of various HTL accounting scenarios, integrating knowledge acquired in the book. The eight workshop tasks aim to cover the main accounting techniques explained within the text in a practical and useful way, vividly demonstrating the power and flexibility of the spreadsheet as a tool in accountancy.

ACKNOWLEDGEMENTS

Although the original book and this second edition have been based upon my own approach to accounting education at this level, I have benefited greatly from the knowledge I have acquired from the combined experience and critical wisdom of colleagues over eleven years while teaching and learning at the Swansea Institute of Higher Education, and from the inspiration provided by colleagues elsewhere, whose approaches to accounting instruction and assessment techniques continually help to add to a deeper and better understanding of this subject.

In particular, I wish to mention Roy Staley, David Trenberth and Owen Lewis, my closest colleagues on the BA (Hons) degree in accounting, who as cohabitants of our office have always found the time and patience to listen to my ideas and approaches, and to challenge them constructively when appropriate. I also wish to acknowledge a retired colleague, Bryan Goss, who originally opened my eyes to the world of computer spreadsheets in the mid 1980s, and for giving me a whistle-stop tour of possibly all the old packages ever to be launched in the mid 1980s until the early 1990s, which have at the same time created and saved hundreds of hours of work.

I also wish to thank Ian Little, the editor at Longman, for conveying to me his enthusiasm about the original book, for letting me have access to feedback from readers, which was mostly encouraging and positive, and for encouraging me to prepare this second edition. I appreciate the faith which Longman have in this title, and hope that in some way it vindicates the investment that I and the publishers have put into the book to date.

Finally, I would like to thank my wife, Julie, for her continuing support during the completion of the second edition, after I had faithfully promised her that I would never again need to spend countless hours of our leisure time staring at a VDU!

Needs, value and exchange

NEEDS AND WANTS

People, like all other living things have needs that must be satisfied in order to survive. Oxygen, food, water, warmth and shelter are essential to life. Beyond these absolutely fundamental needs are those of a higher order such as love and friendship, self-expression and self-esteem along with physical, intellectual and spiritual fulfilment (Fig. 0.1).

These human needs may be expressed as a diverse and intricate web of wants. Wants are the expression of needs in specific terms. For example, a tired and run-down person **needs** a rest and a boost to morale, but may **want** to go on holiday and stay in a luxury hotel, in order to satisfy those needs.

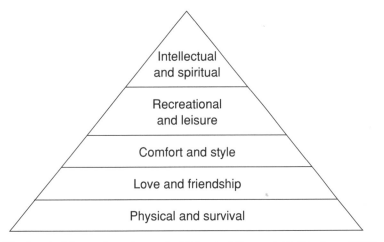

Figure 0.1 Maslow's hierarchy of needs (Adapted from A.H. Maslow, 1954, *Motivation and Personality*, Harper, New York)

EXCHANGE AND MONEY

No man is an island. If he were, or if he were marooned, his basic needs would have to be self-provided. Clearly the range and sophistication of his wants would be extremely limited or would remain largely unsatisfied, and his existence would be primitive indeed.

Individuals and even communities are limited in terms of the wants they can satisfy for themselves. If the necessary lines of communication and distribution exist, exchange allows a greater range of wants to be met. Exchange takes place between two parties. One party agrees to give up a valued product or service for a different product or service which they believe confers a greater benefit or **utility** than the product which they gave up.

Both parties must benefit from exchange or there would not exist the motivation for them both to enter into a voluntary agreement. The outcome of exchange is a transaction, which is the confirmation of exchange. The transaction would be the culmination of the exchange process where the undertaking to exchange would be formally confirmed, either by physically exchanging items of value, or by agreeing to do so at a specific time in the future. In a primitive economic system this would involve swapping objects or services of equivalent value, known as barter. Exchange becomes a much more widespread, versatile and beneficial activity if a common unit of value is used as a medium for this exchange. This is why barter was very soon replaced by monetary exchange, where a valuable commodity could represent consistently the value of what was being exchanged by all parties, and it could be held in store until required.

THE ECONOMIC SYSTEM

A sophisticated modern economy produces a wide range of products and services in order to satisfy the needs of individuals and organizations. The demanders and suppliers of these 'products' are known as economic units; they can be classified broadly as households, firms and government, but they are staffed and controlled by key individuals (Fig. 0.2).

In a private enterprise, or even in a mixed economic system, transactions take place between these economic units on the basis of choices constrained within economic means (disposable income). There are few, if any, explicit barriers or inducements to most transactions. Essentially these economic units supply goods and services to satisfy each other's needs in exchange for monetary value.

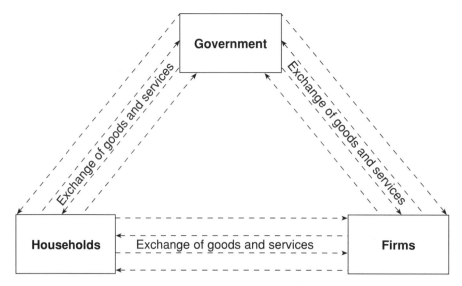

Figure 0.2 A simple model of a mixed economic system

SUPPLY AND DEMAND WITHIN THE HTL SECTOR

The monetary value or price of any good or service is determined by its availability in relation to the effective demand for it. The scarcer and more useful, the higher the price will be in most cases. In response, economic units will be motivated to produce or provide the goods or services that command the highest prices, and all other things being equal, they will yield the greatest profits. As more firms, who wish to share in the profits, add to the supplies of these products or services, the less scarce they become, and the less valuable they will be to potential consumers, so the price will fall in order to get rid of surplus stocks. This is certainly observed in many of the hospitality, tourism and leisure industries, as highly priced 'fashionable' products and services are bought by so-called innovators and opinion leaders, who are then swiftly followed by early then late adopters, and finally as supplies on the market are boosted by new entrants of the 'me too' variety and even by counterfeiters, prices will eventually fall dramatically, leaving 'laggards' to take up these surplus stocks.

At the point within the life cycle of a branded product or service, where suppliers are not making adequate profits, there will be a reduction in suppliers within the market, and the volume of supplies will begin to fall. With products or services for which there is an enduring need, both processes counterbalance one another, effectively maintaining an equilibrium between demand and supply. With products and services in the hospitality, tourism and leisure sector, the process may often continue until supplies are largely exhausted and most producers may have left the market; changes in the forces of supply and demand can be very volatile and unpredictable. These types of markets may even lay dormant, perhaps until reawakened by the renewed interest of nouveau innovators and opinion leaders.

THE SERVICE SECTOR

As an economy and its economic units create and share in greater and greater and wealth, individuals enjoy higher levels of disposable income. As incomes rise and more immediate needs are satisfied (Fig. 0.1), others such as recreational, intellectual and spiritual needs become more powerful. As these activities require leisure time, it is likely that more leisure time will be sought, either by seeking a reduction in the amount of hours worked, or by using spare time more actively in pursuit of their satisfaction. These needs are met largely by the service sector, through the provision of such amenities as hotels, cafes and restaurants; entertainments of all sorts; physical and sporting products and services; and hotels or other travel and tourism opportunities.

Since the 1960s and up to the late 1980s there has been a significant growth in the service sector at the expense of the primary and manufacturing sectors (Table 0.1).

Up to the late 1980s, large industries and firms have multiplied and grown very quickly within the service sector, satisfying the higher-order needs of individuals and households.

Tourism, leisure and hospitality in general has been a major growth area over the past twenty years, recently driving the expansion of the service sector, and it has been a significant generator of exports and a high earner of foreign currency.

Table 0.1 The sectoral shift in UK employment 1971–1995

Sector	Employees (%)		Percentage Change
	1971	1995	
Agriculture	2.0	2.0	nil
Energy and Water	5.0	2.0	−40
Manufacturing	41.0	28.0	−32
Construction	8.0	6.0	−25
Total services	44.0	62.0	**+41**

Source: *Social Trends 1995*

ACCOUNTING FOR ECONOMIC TRANSACTIONS

Within the economy as a whole, firms and the government as economic units engage in a very large volume of transactions, as compared with the individual household over the same period of time. The number, frequency and magnitude of these transactions requires that their financial consequences should be carefully recorded, processed and reported for the benefit of interested parties. Accountancy is the functional expertise required to ensure that the necessary financial and non-financial information is readily available in a form that potential decision makers can use to meet their objectives. Accountancy, like other functions, is required by all businesses and in all business sectors, but the range, variety and form of the information will vary. For example, the type of management accounting information within a business in the service sector will differ greatly from the information in a manufacturing organization. Even within the service sector there are a wide range of business organizations, including those in tourism, leisure and hospitality, which engage in different kinds of transactions, keep a variety of records, and which produce reports that reflect the specific type of business they conduct.

In the final analysis, accounting records and reports prepared by accountants must reflect these differences, but note that accounting information is eventually used for evaluation and as a basis for decision making. The decisions taken will normally be based on a motive to improve the financial performance and status of a business investment, wherever it may be. Therefore, the fundamental financial record-keeping, reporting and decision-making techniques, and the basic principles involved, will be relevant to all.

PART 1

Financial accounting and external reports

CHAPTER 1

Financial position

OBJECTIVES

- ● **Relate exchange with value.**
- ● **Define capital in economic and accountancy terms.**
- ● **Understand the idea of separate entity.**
- ● **Recognize the relationship between assets and liabilities.**
- ● **Identify types of assets and liabilities.**
- ● **Prepare a simple balance sheet from financial information.**

1.1 EXCHANGE AND VALUE

As explained in the introduction, exchange allows economic units within an economy to satisfy the various needs of the individuals within these units. Exchange should benefit the parties that engage in it or it wouldn't take place. Take two people, a boatman and a diver. They both know the offshore whereabouts of a treasure chest filled with a thousand Spanish doubloons and they both want to get hold of it. One owns a boat and fuel; the other has diving-gear and oxygen cylinders. They have no other possessions. Without each other's help they cannot obtain the treasure. Acquiring the treasure requires a means to get to it and a method of bringing it to the surface. Given that both parties know what each has to offer, and can communicate with each other, it would be possible for them to exchange with each other to their mutual benefit.

At the end of the exchange, a transaction might be struck where the contents of the chest were equally shared. The result of this transaction would be to increase the wealth of both parties by a chest full of doubloons between them, which may then be used to exchange with others who have valuable goods or services to offer.

This highly simplified situation introduces the concept of value, in that it is possible to say that the boat and the diving-gear together (assuming no alternative uses) are equivalent in value to the gold. Under these circumstances it is also true to say that neither the boat nor the diving-gear has any value on its own.

Without a medium of exchange, the complementary commodity offered by each party is valueless. If either party wanted to avail themself of the service potential within the other's commodity, each party would be prepared to promise the other up to half the gold in exchange for the use of that commodity. If we assume that the boatman is the only one with the expertise to both navigate and dive, and is willing to undertake the venture alone, he would be prepared to offer up to half the value of the treasure for the other's commodity. He would not offer exactly half, as the diver would be as well off as the boatman after the transaction, despite having made no physical or mental contribution to the venture. The difference between half the gold and the price offered by the boatman to the diver would be equivalent to the agreed value of the service or labour involved in the navigation of the boat and the retrieval of the gold. Let us say that they both agreed that the boatman would pay 400 doubloons to the diver for the use of her gear.

1.2 CAPITAL

Given that the gold coins can be thought of as a standard unit of value, we can say that if the boatman is prepared to dive instead of the diver, then he is worth 600 doubloons, or that his capital is 600 doubloons. We can therefore say that the capital of the diver is 400 doubloons. Capital can be defined as the value of a commodity and its service potential to an individual. This value is a financial expression of the potential capability of the commodity to be used to satisfy a person's needs.

Before the agreed transaction took place, the capital of each was represented by the commodity owned by each individual and by the associated service potential of each party in terms of their individual expertise. If the transaction had been an equal collaboration – the boatman navigated and the diver retrieved – then both would probably agree to split the gold equally between them. In this situation the value of each party's commodity and the associated service potential is 500 doubloons, so each party's capital would reflect this economic reality.

As the boatman effectively buys the diver's gear, not the diver's service, the capital of the boatman is 600 doubloons, and that of the diver is 400 doubloons. In effect, the diver is paying the boatman 100 doubloons for the service of navigating to the treasure and retrieving it.

How does the physical representation of the boatman's capital change after he retrieves the contents of the chest? As the boat and the diving equipment have no alternative use other than to retrieve the treasure chest, they are now useless and accordingly worth nothing, but the boatman is now in possession of 1,000 doubloons.

A number of fundamental concepts are raised by this illustration:

1 The wealth a person possesses in terms of valuable commodities can be defined as capital from that person's financial point of view.
2 Exchange adds value within an economy, and both parties will normally benefit.
3 A commodity only has value if it is useful in some way, i.e. if it can satisfy a need.
4 Provision of a service leads to value in exactly the same way as provision of a commodity.

1.3 FINANCIAL POSITION

The financial position of the boatman as he rows out to the site of the sunken chest will now be examined. His possessions comprise the boat, an engine, diving-gear and his expertise. What are they worth? This can be illustrated in the form of a financial statement, where Dbls = doubloons.

The boatman (financial position)

Possession	Dbls	Obligation	Dbls
Boat, outboard motor, gear, expertise	1,000	Owed to diver	400

The boat, outboard, diving-gear and expertise at this stage are worth 1,000 doubloons. This is because they can be used to retrieve the gold worth that amount. The difference between 1,000 and the 400 owed to the diver, i.e. 600, represents the value to the boatman of the boat, the outboard motor and the expertise at that moment. This is known to be the boatman's capital.

The financial position of the diver is as follows:

The diver (financial position)

Possession	Dbls	Obligation	Dbls
Owed from boatman	400	None	0

Although the diver currently possesses no valuable commodity, she does hold value in terms of a promise or a debt. The promise or debt represents the 400 doubloons that she will receive from the boatman at some future date. In financial terms it can be said that the diver is worth 400 doubloons. As she has no obligation or debt to any other party, this 400 doubloons represents her capital.

How has the financial position of the boatman changed after he has retrieved the treasure chest and arrived on shore?

The boatman (financial position)

Possession	Dbls	Obligation	Dbls
Boat, outboard motor, gear, expertise	0		
Doubloons	1,000	Owed to diver	400

As the boat, outboard motor, diving-gear and expertise have carried out their function – to bring the gold ashore – their usefulness has ceased, so they have no further economic value. Their value is now represented by the gold they have retrieved. The 400 doubloons is still owed to the diver, therefore the capital of the boatman remains unchanged, although its physical form has changed. Describing the financial position of the diver, it could be said that her financial position is unchanged, i.e. that she is still owed 400 doubloons, and that this represents her capital.

How has the financial position of the two parties changed after the gold has been shared out? Consider first the boatman's financial position:

The boatman (financial position)

Possession	Dbls	Obligation	Dbls
Doubloons	600	Owed to diver	0

Note that the number of doubloons held by the boatman is now only 600, as he has discharged his obligation of 400 doubloons to the diver. Although the value of his possessions has reduced, his overall capital, i.e the value attributable to him alone, has again remained unchanged at 600 doubloons.

Let us now look at the new financial position of the diver:

The diver (financial position)

Possession	Dbls	Obligation	Dbls
Owed from boatman	0	None	0
Doubloons	400		

Again the capital or value attributable to the diver has remained unchanged at 400 doubloons. However, the representation of that value has changed; a debt has become doubloons.

1.4 SEPARATE ENTITY

The diver and the boatman could be regarded as business owners instead of as individuals. The capital at each stage is the value within each business that represents the owner's stake in the business or the owner's **claim** on the business. Returning to the financial position of the boatman as he rowed out to the treasure:

The boatman's enterprise (financial position)

Possession	Dbls	Obligation	Dbls
Boat, outboard motor, gear, expertise	1,000	Owed to diver	400
		Owed to Owner	600
Total	1,000		1,000

Considering the boatman as distinct and separate from his business; the business itself can have possessions or own commodities. At the same time, those possessions can be represented by values attributable to a variety of sources. In this case the possessions – the boat, the outboard motor and the diving-gear along with the necessary expertise – are worth 1,000 doubloons, but this value is attributable to the diver, who is owed 400 doubloons, and to the owner, i.e. the boatman. What is owed to the owner is known as capital.

The concept of separate entity determines that, physically and financially, the business is thought of separately from the owner. If this is true, then in all cases the value of the business possessions is represented fully by the value owed to those who provided the value invested in those possessions, including the value invested by the owner.

In the above financial statement, the value of the commodities possessed by the business equals 1,000 doubloons, and the value of the obligations to those who have invested that value, also equals 1,000 doubloons.

1.5 ASSETS AND LIABILITIES

In financial terms, possession or ownership is represented in the form of **assets**. An asset is the generic term for the physical form of value invested in the business. Assets can take a variety of forms. In the earlier example, the boat, the outboard motor, the diving-gear and the contents of the treasure chest can be described as assets. They are physical things which can be seen and touched.

Are there any other assets in this illustration? The debt owed by the boatman to the diver is an asset, from the diver's business viewpoint. The debt is a promise to convey value in physical terms at a future date. The debt can be described as an asset because it represents value.

Liabilities are the opposite of assets. They are best thought of as 'general labels' associated with those assets. Liabilities describe how much of the total value embodied within the variety of owned assets has been invested and how. The total value of all assets is owed to a range of interested parties **outside** the business, perhaps in the form of obligations or debts of various kinds, including the obligation to the owner, i.e. the capital.

The relationship between the assets of a business and its liabilities can be described in the following way:

Assets = liabilities

Assets = capital + other liabilities

This relationship helps to identify the proportion of a business's value that is owed to the owner. This is achieved by adding together the values of all the assets then subtracting from the values owed to other parties **except the owner**:

Assets − other liabilities = capital

1.6 THE BALANCE SHEET

Assets and liabilities have been defined in broad terms, and the fundamental relationship between them has been established. By recognizing that all assets and liabilities should be described in monetary terms, a monetary statement of the financial position of a business can be compiled at any time. Different types of assets and liabilities will now be considered, and how they are presented in a statement of financial position.

Here is a list of values concerned with the owner of Topaz International Travel:

	Monetary value (£)
Offices	50,000
Flat above office (owner's private accommodation)	50,000
Minibus for airport shuttle	18,000
Business loan from bank	12,000
Cash in till	55
Monies owing from customers	65,000
Fixtures and fittings	20,000
Owner's personal vehicle	15,000
Mortgage on flat	10,000
Monies collected and owing to tour operators	54,000
HP owing on private vehicle	10,000
Supplies of brochures and stationery	2,500
Mortgage on offices	35,000
Business bank account	75,000

From these figures the **business** assets and liabilities can be identified. Or put another way, which of the above items are not business assets or liabilities?

	£
Flat	50,000
Mortgage on flat	10,000
Personal vehicle	15,000
HP on personal vehicle	10,000

The above items are the owner's personal assets and liabilities, and under the separate entity concept, they are in no way connected to the business. The rest of the items can be subdivided into business assets and liabilities:

Assets	£	Liabilities	£
Offices	50,000	Mortgage on offices	35,000
Fixtures and fittings	20,000	Business bank loan	12,000
Minibus	18,000	Monies owing to tour operators	54,000
Stationery, etc.	2,500		
Monies owing from customers	65,000		
Bank account	75,000		
Cash in till	55	Owner's capital	?
	230,555		230,555

Before calculating the owner's claim on the business, the essential mechanics of a travel agency should be explained. Broadly, a travel agent collects deposits and subsequent balances on booked holidays from customers on behalf of the principal, the tour operator. The travel agent then pays these monies over to the tour operator, retaining an agreed commission. At any time, the amount owed by the travel agent to the tour operator is the amount collected from customers but not yet paid to the tour operator, minus the travel agent's commission.

Back to the calculation of the owner's capital. The relevant equation is

Assets – other liabilities = capital

Other liabilities are £35,000 + £12,000 + £54,000 = £101,000, so the owner's capital is

£230,555 – £101,000 = £129,555

That is to say, the owner's claim on the business is £129,555.

As shown earlier, the owner had personal assets and liabilities as well as business assets and liabilities. As a distinction has been drawn between the owner's personal and business situations, the extent of the owner's personal wealth can now be calculated.

Owner's financial position (from owner's personal viewpoint)

Personal assets	£	Personal liabilities	£
Claim on business	129,555	Mortgage on flat	10,000
Flat	50,000	HP on car	10,000
Car	15,000		
		Balancing item	
		Personal wealth	174,555
	194,555		194,555

The owner's personal wealth can be established at £174,555.

The personal wealth comprises all the owner's personal assets less the owner's personal liabilities. Note that the assets include the owner's personal investment in his or her business. This is classified as an asset because in effect the business **owes** the owner £129,555. It is therefore a debt representing a value belonging to the owner in the same way as the 400 doubloons were owed to the diver in the earlier example.

1.7 TYPES OF ASSETS AND LIABILITIES

A business can have a whole array of assets and liabilities. It is important to subclassify them under various headings. Assets can be readily subdivided into assets that have relative permanence in the business, such as property, fixtures and vehicles. These assets can be described as the 'bones' of the business, and are known as **fixed assets**.

On the other hand, a business needs to operate on a day-to-day basis; it must produce and rotate goods, debts and cash in order to sustain itself. These types of assets are continually changing as transactions take place, and can be described as the 'muscles, blood and oxygen' of the company. They are formally known as **current assets**.

Returning to the Topaz International Travel business, a statement of affairs or **balance sheet** can be drawn up, showing all the types of business assets and liabilities and how they are described. Check these headings against the original list.

Topaz International Travel
Balance sheet as at December 31, 19x6

	£		£
Fixed assets		Capital	
Premises	50,000	Owners capital	129,555
Fixtures and fittings	20,000	Long-term liabilities	
Vehicles	18,000	Mortgage	35,000
Current assets		Current liabilities	
Stocks	2,500	Creditors	54,000
Debtors	65,000	Bank loan	12,000
Bank	75,000		
Cash	55		
Total assets	230,555	Total liabilities	230,555

The total assets are equal in value to the total liabilities. They have been classified under various subheadings. The assets are conventionally listed from the most fixed down to the most liquid, i.e. from premises to cash. The liabilities are listed from the most long-term, i.e. capital, through long-term loans, down to short-term obligations such as monies owed to suppliers of goods and services and bank overdrafts.

Three new terms have been introduced here. Stocks are the day-to-day commodities that the business either sells or uses in the course of its trade. Debtors are those who owe the business money. Creditors are those to whom the business owes money.

SUMMARY

1 **Exchange creates wealth.**

2 **Wealth in terms of the ownership of valuable commodities can be described as capital.**

3 **The physical existence of valuable commodities or specific rights to them can be described as assets.**

4 **The value invested in assets is owed by a business to external parties, including the owner. The allocation of this value can be described as the liabilities of the business.**

5 **Assets always equal liabilities; assets and liabilities are subdivided into various types.**

6 **The personal possessions and obligations of an individual are entirely separate from the assets and liabilities of a business, and they should be excluded from the balance sheet of a business owned by that individual.**

ASSESSMENT

MULTIPLE-CHOICE QUESTIONS

Question 1
Which of the following best explains exchange?

A A situation where money and commodities are involved
B A situation where someone acquires commodities that they value more by giving up commodities that they value less
C A situation where one person gains and the other loses
D A situation where both parties benefit equally

Question 2
Which of the following are the correct words to fill the gap in the following sentence? In financial terms capital is a measure representing the _____ of the total asset value of a business.

A obligation to lenders as a proportion
B obligation to the owner as a proportion
C fixed asset value as a proportion
D monetary value

Question 3
Given that A = total assets, C = owner's capital and L = liabilities, which of the following is **false**?

A $A - L = 0$ (when L includes owner's capital)
B $C + A = L + C$ (when L does not include owner's capital)
C $L = A - C$ (when L does not include owner's capital)
D $C - A = -L$ (when L does not include owner's capital)

Question 4
Which of these is a current asset?

A Capital
B Fixtures and fittings
C Stocks
D Creditors

Question 5
Select the odd one out.

A Mortgage on business premises
B Trade creditors
C Unpaid business electricity bill
D Bank overdraft on business bank account

EXERCISES

Exercise 1

Fill in the gaps in the following statements regarding a holiday hotel. Choose from fixed assets, current assets, long-term liabilities, current liabilities and owner's capital.

(a) The cash in the safe is included under _____
(b) The unpaid invoice to the suppliers of fresh food is included under _____
(c) The laundry equipment is included under _____
(d) The difference between the total value of the hotel and what is owed to lenders and suppliers is included under _____
(e) A returnable deposit on a booking paid by a potential guest is included under _____
(f) The bank overdraft is included under _____
(g) The drinks in the bar cellar are included under _____
(h) The ten-year mortgage on the land and buildings is included under _____

Exercise 2

At the end of a particular financial period, a restaurateur has lost all the invoices owing to suppliers of food and drink. But the rest of the balance sheet information is available:

	£
Capital invested	50,000
Fixed assets	120,000
Long-term loan	70,000
Stocks of food and drink	5,000
Bank overdraft	2,500

Required
What is the estimated value of the lost invoices?

Exercise 3

At the end of the first year of operations, a travel agent has the following assets and liabilities:

March 31	£
Bank balance (positive)	49,000 (including deposits)
Fixtures and fittings	45,000
Net amounts owing to tour operators	?
Owner's capital as at March 31	?

Other information

Deposits received on holidays booked	£20,000
Balances received on holidays booked	£80,000
Net amounts paid to tour operators in the period	£55,200
The agreed commission percentage retained is	8%

Required

(a) What is the net amount owing at the year-end to the tour operators?
(b) What is the travel agent's capital at the end of the first year of operations?

Exercise 4

The following is a list of assets and liabilities connected with the owner of a cycle-hire business, Mumbles Bike Rental

December 31	**£**
Mortgage on office	20,000
Bikes (20)	4,500
Spares (tyres, tubes, brakes, etc.)	800
Maintenance vehicle	6,500
HP on maintenance vehicle	3,000
Owner's personal vehicle	14,000
Outstanding amounts on bikes purchased	1,200
Bank loan on personal car	8,000
Owner's house	72,000
Mortgage on house	40,000
Hire fees owing from tour operator	200
Hiring office and storage area	30,000
Bank overdraft on business account	1,500

Required

(a) Calculate the financial position of Mumbles Bike Rental by preparing the balance sheet as at December 31.

(b) Calculate the personal wealth of the owner as at December 31, assuming the owner has no other possessions or obligations other than those listed above.

CHAPTER 2

Types of financial transaction

OBJECTIVES

- Record the effects of all transactions on the balance sheet.
- Recognize the dual aspect of transactions and the money measurement concept.
- Define *profit* in terms of its effect on the balance sheet.
- Differentiate between three types of expenditure.
- Identify eight generic types of transaction.

2.1 TRANSACTIONS AND THE BALANCE SHEET

Chapter 1 introduced the balance sheet as a statement of financial position. This chapter will confirm that the financial position of a business changes after each transaction but the equality of assets and liabilities is never violated.

The best way to see the effect of transactions on the balance sheet of a business is to set up an imaginary business from scratch and carefully record its first few transactions. Businesswoman Sue Venir sets up a gift and sweet shop in a popular holiday resort.

2.2 THE DUALITY OF TRANSACTIONS AND THE MONEY MEASUREMENT CONCEPT

The effect of ten transactions on the balance sheet of Sue Venir will now be recorded. Observe the dual aspect of the changes to the balance sheet after each day, and note that all changes are expressed in monetary terms.

Day 1: Sue transfers £35,000 from her private building society account into a business bank account with Redwood Bank

This transaction is where Sue as an an individual sets up the business as a separate entity. The business is thereafter considered as being entirely separate from its owner in accounting terms:

Sue Venir: balance sheet as at day 1

Assets	£	Liabilities	£
		Capital	35,000
Current assets			
Bank	35,000		
Total	35,000		35,000

This transaction creates the initial balance sheet. The business has in a bank account possessions amounting to £35,000. The value backing this asset is owed to the owner, Sue Venir. This claim that she has on the business is known as her capital.

Day 2: Sue pays £30,000 by cheque for a twenty-year lease on a small sales booth
This transaction involves an exchange of assets. She acquires a fixed asset, a leasehold property worth £30,000; but to obtain this asset, her bank asset is reduced by £30,000.

Sue Venir: balance sheet as at day 2

Assets	£	Liabilities	£
Fixed assets		Capital	35,000
Leasehold property	30,000		
Current assets			
Bank	5,000		
Total	35,000		35,000

Note that as the transaction only involved an equal exchange of assets, there was no overall change in the total assets. As assets must always equal liabilities, the capital remains unchanged. The exchange of assets involved the purchase of a fixed asset using current assets; this is an example of **capital expenditure** financed from existing resources.

Day 3: Sue buys £8,000 worth of stock on credit from Nicholas Nack
Sue's business increases its possessions by purchasing goods to sell – the stock. This time the business acquires a current asset by investment from outside. The investment is in the form of an obligation to Nicholas Nack, who has provided valuable commodities for which he has yet to be paid. And as long as the business owes value to him, Nicholas Nack is a trade creditor.

Sue Venir: balance sheet as at day 3

Assets	£	Liabilities	£
Fixed assets		Capital	35,000
Leasehold property	30,000		
Current assets		Current liabilities	
Stock	8,000	Creditors	8,000
Bank	5,000	(Nicholas Nack)	
Total	43,000		43,000

Note that as the stock was financed externally, i.e. by a creditor, the total asset side increases by £8,000. If assets increase by £8,000 then so must liabilities, to keep the equality.

The increase in liabilities is indicated by the inclusion of the creditors under current liabilities, showing that the business owes this amount to Nicholas Nack within a period of one year.

Day 4: Sue sells stock costing £1,000 for £1,500 cash
This transaction involves an unequal exchange of assets. A current asset is sold, stock costing £1,000. In return the business has acquired another current asset, £1,500 cash.

The result of this transaction is that the assets of the business have increased in overall terms. As this increase was internally generated, through trading, the transaction is **profitable**. This causes an increase in the capital owed to Sue.

Sue Venir: balance sheet as at day 4

Assets		£	Liabilities	£
Fixed assets			Capital	35,000
Leasehold property		30,000	Add profit (+500)	+500
Current assets			Current liabilities	
Stock	(−1,000)	7,000	Creditors	8,000
Bank		5,000		
Cash	(+1,500)	1,500		
Total		43,500		43,500

Note that there are three adjustments to be made after this transaction. Stock is reduced by £1,000 and cash is increased by £1,500. The overall increase in assets (profit) has to be added to the liabilities side in order to preserve equality. Therefore, the profit is added to capital, recognizing that the transaction has increased the value of the business which is owed to the owner.

Day 5: Sue pays her assistant £100 cash
This transaction involves reduction in a current asset without an obvious replacement in the form of another asset. Expenditure on wages, rent, rates, insurances, etc., involve a use of resources but do not result in the business having assets which can be included on the balance sheet. The business is paying for services that are useful and necessary in order to trade, but they have no monetary value that can be described as an asset.

The **money measurement concept** states that only expenditure which results in the acquisition of an asset with an objective and observable monetary value can be included on the balance sheet. Services cause a problem in this respect, because although the cost of acquiring the service is a definite recorded amount, the benefits to be derived from this expenditure are less certain. A good example of this is training or advertising expenditure. A business wouldn't pay to train a chef or to advertise for waiters if the benefits in terms of future profit were not expected to outweigh this original expenditure. However, this is an expectation or a hope rather than a certainty. It is possible that the trained chef might leave the restaurant after three months to join another organization, or that no waiters might respond to the advertising.

The **prudence concept** requires that, in the face of such uncertainty, none of the potential future financial benefits to be derived from such revenue expenditure should be shown on the balance sheet as an asset. In order to comply with the money measurement concept and the prudence concept, the value of any expenditure on services is treated as a reduction in the value of the assets of the business. As this reduction on the asset side is **not compensated** by the acquisition of another asset, there needs to be an equivalent reduction on the liabilities side. This reduction must logically come from capital. The owner's claim will therefore have been reduced by the whole amount of the expenditure.

Sue Venir: balance sheet as at day 5

Assets		£	Liabilities	£
Fixed assets			Capital	35,000
Leasehold property		30,000	Add profit	+500
			Less wages	−100
				35,400
Current assets			Current liabilities	
Stock		7,000	Creditors	8,000
Bank		5,000		
Cash	(−100)	1,400		
Total		43,400		43,400

Day 6: Sue sells stock costing £1,200 to CU Orite on credit for £1,000

This transaction involves another unequal asset exchange. The current asset stock is reduced by £1,200 but this is only partly compensated by an increase in another current asset. Sue has agreed to accept only £1,000 as a promise to pay from CU Orite, so the total assets have reduced. The reduction in stock of £1,200 is exchanged for an increase in debtors of only £1,000. The business has therefore reduced its value through trading. Unlike day 4, where it made a profit, the business has now made a loss. This loss has to be borne solely by the owner. Therefore, to keep the balance sheet balanced, the loss must be subtracted from the owner's capital, reducing her overall claim on the business.

Sue Venir: balance sheet as at day 6

Assets		£	Liabilities	£
Fixed assets			Capital	35,000
Leasehold property		30,000	Add profit	+500
			Less wages	−100
			Less loss	−200
				35,200
Current assets			Current liabilities	
Stock	(−1,200)	5,800	Creditors	8,000
Debtors	(+1,000)	1,000		
Bank		5,000		
Cash		1,400		
Total		43,200		43,200

Again there are three adjustments here. The unequal asset exchange is compensated by a downward adjustment to capital (loss £200).

Day 7: Sue buys stock costing £7,000 from Nicholas Nack by business cheque

Sue purchases more stock from Nichols Nack. This time she signs a business cheque to pay for it. Stock increases by £7,000 and bank goes down by £7,000. There is a problem here! The bank only has £5,000 in it. As long as the bank honours the cheque, Sue now has an overdraft, i.e. she owes the bank £2,000. This amount therefore needs to appear on the liabilities side as a current liability, recognizing the fact that £2,000 of the stocks are being financed in the short term by the bank.

Sue Venir: balance sheet as at day 7

Assets		£	Liabilities	£
Fixed assets			Capital	35,000
Leasehold property		30,000	Add profit	+500
			Less wages	−100
			Less loss	−200
				35,200
Current assets			Current liabilities	
Stock	(+7,000)	12,800	Creditors	8,000
Debtors		1,000		
Bank	(−5,000)	nil	Bank o/draft (+2,000)	2,000
Cash		1,400		
Total		45,200		45,200

Day 8: Sue pays the ground rent on the sales booth using £150 from her personal bank account

This transaction is similar to that on day 5, but is really two distinct transactions blurred into one event. This time the expense is being met from the private and separate resources of the owner, not from the assets of the business. In effect, what is happening is that the owner is investing in the business by paying business expenses from private means.

Strangely enough, if we made no change to the balance sheet, this would be correct in outcome, as in net terms neither business assets nor liabilities are affected by this transaction.

In reality what has happened has been an initial increase in the capital of the owner invested in the business as she uses private wealth to pay business expenses. Theoretically this finance initially comes into the business in the form of cash or cheque, and is then spent. The expenditure is then recognized by reducing those assets and the owner's capital back to their original level.

Sue Venir: balance sheet as at day 8

Assets		£	Liabilities	£
Fixed assets			Capital	35,000
Leasehold property		30,000	Add profit	+500
			Less wages	−100
			Less loss	−200
			Capital introduced	+150
			Less ground rent	−150
				35,200
Current assets			Current liabilities	
Stock	(+7,000)	12,800	Creditors	8,000
Debtors		1,000		
Bank	(−5,000)	nil	Bank o/draft (+2,000)	2,000
Cash	(+150 − 150)	1,400		
Total		45,200		45,200

Day 9: Sue borrows £2,000 over five years from Northsea Bank to pay off her overdraft with Redwood Bank

This transaction involves an exchange of liabilities. The current liability, bank overdraft, is replaced by alternative finance from outside, a long-term loan from Northsea Bank.

Sue Venir: balance sheet as at day 9

Assets	£	Liabilities	£
Fixed assets		Capital	35,000
Leasehold property	30,000	Add profit	+500
		Less wages	−100
		Less loss	−200
		Capital introduced	+150
		Less ground rent	−150
			35,200
		Long-term liabilities	
		Loan from Northsea	2,000
Current assets		Current liabilities	
Stock	12,800	Creditors	8,000
Debtors	1,000		
Bank	nil	Bank o/draft (−2,000)	nil
Cash	1,400		
Total	45,200		45,200

Day 10: Sue takes £200 from the till to buy clothes for her children, and pays for groceries worth £50 using the business cheque-book

This time the owner is taking a business asset and increasing a business liability in order to satisfy her own personal needs. The withdrawal of cash reduces current assets by £200, and the use of the cheque increases current liabilities by £50. Any change in the balance sheet of the business caused by the personal transactions of the owner needs to be compensated by making appropriate adjustments to the owner's capital to reflect this. Therefore, the equality of the balance sheet can only be preserved by reducing the owner's claim on the business, i.e. her capital, by the necessary amounts. Where the net assets of a business are reduced by personal transactions of the owner, it is known as **drawings**.

Sue Venir: balance sheet as at day 10

Assets	£	Liabilities	£
Fixed assets		Capital	35,000
Leasehold property	30,000	Add profit	+500
		Less wages	−100
		Less loss	−200
		Capital introduced	+150
		Less ground rent	−150
		Less drawings (200 + 50)	−250
			34,950

Sue Venir: balance sheet as at day 10 (cont'd)

Assets		£	Liabilities		£
			Long-term liabilities		
			Loan from bank		2,000
Current assets			Current liabilities		
Stock		12,800	Creditors		8,000
Debtors		1,000			
Bank		nil	Bank o/draft	(+50)	50
Cash	(−200)	1,200			
Total		45,000			45,000

Note that the original capital invested in the business has been amended by a number of transactions and now stands at £34,950. It was boosted by a profit of £500 after day 4. Thereafter it was eroded by paying wages of £100 on day 5, making a loss of £200 on day 6. It was increased and reduced by £150 simultaneously when ground rent was paid on day 8, and reduced finally by drawings of £200 and £50 for personal use on day 10, finally ending up at £34,950.

2.3 PROFIT DEFINED

Having recorded ten days in the financial position of Sue Venir, it is time to summarize what has been learned.

1 The balance sheet has always been maintained as an equality following each and every transaction.
2 All transactions have a dual effect on the balance sheet, except where the business makes a profit or a loss.
3 Where the business makes a profit or a loss, adjustment to the owner's capital represents the consequent increase or reduction in the owner's claim on the business following that transaction.

Can profit or loss be defined in financial terms? Profit or loss can be defined as a trading transaction that affects the capital of the owner. This is normally caused by an unequal exchange of assets as a result of a transaction. It could in certain rare circumstances be defined as an unequal exchange in liabilities, e.g. a loan being paid off by borrowing a lesser amount from another lender. In the case of a profitable transaction, the reduction of one asset is more than compensated by an increase in another. Loss is caused by a reduction in one asset not being fully compensated by an increase in another. Look back at the effects of the transactions on days 4 and 6 to confirm this.

2.4 TYPES OF EXPENDITURE: THE CAPITAL/REVENUE DISTINCTION

The previous example involving Sue Venir's business transactions reveals three types of expenditure that a business makes. The first is to purchase **fixed assets** by using other assets, or through finance from outside. This is known as **capital expenditure**. The second type is where **stocks** are purchased either using existing resources or through external finance. This is an example of **revenue expenditure** where there is a definable benefit to the business in the acquisition of goods for resale, expressed in monetary terms. This can be called **compensated revenue expenditure**. A third type of expenditure which also comes under revenue expenditure is expenditure on consumable goods and services where no definable monetary benefit can be objectively recognized for inclusion on the balance sheet. The expenditure is treated as an immediate reduction in the value of the business, and this reduction is reflected directly in the owner's claim on the business. This can be called **non-compensated revenue expenditure.**

2.5 GENERIC TYPES OF TRANSACTION

Although all transactions are unique, if the subsequent transactions of Sue Venir were to be recorded, all of them would fall into general categories. It is therefore possible to classify all external transactions in terms of a few broad types, in the way they affect the equality of the balance sheet and affect its constituent parts (Table 2.1).

Try to identify the transactions of Sue Venir's business which fall into the above categories. All of them are included there somewhere! Any transaction will have no net effect on the totals on each side, or it will affect both sides equally.

Table 2.1 How transactions affect the equality of the balance sheet

Type of transaction	Net effect on assets	Net effect on other liabilities	Net effect on capital
1 Asset exchange	+/– (nil)	nil	nil
2 Liability exchange	nil	+/– (nil)	nil
3 Investment by owner			
(a)	+	nil	+
(b)*	nil	–	+
4 Drawings by owner:			
(a)	–	nil	–
(b)	nil	+	–
5 Investment by third parties	+	+	nil
6 Repayments to third parties	–	–	nil
7 Profit	+/– (+)	nil	+
8 Loss	+/– (–)	nil	–

* Investment by the owner could also be represented by the owner meeting business liabilities from his or her private wealth. An example of this might include the owner paying a meat bill for the restaurant using a personal cheque-book. The effect on the balance sheet is to reduce creditors and increase capital.

SUMMARY

1 **All business transactions affect the business balance sheet.**

2 **Transactions have a dual effect in terms of maintaining the equality of assets and liabilities.**

3 **The business can either finance expenditure from its existing resources or from outside in the form of investment made by third parties, including the owner.**

4 **An unequal exchange of assets creates a profit or a loss in financial terms. In this case a third adjustment must be made to the balance sheet – to the capital of the owner.**

5 **Expenditure can be classified in three ways:**
   – Expenditure on fixed assets (capital expenditure)
   – Expenditure on stocks (compensated revenue expenditure)
   – Expenditure on consumables and services (non-compensated revenue expenditure)

6 **All business transactions can be classified under eight generic types.**

ASSESSMENT

MULTIPLE-CHOICE QUESTIONS

Question 1

Which of the following best describes the financial effect of a transaction on a business balance sheet?

A Where an adjustment is made to both sides of the balance sheet
B Where the total assets and the total liabilities both increase equally
C Where the total assets and the total liabilities do not change
D Where the total assets and the total liabilities remain equal

Question 2

Which of the following best replace the missing words in the following sentence? The owner's capital is directly affected by _____.

A expenditure on a business vehicle
B expenditure on advertising
C expenditure on stocks
D expenditure on business equipment

Question 3

Which of these is not affected by a profitable credit sale to a customer?

A Creditors
B Stock
C Debtors
D Capital

Question 4

Which one of these transactions would represent the owner making a further investment into his or her business by paying off a loan from private means?

A Assets up, liabilities down and capital up more
B Assets up and capital up equally
C Capital up and liabilities down equally
D Capital down and liabilities up equally

Question 5

If a balance sheet starts at a balance of £70,000, what would be its balance after these three transactions?

1 £3,500 cash spent on insurances
2 Stock bought on credit for £5,000
3 Stock costing £3,200 sold on credit for £3,150

A £74,950
B £71,450
C £66,450
D £71,500

EXERCISES

Exercise 1

The following transactions take place in a fast-food restaurant during the week:

1 Owner purchases meat on credit from the wholesale butchers.
2 Owner takes cash from the till for personal spending money.
3 Chefs' wages are paid.
4 Owner's father-in-law pays off part of the business mortgage as a gift.
5 Restaurant sells food costing £500 for £1,000.
6 Owner purchases new oven.
7 Owner pays rent from his or her personal bank account.

For items 1 to 7, please select the correct effect on capital out of the following:

– Capital up
– Capital down
– No effect

Exercise 2

The following transactions take place during the first weeks of trading for a whale-watching enterprise in Cape Cod, USA:

1 $200,000 entered in a business bank account.
2 $20,000 cheque paid as rental to boat owner for a month.
3 $12,000 cheque paid for new binocular equipment.
4 Diesel purchased for $5,000 on credit.
5 Takings for the week on eight trips to the whaling grounds, $14,000 cash.
6 Crews wages, $3,500 cash.
7 Donations to a whale preservation society in the United States, $3,000 cheque.

Required

(a) What is the capital of the business at the end of the week?
(b) At what total would the balance sheet of the whale-watching business balance at the end of the week?

Exercise 3

An amusement arcade business has the following assets and liabilities at the beginning of a week's trading at a fair in a provincial town:

	£
Arcade machines and equipment	95,000
Vehicle and equipment	100,000
Fuel stores	300
Cash	7,000
Bank balance	−4,000

During the week, the arcade engages in the following transactions:

		£
1	Cash takings	8,000
2	Fuel purchased by cheque	400
3	Fuel used	500
4	Cash banked	6,500
5	Casual wages paid by cash	900
6	Owner's cash drawings	400
7	New generator purchased by cheque	2,300

Required

(a) Prepare the opening balance sheet and establish the opening capital.
(b) Process the week's transactions and amend the balance sheet accordingly.
(c) By how much is the owner better off at the end of the week than at the beginning of the week?

Exercise 4

A sports consultancy business is facing an enquiry by the tax authorities as to how much profit was made in the previous financial period. The following assets and liabilities were established at the end of the year:

	£
Fixed assets	120,000
Current assets	5,000
Current liabilities	14,000
Long-term liabilities	25,000

At the beginning of the year the business had the following assets and liabilities:

	£
Fixed assets	100,000
Current assets	25,000
Current liabilities	8,000
Long-term liabilities	30,000

The only other information is that the owner had donated a car worth £20,000 to the business during the year from personal property, and had paid off £5,000 of the long-term loan from the proceeds of a personal lottery win. It was also verified that the owner withdrew £500 a week for 48 weeks as drawings. There is no other information regarding the transactions undertaken in connection with the business.

Required

What profit must have been made overall by the business as a result of the transactions undertaken by the business during the year? Show your workings.

CHAPTER 3

Recording, processing and correcting financial transactions

OBJECTIVES

- Systematically process the transactions of a business in ledger accounts, using a double-entry system.
- Determine the balances in the accounts at the end of a financial period.
- Check the accuracy of the double-entry system by the use of a trial balance.
- Recognize types of error not revealed by a trial balance.
- Correct errors by double entry using the journal.

INTRODUCTION

After having read Chapter 2, it may seem as if processing transactions is a cumbersome and time-consuming activity which is wholly impractical. As each transaction alters the balance sheet in some way, it follows that after every transaction the balance sheet needs to be amended.

Although the balance sheet is affected by each and every transaction, is it necessary to record the effect of that transaction on the balance sheet every time, or could it be carried out periodically?

Is there some system where the effects of transactions can be recorded and stored for easy retrieval at a later stage, either to establish the total profit in a particular period, or to establish the financial position at any particular moment or at the end of a financial period?

3.1 THE DOUBLE-ENTRY SYSTEM

Since fifteenth-century Venetian merchants began using a system developed by an Italian mathematician, Pacioli, transactions have been recorded in a particular way that has largely remained unaltered up to the present. The system is a logical and mechanical method for accurately recording and processing financial transactions, recognizing the dual aspect of transactions and their effect on the balance sheet. It is important that this system is understood as it provides the underlying mechanical framework for recording all transactions and reporting and assessing their effects on the financial performance and position of the business. It is also important to recognize that this mechanical framework must be supported by a valid framework of theoretical concepts, conventions and principles as a basis for this system. These concepts must be well understood and strictly adhered to by the accountant, in order to make the output of this system as reliable and comparable as possible.

In mechanical terms the double-entry system is best explained as a simple set of rules governing each transaction:

- A numerical (monetary) amount is recorded in two different accounts.
- Each numerical amount is equal but opposite, a positive number in one account and a negative in the other. (The positive/negative notation will be used as this is conceptually easier to grasp, and lends itself more easily to computerization, particularly to spreadsheets.)

Here are some more specific rules:

- To increase an asset enter a positive amount in the account.
- To reduce an asset enter a negative amount in the account.
- To increase a liability enter a negative amount in the account.
- To reduce a liability enter a positive amount in the account.

Let us try these rules so far by processing these transactions:

May 1: Freddo Gelati opens an ice-cream parlour, putting £50,000 in a business bank account.
May 2: Freddo pays £30,000 by cheque for a leasehold ice-cream shop.
May 3: Freddo buys bulk ice-cream for resale from A. Cauld for £900 on credit.
May 4: Freddo sells £500 of ice-cream to customers for £800 cash.
May 5: Freddo pays the shop assistant £20 cash for a day's wages.

Capital account

Date	Account	£
May 1	Bank	−50,000
May 4	Cash	−800
May 4	Stock	+500
May 5	Wages	+20

Bank account

Date	Account	£
May 1	Capital	+50,000
May 2	Shop	−30,000

Leasehold shop

Date	Account	£
May 2	Bank	+30,000

Stock-in-trade account

Date	Account	£
May 3	A. Cauld	+900
May 4	Capital	−500

A. Cauld account

Date	Account	£
May 3	Stock	−900

Cash account

Date	Account	£
May 4	Capital	+800
May 5	Capital	−20

Note that each transaction should be referenced by a date and should name its opposite account. It is also acceptable to show negative entries within brackets as an alternative notation. Let us look at each transaction in turn and relate it to the rules.

May 1: This transaction recognizes an investment by the owner
When Freddo opened up his business, the dual aspect of the transaction was recorded by entering a positive amount in the asset bank, and a negative amount in the liability capital. This recognizes that the increase in the asset was financed by the business owing more to external parties – in this case to the owner – giving an illustration of the separate entity concept of accounting and its implied effect on the balance sheet.

May 2: This transaction recognizes an equal asset exchange
Here Freddo reduces one asset (bank) with a negative entry and increases another (leasehold premises) with a positive entry.

May 3: This transaction recognizes revenue expenditure on stocks financed from an external party who is not the owner
Here Freddo increases his business's assets by purchasing stock-in-trade financed by a supplier, A. Cauld. Recognizing this, the asset stock is increased with a positive entry, and the obligation to A. Cauld is recognized by the recording of a negative entry.

May 4: This transaction recognizes an unequal asset exchange
The transaction has two parts. The first part recognizes the receipt of revenue when the sale takes place. As cash is received, a positive entry is made in the cash account. Following the primary rules of double entry, a negative entry must also be made. Theoretically a sale increases the capital of the owner as the revenue directly increases the asset cash. However, a sale will almost always have an associated cost. The associated part of the transaction is that stock is reduced by £500, representing the cost of the stock sold. The opposite entry is entered as a positive amount in the capital account (reducing capital).

The overall effect on capital is an increase of £800 − £500 = £300, representing the total increase in assets following the transaction. Therefore the profit made on that transaction is immediately reflected in the liability to the owner.

May 5: This transaction recognizes a revenue expense
Here cash is reduced with a negative entry, so the opposite entry must be a positive. No asset is recognized as having replaced the cash used in paying the wages, so it reduces the capital of the owner, shown by making a positive entry in the capital account.

The sales and cost-of-sales account

The transaction on May 4 demonstrates the theoretically correct effect on the balance sheet of recognizing a sale. In practice it may be difficult to record this, as usually the cost of any particular sale cannot be easily identified without computerized electronic point of sale (EPOS) equipment, which can recognize the bar-code on stock items. This equipment is increasingly being used in large retail outlets where large volumes of stock are being sold.

In non-automated businesses it may be impractical, if not impossible, to establish for every single transaction the cost of the last item sold. If this is the case, we must record sales differently. The alternative method of recording the transaction on May 4 is as follows:

Cash account	Sales account
£	£
+800	−800

From now on we will always recognize an increase in revenue as a positive entry in the asset account and a negative entry in the appropriate revenue account, **not in the capital account**.

The implication of ignoring the 'cost of the sale' is that the stock account will not be reduced as sales are made, nor will the corresponding amount be entered in the capital account. The way to approach this is to have a cost-of-sales account, or a purchases account, which simply records all purchases of stocks made 'available' for sale.

The transaction on May 3 should therefore be recorded as follows:

Cost-of-sales account	A. Cauld account
£	£
+900	−900

As in the transaction on May 5, revenue expenditure can be of many different kinds and will occur frequently. It is impractical to enter them as reductions to capital every time they take place. The conventional way is to enter the positive entry into an **expense** account, classified as wages, rent, insurance, etc. The double entry would therefore look like this:

Cash account	Wages (expense) account
£	£
−20	+20

It is not possible to record the profitability of individual transactions, so there must be some terminal method of calculating the total profitability of a batch of transactions, or as is more common, a method of calculating the profitability of a series of transactions that have been undertaken within a fixed period of time. How this is done is covered in Chapter 4.

Returning to the initial stages of recording the business of Freddo Gelati, the following fifteen transactions take place during the rest of May, and we will record them in our accounts.

6 Freddo sells ice-cream on a bulk order to a credit customer, B. Goode, for £120. Freddo offers him a 10% discount on the price if he pays within seven days.

7 Freddo pays insurance for five months from May 1, to September 30, £150 cash.

8 B. Goode informs Freddo that three of the twelve boxes delivered to him were missing. Freddo checks with the warehouse and confirms this is correct; he sends B. Goode a credit note for the appropriate amount.

9 Freddo pays A. Cauld £500 by cheque on account.

10 Freddo purchases a total of £4,200 of ice-cream on account from A. Cauld during the accounting period.

11 Total cash sales in the period to December 31 amount to £7,600.

12 £500 of the total purchases from A. Cauld were returned to him as unsuitable. Credit notes for the full amount were duly received.

13 Total cash wages paid during the year came to £1,500.

14 Cash banked during the year came to £6,000.

15 Freddo had agreed to sublet part of his premises to Francis Chiser for a sum of £1,200. The agreement was from May 1 to July 31, payable in advance. He paid by cheque.

16 Advertising for May was £2,550 paid by cheque. Additional invoices for May's advertising amounted to £850, which remained unpaid at the end of May.

17 Freddo borrowed £10,000 over a three-year period in order to purchase ice-cream making machinery for installation at the rear of his shop. The interest is payable quarterly in advance starting from May 1. The annual interest rate is 12%.

18 B. Goode settled his account by cheque in full within the fourteen-day period agreed.
19 Total credit sales apart from that made to B. Goode came to £2,200. Of the propor-tion settled, 4% was granted as prompt payment discounts and £500 was still outstanding at the year-end. All debtors settled by cheque.
20 Freddo withdrew £4,800 from the bank for his own personal living expenses.

Below are the accounts already opened and the new accounts. Try to understand how transactions 6 to 20 have been recorded in the double-entry system. Referring to the rules, go through the transactions one by one. The additional rules we must adhere to – rules that emerged from recording transactions on May 4 and May 5 – are as follows:

– To increase an expense enter a positive amount in the appropriate expense account.
– To increase income enter a negative amount in the appropriate income account.

The May transactions are referenced 1 to 20 within parentheses; the account references are missing. For each transaction, it is therefore necessary to verify which two accounts are involved. Remember that an amount in one account will be matched by an equal but opposite amount in another account.

Capital account			*Bank account*			*Leasehold shop account*	
Ref	£		Ref	£		Ref	£
(1)	−50,000		(1)	+50,000		(2)	+30,000
			(2)	−30,000			
			(9)	−500			
			(14)	+6,000			
			(15)	+1,200			
			(16)	−2,550			
			(18)	+81			
			(17)	−300			
			(19)	+1,632			
			(20)	−4,800			

Cost-of-sales account			*A. Cauld account*			*Cash account*	
Ref	£		Ref	£		Ref	£
(3)	+900		(3)	−900		(4)	+800
(10)	+4,200		(9)	+500		(5)	−20
			(10)	−4,200		(7)	−150
			(12)	+500		(11)	+7,600
						(13)	−1,500
						(14)	−6,000

Sales account			*Wages account*			*B. Goode account*	
Ref	£		Ref	£		Ref	£
(4)	−800		(5)	+20		(6)	+120
(6)	−120		(13)	+1,500		(8)	−30
(11)	−7,600					(18)	−9
(19)	−2,200					(18)	−81

Insurance account			*Returns inwards*			*Returns outwards*	
Ref	£		Ref	£		Ref	£
(7)	+150		(8)	+30		(12)	−500

Rent received account

Ref	£
(15)	−1,200

Advertising account

Ref	£
(16)	+2,550

Loan account

Ref	£
(17)	−10,000

Machinery account

Ref	£
(17)	+10,000

Discount allowed

Ref	£
(18)	+9
(19)	+68

Other debtors account

Ref	£
(19)	+2,200
(19)	−68
(19)	−1,632

Drawings account

Ref	£
(20)	+4,800

Interest account

Ref	£
(17)	+300

It is important to follow through each transaction and to recognize the double entries, referring to the transaction date reference numbers and applying the main rules stated above. Some transactions may have caused you more difficulty than others, particularly those involving discounts and returns. Discounts are where the business or its customers are offered a reduction against the invoice value in return for payment within a specified period of time. Returns inwards are sales made by the business which are subsequently returned for some legitimate reason. Returns outwards are purchases made by the business which are subsequently returned to suppliers.

The best approach is to begin with that part of the double entry to which you can best apply a rule, then put the opposite entry in the other account. This way you will quickly become accustomed to efficiently recording all types of transactions by the double-entry method. You will get further practice in the assessment at the end of this chapter.

Batch processing

Although the pure double-entry system of recording transactions is neat and logical, it cannot be operated in practice on a transaction-by-transaction basis, particularly in a business with a high volume of daily transactions. The recording process is often computerized and many of the transactions – recording credit sales invoices, credit purchase invoices, expenditure receipts, returns, discounts, etc. – will be entered in batches in order to save time. The accounts clerk will total up a batch of original documents for a given period of time and enter them as one transaction by following the rules of double entry.

The main original documents that will be processed in this way are:

1 Credit sales invoices
2 Cash sales invoices (till roll)
3 Credit purchase invoices
4 Cash purchase receipts
5 Other expense receipts by category
6 Credit notes (returns inwards)
7 Credit notes (returns outwards)

Some transactions must be entered on a transaction-by-transaction basis. The main ones are cash and cheque receipts and payments, which need to be recorded as they take place for control purposes; and those transactions which are large and infrequent, such as the purchase or sale of fixed assets, or the raising or repayment of loans and other finance.

3.2 PERIODIC BALANCING OF THE BOOKS

The system of recording and processing transactions is carried out in order to produce an output known as the financial report. Meaningful reports need certain important characteristics. For example, they should contain comparable information prepared on a consistent basis. For information to be comparable, it is important to work within a conceptual framework, and a major tenet is that accounts should be prepared on a consistent periodic basis. Partly this is a requirement of tax organizations and other statutory bodies, but mainly it is to set a unit of time within which people can make reasonable and justified performance comparisons. The accounting period is normally taken as one year, but accounts for internal purposes can be prepared more often, perhaps on a monthly basis.

Following the logic of the double-entry system and its rules, there are four broad types of ledger account that we need to process periodically:

- Asset accounts
- Liability accounts
- Expense accounts
- Revenue accounts

If we total them at the end of an accounting period (in this case at the month ended May 31) by summing the total entries within each individual ledger account, what can be said about the results?

1 All asset accounts should have a positive total.
2 All liability accounts should have a negative total.
3 All expense accounts should have a positive total.
4 All revenue accounts should have a negative total.

Traditionally a positive entry has been known as a **debit** and a negative entry as a **credit**. We will refer to a positive entry as a debit and a negative entry as a credit from now on. If we now balance the accounts of Freddo Gelati, we can test this hypothesis.

Capital account			Bank account			Leasehold shop account	
Ref	£		Ref	£		Ref	£
(1)	−50,000		(1)	+50,000		(2)	+30,000
			(2)	−30,000			
			(9)	−500			
			(14)	+6,000			
			(15)	+1,200			
			(16)	−2,550			
			(18)	+81			
			(17)	−300			
			(19)	+1,632			
			(20)	−4,800			
Total	−50,000		Total	+20,763		Total	+30,000

Cost-of-sales account			A. Cauld account			Cash account	
Ref	£		Ref	£		Ref	£
(3)	+900		(3)	−900		(4)	+800
(10)	+4,200		(9)	+500		(5)	−20
			(10)	−4,200		(7)	−150
			(12)	+500		(11)	+7,600
						(13)	−1,500
						(14)	−6,000
Total	+5,100		Total	−4,100		Total	+730

Sales account			Wages account			B. Goode account	
Ref	£		Ref	£		Ref	£
(4)	−800		(5)	+20		(6)	+120
(6)	−120		(13)	+1,500		(8)	−30
(11)	−7,600					(18)	−9
(19)	−2,200					(19)	−81
Total	−10,720		Total	+1,520		Total	0

Insurance account			Returns inwards			Returns outwards	
Ref	£		Ref	£		Ref	£
(7)	+150		(8)	+30		(12)	−500
Total	+150		Total	+30		Total	−500

Rent received account			Advertising account			Loan account	
Ref	£		Ref	£		Ref	£
(15)	−1,200		(16)	+2,550		(17)	−10,000
Total	−1,200		Total	+2,550		Total	−10,000

Ice-cream machinery account			Discount allowed account		
Ref	£		Ref	£	
(17)	+10,000		(18)	+9	
			(19)	+68	
Total	+10,000		Total	+77	

Other debtors account			Drawings account			Interest account	
Ref	£		Ref	£		Ref	£
(19)	+2,200		(20)	+4,800		(17)	+300
(19)	−68						
(19)	−1,632						
Total	+500		Total	+4,800		Total	+300

Having balanced all the accounts, we can recognize that the above hypothesis is true. For example:

The asset cash has a balance of   £+730
The liability loan has a balance of   £−10,000
The expense advertising has a balance of £+2,550
The income rent received has a balance of £−1,200

What else can be logically concluded from examining all the balances of the ledger accounts prepared?

3.3 THE TRIAL BALANCE

The primary rules of double entry dictate that for every **positive** or debit entry in an account there must be an equal **negative** or credit entry in another account. The logic of this dictates that if we total the balances of all the accounts, the result should be zero.

The way to test this is to list the balances of all the ledger accounts of Freddo Gelati in one column and then sum the total. This column is known as the **trial balance**. The trial balance of Freddo Gelati is as follows:

Trial balance: Freddo Gelati as at May 31

	£	Type of account
Capital	−50,000	Liability
Bank	+20,763	Asset
Leasehold shop	+30,000	Asset
Cost of sales	+5,100	Expense
A. Cauld (creditor)	−4,100	Liability
Cash	+730	Asset
Sales	−10,720	Revenue
Wages	+1,520	Expense
B. Goode (debtor)	nil	Asset
Insurance	+150	Expense
Returns inwards	+30	'Expense'*
Returns outwards	−500	'Income'*
Rent received	−1,200	Income
Advertising	+2,550	Expense
Loan	−10,000	Liability
Ice-cream machinery	+10,000	Asset
Discount allowed	+77	Expense
Total debtors	+500	Asset
Drawings	+4,800	'Expense'†
Interest	+300	Expense
Total	0	

* Returns inwards and outwards do not fall neatly into expenses or income. They are sales and purchases of stock which have been cancelled, so they are in a sense 'negative' income in the case of returns inwards, or 'negative' purchases in the case of returns outwards. Theoretically the first can be treated in the double-entry system as an expense and the second as income.

† Drawings do not strictly fall into any of the four main categories identified above. But as far as the rules of double entry are concerned, drawings are recorded as if they were a 'private' expense. This is because, like any other revenue expense, they have the ultimate effect of reducing the capital of the owner. As drawings usually involve business assets being assigned for the personal use of the owner, they cannot be described as a business expense. Business expenses are part of the equation that we will use in order to determine overall profit for a financial period, which will have tax implications. Defining and calculating profitability will be covered in Chapter 4, and the conceptual distinction between expenses and drawings will be reconsidered.

3.4 TYPES OF ERROR

The trial balance is the culmination of the recording and processing system, which summarizes the economic activity of a business in monetary terms. The trial balance can confirm to the accountant that the double entry has been carried out correctly in accordance with double-entry principles and the primary rules of duality.

The trial balance **must** balance if double entry has been carried out correctly, but this does **not** necessarily mean that no errors in recording the transactions have taken place.

This apparently contradictory statement acknowledges an important fact which accountants must recognize after having drawn up a trial balance: some errors in the recording of transactions may not be revealed by the trial balance. Below are some examples of what are generally known as compensating errors:

An error of commission: the wrong debtor may have been credited with a receipt.
An error of principle: the cost-of-sales account may have been debited instead of a fixed-asset account.
An error of omission: a transaction may not have been recorded in the accounts at all.
An error of duplication: a transaction may have been entered more than once.
An error of original entry: an incorrect figure may have been posted to both accounts, or both the negative and positive entries may have been reversed (a transposition error).

None of these errors would be identified by the trial balance, so it can never be taken for granted that such errors have not occurred.

Any other errors which involve the violation of the double-entry rules will be identified by a non-zero sum for the trial balance. The size of the discrepancy does not in any way indicate the quantity or magnitude of such errors, merely that at least one exists, and that it or they must be located and corrected.

The discrepancy on a trial balance is traditionally represented by a **suspense** account, which will leave zero sum total for the trial balance.

3.5 THE CORRECTION OF ERRORS

We return to the transactions of Freddo Gelati for the first five days of May, on this occasion recording three of them incorrectly. When we draw up a trial balance, we can see the function of the suspense account. We will then correct the errors and eliminate the suspense account by the double-entry method:

May 1: Freddo Gelati opens an ice-cream parlour, putting £50,000 in a business bank account.
May 2: Freddo pays £30,000 by cheque for a leasehold ice-cream shop.
May 3: Freddo buys bulk ice-cream for resale from A. Cauld for £900 on credit.
May 4: Freddo sells £500 of ice-cream to customers for £800 cash.
May 5: Freddo pays the shop assistant £20 cash for a day's wages.

Capital account			Bank account			Leasehold shop account		
Ref	£		Ref	£		Ref	£	
(1)	−50,000		(1)	+50,000		(2)	+30,000	
			(2)	−20,000*				
Total	−50,000		Total	+30,000		Total	+30,000	

Cost-of-sales account		A. Cauld account		Cash account	
Ref	£	Ref	£	Ref	£
(3)	+900	(3)	−900	(4)	+80**
				(5)	+20***
Total	+900	Total	−900	Total	+100

Wages account		Sales account	
Ref	£	Ref	£
(5)	−20***	(4)	−800
Total	−20	Total	−800

* First error
** Second error
*** Third error

Interim trial balance: Freddo Gelati

	£
Capital	−50,000
Bank	+30,000
Leasehold premises	+30,000
Cost of sales	+900
A. Cauld (creditor)	−900
Cash	+100
Wages	−20
Sales	−800
Suspense account (difference)	−9,280
	0

The correction of errors is carried out using double-entry transactions. Traditionally these are also recorded as a memorandum in a **journal**, which records the account to be debited first, then the account to be credited, followed by a brief written explanation of the correcting entry, known as a **narrative**. The function of the journal is to explain or corroborate any unusual transactions undertaken, particularly with respect to correcting errors.

The first error

The first error was a double-entry error where the bank account was credited by £20,000 instead of £30,000. To correct this requires the following double entry:

	£
Debit the suspense account	+10,000
Credit the bank account	−10,000

Being the correction of a £10,000 discrepancy between the bank account and the leasehold premises account.

i.e.

Bank account		Suspense account	
Ref	£	Ref	£
Bal b/d*	+30,000	Bal b/d	−9,280
Suspense	−10,000	Bank	+10,000
Bal c/d*	+20,000	Bal c/d	+720

* Note that a ledger account total at the beginning of an accounting period is known as a balance brought down (b/d); a ledger account total at the end of a period is known as a balance carried down (c/d).

The second error

The second error was where cash sales of £800 were debited to the cash account as £80 not £800. To correct this requires the following double entry:

	£
Debit the cash account with (800 − 80)	+720
Credit the suspense account with	−720

Being the correction of the discrepancy between the cash account and the sales account of £720.

i.e.

Cash account		Suspense account	
Ref	£	Ref	£
Bal b/d	+100	Bal b/d	+720
Suspense	+720	Cash	−720
Bal c/f	+820	Bal c/f	nil

Notice that after two of the errors have been discovered and corrected, the suspense account is now cleared. This indicates that the trial balance would now balance. We know that this would therefore hide the last of the three errors, which is a compensating error.

The third error

This error involved recording the entries in both the wages and the cash accounts the opposite way round. The wages account has been recorded with £−20 instead of £+20, and the cash account has been recorded with £+20 instead of £−20, therefore there is a discrepancy of £+40 in the cash account, and a discrepancy of £−40 in the wages account. To correct this requires the following double entry:

	£
Debit the wages account with	+40
Credit the cash account with	−40

Being the correction of a compensating error where the opposite entries were made in the cash and the wages accounts.

i.e.

Cash account			Wages account	
Ref	£		Ref	£
Bal b/d	+820		Bal b/d	−20
Wages	−40		Cash	+40
	———			———
Bal c/f	+780		Bal c/f	+20
	═══			═══

Now all the errors have been corrected, we can redraft the original interim trial balance to show the correct account balances without the inclusion of a suspense account.

Interim trial balance: Freddo Gelati

	Original £	£	Corrections £	Corrected £
Capital	−50,000			−50,000
Bank	+30,000	−10,000		+20,000
Leasehold premises	+30,000			+30,000
Cost of sales	+900			+900
A. Cauld (creditor)	−900			−900
Cash	+100	+720	−40	+780
Wages	−20	+40		+20
Sales	−800			−800
Suspense account (diff)	−9,280	+10,000	−720	nil
	———			———
	0			0
	═══			═══

If this correction procedure is carried out successfully at the end of a financial period, we will be in a position where a column of accounts is balanced correctly, where all negatives equal all positives. Then we are ready to produce reports on the financial performance of the business over the preceeding financial period, and on the financial position of the business at the end of that period.

We will learn in Chapter 4 how to prepare a trading and profit and loss account and a balance sheet for Freddo Gelati.

SUMMARY

1 **Transactions are recorded in a double-entry system.**

2 **The double-entry system operates under strict rules of duality.**

3 **Ledger accounts have a negative balance or a positive balance; the total of all the balances in a ledger should be zero.**

4 **Certain errors will not be revealed by a trial balance.**

5 **Double-entry errors are corrected via a suspense account.**

6 **Corrections are explained in a journal by narrative.**

ASSESSMENT

MULTIPLE-CHOICE QUESTIONS

Question 1
Which of the following pairs of words most suitably fit the gaps in the following statement? The duality principle embodied in the double-entry system is determined by the fact that assets ___ ___ liabilities.

A physically represent
B always affect
C always equal
D finance all

Question 2
Choose the correct pair of ledger entries for this transaction: a business benefits from a 5% discount for paying its £200 account to a supplier within an agreed period of time. All figures are in pounds (£).

A **Debit** discount alld (+10)   **Credit** creditor   (−10)
B **Debit** creditor   (+10)   **Credit** discount recd (−10)
C **Debit** discount recd (+10)   **Credit** creditor   (−10)
D **Debit** creditor   (+10)   **Credit** discount alld (−10)

Question 3
Which account balance brought down at the end of a period is incorrect? All figures are in pounds (£).

A Cash   +500
B Returns in   +30
C Creditors   −350
D Discount allowed −90

Question 4
Which one of the following statements is not true?

A The trial balance can confirm there are no non-compensating double-entry errors.
B A small trial balance discrepancy, either way, indicates there may be only a few insignificant errors to be discovered and corrected.
C Errors of commission, principle, ommission and duplication will not cause a discrepancy in the trial balance.
D As soon as the suspense account has been cleared by double-entry corrections noted in the journal, the trial balance will balance.

Question 5
Choose the appropriate pair of ledger entries to correct the following erroneous entry: the returns outwards account was debited (+50) when £50 worth of goods were returned as damaged from a credit customer. The entry in the debtor account was correct. All figures are in pounds (£).

A **Debit** returns in   (+50)   **Credit** returns out (−50)
B **Debit** suspense   (+50)   **Credit** returns out (−50)
C **Debit** returns out (+50)   **Credit** returns in   (−50)
D **Debit** returns in   (+50)   **Credit** suspense   (−50)

EXERCISES

Exercise 1

Di Dactic decides to set up in her own air and water sports retail business, after being made redundant from her teaching post. The following transactions take place in the first week:

1 Di deposits £20,000 in the business bank account.
2 Fixtures and fittings are purchased for £8,000 by cheque.
3 A pair of surfboards are purchased for £500 each by cheque.
4 £3,500 cash is withdrawn from the business bank account.
5 A hang-glider is purchased from Aerial Ltd on credit for £1,500.
6 A surfboard is sold to a credit customer for £1,000.
7 Jim the shop assistant is paid wages of £150 cash, and the £100 rent for the shop is paid by cheque.
8 The owner puts her own car into the business, to be used by Jim in the course of his duties. The fair value of the car is assessed to be £2,000.
9 The debtor pays half of his debt on account by cheque.
10 At the end of the week £200 cash is taken from the till for the owner's personal expenses.

Required

Process these transactions, balance the accounts and prepare a trial balance to check the accuracy of the double entries.

Exercise 2

The Mangetous restaurant in Boulougne has the following assets and liabilities at the end of a financial period to December 31, 19x6:

	FFr
Owner's capital	−930,000
Fixtures and fittings	+1,400,000
Creditors	−60,000
Long-term loan	−500,000
Cash on hand	+10,000
Balance at bank	+80,000

In the next period the following summary transactions take place:

1 Catering equipment purchased by cheque for FFr 50,000.
2 Takings for food and drink FFr 450,000; 40% in cash, the remainder in cheques.
3 Kitchen and service staff wages FFr 150,000 by cheque.
4 Credit purchases of food and drink FFr 200,000; 70% of them were settled net of 8% discount for prompt payment. FFr 168,800 were paid to suppliers during the year.
5 Food returned to suppliers FFr 25,000 at gross invoice value. (The goods were returned before the invoice was settled.)
6 Establishment expenses of FFr 15,000 by cheque.
7 Fresh fruit and vegetables purchased from the local market for FFr 15,000 cash.
8 Owner's personal cash drawings of FFr 150,000.

Required

Open up the accounts at the beginning of the year and post the summary transaction entries to those and any other necessary accounts. Balance these accounts and draw up a trial balance as at December 31, 19x6.

Exercise 3

Here is the trial balance of the Hotel Shambles at the end of its first year of operations, drawn up by an inexperienced accounts clerk with little idea of the mechanics of formal double-entry bookkeeping.

	£
Takings for accommodation (exc deposits)	+50,000
Land and buildings	+150,000
Purchases of food and drink	−12,000
Sales of food and drink	+20,000
Staff wages paid	+25,000
Electricity paid	+4,500
Insurances paid	−2,000
Non-returnable deposits	+3,000
Purchases of bedlinen	−3,500
Purchases of cleaning materials	−400
Rates paid	+5,000
Discounts received from suppliers	+1,000
Bank overdraft	+4,300
Owner's capital	?

Required

All the figures are correct but some of the signs are incorrect. Correct the signs and calculate the owner's capital invested in the hotel at the year-end.

Exercise 4

Here is the trial balance for a travel agent as at March 31, 19x6.

	£
Owner's capital (31.3.x2)	−50,000
Land and buildings at cost	+200,000
Office equipment	+60,000
Cash and traveller's cheques on hand	+8,000
Mortgage on property	−50,000
Establishment expenses	+12,000
Staff costs	+8,000
Deposits collected on holidays sold	−20,000
Balances collected on holidays sold	−100,000
Bank balance	−25,000
Amounts owing to tour operators net of commission (10%)	−36,000
Commissions on holidays sold	−8,000
Commission on currency and traveller's cheques changed and sold	−6,000
Commission on insurances sold	−10,000
Suspense account	+17,000
Total	0

Several errors were discovered at the end of the year:

1 Establishment expenses had been entered correctly in the bank account but the figure had been transposed in the establishment expenses account.
2 Commission on insurances had been entered correctly in the bank account but had been over-stated by £2,000 in the commission on insurances account.
3 Accountancy fees, paid by cash of £500, had been ommitted from the accounts altogether.
4 An additional mortgage of £5,000 had been arranged during the period. A cheque was duly received at the appropriate time and was debited (+) to the bank account, but had been credited to balances collected from customers for holidays sold, instead of to the mortgage account.

5 Cash drawings of £6,000 had been taken steadily from the business during the year but had not been recorded in a drawings account.

Required

(a) Correct these six errors; use the journal entry format and incorporate a narrative.
(b) Show sufficient working to explain how the suspense account balance would be cleared.

CHAPTER 4

Preparing the final accounts

OBJECTIVES

- Calculate the net profit for a financial period from a trial balance, and recognize its relationship to business assets and liabilities.
- Prepare a trading and profit and loss account in the vertical format.
- Understand how to match costs against revenues in a financial period, according to the accruals concept of accounting, including accounting for stocks on hand.
- Prepare a balance sheet at the end of a financial period.

INTRODUCTION

At the end of Chapter 3, Freddo Gelati's accounts had been balanced, and any errors that may have been made during the double-entry recording stage had been located and corrected. Now that the balances are correct they are ready to be transferred to the final accounts.

4.1 CALCULATING PROFITABILITY

As was explained in Chapter 3, it is impractical if not impossible for businesses without computerized accounting systems to assess profitability after every transaction. It is therefore only at the end of a fixed period of time that the overall profitability of a business is calculated. How can profitability be calculated, given the way the double-entry system works?

Let us remind ourselves of how profit is generated. In Chapter 2 a profitable transaction was recognized as a transaction where there was an unequal exchange of assets. In this situation the total assets of the business increased as a result of the transaction. This increase was then counterbalanced by an equivalent increase in the owner's capital.

Wealth transfer or wealth creation?

Chapter 2 identified four types of transaction that produce adjustments to the owner's capital:

1 Investment by owner
2 Drawings
3 Income generation
4 Revenue expenditure

The first two are direct adjustments to capital. The first is an investment by the owner from their own personal wealth, which is merely a transfer of wealth to the business from their private resources. Drawings constitute the opposite situation; they can be defined as a transfer of wealth from the business. Transfers of value to and from the business by the owner have nothing to do with profitability, as in these situations the capital is being adjusted directly by the owner, not as a result of the trading activities of the business itself.

The third type of transaction is where the owner's capital is directly increased by the generation of income. The fourth type can be subdivided into two types: where the business purchases stock for resale to customers, and where the business purchases consumables and uses services in the course of carrying on its trading activities with customers. Where the business invests in stocks, we record this by debiting a cost-of-sales account. Where the business purchases consumables or services, we record this by debiting an expense account.

The **net profit** for a period is the sum of the values of all transactions that generate income, less the sum of the values of all transactions that incur revenue expenses, i.e. purchases of stock and other expenditure on consumables and services.

By looking again at the final trial balance of Freddo Gelati, it is possible to isolate those accounts which will have an effect on the business profitability and indirectly the capital.

Trial balance: Freddo Gelati as at May 31

	£	Type of account
Capital	−50,000	Liability
Bank	+20,763	Asset
Leasehold shop	+30,000	Asset
Cost of sales	+5,100	Expense
A. Cauld (creditor)	−4,100	Liability
Cash	+730	Asset
Sales	−10,720	Revenue
Wages	+1,520	Expense
B. Goode (debtor)	nil	Asset
Insurance	+150	Expense
Returns inwards	+30	Negative income
Returns outwards	−500	Negative expenditure
Rent received	−1,200	Income
Advertising	+2,550	Expense
Loan	−10,000	Liability
Ice-cream machinery	+10,000	Asset
Discount allowed	+77	Expense
Total debtors	+500	Asset
Drawings	+4,800	Transfer to owner
Interest	+300	Expense
Total	0	

From what was explained above, the accounts that would affect profit are those defined as income or expenses (excluding drawings). Income has the effect of increasing capital, whereas expenses reduce it. The overall difference between income and expenses would indicate the net change in owner's capital due to trading over the whole financial period – the **net profit**.

Here is a partial trial balance extracted from the above trial balance; it comprises only income and expenses.

Revenue/expenses trial balance: Freddo Gelati

	£
Cost of sales	+5,100
Sales	−10,720
Wages	+1,520
Insurance	+150
Returns inwards	+30
Returns outwards	−500
Rent received	−1,200
Advertising	+2,550
Discount allowed	+77
Interest	+300
Net profit	−2,693*

* The net profit is a negative amount. This is because incomes exceed expenses, and income accounts have negative balances. This profit is 'owed' to the owner, and effectively increases the liability to the owner, known as capital. If the balance had been positive, it would have denoted a loss and would correspondingly reduce the capital.

These accounts are known as **nominal** accounts. With the remaining accounts, the assets and liabilities, another partial trial balance can be drawn up.

Assets and liabilities trial balance: Freddo Gelati

	£
Capital†	−50,000
Bank	+20,763
Leasehold shop	+30,000
A. Cauld (creditor)	−4,100
Cash	+730
Loan	−10,000
Ice-cream machinery	+10,000
Other debtors	+500
Drawings†	+4,800
	+2,693‡

† Drawings would be netted off against capital in practice, leaving the net capital at £45,200 before adding the current period's profit.
‡ The difference here is positive, indicating that the assets exceed the liabilities by £2,693. This is the net effect on the assets of all the transactions that have taken place during the financial period.

These accounts are known as **real accounts**. There is a direct relationship between the excess of income over expenditure (profit), and the relationship between the closing assets and liabilities. If the £–2,693 profit were added to the capital, the assets and liabilities would actually balance.

Assets and liabilities trial balance: Freddo Gelati

	£	Adjustment £	£
Capital	−50,000	−2,693	−52,693
Bank	+20,763		+20,763
Leasehold shop	+30,000		+30,000
A. Cauld (creditor)	−4,100		−4,100
Cash	+730		+730
Loan	−10,000		−10,000
Ice-cream machinery	+10,000		+10,000
Other debtors	+500		+500
Drawings	+4,800		+4,800
	+2,693		0

4.2 THE TRADING AND PROFIT AND LOSS ACCOUNT

The partial trial balance comprising the income and expenses contains all the accounts which directly affect the profitability of the business. Although net profits can be calculated by balancing these accounts, their presentation as a financial report in a single column leaves a lot to be desired.

The professional way to report profitability is to arrange the nominal accounts in the following format:

Trading and profit and loss account: Freddo Gelati for the month ended May 31

	£	£
Sales		10,720
Less returns inwards		30
Less:		10,690
Cost of sales	5,100	
Less returns outwards	500	
Net cost of sales		4,600
Gross profit		6,090
Add other income: rent received		1,200
Less expenses:		7,290
Wages	1,520	
Insurance	150	
Advertising	2,550	
Discount allowed	77	
Interest paid	300	
Total expenses		4,597
Net profit		2,693

From now on the profitability of a business will always be shown in this way. Note that no negatives appear in the statement; expenses are merely subtracted from income. Also note that the statement is in two distinct parts: the top part is the trading account. The trading account shows the difference between income from selling goods or services (notice that this excludes other income such as rent received), and the **primary** cost of acquiring or providing those goods or services. In the case of Freddo Gelati, it is the income generated from ice-cream sales less the cost to him of acquiring the ice-cream from his suppliers. Income is shown net of returns from customers, and the cost of sales is shown net of returns to suppliers. The difference between income and the primary cost of generating this income is known as **gross profit,** and this is an extremely valuable measure of the business's basic financial performance. Gross profit as a primary measure of financial performance will be examined more carefully in Chapter 19.

The profit and loss account measures the bottom-line profitability of a business. After gross profit, other non-trading income is added, and expenditure on consumables and services associated with the running of the business is subtracted; this produces the measure known as **net profit.** Net profit tells us how much the capital or net assets of the business have increased during the financial period through commercial transactions undertaken with external parties excluding the owner.

4.3 THE ACCRUALS CONCEPT

As explained in Chapter 3, the reporting of financial performance depends on a conceptual framework of accounting. Perhaps the most important of the concepts that underlie the measurement of profit, and therefore the valuation of assets and liabilities, is the accruals concept. It can be defined in the following way:

The profit recognized in any financial period should be determined by the income attributable to that financial period less the expenditure attributable to that same financial period.

The key word is attributable. What does it mean? In Chapter 1 a transaction was recognized as taking place when an exchange was agreed, not necessarily when the debt was settled. This means that if an invoice is issued to a customer and goods are delivered, a sale is recognized. This sale is known as a contract, and the obligation for eventual settlement of the debt is enforceable by law.

The implication this has on reporting profit is that income recognized in the trading and profit and loss account should be the total value of contracts entered into in a financial period, regardless of the receipts during that same period. In the case of Freddo Gelati, it is the total value of sales invoices issued between May 1 and May 31. This would comprise the total amount from the till roll and the sales invoices issued to credit customers during the period. As Freddo Gelati set up in business on May 1, and was owed £500 by customers at the end of May, total sales attributable to the financial period will be £500 more than the actual cash receipts during that period.

The same applies to the cost of sales. The cost of sales attributable to the period should be those purchases contracted into during the financial period, not the payments made to suppliers during that period. Freddo Gelati started business on May 1 and during the month he purchased £5,100 worth of stock from his supplier, A. Cauld. We should therefore recognize this amount (less returns) as being the cost of sales, regardless of the fact that £4,100 is still owed to A. Cauld at the year-end.

Stocks on hand

We have not assumed that Freddo Gelati had any ice-cream stocks on hand at the year-end. Is this realistic? Probably not. Ice-cream is a perishable item, nevertheless some stocks will be carried on a day-to-day basis, so it is likely that a small amount of stock will exist on May 31. What implication does this have for recognizing profit according to the accruals concept?

If it is assumed that Freddo Gelati carried out a stocktake of ice-cream in his shop on May 31 and valued it at £150, what implication does this information have on the cost of sales to be recognized as attributable to the financial period?

	£
Total purchases of ice-cream (invoice value)	5,100
Less returns to supplier	500
	4,600
Less value of stocks unsold at the year-end*	150
Net cost of sales in the financial period	4,450

* The value placed on closing stocks is subtracted from the net cost of sales as, by definition, if those stocks were not sold during the period, their cost should not be attributable to the cost of sales recognized in that period. The value of closing stock will therefore form part of the cost of sales attributable to the following period. And because it is an asset of the business, it should appear on the balance sheet under the category of current assets at the end of the financial period.

In the following period the net cost of sales would therefore be calculated as follows:

	£
Value of opening stocks at June 1	150
Total invoice value of ice-cream in June	x
	x
Less returns to supplier	x
Net cost of stocks available for sale	x
Less value of stocks unsold at the year-end	x
Net cost of sales in the financial period	x

Gross profit is therefore defined as trading income attributable to the financial period less the net cost of sales attributable to the same financial period. Net profit is gross profit plus other income attributable to that period less other expenses attributable to the same period.

We will now look at the rent received, and remind ourselves of the transaction involving Francis Chiser. Freddo sublet part of his premises to Francis Chiser for a sum of £1,200 quarterly. The agreement applied from May 1 to July 31, payable in advance. Francis paid by cheque.

To record this transaction the double entry was debit bank (£+1,200) and credit the income account; rent received (£–1,200). Under the accruals concept what should be recognized as attributable rental income for the financial period? The answer to this is to establish the amount of rent that should have been paid for there to be no outstanding amount at the end of the period. As the franchise was taken out for three months, one-third of £1,200 is the attributable amount of rental income for the period May 1 to May 31. In other words, if Francis Chiser had paid only £400 to Freddo Gelati by the end of May, nothing would have been outstanding.

The actual situation is that at the end of May, Francis Chiser has paid for three months, and has at this time paid in advance for two months' rental (June and July). How should this be reflected in the profit and loss account? Under the accruals concept, £400 should be entered in the profit and loss account as the attributable rental income for the period. And at that point, Freddo Gelati in theory owes rent of £800 to Francis Chiser as at the end of May.

We will now examine the attributable expenses that should be recognized in the profit and loss account for May. What about the transactions involving the payments of insurance, advertising, and interest?

Freddo pays insurance of £150 cash for the five months ending September 30. The attributable expense chargeable to the profit and loss account should be the insurance for one month as this is the length of the accounting period we are measuring. At the end of the month Freddo has prepaid four months of insurance, amounting to $4/5 \times £150 = £120$. In theory, at the end of May, the insurance company owes this money to Freddo. The amount of insurance that should be entered in the profit and loss account is therefore $1/5 \times £150 = £30$.

The advertising account had an amount of £850 which remained unpaid at May 31. The attributable expense chargeable in this case is the advertising cost due for May, even though £850 of this amount still remains unpaid at the end of May. The total amount of advertising expenditure attributable to May is therefore £2,550 + £850 = £3,400.

In the case of interest paid on May 17, £10,000 was borrowed at an annual interest rate of 12%. The annual interest is therefore £1,200, of which three months, or £300, was paid during May. Of this only £100 was attributable to May, and £200 was paid in advance for June and July.

Formally recording accruals and prepayments

In all cases where the attributable income or expenditure is different from the associated monetary receipts or payments, there will be a discrepancy in the balance sheet unless some formal adjustment is made in order to recognize this discrepancy. To explain this, take advertising as an example. The asset cash is reduced by £2,550, being the payments made in May, but the expense that should be recognized in the profit and loss account is £3,400, being the attributable expense for May. This means there will be a difference of £850 in the balance sheet unless it is accounted for in some way.

The key is to recognize how the discrepancy between attributable income or expenditure in a given period, and the associated monetary receipts or payments in that period represent debts owing to or owed by the business at the end of the financial period.

In the first case, the rent received prepaid of £800 by Francis Chiser is owed by Freddo Gelati to the franchisee. Like a debt owed to a supplier, this should be recognized as a liability in the balance sheet. As the debt will be settled within twelve months, this will be defined as a current liability, and it will appear below trade creditors in that section of the balance sheet, and will be described as an **accrual**.

In the second case, the insurance company effectively owes Freddo Gelati £120. The insurance company is similar to a debtor because it owes £120 within twelve months. Here the amount owed will be recognized as a current asset in the balance sheet and will appear under trade debtors in that section of the balance sheet; it will be described as a **prepayment**.

In the third case, the £850 owed to the advertiser is payable imminently, therefore it will appear as an **accrual** under creditors in the current liabilities section of the balance sheet. The case of the interest is the same as for the insurance, in that the prepaid interest of £200 will appear as a prepayment within the current asset section of the balance sheet.

Looking at the complete trial balance of Freddo Gelati again, it can be seen how all adjustments for stocks, accruals and prepayments can be formally recorded, so the attributable amounts can be entered in the trading and profit and loss account and on the balance sheet.

The double-entry adjustments will be made in an adjustment column, then if both columns are summed horizontally we end up with a final trial balance from which the trading and profit and loss account can be correctly prepared along with the balance sheet.

Trial balance: Freddo Gelati as at May 31

	£	Adjustments £	Final TB £	T/P/B*
Capital	−50,000		−50,000	B
Bank	+20,763		+20,763	B
Leasehold shop	+30,000		+30,000	B
Cost of sales	+5,100	−150	+4,950	T
A. Cauld (creditor)	−4,100		−4,100	B
Cash	+730		+730	B
Sales	−10,720		−10,720	T
Wages	+1,520		+1,520	P
B. Goode (debtor)	nil			
Insurance	+150	−120	+30	P
Returns inwards	+30		+30	T
Returns outwards	−500		−500	T
Rent received	−1,200	+800	−400	P
Advertising	+2,550	+850	+3,400	P
Loan	−10,000		−10,000	B
Ice-cream machinery	+10,000		+10,000	B
Discount allowed	+77		+77	P
Total debtors	+500		+500	B
Drawings	+4,800		+4,800	B
Interest	+300	−200	+100	P
Adjustments				
Closing stock valuation		+150	+150	B
Accruals				
Rent received prepaid		−800	−800	B
Advertising owing		−850	−850	B
Prepayments				
Insurance prepaid		+120	+120	B
Interest prepaid		+200	+200	B
Total	0	0	0	

T = trading account
P = profit and loss account
B = balance sheet

* This indicates in which final account each ledger account should appear. Note that the closing stock valuation, being a current asset, will appear on the balance sheet, and is subtracted from the cost of sales in the trading account.

Having made all the adjustments to the accounts in accordance with the accruals concept of accounting, the corrected trading and profit and loss account, and the balance sheet of Freddo Gelati as at May 31 can finally be prepared.

Trading and profit and loss account: Freddo Gelati for the month ended May 31

	£	£
Sales		10,720
Less returns inwards		30
		10,690
Less:		
Cost of sales	4,950*	
Less returns outwards	500	
Net cost of sales		4,450
Gross profit		6,240
Add other income: rent received		400*
		6,640
Less expenses:		
Wages	1,520	
Insurance	30*	
Advertising	3,400*	
Discount allowed	77	
Interest	100*	
Total expenses		5,127
Net profit		1,513

* Indicates an account that was adjusted in accordance with the accruals concept.

4.4 THE BALANCE SHEET

Note that the net profit is now £1,513 instead of £2,923, the figure before adjustments. This makes a considerable difference to the capital of the owner. It is now possible to prepare the balance sheet.

Balance sheet: Freddo Gelati as at May 31

	£	£	£
Fixed assets			
Leasehold premises			30,000
Ice-cream making machinery			10,000
			40,000
Current assets			
Closing stocks		150	
Trade debtors		500	
Prepayments (insurance and interest)		320	
Bank		20,763	
Cash		730	
		22,463	
Current liabilities			
Trade creditors	4,100		
Accruals (800 + 850)	1,650		
		5,750	
Net current assets			16,713
Fixed assets plus net current assets			56,713
Less long-term liabilities			
Long-term loan			10,000
Net assets			46,713
Financed by			
Owner's capital including capital introduced			
during the financial period:			50,000
Add net profit earned in the financial period			1,513
			51,513
Less drawings made during the financial period			4,800
			46,713

This balance sheet has been prepared in **vertical** format in accordance with generally accepted principles. Up until now the balance sheet has been prepared in **horizontal** format in order to demonstrate more clearly the imperative equality of the balance sheet. There is no difference in theory between the two alternative formats. Both demonstrate the equality of the balance sheet, but are presented from different perspectives.

The horizontal format shows the equality in the following way:

$$FA + CA = C + LTL + CL$$

where   FA = fixed assets
CA = current assets
C = owner's capital
LTL = long-term liabilities
CL = current liabilities

The vertical format restates the equality in the following way:

$$FA + (CA - CL) - LTL = C$$

The vertical format improves the presentation of the report, presenting it from the perspective of the owner and their claim on the business, showing the owner's capital as a balancing figure. It is necessary to become familiar with the vertical format as it is used in financial statements prepared by nearly all types of organization. It will always be used from now on.

SUMMARY

1 **The balancing figure on a partial trial balance of income and expense accounts will normally be a negative amount which represents a net profit for the financial period. If the balance is positive, this represents a net loss.**

2 **The balancing figure on a partial trial balance of assets and liabilities at the end of a period represents an increase in the net assets of the business as a consequence of exchange, which also equals the net profit of a business earned in a given period.**

3 **The accruals concept requires that revenue and expenses attributable to a financial period should be entered in the trading and profit and loss account. Where receipts and payments differ from those attributable amounts, there must exist a measure of debt to or by the business. That debt will be included in the balance sheet as a prepayment if the debt is owed to the business, or as an accrual if the amount is owed by the business.**

4 **The trading and profit and loss account is separated into two distinct parts. The upper half is the trading account; it measures the difference between income attributable to trading and the primary cost of generating this income, known as gross profit. The lower half derives the net profit by adding other attributable incomes to the gross profit and subtracting other attributable expenses.**

5 **The final accounts are prepared in vertical format. The balance sheet presented in vertical format isolates the owner's capital in the following way:**

$$FA + (CA - CL) - LTL = C$$

ASSESSMENT

MULTIPLE-CHOICE QUESTIONS

Question 1
From the following list of accounts at the end of December, calculate the net profit earned and select the right answer from the choice of four.

	£		£
Drawings	200	Cost of sales	6,500
Returns inwards	45	Debtors	2,200
Bank	100	Rent received	560
Discount received	80	Capital (1.1)	30,000
Premises	35,000	Discount allowed	395
Wages	2,700	Creditors	4,600
Insurance	1,100	Sales	13,000

A £2,700
B £2,900
C £2,825
D £3,215

Question 2

Taking the situation in Question 1, if at December 31 the stocks unsold were valued at £400, which one of the following identifies the correct effect on gross profit and net profit?

	Gross profit £	Net profit £
A	−400	−400
B	+400	−400
C	+400	+400
D	+800	+400

Question 3

Which one of these is an accrual?

A Rent received in advance
B Insurance paid in advance
C Interest received in arrears
D Closing stocks undervalued

Question 4

Rent of £2,400 was paid on November 12 by a tenant to a leisure complex business, covering the six months between November 1, 19x3 and April 30, 19x4. Rent of £3,200 was paid on May 8 covering the period May 1, 19x4 until October 31, 19x4, and £3,600 was paid on November 10, 19x4 covering the period November 1, 19x4 to April 30, 19x5.

Each rental payment was made in full and in advance. How much income should the landlord attribute to his or her profit and loss account for the financial period January 1, 19x4 to December 31, 19x4?

A £6,800
B £6,000
C £5,600
D £9,200

Question 5

Having prepared the trial balance for the year ended December 31, 19x3, the following adjustments must be made:

1 Wages of £120 are owing to an employee.
2 One of the sales staff has overclaimed expenses of £50.
3 A tenant has overpaid rent of £150.
4 The stock valuation at December 31 was £80 more than it should have been.

Which one of the following answers is correct in identifying the overall effect on net profit of these adjustments?

	Net profit
	£
A	−140
B	−400
C	no effect
D	−300

EXERCISES

Exercise 1

The following trial balance was extracted for the Alpine classic car spares business as at the year ended May 31, 19x3:

		£
Land and buildings		100,000
Fixtures and fittings		20,000
Spares and parts stocks	(June 1, 19x2)	15,000
Sales		150,000
Purchases of spares and parts		52,000
Mechanics' and engineers' wages		75,000
Rent and rates		4,000
Debtors		1,000
Creditors		1,500
Insurances		3,000
Discounts allowed		500
Discounts received		300
Returns inwards		1,000
Returns outwards		2,500
Bank overdraft		1,500
Carriage inwards		1,500
Carriage outwards		2,500
Drawings		25,000
Light, heat and telephone		4,200
Rent received		4,000
Owner's capital	(June 1, 19x2)	140,900

The following information is available:

1 Closing stocks valued at May 31, 19x3 were £12,000.
2 Mechanics' wages owing at May 31, 19x3 were £900.
3 Rent was half the rent and rates expense and this was paid for the period June 1, 19x2 to September 30, 19x3.
4 Rent received was for the period June 1, 19x2 to January 31, 19x3.

Required

Produce an extended trial balance showing the necessary adjustments (1 to 4) and the final accounts for Alpine, at the end of May 19x3.

Exercise 2

The Triassic model dinosaur theme park opened for business on May 1, 19x3. The business rents land from a farmer. The rent is paid as follows:

May 30, 19x3: 2,500 for the first three months ended July 31, 19x3.
August 22, 19x3: £3,000 for the six months ended January 31, 19x4.
February 15, 19x4: £3,600 for the six months ended July 31, 19x4.

During this period the theme park owners have sublet part of the land to a funfair business that provides amusements and rides. The annual rent for this part of the land is £3,600, the rent has been received as follows:

July 31, 19x3	£900
November 30, 19x3	£800
February 28, 19x4	£1,000

Required
Construct the rent payable and receivable accounts, and calculate the profit and loss account entries for the year ended April 30, 19x4, and the relevant balance sheet entries as at April 30, 19x4.

Exercise 3
Calculate these missing figures for the Getaway travel agent business:

Rates expense	£		Postage and stationery expense	£	
Balance Jan 1	200	accrual		?	
Paid during the year	?			500	
Due for the year	400			1,200	
Balance Dec 31	150	prepayment		300	accrual

Booking-clerk wages	£		Electricity expense	£	
Balances Jan 1	1,100	accrual		320	prepayment
Paid during the year	14,500			600	
Due for the year	?			800	
Balance Dec 31	1,300	accrual		?	

Exercise 4
The following trial balance was extracted from the books of Norbury Trendwear, a leisure clothes retailer, as at December 31, 19x3:

	£
Capital account	−20,500
Cost of sales	+52,800
Sales	−60,900
Repairs to buildings	+848
Motor car	+950
Car expenses	+318
Freehold land and buildings	+10,000
Bank balance	+540
Furniture and fittings	+1,460
Wages and salaries	+8,606
Discounts allowed	+1,061
Discounts received	−814
Drawings	+2,400
Rates and insurances	+248
Trade debtors	+5,213
Trade creditors	−4,035
General expenses	+1,805
	0

Additional information

(a) Stocks of clothing valued at December 31, 19x3 totalled £8,800.

(b) Wages and salaries outstanding at December 31, 19x3 amount to £318.

(c) Rates and insurances paid in advance as at December 31, 19x3 are £45.

(d) During the year the owner withdrew clothes which cost £200 for his family's use.

(e) The repairs to buildings included £650 in respect of an extension to the shop-floor area and a completely new shop-front and window.

(f) It was agreed with the Inland Revenue that two-thirds of the motoring expenses would be classified as business expenditure.

Required

Prepare the final accounts for Norbury Trendwear for the year to December 31, 19x3.

CHAPTER 5

Accounting for fixed assets

OBJECTIVES

- Define a fixed asset.
- Recognize that fixed-asset values depend on a number of factors, and that the business is a going concern.
- Relate the accruals concept of accountancy to the allocation of the periodic depreciation of fixed assets against the revenues they help to generate.
- Describe, justify and calculate the main methods of depreciating the cost of fixed assets.
- Record, process and report depreciation in the accounts and consider its effects on profit and financial position.
- Understand the importance of consistency in the treatment of fixed-asset depreciation.
- Determine and calculate the effects on profitability of purchasing and disposing of fixed assets.
- Define, identify and describe the main sources of intangible fixed-asset values, with reference to the fundamental accounting concepts of accruals, prudence and money measurement.

5.1 DEFINITION OF FIXED ASSETS

Chapter 2 introduced the important conceptual distinction between **capital** and **revenue** expenditure. Capital expenditure occurs when a business utilizes its resources to acquire an asset which has a permanent existence or value within the business. Revenue expenditure occurs when a business uses its resources to acquire assets which don't have a permanent existence, e.g. stocks, or when it makes no recognizable acquisition at all, due to there being no asset value to place on the business balance sheet; perhaps it buys consumables or services. In Chapter 1 the permanent nature of fixed assets was implied by describing them analogously as the 'bones' of the business, providing the infrastructure within which trading can operate. But nothing is permanent. As with the bones in our bodies, fixed assets may become damaged or useless, they may sometimes need replacing, and they will eventually crumble away!

5.2 DEPRECIATION OF FIXED ASSETS

If A. Cooke, a hotelier, purchases kitchen cooking equipment for £30,000 at the beginning of year 1, can it be expected to retain its original 'value' by the end of year 3? The obvious answer is no, but what are the possible reasons for this?

1 The passage of time
2 The level of usage
3 Technological obsolescence
4 Market obsolescence

All of these factors reduce the value of a fixed asset, and will mean that a business will need to replace it at some time. The eventual replacement of a fixed asset must imply an assumption that a business will continue to trade into perpetuity, and that it will not discontinue its activities or become bankrupt. This important but arguably rather naive assumption is known as the **going concern** concept, and to a significant extent underpins the treatment of fixed assets in the accounts.

Depreciation has been defined many times, but the accountancy profession has defined it formally in one of its statements of standard accounting practice (SSAPs). SSAP 12 defines depreciation as

the measure of wearing out, consumption or other reduction in the useful economic life of a fixed asset whether arising from use, effluxion of time or obsolescence through technological or market changes.

This definition encompasses the four factors which were identified earlier, and implies that a fixed asset must therefore have a 'finite economic life'. The 'useful economic life' can be defined as the period over which the present owner of that asset derives economic benefits from its use. If a fixed asset ceases to provide continuing economic benefits from use, it may still have what is known as a residual value. This can be defined as the realizable value less the potential realization costs associated with the realization of this value for the present owner.

5.3 DEPRECIATION AND THE ACCRUALS CONCEPT

The accountancy profession requires that a depreciation 'charge' should be arrived at by allocating the cost or value of fixed assets, less any estimated net residual value, as fairly as possible to the periods expected to benefit from their use. This charge should be made against attributable revenues in those periods.

If there were no accruals concept, it might be acceptable to charge the whole of a fixed asset's purchase cost to the profit and loss account in the year of acquisition. What are the implications of this approach? It would be the same as treating the purchase of fixed assets as expenditure on consumables and services. The whole cost would be 'written off' and no balance sheet value would be recognized.

This creates two major but related problems. Profit would be dramatically and adversely affected in years where major purchases of fixed assets were made, and would be artificially high in other years, possibly misleading users of the profit and loss account as to the underlying financial performance and future potential of the business. And as the existence of the physical form of these 'fixed assets' within the business would not be financially recognized on the balance sheet of the business, the asset values and capital of the owner would be seriously understated.

Using this approach would mean that, although the owner would be deriving continued economic benefit from the 'asset', over a number of years, the cost of that 'asset' would have been charged against the revenue attributable to only one of those years.

The problem in adhering to the accruals concept is how to fairly attribute that proportion of the cost or value of the fixed asset to the appropriate period. A number of specific questions need to be asked:

1 How long will the asset remain in use?
2 How heavily will it be utilized in each financial period?
3 To what extent does this fixed asset in particular, among all the others employed within the business, confer economic benefits on the present owner?
4 To what extent will its technological obsolescence affect the the answers to the first three questions?
5 To what extent does the marketability of the products or services that the business makes available, affect the economic benefits that the owner derives from the fixed asset in any specific period?

The answers to these questions are often very difficult, perhaps impossible, to arrive at with any certainty, and therefore the allocation of fixed-asset cost over its useful life can be a very uncertain practice indeed. It is best to take into account these factors and make an 'appropriate' allocation of costs depending on the class of fixed asset that the business is depreciating.

5.4 METHODS OF DEPRECIATION

Returning to A. Cooke, the hotelier: he has purchased catering equipment for £30,000. The following information is available to the owner regarding this equipment over the next three years. He expects to sell the equipment at the beginning of the fourth year:

	Year 1 £	Year 2 £	Year 3 £	Year 4 £
Equivalent market value at the beginning of each year	30,000	23,500	19,000	12,000
Hourly usage each year	2,500	2,000	1,500	n/a

The straight-line method

The straight-line method involves simply taking the cost price of the asset, then subtracting the net residual value and dividing the result by the number of years over which the asset is expected to confer economic benefit on the owner. This can be described algebraically as

$$D = (C - R)/L$$

where D = annual depreciation
C = cost or original value
R = net residual value
L = asset life in periods

If this formula is used for the catering equipment, it is possible to calculate a periodic depreciation charge:

$$(£30,000 - £12,000)/3 = £6,000 \text{ per year}$$

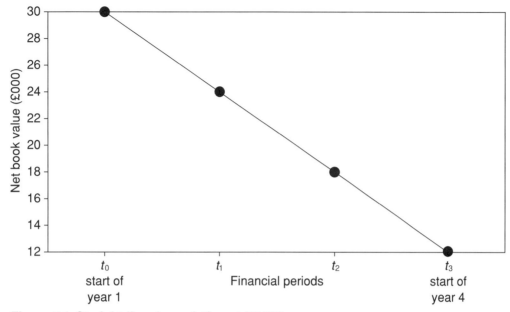

Figure 5.1 Straight-line depreciation at £6,000 per year

This can be depicted graphically showing the linear relationship between the 'value' of the fixed asset and its age (Fig. 5.1).

This method of depreciation uses time as the major factor determining diminution of value; it is convenient but simplistic.

The reducing-balance method

This method recognizes the phenomenon that a new fixed asset tends to lose more value in its earlier years than in its later years. A new car falls in to this category. The way this can be calculated is to take the depreciated 'value' of the fixed asset at the beginning of every period and to depreciate it by a fixed percentage each period. If the catering equipment above were depreciated under the reducing-balance method over the three years at 30%, what residual value would it have at the beginning of year 4?

	£
Cost at start of year 1	30,000
Less 30% depreciation	9,000
Depreciated value at start of year 2	21,000
Less 30% depreciation	6,300
Depreciated value at start of year 3	14,700
Less 30% depreciation	4,410
Residual value at start of year 4	10,290

Notice that the depreciation charge reduces from £9,000 in the first year down to £4,410 in the third year. The only problem here is that the residual value is too low compared with A. Cooke's original estimate. We know therefore that the appropriate

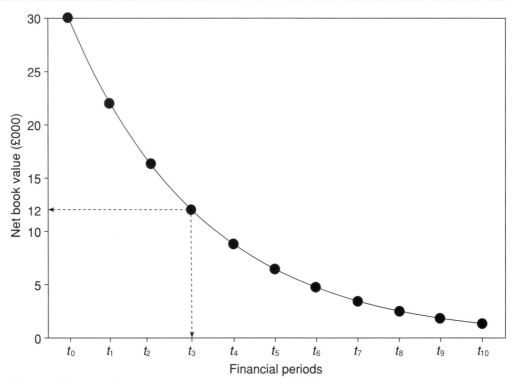

Figure 5.2 Reducing-balance depreciation at 26.32% per year

percentage rate using this method is less than 30%. But what exact fixed percentage rate would need to be used to arrive at the correct residual value at the beginning of year 4 without using a tedious trial and error method?

The formula for deriving the annual fixed percentage rate is

$$D = 100[1 - (R/C)^{1/L}]$$

where D = annual percentage rate
L = expected life in periods
R = net residual value
C = cost or original value

Using our original example, we get

$$D = 100[1 - (12,000/30,000)^{1/3}]$$
$$= 26.32\%$$

By looking at the graphical representation of the reducing-balance method using $D = 26.32\%$, the value of the asset can be plotted and the shape of the function seen (Fig. 5.2). There is an exponential decay in the value of the catering equipment over time. This inevitably means that the asset will never have a zero value. In reality this is a fairly reasonable assumption, as even low-grade scrap may realize some value unless this is outweighed by realization costs, which may be the case with installed machinery.

The formula therefore will not work if a zero value is required, and is a little cumbersome to calculate, but its function does resemble the depreciation pattern of such fixed assets as vehicles.

The sum-of-digits method

The sum-of-digits method is mathematically simpler and accords conceptually with the overall effect of the reducing-balance method. It is calculated by first assessing the total estimated depreciation over the asset's useful economic life:

$$C - R = £30,000 - £12,000 = £18,000$$

then adding up the digits of the period numbers:

$$\text{Yr1 Yr2 Yr3}$$

$$1 + 2 + 3 = 6$$

and apportioning the annual depreciation charge in the following way:

$$\text{Year 1} \quad 3/6 \times £18,000 = £9,000$$

$$\text{Year 2} \quad 2/6 \times £18,000 = £6,000$$

$$\text{Year 3} \quad 1/6 \times £18,000 = £3,000$$

By looking at the equivalent annual depreciation charge under the reducing-balance method for $D = 26.32\%$ it is found there would not be a significant difference in the chargeable amount, so in principle the sum-of-digits method reflects the same assumptions underlying the adoption of the reducing-balance method. Both the reducing-balance method and the sum-of-digits method attempt to take into account other factors such as usage, wear and tear, and market and technical obsolescence. For example, a new car will have done most of its mileage in the first two years of its life and may be almost obsolescent at only a few years of age, as newer models are introduced to the market-place with more advanced features.

Looking at usage as the prime determinant of depreciation, the annual depreciation charge of A. Cooke's catering equipment can be calculated on the basis of the estimated annual hourly usage:

	Year 1	Year 2	Year 3	Total
Annual hourly usage	2,500	2,000	1,500	6,000

The formula here is

$$D = (\text{Annual usage/Total usage}) \times (C - R)$$

In the first year the depreciation charge would be

$$D = (2,500/6,000) \times (30,000 - 12,000)$$
$$= 7,500$$

$$\text{In the first year} \quad D = 7,500$$

$$\text{In the second year} \quad D = 6,000$$

$$\text{In the third year} \quad D = 4,500$$

All these methods are flawed from the point of view that they assume perfect knowledge about the future: the economic life of the asset, the net residual value, and for the sum-of-digits method, the expected productive capacity of the asset over its useful economic life.

The revaluation method

The most objective method, but probably the most costly and time-consuming, requires systematic valuations at the end of each financial period. This may involve reference to trade journals, guidebooks, using available indices, or may even require professional valuation.

In the case of A. Cooke, the valuations (£) given at the end of each of the three years were

Original cost	End of year 1	End of year 2	End of year 3
30,000	23,500	19,000	12,000

The depreciation to be charged in each of the three years would be as follows:

$$£$$

Year 1: $D = 30,000 - 23,500 = 6,500$
Year 2: $D = 23,500 - 19,000 = 4,500$
Year 3: $D = 19,000 - 12,000 = 7,000$

In practice we must accept the shortcomings of most methods of apportioning depreciation, and select a reasonably simple, convenient and cost-effective method. We must also make reasonable assumptions about any uncertainties, based on the past experience of owning and using similar classes of assets.

The most commonly used method is the straight-line method because of its simplicity and ease of calculation. The length of economic life can usually be ascertained by reference to policy, such as sales representatives having their cars changed every two years, or pubs being refurbished every five years, and so on. The residual value can usually be estimated with reasonable accuracy. For example, second-hand car prices fall within certain ranges, and old pub furniture and fittings probably have no residual value when removed.

5.5 RECORDING, PROCESSING AND REPORTING DEPRECIATION IN THE ACCOUNTS

The choice of depreciation method will determine the amount of depreciation attributable as an expense to be charged in the current year's profit and loss account. A. Cooke's catering equipment will be depreciated in his accounts using the straight-line method. Note that the fixed asset is worth less and less every year, so there are implications for the balance sheet. Imagine that A. Cooke's balance sheet comprised the following accounts at the beginning of year 1:

	£
Land and buildings at cost	+50,000
Catering equipment at cost	+30,000
Capital	−105,000
Bank	+25,000
	0

Assume that in the first year no trading actually takes place. In the first year the only 'transaction' that needs to be recognized is the depreciation of the catering equipment. (The recording of depreciation is not a true transaction; the transaction takes place only when the fixed asset is bought, and when it is sold. However, there is a need to record the internal transaction by recognizing the perceived change in economic circumstances of the owner.)

The catering equipment is worth £6,000 less at the end of the first year than it was when it was purchased. It is therefore necessary to subtract £6,000 from the asset value to reflect that the total asset side of the balance sheet has been reduced. It is also necessary to make a compensating entry on the liabilities side of the balance sheet in order for it to remain in balance. The compensating adjustment is made in the capital account, reflecting that the owner is theoretically £6,000 worse off at the end of the year than he was at the beginning of the year.

At the end of the first year the assets and liabilities would be as follows:

	Before £	Adjustment £	After £
Land and buildings at cost	+50,000		+50,000
Catering equipment at cost	+30,000	−6,000	+24,000
Capital	−105,000	+6,000	−99,000
Bank	+25,000		+25,000
	0		0

Although this is the net result of the transaction, in practice the depreciation charge would be recorded as an expense in the accounts, and reported as a deduction from gross profit in the profit and loss account, thereby reducing the net profit available to the owner. The actual double entry for the depreciation in the accounts would be

> **Debit** the depreciation expense account   +6,000

and instead of crediting the fixed asset account:

> **Credit** the provision for depreciation account   −6,000

The reason for not netting off the depreciation against the cost of the fixed asset is that the balance sheet needs to present the original cost of the fixed asset less the **accumulated** depreciation over its economic life to date. The reason for this is to give an indication to users of accounts how much remains of the asset's useful economic life.

In the second year it is assumed that A. Cooke trades normally and makes a net profit before depreciation of £28,000. If all sales, purchases, and expenses are for cash and no stocks are left at the year-end, there will be an increase in cash of £28,000, therefore the net profit declared after deducting the depreciation charge will be £22,000. The closing balance sheet at the end of the second year would be as follows:

Balance sheet (A. Cooke) as at end of year 2

	Cost £	Depreciation £	Net book value (NBV) £
Fixed assets			
Land and buildings	50,000	nil	50,000
Catering equipment	30,000	12,000	18,000
	80,000	12,000	68,000
Current assets			
Bank (25,000 + 28,000)			53,000
			121,000

Balance sheet (A. Cooke) as at end of year 2 (cont'd)

	Cost £	Depreciation £	Net book value (NBV) £
Financed by			
Capital at end of year 1			99,000
Add net profit for year 2 (28,000 − 6,000)			22,000
			121,000

Note that the net profit is shown net of the year's annual depreciation charge, and the fixed asset is shown on the balance sheet at its net book value (NBV), which is cost less accumulated depreciation to date, i.e. (2 × £6,000).

5.6 ACCOUNTING FOR THE ACQUISITION AND DISPOSAL OF FIXED ASSETS

Although it is assumed that fixed assets will be held by a business for a number of financial periods, there will be times when their economic lives are effectively over for any number of reasons, contained within the definition of depreciation quoted earlier.

In addition, as the business is assumed to be a going concern, it will be expected to purchase and sell its fixed assets periodically in order to maintain and expand its level of operations. The decisions about which assets should be purchased from a finite pool of available financial resources, are the responsibility of the management accountant, and we will look at these decisions in Part 2.

When an asset is sold or disposed of, a number of entries need to be made. The entries concerned with the acquisition and disposal of fixed assets will be demonstrated using our example, A. Cooke.

A. Cooke makes a cash profit before depreciation of £24,000 in the third year. If he disposes of his old catering equipment for £12,500 cash on the last day of the third year, and uses the proceeds to contribute towards the acquisition of new equipment costing £35,000 cash on the same day, what are the entries required within the accounts?

Catering equipment a/c		*Provision for depreciation a/c*		*Disposals a/c*	
Ref	£	Ref	£	Ref	£
Bal b/d (yr 2)	+30,000	Bal b/d (yr 2)	−12,000	Cat equip	+30,000
Disposals	−30,000	Depn (yr 3)	−6,000	Prov	−18,000
Bank	+35,000	Disposals	+18,000	Bank	−12,500
Bal b/d	+35,000	Bal b/d	nil*	Bal b/d	−500

Bank account	
Ref	£
Bal b/d (yr 2)	+53,000
Cash profits	+24,000
Disposals	+12,500
Cat equip	−35,000
Bal b/d	+54,500

* There is no balance left on the provision for depreciation account as the old catering equipment has been sold and the new equipment was bought on the last day of the year, so no depreciation has yet been suffered.

The disposal account is used to transfer out the original cost of the disposed asset and the accumulated depreciation on that fixed asset. The remaining balances in those accounts should only relate to fixed assets still held by the business at the end of the current financial period.

The balance of £–500 on the disposal account represents a profit on the disposal of that fixed asset. This is explained by comparing the net book value of the old asset, £30,000 – £18,000 = £12,000, with the proceeds obtained from selling the asset. This exceeded the net book value by £500. In reality this reflects that A. Cooke's business has overprovided depreciation in the past on that asset. To correct this imbalance the 'profit on sale' should be added to the profit declared by the business for the period. If this were a loss, an additional depreciation charge would need to be made against the reported profits of the period.

The balance sheet as at the end of the third year would be as follows:

Balance sheet (A. Cooke) as at end of year 3

	Cost £	Depn £	NBV £
Fixed assets			
Land and buildings	50,000	nil	50,000
Catering equipment	35,000	nil	35,000
	80,000	nil	85,000
Current assets			
Bank			54,500
			139,500
Financed by			
Capital at end of year 2			121,000
Add net profit for year 3			18,500*
			139,500

* The net profit for year 3 = cash profits – depreciation charge for the year + profit on sale of old equipment:

£24,000 – £6,000 + £500 = £18,500

Charging an amount for depreciation over the useful life of the asset effectively reduces the profit available to the owner, reflecting the apportionment of the economic value of the asset dissipated in the current financial period. The depreciation charge is based upon the historic cost of the asset, and in no way takes into account that additional resources may be required to replace the asset at current prices. A business needs to ensure that, in order to maintain its operating capability, it retains adequate resources within the business to allow fixed assets to be replaced as and when required. It is not enough to retain funds generally; it is essential that those funds are available in liquid form to allow replacement at the required time.

5.7 THE CONSISTENCY CONCEPT

A variety of methods can be adopted when depreciating fixed assets. The range of methods and accounting policies can have a considerable effect on the net profit calculated, and as capital expenditure can form a considerable proportion of a business's total expenditure, it is of vital importance that the method used is appropriate to the class of asset concerned, and that it does fairly apportion the cost of the asset to the periods which produce the economic benefits.

It is also important that, once a method and policy has been selected on a sound economic basis, it is used consistently year on year. The reason for this is that users of financial information may be misled if fluctuations in profitability are caused by arbitrary changes in depreciation policies rather than by the underlying financial performance of the business. There may be substantive reasons for changing a depreciation method or policy, but they must be based on a change in economic reality, or reflect a change in a specific business policy; they must not be driven by a need to manipulate reported profitability.

5.8 INTANGIBLE FIXED ASSETS

Fixed assets are usually described as tangible, e.g. land, buildings, plant, equipment, fixtures and fittings, and vehicles. These assets appear on the balance sheet along with the current assets to represent the total book value of the business at any time. But is the business worth exactly this amount, or are there any other values that may have been overlooked?

If a business operating as a going concern is sold, it is usual to find that the buyer will pay more for the business than is indicated by the net asset values disclosed on the balance sheet. What are the reasons for this? Several aspects of a business may not have a monetary value placed on them; here are some examples:

1 A skilled and efficient labour force
2 Excellent labour relations
3 A lucrative market-place or competitive advantage
4 A highly innovative and capable management
5 Well-known and respected brand names
6 A strategic location
7 Patented products, secret formulae or secret ingredients

All these qualities would be valued by a prospective buyer, but nowhere are they normally specifically quantified in monetary terms on the balance sheet. The only exceptions would include recognized brands and patents, where in certain highly specific circumstances, expenditure on them may be included on the balance sheet.

Many types of expenditure, classified as revenue expenditure, are written off in the year of incurment but they may create lasting value. Let us look at some specific examples in the tourism, leisure and hospitality industry:

1 Expenditure on the training and education of chefs
2 Advertising and promotional expenditure on holiday packages
3 Subsidies paid to beat competition for tenders for a bus route
4 A golden hello to appoint a new driver for a racing team
5 Expenditure on research and development of a new aerodynamic racing bicycle

Most of them, it could be argued, add lasting value to the business, although most of that expenditure would not find its way to the balance sheet in the form of business assets.

Referring once again to the accruals concept, are any of the economic benefits to be derived from such expenditure likely to be derived in future periods? If the answer is yes, then it can be argued that an asset needs to be recognized in much the same way as a prepayment is recognized as an asset.

Consider advertising expenditure. If a travel agency spends thousands of pounds in a particular period, advertising itself, its name and its services, it could be argued that, by creating or enhancing awareness of its name in the minds of customers and potential customers, its business receives a lasting financial benefit. It could also be argued that expenditure on providing staff with the interpersonal qualities to satisfy customers, perhaps to leave them with a lasting favourable impression of the service they have received, will confer future benefits in the form of repeat business from existing customers and new business from recommendations.

What about expenditure on acquiring a managing director with the vision and the strategic planning capability that can give the business a competitive advantage in the market-place for years to come, or expenditure on research and development which leads to a product that uniquely meets a specific market need? What about the salary of a master chef whose culinary renown spreads far and wide? What value should be placed on such key personnel?

Although a distinction has been made between capital and revenue expenditure, satisfying the accruals concept and the money measurement concept, this distinction may not in fact be quite so clear. A whole range of revenue expenditure may provide more than an immediate benefit to the business, and it may represent an investment for the business from which future economic benefits will be derived, in just the same way as tangible assets such as land, buildings and plant. The only objective way that the value invested in a business by such revenue expenditure becomes evident is when the business is sold, because it is only then that a monetary price is placed on this surplus value through the offer made by the buyer. This surplus value is known as **goodwill**. Goodwill is therefore defined as

the difference between the value of a business as a whole and the aggregate of the fair values of its separable net assets. (SSAP 22, 1984)

In the context of valuing a brewery, Dr Samuel Johnson once defined *goodwill* as the premium above the aggregate value of all the vats, pipes and boilers which one would be willing to pay for that brewery in order to acquire the 'potentiality to grow rich beyond the dreams of avarice'.

To some extent this sums it up. A business only has value, or its assets only have value, if those assets bring monetary benefit to the owner in future periods. Those assets can therefore be defined as being worth the equivalent of the total economic benefits they will generate in the future for the owner. There are two difficulties with this kind of valuation:

– The future economic benefits are inherently uncertain.
– The identificaton of the exact source of those economic benefits in relation to specific assets is very difficult.

The accountant should always attempt to measure value objectively. It is very difficult to assess how much revenue expenditure is 'investment' for the future and how much is immediately 'consumed'. How much of the training budget can be traced directly to the improved skills of the workforce? How much of the advertising and promotional budget has a lasting impact on consumers? How much of the research and development expenditure leads directly to new products and services? In recognition of this uncertainty, prudence and the money measurement concept require that the value of goodwill can only be recognized on the balance sheet if it has been objectively verified through a buyer paying more for a business as a whole than its aggregated net assets are worth on the balance sheet.

The concept of prudence requires that a going concern, undertaking some of the expenditures we have discussed, should write them off entirely in the current year, and should not recognize any of the value of unexpired economic benefits as intangible assets on the balance sheet, except in very narrowly prescribed circumstances, as recommended by the professional accountancy bodies and allowed under company law. Clearly this prudent approach would confirm that the balance sheet as prepared by accountants does not tell us the whole story about value, and may therefore be criticized for seriously undervaluing the business as a going concern.

SUMMARY

1 **A fixed asset was defined.**

2 **Most fixed assets have a finite economic life.**

3 **Depreciation needs to be fairly charged against the economic benefits derived from such assets over their useful lives, in accordance with the accruals concept, and the most appropriate method of doing this will be determined by economic circumstances and the business policies of the organization.**

4 **Whichever method or policy for depreciation is selected for a particular class of fixed asset should be maintained over the long term, unless there are changes in underlying economic circumstances or business policy. This is a requirement of the consistency concept of accounting.**

5 **Providing for depreciation effectively reduces the net profit available for withdrawal by the owner, indicating the necessity to retain funds within the business for the eventual and inevitable replacement of those assets.**

6 **When an asset is disposed of, there will almost inevitably be a discrepancy between the accounts value of the asset – the net book value (NBV) – and what is realized from its sale. This discrepancy represents an underprovision or an overprovision for depreciation over the asset's useful life. This amount is either deducted from or added to the gross profit in the profit and loss account during the year of the asset's disposal.**

7 **Several qualitative factors mean that the true asset value of the business is understated due to the simple distinction between capital and revenue expenditure. According to the accruals concept, certain revenue expenditure will provide economic benefits in future periods and should therefore be recognized as intangible assets on the balance sheet. The argument for not doing so stems from the lack of certainty about such values, and the need to adhere to the prudence concept and the money measurement concept.**

ASSESSMENT

MULTIPLE-CHOICE QUESTIONS

Question 1
Fixed assets can best be defined as which of the following?

A Assets which cannot easily be moved from their present location
B Assets which will derive economic benefits for the owner more than one year into the future
C Assets which have a relatively high purchase price
D Assets that are financed by long-term liabilities

Question 2
Which of the following methods of depreciation cannot be used if there is an assumption of a zero net residual value?

A Reducing-balance method
B Straight-line method
C Sum-of-digits method
D Revaluation method

Question 3
Which of the following accountancy concepts is described by the following statement? We provide depreciation in order to retain funds within the business for the eventual replacement of an asset by another of the same productive capability.

A Accruals concept
B Prudence concept
C Going-concern concept
D Consistency concept

Question 4
An asset purchased for £10,000 with an expected life of five years and a net residual value of £2,500 is sold during the third year of its life for £8,000. What is the adjustment required in the profit and loss account at the end of the third year, using the straight-line method?

A Add £2,500 to gross profit in the profit and loss account
B Subtract £1,000 from gross profit in the profit and loss account
C Subtract £2,500 from gross profit in the profit and loss account
D Add £1,000 to gross profit in the profit and loss account

Question 5
Goodwill is best represented by which one of the following descriptions?

A Expenditure on assets which cannot be touched or seen
B The difference between the price a buyer is willing to pay for a business and the net value of its separable tangible net assets
C Expenditure on items which directly benefit the customer
D Assets which cannot be defined as tangible or intangible

EXERCISES

Exercise 1
The Otis Hotel is finalizing its accounts for the current year. During the year, a new larger lift was purchased in order to cater for increased demand. The original lift was part-exchanged on the basis of a trade-in, where £5,000 was allowed from the full purchase price of the new lift of £20,000. Before taking account of this disposal and acquisition, and before charging depreciation for the year, the profit arrived at was £30,500. The hotel has a machinery depreciation policy of charging a full year's depreciation in the year of acquisition, and none in the year of disposal.

Other information
The original cost of the old lift was £14,000, and it was three years old at the beginning of the current year.

Required
Find the adjusted profit figure after dealing with the disposal and charging depreciation against profits for the current year under all three of the following choices of depreciation policy for the lifts. (Assume that exactly the same depreciation policy applies to both lifts.)

1 Straight-line method using a rate of 25% on cost
2 Reducing balance method using 30%
3 Sum-of-digits method assuming a four-year life and a £4,000 residual value

Exercise 2
The Ubiety Coach Company made the following acquisitions and disposals over the past three years:

	Year 1	Year 2	Year 3
Acquisitions			
Coach A	12,000		
Coach B	15,000		
Coach C		16,000	
Coach D			20,000
Disposals			
Coach A		8,000	
Coach B			5,000

The depreciation policy of the coach company is 25% straight-line on all vehicles. A full year's depreciation is charged on vehicles in the year of acquisition, none in the year of disposal.

Required

(a) Calculate the total depreciation to be charged on vehicles held at the end of each of the three years.
(b) Calculate the profit and loss on disposal to be charged in year 2 and year 3.

Exercise 3
The Permafrost frozen meat supplies business has the following trial balance as at November 30, 19x3:

	£
Capital account	−96,000
Delivery van at net book value	8,000
Purchases of meat supplies	483,600
Sales of meat supplies	−622,200
Stocks of meat (1.12.x2)	47,000
Trade debtors	52,800
Trade creditors	−41,160
Cabinet freezer (see note)	12,680
General expenses	14,690
Motor expenses	4,180
Rent and rates	6,740
Spare land	37,500
Balance at bank	14,150
Discounts allowed	11,260
Discounts received	−8,710
Wages and salaries	74,620
Lighting and heating	850
	0

The following information must be taken into account:

1 Closing stock of meat supplies, £64,650.
2 Lighting and heating accrued at 30.11.x3, £120.
3 Rates paid in advance at 30.11.x3, £280.
4 The freezer cabinet fixed-asset account had not been properly recorded. It had been completed as follows:

Cabinet freezer account

Ref		£	
1.12.x3	Bal b/d	+2,760	(old cabinet at NBV*)
23.4.x3	Bank	+12,000	(new cabinet)
20.5.x3	Bank	−2,080	(proceeds old unit)
30.11.x3	Bal c/d	+12,680	

* Net book value (cost less accumulated depreciation).

The business depreciates its cabinet freezers at a rate of 20% per annum and charges a full year's depreciation in the year of acquisition, none in the year of disposal.

The delivery van is depreciated at the rate of 25% per annum using the reducing-balance method. It is the policy of the business not to depreciate the land.

Required
Prepare a trading and profit and loss account for the year ended November 30, 19x3 and the corresponding balance sheet.

Exercise 4
The Delta TEFL language school based in the Greek islands is a cash-based business, where customers attend courses in-house and pay for them when they enrol. The business carries no stock-in-trade, and all its fittings and equipment are treated as fixed assets. The business has the following assets and liabilities as at July 31, 19x7:

	Dr
Land and buildings	1,000,000
Furniture and fittings (F + F)	800,000
Equipment	720,000
Provision for depreciation (F + F)	−400,000
Provision for depreciation (equip)	−240,000
Stocks of video- and audiotape (NBV)	100,000
Bank balance	500,000
Long-term loan (fixed rate, 12%)	−700,000
Capital	−1,780,000
	0

During the next three months the business made a cash surplus on providing its language services, before interest and depreciation of Dr 180,000. The interest on the long-term loan is paid quarterly in advance by standing order from a bank. The depreciation policy of the language school is to use the straight-line method as follows:

– Furniture and fittings are depreciated at 20% of cost per annum.
– Equipment is depreciated on the straight-line basis over a three-year period, assuming no residual value.
– Stocks of tapes are depreciated at 20% per annum using the reducing-balance method.

It is also known that EuroLang, a multinational language school, is prepared to pay Dr 2,000,000 for the business excluding cash as at October 30, 19x7.

Required

(a) Prepare the balance sheet of Delta TEFL as at October 30, 19x7.
(b) Calculate the value of the intangible assets, or goodwill, as at October 30, 19x7, assuming the EuroLang offer is acceptable to Delta.

CHAPTER 6

Accounting for stocks

OBJECTIVES

- Identify the main types of stocks to be found in the tourism, leisure and hospitality industries.
- Understand the impact that stock valuations have on profitability.
- Identify and explain methods of verifying the quantity and quality of deliveries, and methods of checking for fraud and deception.
- Describe and operate a system of stock control that checks for leakage and theft, and accounts for perquisites.
- Value stocks by several different methods, understand their impact on profitability, and justify their use against the framework of generally accepted accounting concepts.

6.1 TYPES OF STOCK

In most trading businesses, a key asset held at any moment is stock-in-trade. This can be defined as the assets which a business acquires solely for the purpose of selling, and from which its major income is derived. In the case of Freddo Gelati (Chapter 3) it was ice-cream. For a business selling souvenirs it would be the stocks of souvenirs, etc., found in the shop and the storeroom. Some businesses hold vast amounts of stock such as cash-and-carry warehouses, whereas others carry very little stocks at all, such as a small fishmonger, where freshness is paramount.

In the tourism, leisure and hospitality industry, which generates its income by providing services rather than supplying goods, there may not be any trading stocks at all. Examples of this type of business are a travel agent, a fitness gymnasium and a snooker hall. The organization may purchase stocks of supplies, such as brochures, leaflets, stationery, cleaning materials and fuel, but they are for immediate consumption, not to be sold for profit; and they are treated as revenue expenditure in the profit and loss account. Stocks of these items may need to be accounted for if amounts are material, and a control may need to be kept on their order and stock levels.

The main types of trading stocks to be found in the hospitality, tourism and leisure (HTL) industry, apart from consumer goods, are perishable commodities such as fresh food and drink, which are a major source of income for organizations like hotels and pubs, entertainment complexes and sporting facilities. Stock levels may be significant for HTL businesses, so costs need to be controlled and managed carefully to maintain profitability.

6.2 STOCK VALUATION AND PROFITABILITY

The quantity and value of trading stocks on hand at the end of an accounting period will have a direct impact on the gross profit of the organization, which in turn will have an effect on the net profit. If they are significant, stocks of consumable stores, such as stationery and fuel, will also need to be accounted for, in order to charge the correct expense to the profit and loss account. The extent to which these stocks are consumed in a particular period will have a material effect on the reported net profit of the business.

Here is an example. The Herts Break Hotel in Welwyn Garden City provides bed and breakfast to its clients and its central heating system runs on oil. At the beginning of the year, stocks on hand of food and beverages were valued at £1,350, and stocks of fuel were valued at £800.

The hotel proprietor purchased food and beverages every month at the cash and carry. The average amount purchased amounted to £2,650. Oil was delivered to the storage tank once a quarter. During the two winter quarters £3,200 worth of oil were delivered. Half that amount was delivered during the other two quarters. Stocks of food and beverages at the end of the financial period were valued at £500, and stocks of fuel were valued at £2,700. Weekly wages and other expenses totalled £1,150.

The hotel had twenty single rooms costing £20 a night and eight double rooms costing £30 a night. On average throughout the year, the single rooms were 60% utilized and the double rooms 50%. How will the profit for the year be calculated, and what impact do the stock levels have on the reported profit? To begin,

$$\text{Sales} = (12 \times £20 \times 365) + (4 \times £30 \times 365) = £131,400$$

Calculation of profit ignoring stocks on hand

	£	£
Sales		131,400
Less cost of sales:		
Food and beverages (2,650 × 12)		31,800*
Gross profit		99,600
Less expenses:		
Fuel (6,400 + 3,200)	9,600*	
Wages, etc. (1,150 × 52)	59,800	
		69,400
Net profit		30,200

* The cost of food and fuel charged to the trading and profit and loss account comprises the aggregate purchase value of these items during the year. As it can be argued that stocks on hand represent a material amount, the accruals concept is violated by not taking them into account.

To calculate the true cost of food and beverages sold, and the fuel used during the year, the following calculations need to be made:

	Food + beverages £	Oil £
Opening stocks	1,350	800
Add purchases in period	31,800	9,600
Total available to use	33,150	10,400
Less closing stocks	500	2,700
Cost of stocks used	32,650	7,700

Now we take account of the stocks on hand.

Calculation of profit including stocks on hand

	£	£
Sales		131,400
Less cost of sales:		
Food and beverages		32,650*
Gross profit		98,750
Less expenses:		
Fuel	7,700*	
Wages, etc. (1,150 × 52)	59,800	
		67,500
Net profit		31,250

* These are now the costs of stocks **used** in the period, not the costs of stocks **purchased**, in accordance with the accruals concept of accounting.

Herts Break reports a profit more than £1,000 higher by including its stocks on hand – a significant difference. It is therefore very important that the value of stocks on hand are ascertained periodically so the above adjustments can be accurately made. For the financial accounts, all that needs to be carried out is an annual physical stocktake, but a well-run and efficient organization will operate a formal stock control system, to ensure that no leakage, loss, theft or deception is taking place.

6.3 CONTROL AND VERIFICATION OF PURCHASING AND RECEIVING

It is very important that the purchasing of stocks is carefully monitored so their true value may be ascertained. In particular, with foods and beverages, if quantities, quality and values are not exactly verified, a significant wastage or leakage may be taking place unnoticed, even before stocks are delivered, adversely affecting the reported profit of the organization.

The quality of the food or drink must be decided upon according to the needs of the business and its customers. Price will usually be a factor, but it is important that the business knows its suppliers and trusts them to give consistent quality at the price charged. This is particularly relevant to perishable food items, which have an extremely short shelf-life. Products such as dairy, bakery, fresh meat, poultry and seafood will be ordered on a daily basis and consumed immediately. Dairy and bakery products may be ordered by standing order if their usage is reasonably consistent over a period of time.

In order to verify quality and quantity, periodic food tests need to take place. This is normally done on an informal sampling or spot-check basis, but can be carried out statistically if necessary. Numerous methods can be used to defraud or decieve customers in supplying foods. Here are some examples:

1 Failing to provide the product at the right weight or quantity
   – underproviding
   – substitution of product by excess ice, water, etc.

2 Failing to meet the agreed specifications on quality
- supplying inferior quality steaks
- excess fat on meat
- fish size inappropriate
- incorrect class of potatoes or apples
- delivery in wrong bags or boxes
- correct product in the top layer only

3 Delivering and invoicing more than was agreed
- a representative on commission able to increase an order
- orders phoned in without consulting the buyer
- double orders placed before going on holiday

4 Scheduling early delivery dates

5 Overcharging on invoices

Most of these frauds happen through lax or non-existent control mechanisms at the receiving end. Certain standard procedures such as checking all deliveries, weighing and counting stocks, and verifying quality and specification can detect and prevent fraud. Taking control of ordering by operating a formal stock card with agreed order and delivery dates, with current invoice prices, is preferable to devolving stock control to company representatives, and can avoid the problems of overordering and badly timed deliveries.

6.4 STOCK CONTROL SYSTEMS

Ordering in a big establishment such as a hotel or restaurant is probably achieved by a combination of standing orders for daily perishable items and a stock card system for non-perishable goods. The stock card system, sometimes known as the perpetual inventory system, records opening stock, receipts of stock and requisitions, then maintains an account of the quantity and value of stock held in store at any time; it measures the value of stock used within the business. These non-perishable items would be kept securely, controlled by a trusted individual, perhaps the owner. Stock may be counted and valued quarterly.

All receipts of goods (verified as being exactly what was invoiced) are sent to the stores and recorded as received on each stock card. The purchase invoices are then sent up to the accounts office to be recorded in the double-entry system. In large organizations, requisitions for stocks by any department are made by completing a signed and authorized requisition form. The quantity and price are recorded on the requisition form and the relevant stock card, maintaining an up-to-date record of quantities and values of all stock items at any moment, and giving each department a record of the value of the stocks they have used during an accounting period. The physical stocktake of all or some of these items in rotation will verify over the accounting period whether any leakage or theft has taken place by reference to the size of any discrepancy between the recorded stock valuation and the result of the physical stocktake. This may be demonstrated with a numerical example.

The Delboy hotel buys its beer in 20-litre barrels costing £10 a barrel. The hotel has three separate bars and a central cellar used for storing beer. Prices remain constant throughout the year. Beer sells for £1 a litre. During the year the following transactions take place:

Date			Bar 1	Bar 2	Bar 3
	Barrels		Barrels	Barrels	Barrels
Opening stock	25		4	2.5	3
Purchases		Issues			
Jan	120		25	50	40
April	170		40	60	60
July	250		60	70	140
Nov	90		20	30	25

At the end of the year there were 30 barrels left in the hotel cellar, 4.5 barrels in bar 1, 5 barrels in bar 2, and 8 barrels in bar 3; all three bar staff had been given a barrel each as a Christmas present. How are the transactions recorded within a stock control system? How is leakage assessed? How are the profits calculated for each bar and for the hotel as a whole?

Sample stock control card, main cellar (beer barrels)

Date	Opening stock	Cellar purchases			Cellar issues	Closing stock
	£	£			£	£
Jan 1	250					250
Jan		1,200				1,450
Jan			Bar 1		250	1,200
Jan			Bar 2		500	700
Jan			Bar 3		400	300
April		1,700				2,000
April			Bar 1		400	1,600
April			Bar 2		600	1,000
April			Bar 3		600	400
July		2,500				2,900
July			Bar 1		600	2,300
July			Bar 2		700	1,600
July			Bar 3		1,400	200
Nov		900				1,100
Nov			Bar 1		200	900
Nov			Bar 2		300	600
Nov			Bar 3		250	350
Dec 31						350
Totals	250	+ 6,300		–	6,200	= 350
Actual						300
Discrepancy						50

The cost of beer issued to the bars of the hotel is calculated from opening stock + purchase invoices – closing stock. In this case £50 of beer, or five barrels, are unaccounted for in the cellar, which would have to be explained by the cellar manager. Possible reasons:

1 Opening or closing stocktake was incorrect.
2 Purchases were overrecorded or deliveries were not checked in properly.
3 Requisitions by bars were greater than those recorded.
4 There was theft by the cellar manager or somebody else.

Here are the individual bar stocks:

	Bar 1 £	Bar 2 £	Bar 3 £
Opening stock	40	25	30
Requisitions:			
Jan	250	500	400
April	400	600	600
July	600	700	1,400
Nov	200	300	250
Available to sell	1,490	2,125	2,680
Less:			
Perquisites	10	10	10
Cost of sales*	1,435	2,065	2,590
Closing stock	45	50	80

* The cost of sales and losses here is the balancing figure

Stock available for sale – perquisites – closing stock

If there has been no leakage, wastage or theft, the sales generated by each bar should be twice the cost of sales, as the beer is sold for £1 a litre and each barrel contains 20 litres.

The actual till receipts for each bar are as follows:

	Bar 1 £	Bar 2 £	Bar 3 £
Sales	2,700	4,000	4,300
	Bar 1 £	**Bar 2** £	**Bar 3** £
Cost of sales, theft and waste	1,435	2,065	2,590
Cost of recorded sales	1,350	2,000	2,150
Cost of stock stolen, wasted, etc.	85	65	440
Percentage discrepancy	5.9%	3.14%	17.0%

Clearly there is a problem with the management of the bars. All the percentage losses are significant, with bar 3 showing a big loss, which would need to be urgently investigated. Possible reasons:

1 Incorrect stocktake
2 Incorrectly completed requisition cards
3 Theft of beer
4 Theft of cash from till

It is unlikely the requisition cards were completed incorrectly if there is no similar discrepancy at the central cellar. A trading and profit and loss account can now be prepared by bar and in total, correctly recognizing the different categories of expense.

	Bar 1 £	Bar 2 £	Bar 3 £	Total £
Recorded sales	2,700	4,000	4,300	11,000
COS (50%)	1,350	2,000	2,150	5,500
Gross profit (50%)	1,350	2,000	2,150	5,500
Less expenses:				
Perquisites	10	10	10	30
Cost of leakage	85	65	440	590
Discrepancy in central cellar				50
	1,255	1,925	1,700	4,830

The total hotel net profit on drinks can be reconciled by presenting it this way:

		£
Total beer sales		11,000
Opening stock:		
Cellar	250	
Bars	95	
	345	
Add purchases	6,300	
	6,645	
Less closing stock:		
Cellar	300	
Bars	175	
		6,170
Net profit		4,830

The problem with presenting it this way is that the gross profit, which should be 50% of sales, is not separately identified, nor are the separate expenses incurred by providing perquisites, suffering waste and being defrauded. Separately identifying these items is of the utmost importance in managing and controlling the business, to minimize waste, inefficiency and fraud.

6.5 STOCK VALUATION WHEN INPUT PRICES ARE CHANGING

It is usual during a financial period for the cost of purchases to rise at some point. If the stores contain stocks purchased at different prices, then it has to be decided how to assign a value to any particular requisition. Some alternative approaches can be illustrated using an example of a wine merchant, and the sales of one particular line of a full-bodied red, Château Cherv, sold in cases of twelve bottles.

Opening stock 5 cases at a cost of £37.92 per case
Week 1 purchases 8 cases at a cost of £39.60 per case.
Week 2 purchases 4 cases at a cost of £41.52 per case.
Week 3 purchases 6 cases at a cost of £42.96 per case.
Week 4 purchases nil

Sales all at £5.95 were as follows:

Week 1   110 bottles
Week 2   55 bottles
Week 3   70 bottles
Week 4   20 bottles

It is possible to set up a sample stock card for this stock item and calculate the cost of sales (known as requisitions when internal) and the valuation of the closing stock of this line at the end of week 4. The first method that we will examine is the first in, first out method (FIFO). Under this method it is assumed that, in value terms, the oldest stock is issued first:

Date	Purchases (bottles)	Cost £	Sales (bottles)	Cost £	Stock quantity (bottles)	Stock price £	Stock value £
Opening bal	60	189.60			60	3.16	189.60
Week 1	96	316.80			96	3.30	316.80
					156		506.40
Week 1			110	354.60*	110		354.60
					46	3.30	151.80
Week 2	48	166.08			48	3.46	166.08
					94		317.88
Week 2			55	182.94**	55		182.94
					39	3.46	134.94
Week 3	72	257.76			72	3.58	257.76
					111		392.70
Week 3			70	245.92***	70		245.92
					41	3.58	146.78
Week 4			20	71.60****	20	3.58	71.60
Total	276	930.24	255	855.06	21	3.58	75.18

		£
* Issues in week 1	60 bottles × £3.16 =	189.60
	50 bottles × £3.30 =	165.00
		354.60
** Issues in week 2	46 bottles × £3.30 =	151.80
	9 bottles × £3.46 =	31.14
		182.94
*** Issues in week 3	39 bottles × £3.46 =	134.94
	31 bottles × £3.58 =	110.98
		245.92
**** Issues in week 4	20 bottles × £3.58 =	71.60

Under this method all the oldest stocks (the cheapest stocks during a period of rising prices) are recorded as issued first. The FIFO method means that the more expensive stocks are left at the end and the issues are relatively cheaper. The effect that has on profitability is shown later in the chapter.

Particularly with perishables or foods with a finite shelf-life, **physical** stock rotation should always be conducted according to the FIFO system. This is a matter of efficient stores management. What we are examining here is the **financial** stock recording and measurement, and how we **account** for the issues of stock, not how we carry out the operation of physical stock storage and movement in and out of the stores.

The next method to examine is the last in, first out method (LIFO). Under this method, stock is accounted for by assuming that, in value terms, the most recently acquired stocks are issued first. In this situation the closing stocks will tend to be valued as the older, normally least expensive stocks, and the issues will tend to be the more expensive stocks; this will have an impact on the reported profitability.

Date	Purchases (bottles)	Cost £	Sales (bottles)	Cost £	Stock quantity (bottles)	Stock price £	Stock value £
Opening bal	60	189.60			60	3.16	189.60
Week 1	96	316.80			96	3.30	316.80
					156		506.40
Week 1			110	361.04*	110		361.04
					46	3.16	145.36
Week 2	48	166.08			48	3.46	166.08
					94		311.44
Week 2			55	188.20**	55		188.20
					39	3.16	123.24
Week 3	72	257.76			72	3.58	257.76
					111		381.00
Week 3			70	250.60***	70	3.58	250.60
					39	3.16	123.24
					2	3.58	7.16
					41		130.40
Week 4			20	64.04****	20		64.04
Total	276	930.24	255	863.88	21	3.16	66.36

			£
* Issues in week 1	96 bottles × £3.30 =	316.80	
	14 bottles × £3.16 =	44.24	
		361.04	
** Issues in week 2	48 bottles × £3.46 =	166.08	
	7 bottles × £3.16 =	22.12	
		188.20	
*** Issues in week 3	70 bottles × £3.58 =	250.60	
**** Issues in week 4	2 bottles × £3.58 =	7.16	
	18 bottles × £3.16 =	56.88	
		64.04	

Under this method all the newest stocks (the most expensive stocks during a period of rising prices) are recorded as issued first.

The third method of valuing stocks is known as the average cost method. There are several versions of this method but conceptually the most appropriate is the weighted average cost method (WAVCO). This aggregates the total invoice value of all stocks on hand at any time then divides it by the number of units to arrive at a weighted average value.

Date	Purchases (bottles)	Cost £	Sales (bottles)	Cost £	Stock quantity (bottles)	Stock price £	Stock value £
Opening bal	60	189.60			60	3.16	189.60
Week 1	96	316.80			96	3.30	316.80
					156	3.25	506.40
Week 1			110	357.50*	110	3.25	357.50
					46	3.25	148.90
Week 2	48	166.08			48	3.46	166.08
					94	3.35	314.98
Week 2			55	184.25**	55	3.35	184.25
					39	3.35	130.73
Week 3	72	257.76			72	3.58	257.76
					111	3.50	388.49
Week 3			70	245.00***	70	3.50	245.00
					41	3.50	143.49
Week 4			20	70.00****	20	3.50	70.00
Total	276	930.24	255	856.75	21	3.50	73.49

		£
* Issues in week 1	110 bottles × £3.25 =	357.50
** Issues in week 2	55 bottles × £3.35 =	184.25
*** Issues in week 3	70 bottles × £3.50 =	245.00
**** Issues in week 4	20 bottles × £3.50 =	70.00

The new weighted average value is recalculated after each and every delivery received at a different price. Note that there will normally be a small rounding error built into this average. Issues have no effect on the weighted average as they are issued at the previous value for the average.

Each method of assigning values to issues causes two interdependent effects:

1 The value of issues will be different, causing a difference in the cost of sales.
2 The closing stock valuation will be different.

As these methods are simply alternative ways of measuring the value of issues, the values of purchases are unaffected, as are the quantities of stock on hand at any moment. The effects of these methods on profitability can be summarized by calculating the gross profit reported under each of them.

	FIFO method	LIFO method	WAVCO method
	£	£	£
Sales (255 × 5.95)	1,517.25	1,517.25	1,517.25
Cost of sales	855.06	863.88	856.75
Gross profit	662.19	653.37	660.05

Note that the FIFO method reports the highest level of profit, LIFO the lowest, and WAVCO something in between. How close the WAVCO figure is to either of the others depends on the volume of receipts at various prices. In this example the differences in percentage terms and absolute terms are small. In severe inflationary conditions where a business is purchasing and issuing high volumes of goods, the impact of choosing one method as against another becomes more important. Most businesses adopt FIFO or WAVCO, or a standard cost method (standard costing will be covered in Chapter 17).

FIFO is most commonly used in the United Kingdom as it is conceptually consistent with the physical stock rotation method; it is preferred by the Inland Revenue because it tends to reveal a higher profit. WAVCO leads to lower profits than FIFO, is much easier to account for, and is also acceptable to the tax authorities. LIFO is not much used in the United Kingdom but does have the conceptual advantage in that issues are valued at the most recent prices, adhering to the accruals concept of accounting, and producing a more prudent recognition of profit earned within a period. The disadvantage with this method is that it shows a more out-of-date, though prudent, valuation of stock on the balance sheet.

The choice of method is a management decision, and the method adopted should be maintained from period to period, in order to comply with the consistency concept of accounting. In the final analysis, control of stocks and their appropriate valuation will have a major impact on the financial results of most organizations. To some degree, nearly all businesses will buy goods or consumables for resale or for carrying out their business. Incorrect valuation of any of these types of stock will affect reported profits and stock values.

Several methods of valuing issues and stocks have been examined, but all of them are cost based, in that the values assigned to the stocks are derived from their purchase cost. Under the concept of **prudence** a very important valuation rule overrides any management decision to value stocks under different cost-based methods such as FIFO, LIFO, WAVCO or any other:

Stocks should be valued at their cost, however defined, or their net realizable value (NRV), whichever is the lower.

This means that if a business possesses stocks for which it believes it could not receive more from their disposal than they cost to acquire, then the lower amount should be used as the basis for valuation. In accordance with this rule, the NRV would be used only in exceptional circumstances, e.g. with particular batches of stocks that have become obsolescent through market changes, or have become damaged.

Applying NRV generally would go against the **going-concern** concept, in that no business would be willing to pay more for its stocks than it could realize from their sale in normal circumstances, and any that did would not remain in business for very long. The best examples of businesses that would apply NRVs appropriately to their stocks, and perhaps to other assets, are those which are imminently facing liquidation. If solvent businesses broke the rule and generally valued their stocks at NRV, which in this situation would be higher than the cost price, they would be violating the **prudence** concept by recognizing profits before stocks were sold and overvaluing them on the balance sheet.

SUMMARY

1 **Where food is served, stocks in the tourism, leisure and hospitality industry will often include perishable and non-perishable goods as well as consumable stores.**

2 **Stock valuation based on the accruals concept affects reported profitability.**

3 **Stock receipts, storage and movement must be strictly controlled.**

4 **There are several cost-based methods for valuing issues of stock; they give different results for profitability and stock valuations.**

5 **The concept of prudence dictates that stocks should be valued at their cost or their net realizable value, whichever is the lower.**

ASSESSMENT

MULTIPLE-CHOICE QUESTIONS

Question 1
Which pair of words best fit the gaps in the following statement? Businesses in the tourism, leisure and hospitality sector do not _____ carry trading stock-in-trade but they _____ carry perishable or non perishable food and beverage stocks.

A ever/sometimes
B often/always
C usually/often
D always/usually

Question 2
A small hotel has the following figures: opening stocks of fuel £200, purchases £1,250, theft of fuel from tank £50, and closing stock £120. What is the cost of fuel consumed by the hotel during this period?

A £1,280
B £1,330
C £1,070
D £1,620

Question 3
If there is a discrepancy between the recorded closing stock valuation at the central store area and the physical result of the stores stocktake, which one of the following four reasons could not be the cause?

A Storeworker incorrectly recording receipts or issues
B Ordered items neither supplied nor invoiced
C Stocks stolen from stores
D Opening stocktake incorrect

Question 4
Which of the following stock valuation methods would result in the highest stock value being reported on a solvent business's balance sheet at the end of a period of inflation?

A WAVCO

B FIFO

C LIFO

E NRV

Question 5
If NRV is correctly used as the basis for valuing all of a business's stock items, which of the fundamental accounting concepts is being most contradicted?

A Consistency concept

B Accruals concept

C Prudence concept

D Going-concern concept

EXERCISES

Exercise 1
CD Sounds, a retailer of CD records, starts up in business and makes the following purchases and sales during a six-month period:

	Cost price	CDs purchased	CDs sold
Jan	£1.00	10,000	4,000
Feb	£1.05		
March	£1.10	6,000	2,000
April	£1.15		6,000
May	£1.20	12,000	
June	£1.25		10,000

CDs were always sold at a price based on the current month's purchase cost + 50%.

Required
Calculate the trading (gross) profit of CD Sounds for the first six months using (a) FIFO stock valuation and (b) WAVCO stock valuation.

Exercise 2
The stocks of drink at a public house called the Border Arms in Berwick were valued at £4,350 as at October 1, 19x3. Due to absenteeism, no physical stocktake took place on December 31 (the end of the financial year). In order to prepare the final accounts, it is necessary to calculate the closing stock valuation based on accounting records for the last quarter. The pub made a 'normal' gross profit margin of 20% on retail prices for the majority of its stocks, unless otherwise stated. The following information is available:

1 Total stocks purchased from the brewery amounted to £22,500 between October 31, 19x3 and December 31, 19x3 at cost price.

2 A former employee had stolen £300 of drinks at cost between October 10, and the end of November.

3 Between October 1 and December 31, 19x3, £1,200 of stocks at cost were returned to the brewery because they were unfit for sale.

4 Total takings of £24,500 for the quarter were banked between October 1 and December 31, 19x3, this amount is after cash wages and cash purchases had been paid directly from cash in the till.

5 £160 of beer at retail prices had been returned to the bar by customers unhappy with cloudy or tainted beer served to them between October 1 and December 31, 19x3.

6 Cash purchases of drinks from the local cash and carry amounted to £2,100 during the quarter. All this stock was sold by the year-end, for a gross profit of 30% on retail price.

7 A promotion on a popular beer achieved total sales of £2,400. The beer had been sold on a basis of 'buy four, get one free'.

8 £1,500 of spirits at cost had been transferred on December 28 to a neighbouring Scottish hotel in order to help them meet the increased demand at Hogmanay.

9 Due to negative customer attitudes, a quantity of non-alcoholic beer, which normally earns a gross profit of one-third on selling price, is now believed to be worth only 40% of its retail value. The cost of the product was £210.

10 Bar staff had been paid £1,900 cash directly from the till as wages between October 1 and December 31, 19x3.

Required

Based upon the information given above, calculate what the stock valuation should have been at December 31.

Exercise 3

The following trial balance was extracted from the ledger accounts of Du Pain Frais, a small baker, as at April 30, 19x3:

	FFr
Plant and equipment at cost	300,000
Provision for depreciation as at 1.5.x2	−120,000
Delivery vehicle at cost	95,000
Provision for depreciation as at 1.5.x2	−65,000
Capital account as at 1.5.x2	−214,000
Bank account	−45,000
Rent	32,000
Rates	16,000
Insurance	8,000
Baking raw material stocks as at 1.5.x2	9,000
Finished goods stocks as at 1.5.x2	18,000
Debtors	15,000
Creditors	−14,000
Purchases of raw materials	75,000
Sales of finished goods	−250,000
Wages and salaries	90,000
Stocks of oil as at 1.5.x2	5,000
Purchases of oil	45,000
	0

The following information was available:

1 The stocktake at the end of the year revealed the following information:
  - Stocks of raw materials for baking, FFr 13,000 at cost.
  - Finished stocks of bread, FFr 22,000. Of this it was estimated that 15% would need to be sold at 20% below cost if it were to be sold before it became stale.

- Stocks of oil in the tank at the year-end were calculated to be worth FFr 8,000. However, during the year, an insurance claim was lodged for a theft of FFr 2,500 worth of oil during a recent robbery. The claim has yet to be settled by the insurance company, and no entries were recorded in the ledger accounts.

2 Straight-line depreciation is charged at 15% of cost on equipment and at 25% on the reducing balance for the vehicle.

Required

Produce a trading and profit and loss account for Du Pain Frais for the year ended April 30, 19x3, and a balance sheet as at April 30, 19x3.

Exercise 4

Riviera, a beach bar that sells food and drink, is only open for sixteen weeks during the summer season. The following information is available at the beginning of the holiday season:

	Opening stock FFr	Normal mark-up %
Food and snacks	117,000	100
Drinks	95,000	33.33
Cash on hand at start of season	7,100	

FFr 220,000 was banked during the season and FFr 5,500 was left unbanked on the last day. The owner estimates that, based on records for previous seasons, drink accounts for 60% and food for 40% of normal sales value.

Wages and purchases all came from bar takings:

	FFr
Serving-staff wages per week	2,000
Cleaning per week	600
Cash purchases:	
Food	80,000
Drink	135,000

The bar supplied the local hotel with a quantity of snacks during the season, to help them over a temporary shortage. The mark-up on these snacks was 25%, and the hotel paid Riviera FFr 5,000 on delivery.

The owner of Riviera threw a party on the last day of the season to celebrate a good trading period, and to thank staff for their efforts. A buffet costing FFr 800 was laid on and the guests could eat free of charge. Drinks, however, were sold to staff and their friends at half price. Total takings from the party came to FFr 2,000.

After the party was over, the owner had to leave, taking the contents of the till with him. He left staff to clear away and lock up. Unfortunately, the owner's trust in his staff was misplaced. A quantity of drink was stolen. Furthermore, it was not insured.

The closing stock on the premises next morning was valued as follows:

	FFr
Drink	98,000
Food	12,000

Required

(a) Perform a calculation based on the information above, indicating the cost of the drink that was stolen after the party.

(b) Prepare a trading and profit and loss account for the season, assuming the stock loss was treated as abnormal.

CHAPTER 7

Accounting for credit transactions

OBJECTIVES

- Differentiate between cash and credit transactions.
- Record transactions that affect debtor and creditor accounts.
- Reconcile business records with statements received.
- Operate credit control systems, including in a travel agency.
- Provide for bad debts, under the prudence concept.

7.1 CASH AND CREDIT TRANSACTIONS

A transaction is completed when exchange of value is agreed. The timing of the actual exchange of value in the form of a monetary transfer need not take place at the same time as the contract is entered into. If monetary exchange takes place simultaneously with the contract to exchange, this is known as a cash transaction. If there is a delay in the monetary settlement, this is known as a credit transaction.

In the tourism, leisure and hospitality industry many of the sales generated are cash based. In a hotel, a bar, an amusement arcade, an art gallery or any retail outlet, the customer will have paid for the goods or services received before they leave the premises. Guests in a hotel may build up credit overnight or over a few days as they avail themselves of goods and services on offer. At the end of their stay, the credit will be settled as the bill is paid. In these situations the hotel management will need to keep an accurate record of this indebtedness, so the correct amount can be charged when the customer checks out. Some tourism, leisure and hospitality businesses will offer credit over a longer period and a substantial amount of their sales will be generated in this way. Examples include holiday companies dealing with travel agents, and car-hire companies dealing with corporate customers.

Most businesses will receive credit from suppliers. If any supplies or services are regularly purchased in the normal course of trading, the supplier will probably offer credit terms of payment, such as a monthly account. The extent to which credit is given or received will have an important impact on the cash position of a business, and it is vitally important to record and control this indebtedness very carefully.

7.2 DEBTORS AND CREDITORS

If a sale or purchase is made on credit, an account has to be opened or updated to record the change in indebtedness. This account will then be updated each and every time a transaction affecting this indebtedness takes place. In theory, by doing this, the business should be aware at all times of the amounts owing from specific customers and to specific suppliers. These individual or personal accounts are kept in separate 'files', either physical or electronic, which are collectively known as the sales and purchases ledgers. The total amounts owing from customers at the end of a financial period are entered under current assets on the balance sheet, and total amounts owing to suppliers at the end of a financial period are entered under current liabilities on the balance sheet.

It is important that customers are reminded regularly of the extent of their indebtedness in order to encourage them to settle their debts sooner rather than later. As shown in Chapter 3, a business may encourage prompt payment by offering discounts to its customers, which would help to improve its cash position. It is important when deciding on the size of a prompt-payment discount to ensure that the revenue foregone by allowing the discount does not outweigh any resulting benefits to the cash flow.

Recording and processing a credit account

The personal account of a debtor or creditor can have a number of transactions affecting it during a financial period, and keeping a record of the amount owing needs to be carried out carefully. Here are some transactions that concern a customer, A. Debtor:

1 Credit sales £520
2 Settlement of account six days later taking a 5% discount
3 Credit sales £600
4 Returns from customer £120 (faulty goods)
5 Credit sales £100
6 Settlement on account £400
7 Cheque for £400 bounces
8 Customer is considered to be insolvent
9 Customer pays 75% of the outstanding debt
10 Credit sales £250
11 £450 paid on account

These eleven transactions can be recorded in the account A. Debtor:

A. Debtor account

Ref	£
1 Sales	+520
2 Discount alld	−26
2 Bank	−494
3 Sales	+600
4 Returns in	−120
5 Sales	+100
6 Bank	−400
7 Bank	+400
8 Bad debts	−580
9 Bad debts	+580
10 Bank	−435
11 Sales	+250
12 Bank	−450
Bal c/d	−55

Follow through each one of the above transactions in order to understand the double entries involved. They leave the account with a negative balance of £55. What has happened is that the customer seems to have ultimately overpaid their account. The overpayment transforms the debtor into a creditor. This type of error will result in the presence of a few creditors in the sales ledger and vice versa. These 'rogue' accounts, when identified, will be settled in due course by payment or by adjusting subsequent invoices.

Bad debts

The knowledge that the cheque bounced (item 7), requires that the business credits the bank account (–), reducing it by £400 and debits (+) the debtor account with the £400 debt. This is known as reinstating the debt. The realization that the debtor may be insolvent requires the business to write off the whole balance on the account at that time by recording a credit (–) of £580 in the account and recording a debit (+) of £580 in a bad debts account. The bad debts account is an expense account which recognizes the financial loss to a business should a debtor not settle a debt. At the end of the financial period this expense should be included with other expenses in the profit and loss account. The business should adhere to the concept of prudence, and write off a debt as soon as there is a reasonable doubt about its eventual collection. The subsequent partial settlement by the debtor indicates that the debtor is not insolvent, as previously thought, so the entries required are to redebit (+) the previous outstanding amount to the debtor account, and to credit (–) the bad debts account. Finally it is necessary to debit (+) the cash received to the bank account and credit (–) the debtor account.

Here are some transactions for the first month of trading with a new credit supplier, A. Creditor:

May 1: £300 stock purchased on credit.
May 12: £50 returned to supplier as not suitable.
May 18: debt settled in full net of a 2% settlement discount.
May 24: £250 stock purchased.
May 28: £200 cheque paid on account.
May 31: £245 goods purchased.

A. Creditor account

Ref		£
May 1	Cost of sales	–300
May 12	Returns out	+50
May 18	Discount recd	+5
May 18	Bank	+245
May 24	Cost of sales	–250
May 28	Bank	+200
May 31	Cost of sales	–245
	Bal c/d	–295

The creditor is owed £295 by the business at the end of the financial period. Follow through the entries carefully yourself.

7.3 RECONCILIATION OF STATEMENTS AND LEDGER ACCOUNTS

In large businesses there will be many credit customers and suppliers. It is usual to have many more credit customers than suppliers, but there is a need to keep all their accounts up to date and accurate. As far as customers are concerned, a monthly statement should be sent to them to remind them of what they owe and to request payment. The statement is useful as it can be used by the customers to check their records. Supplier statements can be similarly used by the business to check their own records.

Where there is a heavy volume of credit transactions between two parties, it is unlikely that at the end of any month the statement and the balance on the account will agree exactly. The reasons for this will lie in the timing difference between the issue of goods and the payments, or in errors made by either or both parties. Here is a monthly statement from A. Creditor:

A. Creditor in account with A. Customer
Monthly statement of account

	£ (+)	£ (−)	£
May 1 GDS			+300
May 16 CHQ		245	+55
May 16 DISC		5	+50
May 20 GDS	250		+300
May 26 GDS	254		+554
May 31 GDS	100		+654
May 31 BCE			+654

BCE = balance   CHQ = cheque
GDS = goods   DISC = discount received

There is a discrepancy of £654 − £295 = £359 between the two balances. What is the explanation? Can you spot the differences?

1 The returns of £50 do not seem to have been acknowledged by the supplier. Has the supplier received the goods or the notification, or has the entry been omitted in the supplier's account?
2 The £200 cheque sent by the customer to the supplier has not been received or has not been recorded.
3 £100 of goods despatched by the supplier has not been received or recorded as received by the customer.
4 The goods supplied to the customer on May 28 was recorded by the supplier as £254 and by the customer as £245. Assume that the supplier's account is correct.

It is now necessary to prepare a statement reconciling the two balances for the above differences:

	£
Closing balance (statement)	+654
Less returns	−50
Less cheque not received by supplier	−200
Corrected closing balance	+404
Closing balance (creditor account)	−295
Add goods not yet received and recorded	−100
Add difference caused by transposition error	−9
Corrected closing balance	−404

The corrected balances now agree at £404. The supplier's statement is a positive amount because the supplier sees the customer as a debtor and an asset. The creditor account balance in the customer's own accounts is negative because the customer sees it as a liability to the supplier.

7.4 CREDIT CONTROL

The first important requirement of a good credit control system is that credit should be extended prudently, the second is that the business should know who owes it money, how much and when it is due. The third important facet of a credit control system is that specific action is taken at every stage of the life cycle of a debt, in order that it may eventually be collected.

The first stage in operating a credit control system is to ensure as far as is possible that the business only lends to customers who are likely to repay the debt. This can be achieved by searching a credit database to obtain credit ratings for prospective customers. If customers have a low rating or have outstanding county court judgements against them, it would be best either to refuse credit or to supply goods on a pro-forma basis, where delivery is made only when payment is guaranteed. Checking each potential customers credit rating is no guarantee of payment once credit is offered. Every bad debtor defaults for the first time at some time, and therefore every business must expect that where credit is offered, a proportion of those debts may not eventually be collected.

The tourism, leisure and hospitality industry offers less credit than other sectors of business. In many cases tourism or leisure services are offered on a 'negative' credit basis, where cash is paid over by the customer and the service is offered at a later date, such as with many ticket-based services; examples are theatre, rail and airline tickets. However, considerable amounts of credit may be offered by tour operators and car-hire companies, and where such businesses operate there needs to be an effective system of control. We will examine the specific credit control system for a travel agency at the end of this section.

Credit should be offered on systematic terms, so that control is easier. It is possible, but not advisable, to have differential credit terms for different classes of customers, but competition may dictate otherwise. A customer is usually offered a monthly account. A discount may be offered for prompt payment, perhaps within ten days. As soon as the sale is agreed, an invoice is sent to the customer. The invoice should state clearly the date of the sale, the amount to be paid net of any cash, trade, or quantity-based discount, and inclusive of any tax. The due date of payment for the prompt-payment discount should be indicated, and the normal period of credit should be stated. Most computer-based accounting systems register the date of the sale and the date of any payment. The system is then able to identify whether or not the customer has qualified for a prompt-payment discount. More important, it can identify debtors who have not met their payment deadlines.

Where there are credit customers who have not met their due dates of payment, the system should highlight them and may automatically generate statements or requests for payments. And computerized systems can produce an analysis of outstanding debts and their age for any point in time:

Ageing debtor schedule as at June 30, 19x3

	£
Debts outstanding for:	
Up to 1 month	3,500
From 1 to 3 months	1,500
Over 3 months	350
Total debtors	5,350

The credit control system should differentiate between the ages of these debts in the responses it generates. Debtors of one to three months may be reminded at the end of each month with a statement and a supporting letter firmly requesting payment. Debtors of over three months may be sent letters advising them of their legal position and notifying them of an intention to start legal proceedings for recovery. In extreme cases, phone calls, personal visits or litigation may be necessary.

As far as creditors of the business are concerned, the only control is to ensure the statements received are accurate (section 7.3) and payments are made at appropriate times. They should not be made too early unless a discount is worth claiming; and they should not be made too late, perhaps jeopardizing a good source of supply or the business's credit rating.

Credit control and travel agents

At the end of Chapter 1, a balance sheet of a travel agency was introduced. It was explained in broad terms how the core business of a travel agency is carried out. Travel agencies operate heavily on a credit basis, where holidays are booked by customers who pay a deposit then make final payments or pay by instalments, and where the agent who collects these monies then pays the tour operator or holiday company by a certain date, net of an agreed commission which may be retained. A customer is a **third party** that owes money to the **agent** on behalf of the tour operator, called the **principal**. In the agent's books are the customer accounts, which are debtor accounts, and the tour operator accounts, which are creditor accounts. There might be several variations in how the bookkeeping is managed, but the following example will illustrate the basic approach.

Travel agency Routs Tours sells package holidays, and the following information was available at the beginning of the previous month:

	£
Customer account (amounts owing)	+30,000
Tour operator account (amounts owing)	−40,000
Bank account	+40,000
Fixed assets at valuation	+200,000
Capital account	−230,000
	0

During the month the following transactions took place

1 £100,000 of holidays were booked.
2 £60,000 was collected as deposits and instalments from customers.
3 £45,000 was paid over to the tour operator.
4 General expenses of £4,000 were incurred.

Additional information

1 The agreed commission is 10% of the value of the holidays sold, recognized at the point when the booking is made.
2 Interest is earned on the average bank balance held between the beginning and end of the month at a rate of 1% per month (ignoring any interest earned).

The ledger accounts for this business might be recorded as follows:

Tour operator (creditor) account		*Customer (debtor) account*	
Ref	£	Ref	£
Balance b/d	−40,000	Balance b/d	+30,000
Customers	−100,000	Tour operator	+100,000
Commission a/c	+10,000	Bank	−60,000
Bank	+45,000		
Bal c/d	−85,000	Bal c/d	+70,000

Commission retained account		*Bank account*	
Ref	£	Ref	£
Tour operator	−10,000	Bal b/d	+40,000
		Tour operator	−45,000
Bal c/d	−10,000	Customers	+60,000
		Expenses	−4,000
		Interest*	+455
		Bal c/d	+51,455

Interest received account		*General expenses account*	
Ref	£	Ref	£
Bank account	−455	Bank account	+4,000
Bal c/d	−455	Bal c/d	+4,000

* Interest is calculated as $\frac{1}{2}$(£40,000 + £51,000) × 0.01 = £455

We will now calculate the profit made by the business during the month:

Profit and loss account (Routs Tours)

	£
Commission earned	10,000
Interest received	455
Gross income	10,455
General expenses	4,000
Net profit	6,455

The balance sheet at the end of the month would be as follows:

Balance sheet (Routs Tours)

	£	£
Fixed assets		200,000
Current assets		
Debtors (customers)	70,000	
Bank	51,455	
	121,455	
Current liabilities		
Creditors	85,000	
Net current assets		36,455
Net assets		236,455
Financed by		
Opening capital		230,000
Add net profit		6,455
		236,455

This complete example illustrates the basics of a travel agency business. Control accounts for the debtors and creditors are the hub of the business. Remember that technically these debtors and creditors are directly indebted to each other. In theory the travel agent is not owed anything personally from third parties, nor owes anything personally to principals, but acts as a collecting and paying agent. The main income earned by the travel agent is therefore the commission which may be retained from the monies collected, and also the interest earned on the monies held by the travel agent, between the time they are collected from customers and the time they are paid over to the tour operator. The commission retained could be calculated in one of two main ways:

1 On the invoice value of the holidays booked
2 As a percentage of the monies remitted to tour operators

The above example was based on the first of these methods. An important accounting issue is raised in connection with this. Although the choice of method does not affect the cash position of the travel agency, it does affect the timing of any commission to be recognized in the profit and loss account for any financial period.

Under the first method, the commission is recognized as soon as the holiday is booked and the debt from the customer recorded. The double entries would be as follows:

	Debit (+) £	Credit (−) £
Customer (debtor a/c)	100,000	
Tour operator (creditor a/c)		100,000
Tour operator (commission retained)*	10,000	
Commission a/c		10,000

* Commission = (1/10) × invoice value of holiday.

Under the second method, the travel agency cannot recognize the commission until such time as the money already collected from customers is remitted to the tour operator. The double entries would be as follows:

	Debit (+) £	Credit (−) £
Tour operator (monies remitted)	45,000	
Bank a/c		45,000
Tour operator (commission retained)†	5,000	
Commission a/c		5,000

† Commission = cash remitted × 10/(100 − 10) = (1/9) × cash paid to creditors.

The method that should be adopted, in accordance with the accruals concept, is the first one, because the sale of the holiday becomes a legally binding contract when the booking form is signed. However, if the commission is to be physically earned in the form of cash, it is necessary for the agent to ensure that the outstanding amounts from holidays booked are eventually collected from the customers concerned.

7.5 PROVISION FOR BAD DEBTS

The concept of prudence requires that an asset should not be valued in the balance sheet at more than it is genuinely considered to be 'worth'. In the case of fixed assets this is normally the historical cost less an amount for depreciation, and stocks are valued at cost or net realizable value (NRV), whichever is the lower. Debtors, however, should be valued using the NRV, because each is only worth the proportion of the outstanding debts eventually expected to be recovered, almost always less than the original book value. At any time it cannot be known with any certainty how much will not be collected, which makes it difficult to put a true value on these debts. What is certain in most cases is that a business will not collect all the debts recorded in the debtors' personal accounts. Consequently, a prudent business must make a reasonable estimate of how much debt may not be collected, make a provision for this in the accounts, and show the debtors on the balance sheet net of this provision. A reasonable estimate can be made in two ways:

1 By examining the historical data on the level of bad debts for this business, and for this type of industry in general. This information may be available from trade journals, etc.
2 By examining specific debts outstanding at the time, assessing the likelihood of collection, given customer history, and the current ages of the debts.

Netscope Newspapers operates a credit sales system for its newspaper advertising. At the end of April 19x3, the ageing debtors schedule reveals the following information:

Ageing debtor schedule as at April 30, 19x3

	Total	Under £20
	£	£
Up to 7 days	2,790	1,500
7 to 14 days	1,200	600
14 to 28 days	800	450
Over 28 days	300	120
Over 2 months	100	40
Total debtors	5,190	2,790

Netscope Newspapers offers credit over the telephone for small advertisements. The terms are seven days for the prepaid rate, which is the discount rate. The normal price is available up to a fortnight, beyond this the accounts are considered overdue. The trade journal for local and regional newspapers reveals that bad debts average 5% of debts. On examination a £30 debt which is over two months old is from a customer who, when his credit rating was checked, was discovered to be a regular defaulter.

The company has a policy of writing off all debts of under £20 as bad debts, if they are over 28 days old, and makes a general provision for bad debts of 5% against all other debts outstanding at the end of the month, except those debts for which a specific provision might be made. The debtors are reviewed monthly. What are the accounting entries required to operate the overall credit policy of Netscope Newspapers?

Ledger accounts as at April 30, 19x3

Total debtors a/c		Bad debts a/c		Provision for bad debts a/c	
Ref	£	Ref	£	Ref	£
Bal b/d	+5,190	Debtors	+160	Bad debts	−30
Bad debts	−160	Provn BD	+30	Bad debts	−250
		Provn BD	+250		
Bal c/d	+5,030	Bal c/d	+440	Bal c/d	−280

BD = bad debt

Firstly the actual bad debts are written off. All those debts of under £20 which are over 28 days old are credited (−) to the individual debtor accounts, and debited (+) to the bad debts expense account. They come to £160. The £30 debt is separately identified as likely to be confirmed bad in the future; it receives a different treatment. As Netscope Newspapers is not definitely writing off this debt, the individual debtor account will not be credited. Instead the company creates a **provision** for this debt.

Creating a provision means that, out of prudence, Netscope Newspapers is going to treat the doubtful debt as an expense in the profit and loss account for the current accounting period, and it will show the debtors net of this provision on the balance sheet. Finally, as the business is creating a general provision for bad debts, it will take 5% of the debtors at the year-end, (£5,030 − £30) × 0.05 = £250, and charge this as a provision against the profit and loss account. The double entry is to debit the bad debts account (+), and credit the provision for bad debts account (−) with these provisions. The total provision for bad debts now recognizes the doubtfulness of the specific debtor for £30, and additionally the fact that, at any moment, it is likely that 5% of other bad debts outstanding will probably never be collected. Here is the balance sheet valuation placed on the debtors as at the end of April 19x3:

Balance sheet extract

	£	£
Current assets:		
Debtors	5,030	
Less provision for bad debts c/d	280	
		4,750

Adhering to the prudence concept, the business is not counting these doubtful debts as part of its assets, and has reduced its profit and therefore its capital by the total of this provision, as created in past accounting periods. The debtor position as at the end of May will now be reviewed with regard to bad and doubtful debts.

Ageing debtor schedule as at May 31, 19x3

	Total £	Under £20 £
Up to 7 days	2,400	1,100
7 to 14 days	900	500
14 to 28 days	650	315
Over 28 days	240	80
Over 2 months	70	50
Total debtors	4,260	2,045

At the end of May it is decided the overall policy for bad and doubtful debts is to be maintained as it is. Confirmation from the solicitors has been received with regard to the specific debt of £30. It is decided to write off this debt.

Ledger accounts as at May 31, 19x3

Total debtors a/c	£	Bad debts a/c	£	Provision for bad debts a/c	£
Bal b/d	+4,260	Debtors	+130	Bal b/d	−280
Bad debts	−130			Debtors	+30
Provn BD	−30	Provn BD	−45*	Bad debts	+45*
Bal c/d	+4,100	Bal c/d	+85	Bal c/d	−205

* In April Netscope Newspapers created a general provision of 5% of debtors (£250). At the end of May the provision need only be £4,100 × 0.05 = £205, so the present provision is now too large by (£280 − £30) − £205 = £45. To adjust the general provision back to £205 it is necessary to reduce the provision by £45 and to reduce the total bad debt expense charged to the profit and loss account for May by £45.

The first adjustment is to write off the actual bad debts written off as policy (the debts of £20 or less); this comes to £130. Then the specific bad debt which was **previously provided for** is written off against the specific debtor account, but instead of debiting the bad debts account, the provision for bad debts account should be debited. The debt has already been charged as an expense in last month's profit and loss account, and it forms part of the present provision against bad debts, so it would be incorrect to make a further charge against profits this month. Finally the general provision for bad debts is reviewed. The balance sheet extract of the debtors as at the end of May would look like this:

Balance sheet extract

	£	£
Current assets:		
Debtors	4,100	
Less Provision for bad debts c/d	205	
		3,895

Finally here is a review of the company's debtors at the end of June 19x3:

Ageing debtor schedule as at June 30, 19x3

	Total	Under £20
	£	£
Up to 7 days	3,150	1,300
7 to 14 days	1,350	700
14 to 28 days	950	450
Over 28 days	390	130
Over 2 months	120	20
Total debtors	5,960	2,600

Due to the high rate of collection for small debts between 28 days and 2 months old, it is now decided that such debts will no longer be written off automatically, and that only debts of under £20 which are over 2 months old will be written off. It is also decided, due to the experience of the past two months, to reduce the general provision from 5% to 2% of outstanding debts at the end of the month. A specific debt of £40 is now identified as being a definite risk, and a specific provision is to be made against it. And a bad debt that was previously written-off is now recovered; the amount is £15.

Ledger accounts as at June 31, 19x3

Total debtors a/c		Bad debts a/c		Provision for bad debts a/c	
Ref	£	Ref	£	Ref	£
Bal b/d	+5,960	Debtors	+20	Bal b/d	−205
Bad debts	−20	Provn BD	+40	Provn BD	−40
		Provn BD	−87*	Bad debts	+87*
		Cash	−15		
Bal c/d	+5,940	Bal c/d	−42*	Bal c/d	−158

* The general provision has been adjusted by £205 − 0.02(£5,940 − £40) = £87; this further reduction of £87 reduces the total provision to (£5,900 × 0.02) + £40 = £158.

The bad debts written off this month include only the debts under £20, each of which is more than 2 months old (£20). A specific provision for £40 against a particular debtor is also created. The bad debt previously written off and recovered is dealt with by a debit (+) to the cash account and a credit (−) to the bad debts account, making a further reduction in the bad debts account for this month, to compensate for the £15 charged against profits in a previous period. As a result, the net balance of £42 carried down in the bad debts account is negative, indicating this now represents a net addition to profit instead of a charge against it. This recognizes that Netscope Newspapers has overprovided for debts in the past, and now they must redress this by increasing reported profit. The balance sheet extract showing the net value of debtors as at the end of June would be as follows:

Balance sheet extract

	£	£
Current assets:		
Debtors	5,940	
Less Provision for bad debts c/d	158	
		5,782

To summarize, the following rules apply:

1 Actual bad debts should be charged as expenses against gross profit in the profit and loss account as they are confirmed, either by communication from these debtors or their representatives, or as a matter of policy as decided by the business itself.

2 A prudent business recognizes that, at any moment, not all outstanding debts will be collected. For those debts that are not likely to be collected, a provision should be made against the profits of the period in which the possibility of default has been recognized. This provision can be based on debts which have been specifically identified as doubtful, or on a general percentage of outstanding debts at the end of the relevant accounting period. At the end of each period the provision should be adjusted appropriately:
   – If the present provision is inadequate, it should be increased.
   – If the present provision is too large or is no longer required, it should be reduced.

The change in the provision for bad debts should either be added to the actual bad debts written off, if the provision is to be increased, or subtracted from the actual bad debts if the provision is to be reduced. The net bad debts are then charged to the profit and loss account as an expense. If the balance on the bad debts expense account at the end of the period is negative, which is possible in some periods (see June), the amount should be treated as income in the profit and loss account and added to the gross profit.

SUMMARY

1 **Credit transactions require records of indebtedness to be kept accurately in individual debtor and creditor accounts.**

2 **Supplier statements should be reconciled with the balances on the creditor accounts, to check for timing differences and errors.**

3 **Debts owing to the business need to be managed within an overall credit control system.**

4 **The prudence concept requires that a proportion of the debts owing to the business need to be provided for by making a charge against current profits.**

ASSESSMENT

MULTIPLE-CHOICE QUESTIONS

Question 1
Which one of the following would be the correct entry in a personal account to record when a customer's cheque bounces?

A Debit (+) the creditor account
B Credit (–) the debtor account
C Debit (+) the debtor account
D Credit (–) the creditor account

Question 2
What would be the total difference between the supplier's statement and the balance on the creditor account if these facts were known at the end of the month?

1 A delivery valued at £120 was wrongly recorded by the customer as £210 in the creditor account and the cost-of-sales account.
2 A delivery recorded in the supplier's books valued at £50 has not been received by the customer.
3 The customer has taken a discount of 2.5% on a £240 purchase although the payment is just outside the permissible period.
4 A return valued at £25 has not been received by the supplier.

A £171
B £9
C £59
D £34

Question 3
If actual bad debts written off in a financial period are £120, if the provision for bad debt is reduced from £550 to £400 in that financial period, and if the closing debtors are valued at £4,500, which of the following reflects the correct entries in the profit and loss account and on the balance sheet?

	P+L account	Balance sheet
A	Expense £520	Debtors £4,100
B	Expense £120	Debtors £4,100
C	Expense £270	Debtors £3,980
D	Income £30	Debtors £4,100

Question 4
During a financial period the bad debts incurred were £880. Credit sales were £22,000, opening debtors were £3,200, monies received from debtors amounted to £18,500, sales returns were £620, discounts allowed were £1,200 and the provision for bad debts was to be maintained at 5% of debtors. By how much should the provision for bad debts have been changed between the beginning of the year and the end of the year?

A Reduced by £40
B Increased by £71
C Increased by £40
D Reduced by £100

Question 5

In which one of the following ways would it not be possible to reduce the provision for bad or doubtful debts?

A Offer discounts for prompt payments by debtors
B Offering bulk-buying discounts
C Putting known defaulters on to pro-forma payment
D Set up a cash discount structure

EXERCISES

Exercise 1

Warsaw Packed Meals have the following balances at the end of April 19x3 on their debtor and creditor control accounts.

Debtor control account		Creditor control account	
Ref	£	Ref	£
Bal b/d	+27,500		−16,000

Here are details of transactions undertaken during the period:

		£
1	Credit sales	240,000
2	Credit purchases	145,000
3	Receipts from credit customers	230,000
4	Payments to creditors	140,000
5	Cheque to supplier not honoured	5,000
6	Discounts received	7,000
7	Discounts allowed	9,000
8	Returns to suppliers (damaged goods)	14,000
9	Refund to credit customer for overpayment	200
10	Bad debts	1,500

Required
Complete the debtor and creditor control accounts by recording transactions 1 to 10.

Exercise 2

Sun Drench, a canned drinks wholesaler, receives the following statement from its main supplier in May:

Big Can Co in account with Sun Drench wholesalers
Monthly statement of account for May 19x3

	£ (+)	£ (−)	£
May 1 BCE			+51,000
May 16 CHQ		20,900	+30,100
May 16 DISC		1,100	+29,000
May 20 GDS	21,000		+50,000
May 22 RET		8,000	+42,000
May 26 GDS	15,000		+57,000
May 28 CHQ		36,100	+20,900
May 31 GDS	10,000		+30,900
May 31 BCE			+30,900

BCE = balance   CHQ = cheque   DISC = discount received
GDS = goods   RET = returns

Unfortunately, this balance did not correspond with the balance on Sun Drench's creditor control account as at the end of May, which stood at £800. The following discrepancies were discovered:

1 Goods delivered by the supplier had been entered in Sun Drench's creditor control account on May 20 as £12,000 instead of £21,000.
2 Sun Drench had sent a cheque for £4,750 to Big Can on May 30, net of a legitimate 5% settlement discount.
3 The goods sent out by the supplier on May 31 had not been received by Sun Drench as at the end of the month, and no other documentation had been received in connection with this order.
4 The cheque sent by Sun Drench for £36,100 was net of a 5% settlement discount, which Sun Drench had recognized in its creditor control account. Big Can rightly disallowed the discount as the payment was made outside the agreed time limit.
5 Of the cans despatched on May 20 and subsequently received by Sun Drench, it was discovered at goods inwards that 20% had been delivered with an out-of-date promotional label. The goods had recently been sent back to Big Can on one of their own delivery vehicles, and a credit note for this had been issued by the driver.

Required
Reconcile the statement from Big Can with the closing balance on the creditor control account of Sun Drench.

Exercise 3
Vosges Travel Service (a travel agency) had the following assets and liabilities as at the end of March 19x3:

	SwFr
Capital account	−1,000,000
Fixed assets	+800,000
Owed to tour operators	−120,000
Owed from customers	+150,000
Bank account	+170,000
	0

The travel agency generates its income by retaining a commission. The agreement between the agency and the tour operator is that a 10% commission is to be retained from all payments made to the tour operators. Interest is earned on a positive balance in the bank account, and is based on the average balance held in the account during the month (ignoring interest). The prevailing interest rate is 0.75% per month. The following transactions take place during May 19x3:

1 Payments to tour operators, SwFr 450,000 (net of commission)
2 Invoice value of holidays booked, SwFr 620,000
3 General expenses incurred and paid, SwFr 28,000
4 Deposits and other monies received from customers, SwFr 650,000

Required
Prepare the necessary ledger accounts for the Vosges Travel Service during the month of May, the profit and loss account for May, and the balance sheet as at the end of May.

Exercise 4
On January 1, 19x3 the total debtors on the debtor control account of the Teganau Toy Warehouse stood at £21,400. At that time, specific provisions had been made against three debtors whose accounts had not been settled within six months:

	£
Jones	120
Gray	80
Harris	100

These accounts had been identified from the ageing debtor schedule. In addition the business had a consistent policy of making a general provision of 4% against all other debtors. During 19x3 the following transactions took place:

1 Credit sales, £130,000
2 Bad debts written off:
   – General bad debts, £4,500
   – Gray and Jones declared bankrupt, debts written off
3 Discounts allowed, £3,200
4 Sales returns, £5,200.
5 Receipts from debtors, £120,000
6 At the year-end two additional debtors required a specific provision totalling £800

Required
Prepare the debtor control account, the bad debts expense account and the provision for bad and doubtful debts account.

CHAPTER 8

Accounting for cash

OBJECTIVES

- **Recognize the importance of cash management.**
- **Reconcile the bank account with the bank statement.**
- **Manage and control cash and credit card takings from tills.**
- **Record and control expenditure in a petty cash system.**
- **Account for the exchange of foreign currency.**
- **Describe a ticketing system.**
- **Prepare a simple cash flow statement for a sole trader.**
- **Understand the difference between cash flow and profit.**

8.1 THE IMPORTANCE OF CASH MANAGEMENT

Current assets were described in Chapter 1 as the 'muscles', 'blood' and 'oxygen' of the business entity. Being more specific with the analogy, cash could most appropriately be identified as the 'oxygen' of the business. Starved of cash, the business will swiftly expire. Profits are the fruit of the successful business which gives customers what they want, when they want it and at a price they will accept. The business can only continue to exist if these profits generate cash and enough of it is maintained within the business to meet its ongoing obligations. 'Look after the pennies, and the pounds will look after themselves' expresses the notion that if positive cash flow is maintained through careful planning and control, profitable growth and prosperity will follow.

Failure to ensure that the flow of cash is continuous and adequate is the surest way to failure, and many profitable or potentially profitable businesses have become bankrupt as a result. The capital of the owner is the difference between the value of all the business's assets and the total value of its liabilities to third parties. This capital is described in monetary terms, but in reality it will be represented by a wide range of assets. Even if the owner's capital is considerable and growing each year, due to profitable transactions, it is important that enough of these assets are in the form of cash or its near equivalent.

Creditors will need to be paid in money, and will not readily accept payment in any other form. A business that may have used up most of its cash received from customers in order to purchase fixed assets, could put itself in a position where it needs to sell some of them in order to meet short-term obligations. This type of activity could seriously reduce the business's operating capability and may affect the business as a going concern.

Chapter 7 highlighted the importance of managing and controlling debt. Debt management also helps to ensure the continuity of supplies and allows suppliers to be paid regularly and promptly. It is imperative that the business is punctual in meeting its obligations to lenders and its tax obligation to government authorities, e.g. value added tax (VAT), pay-as-you-earn (PAYE) and National Insurance (NI).

8.2 THE CASH BOOK

Having understood that the business needs adequate cash to meet its short-term obligations to lenders, suppliers and authorities, it is important that knowledge of cash availability is accurate and timely. The business needs to know exactly how much cash it has, both ready cash and cash at the bank. Similar to the reconciliation of personal accounts with monthly supplier statements, the business should reconcile its own cash account records with the statement produced by the bank. Businesses traditionally keep a cash book to record receipts and payments, both in pure cash terms, and to and from the business bank account. It combines the cash and the bank account in one overall account.

The transactions of Supersurf, a water sports retailer, in March will now be recorded:

Opening balances: cash £75, bank £270 overdrawn
Mar 1: till receipts £500
Mar 2: cheque received from debtor £950, net of discounts allowed of 5% (£50)
Mar 5: cheque payment to supplier £720, net of a 10% discount received
Mar 8: rent received from tenant, £200 cheque
Mar 10: till receipts £650
Mar 15: cash deposited in bank account £1,100
Mar 18: cheque received from debtor £470, net of 6% discount allowed
Mar 20: cheque from debtor £95, net of 5% discount
Mar 21: fixed asset purchased by cheque for £500
Mar 25: cheque payments to creditors £350, late payment
Mar 31: cheque from debtor on March 20 dishonoured

Using the positive/negative format for the accounts, the cash book would be recorded in the following manner:

Cash book

Ref	Discount allowed £	Discount received £		Cash column £	Bank column £
Mar 1 Bal b/d				+75	−270
Mar 1 Sales				+500	
Mar 2 Debtors	+50				+950
Mar 3 Creditors		−80			−720
Mar 8 Rent					−200
Mar 10 Sales				+650	
Mar 15 Contra*				−1,100	+1,100
Mar 18 Debtors	+30				+470
Mar 20 Debtors	+5				+95
Mar 25 Fixed asset					−500
Mar 30 Creditors					−350
Mar 31 Debtors	−5				−95
Total discounts	+80	−80	Bal c/d	+125	+480

* Contra (contradictory entry) is the term for making a reciprocal entry between two equivalent but opposing accounts.

Note that a record of discounts allowed and received is kept in the cash book. At the end of a specified period, the totals from the discount columns are posted to the respective discount accounts, avoiding the need to make individual entries in those accounts with every transaction undertaken. The cash book is a very important record. Not only is it the busiest in terms of the volume of transactions that affect it, but it provides a snapshot of the liquid position of the business at any particular moment.

8.3 BANK RECONCILIATIONS

The snapshot of the liquidity position of the business is important, both to see whether current commitments can be met by cross-referring to the level of indebtedness in the personal accounts, but also to help the business look forward and evaluate whether it is possible to commit resources to the acquisition of higher levels of stock, or to the replacement or expansion of the fixed assets, and whether further finance will be required. It is vitally important when making such an evaluation that the information the business has about its cash position is accurate and up to date. Every month the business receives a statement from the bank indicating all receipts that have been deposited in the account, and all payments that have been made from it. A bank statement is usually laid out in the following format. Here is the bank statement from Clydewest Bank for Supersurf for March.

Supersurf Ltd   **Statement of account**

Clydewest bank   *Flexible business a/c*
High Street
Inverhampton
Tel: 01792 456789

Supersurf Ltd
Watch Bay Street
Water Beach
Inverhampton
IA2 5AA

Details	Payments £ (−)	Receipts £ (+)	Date	Balance £ (+/−)*
Balance forward			March 3	−270
J.O. Hasselhoff STO	150		March 3	−420
East Glam BGC		800	March 4	+380
Cheques		950	March 12	+1,330
100886	720		March 14	+610
Interest	15		March 14	+595
Unauth O/D fee	35		March 14	+560
Cash deposit		1,010	March 15	+1,570
Deposit		470	March 28	+2,040

STO = standing order

BGC = bank giro credit

* On UK bank statements, where the customer has funds in the bank account, or funds are deposited into the account, these entries are denoted as credits (CR), whereas overdrawn balances or withdrawals from the account are shown as debits (DR). The reason for this is that the bank statement sent to customers traditionally showed the account from the bank's point of view, not the customer's. If the customer has funds invested in the bank account, the customer is identified as a **creditor** of the bank, explaining why the bank shows this as a credit balance. When the customer is overdrawn, the customer is a **debtor** of the bank and therefore this type of balance is shown as a debit balance. Banks are now increasingly using the positive/negative notation, and are showing the statement from the customer's perspective, as it is much less confusing.

At the end of the month, the following errors are discovered in Supersurf's own accounting records:

1 On March 15 the cash deposited in the bank was £1,010, not £1,100 as recorded in the cash book.
2 The rent paid, recorded in the cash book on March 8, was in fact rent received from a tenant.

The possible causes of the difference between the closing bank balance as per the cash book (£+480) and the closing balance on the bank statement (£+2,040) will now be examined. The bank balance from the bank statement should give the situation of the bank account as it really is, not as it might be, under the assumption that the bank is more likely to have an accurate and verifiable record of the current position of the account. The bank also makes vicarious or unilateral adjustments to the account with regard to such items as direct debits, standing orders, bank giro credits, bank interest payable/receivable, and sundry charges and fees. It is likely that some of these items may not have been accounted for by the business in its cash book. Another major reason for any discrepancy between the closing balances is the time lag between the issue of a cheque and its eventual processing through the banking system.

Discrepancies may commonly be caused by errors made in the accounting records of the business, and possibly even by the bank itself. The steps involved in reconciling the bank statement and the bank account balance in the cash book are as follows:

1 Take the closing bank statement balance and update it with the entries not yet processed through the banking system:
   – **Subtract** from the balance the total of **unpresented** cheques.
   – **Add** to the balance the total of **uncredited** cheques.
2 Take the closing bank balance in the cash book and update it with the items that the bank will have included, but of which the business was unaware, or ommitted to record:
   – Bank charges
   – Interest payable/receivable
   – Direct debits
   – Standing orders
   – Bank giro credits
   – Other deposits made by third parties
3 If the balances remain unreconciled, check through the entries in the cash book for any errors and amend accordingly.

Bank reconciliation statement (Supersurf) as at March 31

		£	£
Bank statement balance			+2,040
1a Less unpresented cheques:			
	Mar 25	500	
	Mar 31	350	
		850	
			1,190
1b Add cheques not yet credited:			
	Mar 8	200	
Updated bank balance			1,390
Closing cash book balance			480
2a Less bank charges		35	
2b Less bank interest payable		15	
2c Less standing order		150	
			−200
			+280
2d Add Bank Giro credit			+800
			+1,080
Correction of errors:			
3a Less cash deposit error (1,100 − 1,010)			−90
			+990
3b Add rent treated as expense (2 × 200)			+400
Corrected cash book balance			1,390

The discrepancy between the closing balances has now been fully explained following the steps outlined earlier. From the point of view of Supersurf, the updated balance of £1,390 is £900 more than was originally indicated in the cash book. This significant difference puts a completely different perspective on the cash position of the business and may influence any evaluation of its position with regard to the conduct of its financial affairs in the immediate future. It is important that this type of reconciliation is carried out promptly and regularly at the end of the month. It is unlikely to be worthwhile or possible to do it more often, but the business might lose sight of its liquidity if it were to do it any less frequently.

8.4 TILL AND TAKINGS MANAGEMENT

Many businesses in the tourism, leisure and hospitality sector are cash based. In this sector the customers or clients pay in advance by purchasing tickets, e.g. for entertainment; they pay immediately for every transaction, e.g. in an amusement arcade or currency exchange bureau; or on their departure, perhaps from a hotel or restaurant, they pay a single bill that totals a number of individual transactions. In these businesses it is commonplace to receive many of the payments from customers in the form of cheques, and increasingly in the form of credit card vouchers, but a significant proportion of takings will still be in the form of cash. It is important to record cash receipts accurately, and the physical control of these takings should be correctly handled and managed, in order to avoid loss and theft.

As far as cash is concerned, it is important that adequate amounts of change are available in order to meet the expected demand. This change should be in note and coin denominations. It is therefore necessary to keep a float at each cash collection point, in order to meet this expected demand, and there is also a requirement to reconcile electronic records of cash and other takings with the physical quantities of these takings in the till itself. A till should record receipts and payments as keys are depressed. Some computerized cash collection systems recognize the price and possibly the cost of a product when an electronic scanner reads its unique bar-code. This system automatically integrates cash collection with stock control and the accounting system.

Most cash registers, however, are much less sophisticated and may not be part of an integrated system, but they will have a till roll, which is a printed record of these transactions as they occur, perhaps timed by the register's internal clock. What is important is that the totals on this roll should reflect the physical payments to and from the till and highlight any error or fraud that may have taken place. In supermarkets where several tills are operated by different cashiers, all till rolls will need to be separately identified as to their till position, and they should indicate which cashier was operating the till and when.

Here is a simple system for till control and management. The Spoon Cafe, owned by G.R. Easy, takes approximately the same takings every day. All takings are in the form of cash. The following details were available for one day:

	£	£
Float left at the end of the day		
Notes		25.00
Coins £1 and silver		10.00
Copper		5.00
		40.00
Cash removed from till		
Notes	155.00	
Coins £1 and silver	43.50	
Copper	22.24	
		220.74
		260.74
Less float at the beginning of the day		
Notes	35.00	
Coins £1 and silver	11.50	
Copper	5.25	
		51.75
Total cash sales		208.99
Less till roll total		220.99
Discrepancy		−12.00

This is an example of a cashing-off slip, which should be completed every day for each till. The first step is to decide on the float to retain in the till, then the remaining contents are emptied and counted. The total contents of the till at the end of the day less the float at the beginning of the day should represent the cash sales for that till. Any discrepancy between the sales and the total on the till roll will indicate one of four things:

1 The cash contents of the till have been miscounted.
2 The opening or closing float has been wrongly counted or recorded.
3 The cashier has done one of two things:
   – Keyed in the wrong amount in the till compared to what was correctly taken or rendered.
   – Accepted or rendered the wrong amount compared to what was correctly keyed in the till.
4 Cash has been entered in the till without being recorded, or cash has been removed from the till without being recorded (used to pay expenses, etc., or theft).

The cashing-off slips are the originating documents that should be submitted to the accounting department in order to enter as a debit (+) in the cash book and as a credit (−) in the sales account.

8.5 CREDIT CARDS

Credit cards are increasingly being used as a method of payment. Many customers use cards to do their everyday shopping as well as to buy large one-off items. Most traders offer credit facilities to customers, no longer to increase their sales, but merely to maintain their sales level in comparison with competitors, who offer the same service.

The business completes a credit sales voucher, then the customer authorizes it with a signature and retains the top copy. The voucher itself is stored in the till and is counted along with cheques and cash. The business then retains one copy for their records and remits the other copy to the credit company. This is probably carried out on a daily basis to maximize cash inflow. The credit company automatically credits the business's account by bank giro credit after a handling commission has been deducted. These commission rates vary from customer to customer, depending on the average transaction size and the volume of transactions.

The latest technological development which eases handling and improves cash flow is the electronic card reader. This system automatically produces the credit sales voucher like a till roll which has two copies, one given to the customer and one retained for the business's own records. A transaction entered on this system is automatically transmitted to the business's account at the credit card company, and is immediately credited to the customer's bank account, net of the retained commission. The same electronic system is also used for debit cards, such as Switch, which customers use instead of cheques. In this situation the transaction is instantly registered in both the business's account and the customer's personal bank account.

8.6 THE PETTY CASH SYSTEM

Although tills in large organizations like supermarkets and department stores are used exclusively for storing takings and issuing change, in many smaller organizations such as the corner shop or the local cafe, takings in the till may need to be used for paying minor expenses or making minor purchases.

In Nosey Parkers, the newsagent, the following transactions take place on a particular day:

1 Opening float in the till, £35.
2 Milkman is paid £8.50 for personal milk delivered to shop.
3 Fresh flowers purchased from florist by cash, £80.
4 Cash paid to window cleaner, £5.
5 £10 cash returned to customer for faulty goods sold yesterday.
6 Cash given to paper-boy as wages, £15.
7 Assistant takes £3 from the till to pay business postage.
8 Total takings as per the till roll, £320.
9 Cash counted at the end of the day is £180.50 excluding the float retained.
10 Closing float left in till at the end of the day, £48.

How much was the discrepancy at the end of the day? The question can be answered by producing a cashing-off slip for the till:

	£	£
Float in the till at the end of the day		48.00
Cash takings removed from till		180.50
		228.50
Add amounts paid from till:		
2 Milk bill (drawings)	8.50	
3 Flowers (purchases)	80.00	
4 Windows (expenses)	5.00	
5 Cash returned (returns inwards)	10.00	
6 Wages (expenses)	15.00	
7 Postage (expenses)	3.00	
		121.50
		350.00
Less float at the beginning of the day		35.00
Total cash sales		315.00
Less till roll total		320.00
Discrepancy		–5.00

In larger organizations, where there are many minor cash transactions besides sales, it can be inefficient, time-consuming, and above all it may project a poor image to customers if the till is used for anything except the receipt of cash and the rendering of change. Rather than using the till, there may be a need for a petty cashier to handle these types of transaction.

The commonest type of petty cash system is known as the imprest system, where a fixed float of cash is kept in a separate till or secure box from which minor transactions are undertaken. At the end of a fixed period (possibly a week), the cash is counted and is restored to its original level by a transfer from the main cash book. Physically this might be done by taking money from the till. If Nosey Parkers operated a petty cash system, with a fixed float of £200 to be maintained daily, the records might look something like this:

Petty cash book

Date	Details	Drawings	Purchases	Expenses	Returns	Total (rec/pmt)
		£	£	£	£	£
Mar 1	Bal b/d					200.00
Mar 1	Milk bill	−8.50				
Mar 1	Flowers		−80.00			
Mar 1	Windows			−5.00		
Mar 1	Returns in				−10.00	
Mar 1	Wages			−15.00		
Mar 1	Postages			−3.00		
Total payments		−8.50	−80.00	−23.00	−10.00	−121.50
Mar 1	Bal c/d					+78.50
Mar 2	CB (float reimbursement)					+121.50
Mar 2	Bal b/d					+200.00

The balance brought down of £200 is used to make the minor payments. These payments are usually analysed by expense type, totalled at the end of a specified period, and transferred to the main accounts. The float is then made up at the end of that period to its original fixed level, by a single transfer from the main cash book (CB), and the system continues. In this way the cash book itself is not cluttered by a whole host of minor cash entries.

As far as physical handling of cash is concerned, the contents of the tills, which are removed daily or more often, should be bagged and securely transferred to the cash office, which should be in a secure room accessible only to trusted keyholders. The room should preferably have windows which cannot be seen through from outside, as the sight of staff counting large amounts of cash may cause unnecessary temptation. It is very important that the cash is promptly and regularly taken down to the bank, so that no build-up of cash is allowed. Many firms will use private security firms to undertake this risky function.

8.7 FOREIGN CURRENCY EXCHANGE

Many businesses in the hospitality, tourism and leisure sector, particularly in Europe, will offer services to exchange cash into different currencies. Apart from banks, businesses such as hotels and travel agents, even supermarkets near border areas, may offer such services. And there are very many specialist change businesses in tourist venues, all competing to offer instant exchange facilities for visitors.

Suppliers of currency make a profit by buying or selling currency at below or above a central rate at which they can change currency themselves. There will usually be a commission charge based on the value of the transaction or a flat fee, perhaps possibly a combination of both.

Here is a very simple example to explain the basic principle of foreign currency transactions. Guy Hedges, a currency exchange retailer in London's West End, deals in three currencies: the **pound** (sterling), the **dollar** and the **Deutschmark**. Guy makes his money by buying and selling currency at 10% either side of a central rate, which is the exchange rate available to him. The central rates on a particular day for the pound with respect to the two foreign currencies that he deals in are as follows:

$$£1.00 = \$1.50 \qquad £1.00 = DM\ 2.50$$

Guy buys foreign currency at 10% higher than those rates, and sells at 10% lower than those rates. He uses the closing central rate every day to translate his stocks of currencies into sterling equivalent values. Therefore the currency buying and selling rates posted for the day are as follows:

Dollar		*Mark*	
Buy	Sell	Buy	Sell
£	£	£	£
1.65	1.35	2.75	2.25

The following transactions take place during the day:

1 An American comes in to exchange $1,650 into pounds.
2 A German wishes to exchange DM 550 into pounds.
3 An Englishman comes in to exchange £800 into dollars.

Guy charges commission of 5% of the sterling equivalent value of any transaction by retaining that proportion of the value as commission. Guy starts the day with £2,000 worth of exchange in each currency. How much income does Guy make during the day, and how much of each currency does he have at the end of the day?

Cash book	£	$	DM
Balance b/d (valued at central rate in sterling)	2,000	3,000	5,000
1 (1,650/1.65) × 0.95	−950	+1,650	
2 (550/2.75) × 0.95	−190		+550
3 (800 × 1.35) × 0.95	+800	−1,026	
	——	——	——
Bal c/d	1,660	3,624	5,550
Other currencies in sterling central rates:			
$ (3,624/1.5)	2,416		
DM (5,550/2.50)	2,220		
	——		
Total sterling	6,296		
	≡≡≡		

The position of Guy Hedges at the end of the day can be summarized as follows:

	£
Closing cash in sterling equivalent	6,296
Opening cash in sterling equivalent	6,000
	——
Income	296
	≡≡≡

This increase in cash can be broken down transaction by transaction. First, currency gains:

	Profit
	£
1 (1,650/1.65) – (1,650/1.50)	100
2 (550/2.75) – (550/2.50)	20
3 (800 × 1.50) – (800 × 1.35)/1.50	80
	———
	200
	═══

Second, commissions:

	Commission
	£
1 (1,650/1.65) × 0.05	50
2 (550/2.75) × 0.05	10
3 (800 × 1.35) × 0.05/1.50	36
	———
	96
	═══

This accounting system easily lends itself to computerization, and if set up properly it can be a very easy business to operate and account for. In this type of business the cash book is the central account from which profitability is derived. There is still a need, however, to operate the double-entry system in the normal way. The double entries for the receipts and payments in the cash book would be made in the sales and cost-of-sales accounts. The commission would be credited (–) to an income received account. In this way the total value of business undertaken is shown in the profit and loss account, as is the breakdown of profit on currency exchange, and on commissions.

8.8 TICKET SYSTEMS FOR CASH SALES

Tickets are a useful mechanism for the management and control of sales where there are physical constraints on the numbers of customers that can be accommodated. Airlines, trains, theatres, cinemas and sporting venues are examples of businesses that operate under these constraints. Other advantages of tickets are that they may be sold in advance of providing the service. This is beneficial from a cash flow perspective, and they enable the business to keep an accurate and up-to-date picture of the latest sales situation, and may indicate whether they should step up the marketing effort or curtail it.

Tickets are also an effective vehicle for differential pricing, reflecting the type and quality of the service available to different customers. For example, an airline might operate three tiers of prices: first class, club class and standard class. This differentiation can be used to charge the appropriate price, taking into account the quality and cost of the service offered, the availability of seats and the ability of the customer to pay. Tickets are the mechanism by which such differences in price can be charged and the seats appropriately controlled and allocated. The theory underlying possible pricing policies is discussed more thoroughly in Chapter 14.

Tickets sold can be thought of as the originating documents (sales invoices), from which the totals are posted to the cash book and to the sales account. The customer gets the ticket itself, or the top copy of the document where multiple copies are produced. The sale is then recorded manually or electronically. If appropriate, the position of the ticket should be recorded so that the number and location of unsold tickets is readily obtainable; this is often useful with theatre tickets. There is considerable scope for a computerized database in this type of operation; each data record is a specific seat and there are separate fields for price, category, position, smoking or non-smoking. This allows customers to be quickly informed of whether their requirements can be met, and what their alternatives might be.

The Hamlet Theatre in Startford-under-Nova is presenting a Shakespeare play shortly. The following information is available on the type, price, availability and type of sales made to date:

	Front stalls	Rear stalls	Circle	Upper circle
Total seats	200	300	400	250
Available	55	100	145	104
Prices (£)	6.00	5.50	9.00	8.50
Cash sales	90	140	130	96
Credit sales	55	60	125	50

The credit card company charges 4% commission for handling credit card vouchers. If the theatre sells no more tickets between now and the date of the performance on a particular day, how many sales would the theatre have generated for this performance?

Total revenue generated for the performance

		£	£
Cash sales	90 × £6		540.00
	140 × £5.50		770.00
	130 × £9.00		1,170.00
	96 × £8.50		816.00
			3,296.00
Credit sales	55 × £6.00	330.00	
	60 × £5.50	330.00	
	125 × £9.00	1,125.00	
	50 × £8.50	425.00	
		2,210.00	
Less handling charge	(£2,210 × 0.04)	88.40	
			2,121.60
Total revenue			5,417.60

All of this money would have been collected through the till or automatically credited to the theatre's bank account by the credit card company. A high proportion of the credit sales will have been booked by telephone, by customers wishing to save a needless journey to a theatre that may be many miles away from their home. Such bookings should be recorded by the theatre staff by producing a credit sales voucher from the phone call, including the serial number of the customer's credit card. The tickets for such sales are either sent back to the customers, or may be retained by the box office until they are collected on the day of the performance.

8.9 INTRODUCTION TO CASH FLOW STATEMENTS

As was emphasized in section 8.1, cash movement and management is extremely important to an organization, and can be critical to its immediate survival. For this reason there
is a need to have a financial statement explaining fully the cash movements within a
given period. This is achieved by the preparation of a cash flow statement. In 1990,
following pressure from academic and practising accountants, the Accounting Standards
Board (ASB) introduced a compulsory cash flow statement for the financial reports of
larger companies. This recommendation was incorporated in the first ASB financial reporting standard (FRS), known as FRS1. FRS1 was revised in 1996 in order to improve the
transparency of the statement in identifying cash movements within a business. Essentially
the cash flow statement explains the sources and uses of cash in a financial period. The
basic aspects of the statement may be explained using a very simple example where a
hotel has the following balance sheets at the beginning and end of a financial period:

Hotel Arizona balance sheet as at December 31, 19x6			Hotel Arizona balance sheet as at December 31, 19x7		
	$	$		$	$
Fixed assets		200,000			250,000*
Current assets:					
Stocks	10,000			12,000	
Debtors	22,000			17,000	
Bank	11,000			n/a	
	43,000			29,000	
Current liabilities:					
Creditors	12,000			14,000	
Bank	n/a			2,500	
	12,000			16,500	
Net current assets		31,000			12,500
Net assets		231,000			262,500
Financed by:					
Capital Jan 1, 19x5		190,000			231,000
Capital introduced		nil			15,000*
Profit 19x6		62,000			30,000
		252,000			276,000
Less drawings		21,000			13,500
		231,000			262,500

* No fixed assets were sold during the year, and the owners transferred $15,000 into the business from a
  private bank account.

What can we tell about the cash position of the hotel between December 31, 19x6 and
December 31, 19x7? Only that the bank account has reduced by £11,000 + £2,500 =
$13,500 over the year. However, this doesn't indicate very much about what in particular

has caused the overall deterioration in cash. This is where a full cash movement analysis is necessary. The way to do this in simple terms is to look at the changes between the two balance sheets on a line-by-line basis, ignoring the difference in the bank as this is what is being explained.

Hotel Arizona balance sheet as at December 31, 19x6

	$	$	Change in cash (+/−) $
Fixed assets	200,000	250,000	(1) −50,000
Current assets:			
Stocks	10,000	12,000	(2) −2,000
Debtors	22,000	17,000	(3) +5,000
Bank	11,000	n/a	Ignore
	43,000	29,000	
Current liabilities:			
Creditors	12,000	14,000	(4) +2,000
Bank	n/a	2,500	Ignore
	12,000	16,500	
Net current assets	31,000	12,500	
Net assets	231,000	262,500	
Financed by:			
Capital			
Jan 1, 19x5/6	190,000	231,000	
Capital introduced	nil	15,000	(5) +15,000
Profit 19x6	62,000	30,000	(6) +30,000
	242,000	266,000	
Less drawings	21,000	13,500	(7) −13,500
	231,000	262,500	−13,500

The reasons for the decline of $13,500 in the cash position of the Arizona hotel will now be explained in full:

1 The hotel purchased fixed assets for $50,000. All other things being equal, this reduced cash by $50,000.
2 The stocks of the hotel increased by $2,000 over the year. All other things being equal, the increased investment in stocks has reduced cash by $2,000.
3 Debtors reduced by $5,000. All other things being equal, there has been a net increase in cash because $5,000 less is owed by customers than was the case a year previously.
4 Creditors have increased by $2,000. All other things being equal, this means a net increase in cash because the hotel has increased its indebtedness to suppliers, thereby retaining this amount of cash within the business.
5 The owners of the hotel have transferred $15,000 from their private bank account to the business. All other things being equal, this has the effect of increasing cash by $15,000.

6 The hotel made a profit of $30,000 in the year. All other things being equal, the business has increased its cash by this amount over the year through profitable exchange. In reality the profit declared for the year will not equate to cash flow, because of adjustments 2, 3 and 4, already dealt with; other possible factors will be explained in a more comprehensive example later on.

7 The owners of the hotel have in 19x6 withdrawn $13,500 for their own living expenses. All other things being equal, cash within the business has been reduced by this amount. Summing changes 1 to 7 fully explains the total difference between the bank account at the beginning and at the end of the accounting period.

A more comprehensive example should give a more detailed explanation of the cash flow statement recommended in FRS1. Here are the accounts of a fast food outlet called Fast Break:

Profit and loss accounts for Fast Break for the years to March 31, 19x2 and 19x3

	19x2		19x3	
	£000	£000	£000	£000
Sales		630		870
Less COS		525		740
Gross profit		105		130
Expenses, including depn, etc.	50		60	
Loan interest	nil		2	
		50		62
Net profit		55		68

Balance sheets for Fast Break

	At March 31, 19x2		At March 31, 19x3	
	£000	£000	£000	£000
Fixed assets				
Fixed assets at cost		195		200
Provision for depreciation		15		30
		180		170
Current assets				
Stocks of food	50		100	
Debtors	3		1	
Cash at bank	5		nil	
	58		101	
Less current liabilities				
Creditors	(112)		(166)	
Bank overdraft	nil		(10)	
Net current assets		(54)		(75)
		126		95
Less long-term loan		nil		(20)
Net assets		126		75

Balance sheets for Fast Break (cont'd)

| | At March 31, 19x2 | | At March 31, 19x3 | |
	£000	£000	£000	£000
Financed by				
Opening capital		100		126
Add net profit		55		68
		155		194
Add introductions of capital		50		20
		205		214
Less drawings		79		139
		126		75

Heated food storage units were sold during the year, which produced a loss on sale of £2,000 on the disposal. The cost of the equipment was originally £20,000 and the proceeds were £5,000.

In order to prepare a cash flow statement it is necessary to reconcile net profit with net cash flow from operations. This is achieved by taking the net profit before interest and tax then adjusting it for those items which account for the difference between cash flow and net profit. The net profit before interest and tax (BIT) in these accounts is £68,000 + £2,000 = £70,000.

The first item to deal with is depreciation. In most businesses which carry a large investment in fixed assets, depreciation will involve a significant adjustment. Depreciation needs to be added to profit to recognize cash flow; this is because depreciation is not a cash outflow, but an allocation of the original cost of an asset over its economic life, as a periodic expense charged in the profit and loss account (Chapter 5). Therefore, depreciation reduces profit but has no effect on cash. The workings for depreciation and the changes in fixed assets over the period are dealt with as follows:

Depreciation working

Equipment at cost a/c		Provn for depn a/c		Disposals a/c	
Ref	£	Ref	£	Ref	£
Bal b/d	+195,000	Bal b/d	−15,000	Equip	+20,000
Cash*	+25,000	Disposal	+13,000	Provn*	−13,000
Disposal	−20,000	Depn*	−28,000	Cash	−5,000
Bal c/d	+200,000	Bal c/d	−30,000	Loss	−2,000

* Balancing items in the respective accounts.

The loss on sale is also added to the profit to arrive at the cash flow, as this 'loss' is merely a recognition that the depreciation of the fixed asset has been underprovided during its useful life. If a 'profit' were made on a disposal, the reverse would be true. Changes in stocks, debtors and creditors are the other items that account for the difference between net profit and cash flow under the accruals concept. Their effects were explained in the previous example. As far as Fast Break is concerned, in order to arrive at the net cash flow, the total adjustments to the net profit BIT are as follows:

Reconciliation of operating profit to net cash inflow from operating activities for 19x3

	£	
Net profit BIT	70,000	
Add depreciation	28,000	(see working above)
Add loss on sale	2,000	(see working above)
Increase in stocks	(50,000)	(100,000 – 50,000)
Decrease in debtors	2,000	(3,000 – 1,000)
Increase in creditors	54,000	(166,000 – 112,000)
Net cash inflow	106,000	

Once the net profit before interest and tax has been reconciled with the net cash flow from operations, the cash flow statement itself can be prepared:

Fast Break cash flow statement for the year to March 31, 19x3

	£	£
Net cash flow from operating activities		106,000
Returns on investments and servicing of finance		
Interest on loan	(2,000)	
Drawings	(139,000)	
		(141,000)
		(35,000)
Capital expenditure		
Fixed assets purchased	(25,000)	
Proceeds from disposals	5,000	
		(20,000)
		(55,000)
Management of liquid resources		
Capital introduced	20,000	
Loan raised	20,000	
		40,000
Decrease in cash		(15,000)*

* As the cash position has moved from £5,000 positive position to £10,000 negative, we have fully explained where it came from and where it went to.

It appears as if the owner has been withdrawing an excessive amount of cash from the business, which may threaten its survival.

8.10 CASH AND THE ACCRUALS CONCEPT

The pressure to provide the cash flow statement as recommended by the Accounting Standards Board has alleviated some of the disquiet that existed within the accountancy profession and in the wider business community about the validity, reliability and general usefulness of the traditional trading, profit and loss account and the balance sheet.

Much of the disquiet revolved around a lack of objectivity in some accounting practices based on the accruals concept, which required accountants to 'adjust' profits by matching revenue with attributable expenditure. Many of these practices, where provisions were created and adjusted, made it hard to compare cash movements with reported profitability.

The evidence that vulnerability to failure is heavily linked with reported liquidity and indebtedness makes it imperative to provide a transparent and objectively prepared statement of cash generated and used in a period. The user can then assess reported profitability in its proper context.

SUMMARY

1 **Cash collection, management, control and record keeping should be carried out efficiently and promptly.**

2 **Periodically reconcile the accounting records of cash on hand with the statements produced by the bank.**

3 **Account for and manage cash takings from tills and explain any discrepancies.**

4 **Account for petty cash transactions as a subsidiary account of the cash book.**

5 **There are special methods to account for cash within a foreign exchange business.**

6 **Businesses in the hospitality, tourism and leisure sector operate ticket systems for many of their activities.**

7 **A report and supporting notes for a cash flow statement should follow recommended practice.**

8 **Adherence to the accruals concept has been partly at the expense of objectivity in accounting. Cash flow statements help to put information on profitability in a clearer and more transparent context for users of accounts.**

ASSESSMENT

MULTIPLE-CHOICE QUESTIONS

Question 1
If the closing balance on the bank statement of a business is correctly shown to be £36 higher than the balance as brought down on the cash book of that business at the same date, which one of the four reasons below could not be the cause of the discrepancy?

A A transposition error by the business crediting (–) the cash book with £495 instead of £459.

B Credit card vouchers of £37.50 not entered in the cash book, which were credited automatically to the business bank account and subject to 4% commission payable to the credit card company.

C Dividends of £36 directly credited to the bank account by bank giro credit, but not accounted for by the business.

D An £18 cheque paid to a supplier was debited to the cash book.

Question 2

Suppose the opening cash float in the till is £35, the till roll total for the day equals £350, there is a total of £25 in miscellaneous cash expenses paid from the till, and the total takings counted at the end of the day come to £360 including the closing float of £45. What is the discrepancy between the till roll total and the takings at the end of the day?

A Nothing

B £35

C £45

D £5

Question 3

A petty cash imprest system can be best described as which of the following?

A An account which deals exclusively in coinage

B An account which only contains small expenditure items

C An account operated by a trainee cashier

D An account maintained from the cash book through which minor transactions are made

Question 4

The buying rate of £1 in US dollars is $1.44 and the selling rate is $1.36 on a particular day; the central rate is $1.40. If an American wants to exchange £2,016 for dollars, how much profit does the dealer make in exchange difference and on commission if he charges a flat rate of £15 for all transactions and 5% on the value of the deal in sterling terms over £500?

A £100

B £160

C £110

D £50

Question 5

Suppose the profit after depreciation was £20,000, the depreciation for the year was £2,500, the increases in stocks came to £1,500 during the year, the reduction in debtors was £500, the increase in creditors was £3,000, and the loss on disposal of tangible fixed assets was £2,000. What was the cash inflow from operating activities during the year?

A £17,800

B £26,500

C £28,500

D £19,500

EXERCISES

Exercise 1

On May 15 Lakeshore country club received their monthly bank statement for the month ended April 30. The bank statement was as follows:

Lakeshore Country Club: statement of account with Enterprise Bank Limited

Date	Particulars	Payments (−)	Receipts (+)	Balance (+/−)
April 1	Balance			+1,100.00
April 2	245127	210.70		+889.30
April 3	SC		180.45	+1,069.75
April 6	245126	150.00		+919.75
April 6	BC	15.00		+904.75
April 9	245129	45.23		+859.52
April 10	245131	15.40		+844.12
April 12	245128	300.00		+544.12
April 17	SO	28.35		+515.77
April 20	SC		525.65	+1,041.42
April 23	245130	423.60		+617.82
April 24	BGC		45.00	+662.82
April 25	SC		357.00	+1,019.82
April 27	SC		421.00	+1,440.82
April 30	245133	136.54		+1,304.28

SC = sundry credit   BC = bank charges
BGC = bank giro credit   SO = standing order

For the corresponding period, the bank ledger account of Lakeshore country club was as follows:

Bank account

Date	Details	£
April 1	Balance	+1,069.75
April 2	Rates	−150.00
April 3	Super veg	−54.23
April 5	Petrol	−15.40
April 7	Printer	−300.00
April 16	Cash sales	+525.65
April 18	Cash sales	+357.00
April 21	Cash sales	+421.00
April 24	BGC (int)	+45.00
April 26	Wages	−500.00
April 26	Telephone	−136.54
April 30	Cash sales	+280.35
		————
Bal c/d		+1,542.58
		════

Required
Prepare a statement reconciling the balance at April 30 as given by the bank statement with the balance at April 30 as stated in the bank account.

Exercise 2

The Chameleon Theatre has the following entries at the end of the previous month:

	£
Capital	−85,000
Fixed assets	+100,000
Bank account	−12,500
Cash float	+1,000
Owing from credit card company	+5,000
Owing to creditors	−8,500
	0

The following transactions take place during the month:

1 Total sales from tickets:
  − Cash sales including cheques, £36,000
  − Credit card sales (before 4% commission), £14,000
2 Total expenses:
  − Paid by cheque to creditors, £13,740
  − Paid from the till, £2,500
3 Cash banked, £30,000
4 A cashier left suddenly during the month, coinciding with a loss of cash from the till

At the end of the month, the entries for the theatre are as follows:

	£
Capital	−120,000
Fixed assets	+100,000
Bank account	+15,200
Cash float	+3,500
Owing from credit card company	+7,000
Owing to creditors	−5,700
	0

Required

(a) Calculate the amount of cash that was stolen.
(b) Prepare the trading and profit and loss account of the theatre for the month of June; show the necessary ledger accounts and workings.

Exercise 3

Intercurrency is based in London and deals in foreign exchange. Here is some information about it.

Opening stocks of currency

DM	48,000
$	13,125
FFr	37,600
£	19,000

Exchange rates (buying and selling) in sterling terms

Deutschmark		*Dollar*		*Franc*	
Buy	Sell	Buy	Sell	Buy	Sell
2.50	2.35	1.80	1.70	9.50	9.30

The central rates are as follows:

Deutschmark	*Dollar*	*Franc*
DM 2.40	$1.75	FFr 9.40

Currency dealing in one day at the above rates

Currency sold	
DM	42,300
$	17,000
FFr	37,200

Currency bought	
DM	25,000
$	16,200
FFr	47,500

Required

Draw up a cash book statement showing the increase in sterling equivalent value accumulated during the day. Reconcile the cash book balance with the profit made on each individual transaction. Ignore commissions.

Question 4

Here are the final accounts of Piccadily Hotels:

Trading and profit and loss account (Piccadily Hotels) for the year ended Jan 31, 19x3

	£	£
Sales		400,000
COS		250,000
Gross profit		150,000
Expenses excluding interest and depreciation	95,000	
Interest	10,000	
Depreciation	7,500**	
Loss on disposal of coach	1,000*	
		113,500
Net profit		36,500

* During the year a coach costing £50,000 was purchased. The old coach was used in part-exchange, attracting a trade-in allowance of £14,000 against the new vehicle. This incurred a loss on sale of £1,000 on the disposal.

** Depreciation is charged at a rate of 15% on cost.

Balance sheet (Piccadilly Hotels) as at Jan 31, 19x3

	Cost £	Depn £	NBV £
Fixed assets			
Land and buildings	150,000	nil	150,000
Vehicles	50,000	7,500	42,500
	194,500	32,000	192,500
Current assets			
Stocks of food and materials .		12,000	
Debtors		23,000	
		35,000	
Current liabilities			
Creditors	12,500		
Bank overdraft	5,000		
		17,500	
Net current assets			17,500
			210,000
Long-term liabilities			
Mortgage			94,500
			115,500
Financed by			
Opening capital as at 1.2.x2			100,000
Add net profit			36,500
			136,500
Less drawings			21,000
			115,500

Notes

As at 1.2.x2 the assets and liabilities of Piccadilly Hotels were as follows:

	£
Land and buildings at cost	+150,000
Vehicles at cost	+30,000
Provn for depn, vehicles	−15,000
Stock	+15,000
Debtors	+19,000
Creditors	−22,000
Bank	−15,000
Mortgage	−62,000

Required

As financial accountant for Piccadilly Hotels, you are required to prepare a cash flow statement for the business, for the year ended 31.1.x3.

CHAPTER 9

Accounting for employees

OBJECTIVES

- Recognize the significance of employee costs as a proportion of total business costs.
- Describe alternative methods of employee remuneration.
- Understand how to record and calculate employee remuneration and deductions within a payroll system.
- Record the accounting entries for employee remuneration.
- Identify the minimum disclosure requirements of companies in relation to employee costs.

9.1 THE SIGNIFICANCE OF EMPLOYEE COSTS IN HTL BUSINESSES

The single largest category of costs that most hospitality, tourism and leisure (HTL) businesses have to bear, is the total cost of employing their workforce. Whether a business is capital- or labour-intensive will determine whether, and to what extent, remuneration is the major cost. A business such as a major hi-tech fairground ride may well find that depreciation is its largest annual expense, particularly when equipment is new. Employee remuneration is the main cost category for most businesses in the HTL sector because service-based businesses rely heavily on the technical and artistic skills of people, such as in the entertainment business. But many HTL businesses also require a high degree of interpersonal communication and personal care. In hotels and restaurants, personal service at reception, from table and catering staff, and by laundry and cleaning workers means that a large number of people are required. It is therefore very important that the deployment of labour delivers the services both effectively and economically. An efficient and productive workforce is a key factor in a profitable business.

Employee remuneration is usually defined as revenue expenditure to be charged periodically to the profit and loss account, but many costs involved in the recruiting, selecting, training and rewarding of staff will provide lasting economic benefits to the company. Chapter 5 looked at intangible assets, and a key element in the intangible value of any business is the value of the workforce, particularly the effectiveness of its managers. The better their recruitment, their training and their remuneration, the better will be the output of the staff, and the greater the economic benefits to the business.

9.2 REMUNERATION METHODS

Employees are recruited to provide a service for the company in exchange for financial compensation or reward. The service each employee provides will depend on his or her skills, aptitudes and abilities.

Some staff will be recruited and trained to make a product, or to provide a service directly, such as swimming instructors, ski instructors and chefs. Other staff are recruited for their specialist functional experience, knowledge and skills in such areas as administration, finance, marketing or general management, all of which support the main commercial activity of the organization. Although employed by the same employer, different staff will have very different functions within the organization.

Employees directly engaged in making a product or providing a service will normally be paid on an hourly basis, particularly when the work undertaken is highly skilled, time constrained and discrete, such as instruction, or when the work is unskilled but intense in its nature, or when work is part-time or temporary, such as assisting customers in a retail outlet. The business will normally offer a rate of pay that depends on many factors such as the qualifications and experience required, the skill demonstrated and the physical demands of the job itself. However, pay is constrained more broadly by the economic, statutory and competitive environment in which the employer operates. Premium rates of pay or overtime may be earned for working more than the standard hours in a day or working unsociable shifts.

Support staff are usually salaried on a monthly basis as their contribution is normally non-specific on an hour-to-hour basis and the job may require flexibility and versatility of effort, or involve a creative content that is not necessarily related to the time actually spent at the place of work. The general rule to apply is to decide whether the productivity of the job is directly dependent on, and related *pro rata* to the time spent at that work, or whether the relationship is less clear-cut.

Where its staff are paid on a temporal basis, a business needs to ensure that the output of each staff member is monitored and evaluated, so the required efficiency is maintained, or else profitability may be adversely affected. Unless a standard of service or productivity is ensured, the business will find itself incurring staff costs that may not be contributing to profits, and at worst they may be positively damaging.

Where the output of staff can be defined exactly, such as with the work of direct staff in a manufacturing process, it may be possible to relate pay to the output itself. For example, chefs can be paid by the number of meals they provide. Different rates of pay may apply to different types of meal, such as making a distinction between bar meals and restaurant meals. Direct staff in service businesses such as restaurants and cafes may be paid partly on the quality of service they offer. In most catering establishments this may be on an informal basis such as the receipt of supplemental income provided by gratuities from satisfied customers. In cafes or restaurants, pay may be partly determined by the formal feedback of customers. In the United States, and occasionally in the United Kingdom and other countries, formal feedback from customers is recorded and used as a measure to evaluate and monitor the quality of service. In extreme cases it could be used solely as a method of determining the remuneration of staff. Such systems require the staff to be identified by a name or a number; this identifier is recorded on the customer's bill and on an evaluation slip given to the customer after they have been served. The customer completes the evaluation slip, perhaps using a scale from 1 to 5, judging the quality of the service they received against a number of key criteria.

It could be that the aggregate score of each waiter and waitress may be used as the measure for allocating gratuities or the service charge among staff at the end of the day, week or month. Whatever the specific job, there should be a suitable method for providing remuneration that adequately compensates that member of staff for the quantity and quality of their contribution, and rewards them for their achievements. A reward system, if appropriately implemented, should instil loyalty and may motivate the employees in their future performance. In most situations the method of remuneration will be a combination of more than one measurement basis, such as offering a wage based on hours worked but supplemented by an output-based bonus where possible. It might be possible to offer a bonus based on one or more qualitative factors that can be continuously appraised.

Indirect staff can be appraised periodically on their qualitative contribution to the organization; the outcome would then determine the appropriate level of remuneration for that staff member within a pay structure. It can also identify the training needs for individual members of staff.

Let us take the example of the Expresso Taco bar in Mexico City. There are four waitresses and they are paid on an hourly basis, supplemented by a productivity and quality of service bonus. The system works in the following way. The waitresses are paid hourly in pesos, supplemented by a bonus of 10% of sales generated. All meals include a 10% service charge. This bonus is shared at the end of each week among the four waitresses on the basis of their individual points aggregates accumulated on the service evaluation slips, divided by the total number of points accumulated by them all. Here are the details for one week:

	Hours worked	Takings generated P000	Points total
Waitress 1	60	88	1,200
Waitress 2	75	99	1,000
Waitress 3	40	44	800
Waitress 4	20	55	200
Total		286	3,200

If the hourly basic wage is P300, how many pesos does each waitress earn?

			P
Waitress 1			
Basic	60 × 300	=	18,000
Productivity	88,000 × 10%	=	8,800
Quality	1,200/3,200 × (286/11)*	=	9,750
			36,550

Waitress 2			
Basic	75 × 300	=	22,500
Productivity	99,000 × 10%	=	9,900
Quality	1,000/3,200 × (286/11)*	=	8,125
			40,525

Waitress 3			
Basic	40 × 300	=	12,000
Productivity	44,000 × 10%	=	4,400
Quality	800/3,200 × (286/11)*	=	6,500
			22,900

			P
Waitress 4			
Basic	20 × 300	=	6,000
Productivity	55,000 × 10%	=	5,500
Quality	200/3,200 × (286/11)*	=	1,625
			13,125

* The quality bonus is calculated by taking 1/11 of the gross takings (which includes the 10% service charge) and multiplying this by the service points earned by that waitress as a proportion of the points earned by all waitresses.

The advantage of this fairly sophisticated method of remuneration is that it provides incentives in three key areas. The waitress is rightly paid for the time that she is at work, but she is also rewarded for encouraging the customers to spend as much as possible, and finally she is rewarded in relation to the satisfaction given to the customer. The most highly paid waitress works the greatest number of hours, generates the most revenue and ensures the highest levels of repeat business by providing the best service.

The performance of waitresses can be evaluated by this method of remuneration and their training needs can be identified. As a part-timer, the fourth waitress appears to be very successful in getting customers to spend their money, but she is singularly unsuccessful at impressing them with her personal service.

9.3 THE PAYROLL SYSTEM

The mechanics of accounting for wages can be complex and problematical unless a proper system for employee remuneration is operated. The employer is responsible for calculating and deducting the employee's income tax under the pay-as-you-earn (PAYE) scheme; the employer must calculate and deduct the employee's contribution to social security under the National Insurance system (employee's NI); and the employer must make an additional contribution towards social security (employer's NI). There may also be further adjustments for such items as pension contributions, by both the employee and the employer, and for union dues or charitable contributions. There is sometimes a need to calculate the statutory sick pay (SSP) due to an employee taken ill or in some other way incapacitated, or statutory maternity pay (SMP).

In the United Kingdom the various thresholds for paying tax and the rates of tax, National Insurance and SSP/SMP depend on the annual Budget of the Chancellor of the Exchequer, and they are a key part of government fiscal policy. The latest information on thresholds, bands and rates of tax is available from the Inland Revenue. The PAYE system was introduced in order to make it easier for the collector of taxes to collect tax and National Insurance on the many millions of Schedule E taxpayers (employed persons). The employer is held responsible for paying over the income tax and National Insurance liabilities of all employees on a monthly basis. The deadline for payment is the nineteenth of the month following the month in which the remuneration was paid. The employer must keep the following information either on the Inland Revenue's Deductions Working Sheet (form P11) or on computerized files:

1 National Insurance contributions
2 Gross pay for the week
3 Cumulative pay for the tax year to date
4 Total free pay to date (total tax allowances)
5 Total taxable pay to date (item 3 − item 4)
6 Total tax due to date
7 Tax to be paid or repaid for the period

Here is an example of a standard pay slip:

Crown Amusements, London   *Windsor E.R.*
                                               Emp No: 100045

NI No: YZ37777OD
Tax code: 550L   Week No: 12
Period ended June 21, 19x6
Pay and allowances   *Deductions*   *Balances*

Description	Hours	Rate	Value £		£		£
Salary			375	Pension	36.75	Gross pay to date	5,900
Overtime	20	7.50	150	Tax	100.61	Tax to date	955.38
				NI	41.54	NI to date	437.00
				Union	10.00	Annual salary	19,500
						Pension	7%
				Gross pay	525.00		
				Deductions	188.90		
				Net	336.10		

This pay slip can be explained in the following way. The first important piece of information is the tax code. This is obtained from the personal allowance of the employee. An employee's personal allowance is determined by his or her personal circumstances, whether he or she is single, married or a pensioner. Personal circumstances are denoted by the letters H,L,V,P or T. In this case the employee is a single person – code L. The number 550 is his or her total annual personal allowance divided by ten and rounded down to the nearest whole number. Here the total allowance is a £4,910 personal allowance with an additional allowance of £590, making a total of £5,500. Then 5,500/10 = 550 so the complete code is 550L.

The basic rate of tax will be taken as 20% for the first £3,900 of taxable income, and 24% thereafter. We will ignore the fact there is currently a higher marginal rate at 40%, as this employee does not earn enough for it to be relevant. We will assume that the National Insurance contribution (Class 1 for employees) is based on the Inland Revenue's Table A for non-contracted out employees at 2% for the first £62 per week and at 10% from £62 up to a maximum of £465 a week.

The free pay per week for the above employee = £5,500/52 = £105.77. The total free pay to date, given that the tax year starts on April 6 is £1,269.24 (12 weeks × £105.77); the gross pay to date is £5,900. As the taxable income up to this week is £5,900 − £1,269.24 = £4,630.76, the tax due to date is therefore

$$(£3,900 \times 20\%) + (£4,630.76 - £3,900) \times 24\% = £780 + £175.38$$
$$= £955.38$$

The total taxable pay this week for this type of employee would normally be obtained from the tax deduction tables available from the Inland Revenue. The tables indicate the total tax payable, week by week, for different classes of taxpayer at various levels of earnings. If the total tax payable up to the previous week is subtracted from the total tax payable to date, we can calculate the amount of tax to deduct from this week's pay. This can also be done without tables:

$$\text{Free pay to last week} = 11 \times £105.77 = £1,163.47$$

$$\text{Gross pay to last week} = £5,900 - £525 = £5,375$$

The taxable pay due up to last week is $£5,375 - £1,163.47 = £4,211.53$, therefore the tax due up to then is

$$(£3,900 \times 20\%) + (£4,211.53 - £3,900) \times 24\% = £780 + £74.77$$
$$= £854.77$$

Although this figure would be more readily available from a tax table, it is worked through here in order to explain, step by step, how the figures in the tables are actually derived. The tax payable this week is therefore $£955.38 - £854.77 = £100.61$. Refer back to the pay slip and see that it matches the tax entry in the deductions column.

The employee's NI is calculated on a flat rate of

$$(£62 \times 2\%) + (£465 - £62) \times 10\% = £1.24 + £40.30$$
$$= £41.54$$

The NI payable to date is the cumulative NI payable over the 12 weeks of the tax year so far. The amount payable each week will depend on how much overtime was earned by this employee in any particular week.

Besides paying PAYE and NI on behalf of the employee, the employer also has to pay NI to supplement the employee's contributions. The rate of NI payable by the employer is calculated at a different flat rate that depends upon the weekly/monthly/annual amount of the employee's total wage or salary. In order to explain how the system works, we will assume the rates are as follows:

Weekly earnings (£)	Rate of tax payable on all income (%)
0–62	3.00
62–110	5.00
110–155	7.00
Over 155	10.00

We will now calculate the employer's total contribution for the employee this week. As the employee's gross pay is £525 per week, the employer has to pay him the 10% rate of NI for the whole £525, giving a liability of $£525 \times 10\% = £52.50$. Note that the employer's NI does not appear as a deduction on the pay slip of the employee as the employee is not liable for this tax. The employer's NI is treated in the accounts of the business as an expense to be charged to the profit and loss account.

If an employee is unwell, is certified medically as being unfit for work or is pregnant, the employer has an obligation to pay statutory sick pay (SSP) or statutory maternity pay (SMP), as a minimum, to the employee during a period of incapacitation or absence. The rules governing SSP and SMP are available from the Department of Social Security (DSS), and will change periodically. The calculations and accounting treatment of these benefits will not be covered in this text.

At the end of each tax year, the employer is required to furnish the Inland Revenue with form P35 for each employee, detailing their earnings, their PAYE and their NI contributions for the tax year. This information is available from form P11 (see above) or the employer's computerized records. The employer is also required to give the employee a certificate of gross earnings for the year and the amount of income tax deducted under PAYE; this is known as form P60. If an employee leaves their present employment, the employer is required to complete form P45, a summary of the employee's pay and deductions recorded on form P11. The employee then gives the P45 to their new employer.

9.4 ACCOUNTING FOR EMPLOYMENT COSTS

The total cost of remunerating staff is treated as a revenue expense in the profit and loss account. The simple double entry is to credit (–) cash and debit (+) a wages or salaries expense account. The obligations that the employer has to the Inland Revenue to pay PAYE and NI make the entries a little more complicated in practice. We will take the employer in the previous example, Crown Amusements; the following summary information is available at the end of April for all its employees:

	£
Gross wages and salaries	56,000
Employee's PAYE	12,200
Employee's NI	3,355
Employer's NI	5,100

What are the double entries required?

Cash book			*Wages account*		
Ref		£	Ref		£
Apr	Wages a/c	−40,445	Apr	Cash book	+40,445
			Apr 30	Employee's PAYE	+12,200
			Apr 30	Employee's NI	+3,355
			Bal c/d		+56,000*

Employee's PAYE a/c			*National Insurance a/c*		
Ref		£	Ref		£
Apr 30	Wages a/c	−12,200	Apr 30	Wages a/c	−3,355
			Apr 30	Employer's NI	−5,100
			Bal c/d		−4,115

Employer's NI (expense) a/c		
Ref		£
Apr 30	NI account	+5,100

* Net wages = £56,000 − (£12,200 + £3,355)

The net wages are paid continuously throughout the month, probably on a weekly basis. At the end of the month, the total deductions are summed for all employees, both PAYE and employee's NI. The employee's PAYE and NI deductions are debited (+) to the wages and salaries account and credited (–) to the PAYE/NI (creditors) accounts. The employer's NI, being an additional staff cost, is debited (+) to an employer's NI expense account and credited (–) to the NI (creditors) account. The liability to the Inland Revenue will remain on the books until they are paid, sometime between the end of the month and up until the deadline on May 19. These accounts are then closed off as the payments are made from the cash book.

These explanations indicate that calculating, recording and reporting of employee costs can be a complicated process. The specific details on total thresholds, bands, and rates of tax and contributions are revised annually in the Budget, and the changes must be taken into account. Although the system may appear complicated and costly to administer, it can easily be operated using computerization, which can save much valuable clerical time and effort. Large organizations will find it economical to have their own computerized payroll system, whereas smaller organizations may find it more economical to subcontract this part of the accounting function to specialist payroll businesses or to their accountants.

9.5 REPORTING EMPLOYEE COSTS

Although the accounting department will keep detailed records of staff costs and liabilities to income tax, national insurance and SSP analysed by department, the Companies Act 1985 only requires that the overall total of staff costs is disclosed, broken down between directors' remuneration and other staff costs. This is either to be shown on the accounts themselves or as a note to the main accounts. The information on employees required in a company's financial reports includes the following items:

- Wages and salaries paid in the finanacial year (PAYE inclusive).
- Social security costs incurred by the business on each employee's behalf (employee's and employer's NI).
- Other pension costs incurred by the company on each employee's behalf.
- Directors' 'emoluments', including any monies paid to directors in their official capacity.
- The chairperson's emoluments and the emoluments of the most highly paid director if it is not the chairperson.
- The numbers of directors whose total emoluments fall into brackets of a scale starting with zero and continuing in multiples of £5,000.
- Compensation to directors for loss of office, including benefits in kind.

SUMMARY

1 Employee costs in an HTL business may be a major cost, if not the single largest cost.

2 Among other external factors, the contribution of an employee to a business will largely determine the type of remuneration package offered, and the manner in which it is paid.

3 Employers calculate, record and operate the payment of employee wages, salaries and deductions within an overall payroll system.

4 Certain accounting entries are required for employee remuneration and to satisfy the Inland Revenue.

5 Limited companies must obey certain minimum disclosure requirements with regard to staff costs.

ASSESSMENT

MULTIPLE-CHOICE QUESTIONS

Question 1
Which of the factors below has the least significance in determining the total employee costs faced by a business in the HTL sector?

A Whether the business is mainly capital- or labour-intensive
B Whether the business offers a bought-in product or provides a personal service
C Whether most employees are hourly paid or salaried
D The economic, legal or commercial environment faced by the business

Question 2
Which of the following criteria of employee performance would be the most appropriate as a measure to determine the fee of a concert pianist?

A Performance length
B The quality of the performance and the perceived difficulty of the pieces played
C The extent to which the capacity of the concert hall has been filled and the amount of revenue received
D The capacity of the concert hall

Question 3
From the following information, which of the amounts below is the correct total tax deducted for the employee to date this year?

Gross pay this week	£300
Gross pay to date	£1,200
Week number in tax year	4
Total annual free pay	£5,200
Tax rate on all taxable earnings	25%

A £100
B £200
C £300
D £400

Question 4
Which of the following is the correct treatment of employee remuneration in the accounts of a business?

A Debit (+) the net pay of the employee in the wages/salaries account, and credit (−) the cash book.
B Debit (+) the gross pay to the wages and salaries account and credit (−) the cash book.
C Debit (+) the wages/salaries accounts with the gross pay excluding employer's NI and debit (+) the employer's NI to an expense account; credit (−) the cash book with the net pay and credit (−) the NI and PAYE accounts with the total monthly tax payable.
D Debit (+) the wages/salaries accounts with the gross pay including employer's NI and credit (−) the cash book with the net pay; credit (−) the NI and PAYE accounts with the total monthly tax payable.

Question 5

According to the Companies Act 1985, which of the following items of information are not required to be disclosed in the accounts of limited companies?

A Pension costs incurred by the employer on behalf of employees
B Total directors' emoluments
C Total social security costs incurred by the employer on behalf of employees
D Total PAYE paid by the employer on behalf of employees

EXERCISES

Exercise 1

In the following businesses, identify one type of job which could be defined as directly operational and one that could be defined as administrative or supporting. No one type of job should be included more than once.

(a) An hotel
(b) A restaurant
(c) A travel agency
(d) A book publisher
(e) A horse-racing training stable

For each job, identify the most relevant performance measurement criterion from the following list. You may use a performance measurement more than once if applicable.

1 The number of hours worked
2 The level of productivity in physical terms
3 The level of productivity in financial terms, i.e. revenue earned
4 The level of satisfaction provided
5 The level of economy achieved, i.e. cost control, savings
6 The unsociableness of the hours worked
7 The skill, experience and qualifications possessed

Exercise 2

The Black Hart restaurant in Dorset is a busy outlet for meals and drinks, concentrating on bar meals and snacks. There are three waiters and they are paid on an hourly basis, supplemented by a productivity and quality-of-service bonus. The system works in the following way. The waiters are paid hourly, supplemented by a bonus of 5% of sales generated. All meals include a 10% service charge. This bonus is shared at the end of each week among the three waiters on the basis of their individual points aggregates accumulated on service evaluation slips, divided by the total number of points accumulated by them all. Here are the details for one week:

	Hours worked	Bill totals excluding service charges £	Points total
Waiter 1	40	1,200	900
Waiter 2	30	900	1,500
Waiter 3	60	600	600
Total		2,700	3,000

Required

If the hourly basic wage is £2.50, how much should each waiter earn? Make a brief assessment of each waiter's performance during the week.

Exercise 3

Here is the pay slip of J.W. Curtis, who works for a travel agency.

Globe Trotter Travel   *Curtis J.W.*
                                                Emp No: 124612

NI No: YZ478560D
Tax code: 390L   Week No: 20
Period ended 21.8.x7

Pay and allowances				*Deductions*		*Balances*	
Description	Hours	Rate	Value				
			£		£		£
Salary			280	Pension	?	Gross pay to date	5,950
Overtime	16	4.25	68	Tax	?	Tax to date	?
				NI	?	NI to date	495.80
				Union	8.00	Annual salary	14,560
						Pension	5%
				Gross pay	348.00		
				Deductions	?		
				Net	?		

Income tax is levied at 20% up to the first £3,900 of taxable income, and 24% thereafter. Employee's NI is 2% on the first £62 of earned income, and 10% on weekly gross income within the range £62–465 a week.

Required

Calculate the missing figures on the pay slip. Show all your workings.

Exercise 4

The following summary information is available for Gunsmoke City adventure park, as at the end of June for all employees of the business:

	£
Gross wages and salaries	45,000
Employee's PAYE	10,100
Employee's NI	3,105
Employer's NI	4,800

Required

(a) Prepare the ledger accounts in the books of Gunsmoke City adventure park, analyse the pay between net and gross, and show the liabilities to the tax authorities.
(b) Determine the total cash outflow from the business with respect to remuneration in the month of June.

CHAPTER 10

Accounting for VAT

OBJECTIVES

- Outline the fundamental principles of value added tax (VAT).
- Distinguish between standard, zero-rated and exempt items.
- Calculate the VAT liability to Customs and Excise.
- Complete a VAT return and meet payment deadlines.
- Record and process VAT in the accounts.
- Recognize the specific problem of calculating the VAT liability of tour operators and travel agents.

INTRODUCTION

Value added tax (VAT) is a tax on consumer expenditure; it was introduced in the United Kingdom on April 1, 1973. The introduction of VAT in the United Kingdom was in support of the long-standing objective of what was then the European Economic Community (EEC) to partly transfer the tax burden from direct taxation to indirect taxation, and for some of the proceeds of this tax to be used centrally by the community to carry out its economic policies. There was also an overriding objective to harmonize the burden of the tax in all member countries, in order to avoid economic distortions to trading activities between member states. In order to do this the tax rates and the scope (the products and services to which they applied) needed to converge. Despite some progress in narrowing any differences, convergence is still far from complete.

10.1 THE PRINCIPLES OF VAT

Although VAT is a tax on consumer expenditure, it is not a sales tax, which is simply a percentage on the selling price payable to the tax authorities. VAT is collected in stages by all businesses that 'add value' to a product or provide a service. The advantage of VAT is that the businesses act as tax collectors, and remit the tax to the relevant authority (Customs and Excise). The tax is collected as value is added, not only when the product or service is ultimately consumed. The definition of added value is

Sales value – cost of bought-in goods and services

To understand how the tax works, consider the progress of consignments of willow from an exporting forester to a sports shop in another country.

	Price ex VAT	VAT at 10% £	VAT payable at 10%	£
Manufacturer imports willow from England	1,000	100		100*
Manufacturer sells bats to wholesaler	2,750	275	(275 − 100)	175
Wholesaler sell bats to sports shop	3,400	340	(340 − 275)	65
Sports shop sells bats to consumers	4,500	450	(450 − 340)	110
			Total	450

* The importer pays the VAT-exclusive price to the exporter, but pays to the tax authorities the standard rate of VAT for the country to which the goods were imported.

The tax works in the following way. As the product moves up through the chain of value to the consumer, each business charges a VAT-inclusive price to its customer. Each business has therefore also paid VAT on the product and other bought-in goods and services when it was purchased, therefore the VAT on the purchase may be subtracted from the VAT in the sale, and **the difference** paid to the tax authorities. Notice that, although each business in the value chain pays over VAT to the authorities, it is collecting tax paid to it by its customers and it is not a tax borne by them. It is the final consumers who bear the total tax in the price that they pay for the final product or service. Although the tax authorities receive the tax in separate payments of £100, £175, £65 and £110 from the businesses in the chain, the tax burden falls ultimately on the consumer, who pays £4,500 × 10% = £450 in the final price of the bats purchased.

10.2 RATES AND SCOPE OF VAT

Most goods and services sold are covered by VAT. However, there are certain items which are exempted from VAT altogether. The reason for this can be based on past political decisions not to tax these items on grounds of either maintaining a minimum quality of life, and facilitating social and economic exchange, or because they are taxed in some alternative way. The main exempt groups of products and services are financial and insurance services, postal services, health and education services, gambling, burial and cremation, membership of trade unions and professional bodies, sports competitions, and certain works of art and fundraising schemes. Businesses that supply VAT-exempt products and services do not need to register for VAT, so they cannot claim back any VAT paid on taxable purchases if any of them attract a positive rate of VAT.

For the products and services that are covered by the VAT system, the UK rates, current at the time of writing, are zero and 17.5%. Differential rates reflect national economic and political priorities, and will reflect the values of the country in which the rates apply. In the United Kingdom there was once a third differential rate to cover so-called luxury items, which was set higher than the standard rate.

The zero rate applies at the time of writing broadly to those goods and services which are either considered to be 'necessary' such as sewerage, water, clothing, foods, domestic fuel, non-alcoholic drinks and medicines; or to those which are 'educational' such as books, newspapers and talking books and tape recorders for the blind; or to those which facilitate and encourage commerce and trade, such as gold and bank notes, construction of new buildings, and certain transport and international services.

Those businesses which supply zero-rated goods or services charge no VAT on their sales, known as **outputs**, but may claim back the VAT on their purchases, known as **inputs**, if any of them are taxed at a positive rate. In these situations the customs and excise will refund the amount of VAT paid by the zero-rated suppliers on their positive inputs.

Businesses that supply products or services covered by VAT at whatever rate, must register for VAT if the total value of those supplies (or turnover) exceeds a certain annual value. This limit is revised periodically to take into account inflation and to recognize the costs/benefits of requiring very small traders to be in a system that requires a considerable amount of paperwork and bookkeeping. Businesses that exclusively supply zero-rated products and services may apply to be exempted from VAT. This would mean that those businesses would not be able to claim back VAT on rated inputs. All small businesses which do not reach the annual turnover limit for VAT registration are treated in exactly the same way as those businesses which supply exempt goods and services.

10.3 CALCULATING VAT LIABILITY

To see how these rules apply to businesses and to the calculation of their periodic liability to VAT, consider the example of Moduron Coach Tours. Moduron Coach Tours run passenger tours wholly within the United Kingdom. It is a subcontracting operation for a holiday package business and supplies only the travel and onboard food and drink. Overnight accommodation is not supplied by the company. The details for the quarter ended June 30, 1993 are as follows:

	£
Total ticket sales (including food)	13,350
Total sales value of food and drink	2,350
Cost of food	1,410
Cost of diesel	3,290
Wages	3,000
Insurance	500
Road tax	1,000

The VAT due or reclaimable at the end of this quarter for Moduron Coach Tours will now be calculated. The supply of passenger transport services carrying twelve or more passengers within the United Kingdom is zero-rated for VAT; the supply of food is charged at the standard rate. If the standard rate is taken to be 17.5%, then the VAT due to Customs and Excise on outputs less the VAT on inputs is calculated in the following way. As the amounts shown above are **inclusive of VAT**, the VAT element of the inclusive amount will need to be calculated for those items charged at the standard rate.

The total ticket charge for travel and food costs comes to £13,350. Of this, the standard rate supplies are valued at the inclusive amount of £2,350. This amount represents 17.5/100 of the exclusive amount, or put another way the VAT in this inclusive amount = 17.5/117.5 of the inclusive amount. Reduced to its lowest common denominator, this fraction equals 7/47; it is easily remembered as the **Jumbo jet fraction**. But if the standard rate is changed, the fraction will change and so will the mnemonic.

Using this rule, we can calculate the standard-rate VAT elements of the outputs and inputs of Moduron Coach Tours for the last quarter:

	Value inc VAT		VAT
	£	Rate	£
Total ticket sales (excluding food)	11,000	zero	nil
Total charge for food and drink	2,350	std	350
Cost of food	1,410	std	210
Cost of diesel	3,290	std	490
Wages	3,000	n/a	nil
Insurance	500	exempt	nil
Road tax	1,000	n/a	nil

The travel charge is zero-rated, so no VAT is charged or due. The food and drink cost is at the standard rate when supplied as catering services; but if purchased as groceries for private consumption, it is at the zero rate. The diesel costs are at the standard rate. Wages are not applicable as they are not defined as a bought-in good or service. Road tax does not attract VAT as it is another form of tax. What will Moduron have to pay to or claim from Customs and Excise?

$$\text{VAT on outputs} - \text{VAT on inputs} = £350 - £700$$
$$= £350$$

In this case, as the VAT on Moduron's inputs is greater than the VAT on its outputs, the company is entitled to claim £350 from Customs and Excise.

10.4 COMPLETING A VAT RETURN AND PAYING VAT

The VAT return is a form issued by Customs and Excise to all businesses registered for VAT. These forms can be completed monthly or quarterly, usually depending on whether the business is a net payer or net claimer of VAT. The VAT return contains the summary of the VAT-based transactions undertaken during the last return period. The main information required on each form includes the total VAT due on outputs and inputs, and the difference between them. Businesses are also required to disclose the total VAT-exclusive value of all outputs and inputs, including outputs to and inputs from other members of the European Union (EU). Here is the format of the VAT return (VAT 100):

Value Added Tax Return for the period (VAT 100)
01 04 x3 to 30 06 x3

Moduron Coach Tours	Registration No	Period
Bus Depot	587 9308 82	06 x3
NORTHWICK		
Cheshire	Due date: 31 07 93	
Your VAT Office telephone number is 01972 459945		

		£ p
VAT due this period on **sales** and other outputs	1	350.00
VAT reclaimed in this period on **purchases** and other inputs	2	700.00
Net VAT to be paid to Customs or reclaimed by you (Difference between boxes 1 and 2)	3	350.00
Total value of **sales** and all other outputs excluding VAT. Include your box 6 figure	4	13,000.00
Total value of **purchases** and all other inputs excluding VAT. Include your box 7 figure	5	4,000.00

Total value of all **sales** and related services to other
EC Member States   6
Total value of all **purchases** and related services from other
EC Member States   7
Retail schemes.* If you have used any of the schemes in the period
covered by this return please enter the appropriate letter(s) in this box.

If you are enclosing a payment tick this box: DECLARATION by the signatory to be
completed by or on behalf of the person
named above.

I . . . . declare
that the information given above is true
and complete.

* Retail schemes are schemes whereby certain businesses that find it difficult to account for VAT on
a transaction-by-transaction basis, or who supply products or services with different rates of VAT can
systematically estimate their liability to VAT.

The sales and purchases exclusive of VAT that are entered in boxes 4 and 5 should not
include exempt supplies, wages and salaries and deductions, or taxes such as road fund
licences. The standard tax period for net payers of VAT is three months. Businesses will
be allocated VAT tax periods in one of three groups:

– Those with periods ending on the last days of June, Sept, Dec and March.
– Those with periods ending on the last days of July, Oct, Jan and April.
– Those with periods ending on the last days of Aug, Nov, Feb and May.

The VAT due or reclaimed in any tax period must be notified on the VAT return to
Customs and Excise by the end of the month following the final month of the latest tax
period. There is an option to make an annual return on the annual accounting scheme.
Under this scheme the business uses direct debit to make nine monthly payments of
estimated VAT. The tenth transaction, a balancing payment or claim, comes two months
after the end of the year when the actual net VAT amount for the year has been calculated. When payment is made, it is necessary to quote the business's VAT registration
number on the back of the cheque or the giro transfer slip, in case the Customs form
is separated from the payment.

10.5 ACCOUNTING FOR VAT

The VAT return is the last stage in the process of accounting and recording entries for
VAT. As each transaction takes place, the VAT should be calculated, recorded and eventually processed. This is easily achieved under a computerized accounting system, and
the summary figures required for the VAT return are available instantly. It is important
to understand the mechanics of recording and processing transactions that are subject
to VAT.

VAT can be accounted for on an invoice basis or on a cash basis. Let us begin with the
cash basis. The system is straightforward. As soon as the cash is received for a VAT sale,
the liability for VAT (the tax point) is recognized, but not before. The same applies to
VAT purchases. As soon as the invoice has been settled, the VAT claim can be recognized.
If we return to Moduron Coach Tours, we can demonstrate how the system might work.

Moduron Coach Tours

	£	Rate	VAT £
Total ticket sales (excluding food)	11,000	zero	nil
Total charge for food and drink	2,350	std	350
Cost of food	1,410	std	210
Cost of diesel	3,290	std	490
Wages	3,000	n/a	nil
Insurance	500	exempt	nil
Road tax	1,000	n/a	nil

These summary transactions will now be entered in the accounts:

Sales account

Ref	£
Cash book	−13,000*

Cash book

Ref	£
Sales	+13,000*
VAT	+350
COS	−1,200
VAT	−210
Diesel	−2,800*
VAT	−490
Wages	−3,000
Insurance	−500
Road tax	−1,000
Bal c/d	+4,150

VAT account

Ref	£
Cash book	−350
Cash book	+210
Cash book	+490
Bal c/d	+350

Cost of sales (COS)

Ref	£
Cash book	+1,200

Diesel expense a/c

Ref	£
Cash book	+2,800*

Wages expense a/c

Ref	£
Cash book	+3,000

Insurance expense a/c

Ref	£
Cash book	+500

Road tax expense a/c

Ref	£
Cash book	+1,000

* Note that the 'nominal' accounts are posted with the VAT-exclusive amounts, and the VAT due on outputs or VAT reclaimed on inputs are posted to the VAT account. The balance on the VAT account at the end of the quarter represents the amount owing to or from Customs and Excise. In this case the positive balance represents £350 owing from Customs and Excise to Moduron Coach Tours.

Where businesses predominantly generate their revenue on a cash basis, but **pay their suppliers on credit terms**, it might be beneficial from a cash flow perspective to elect to have VAT calculated on an invoice basis. The benefit to them is that they can claim back their input tax as soon as they are invoiced. This might afford considerable cash flow benefit if the amounts involved, or the settlement periods allowed by suppliers, were substantial.

Here is an example of a leisure centre which purchases £1,000 of chlorine, excluding VAT, on credit from a chemical supplier for its heated swimming-pool.

COS account		Creditor account		VAT account	
Ref	£	Ref	£	Ref	£
Creditor	+1,000	COS	−1,000	Creditor	+175
		VAT	−175		

Note that here the VAT is actually recognized as the invoices are processed, and in this case the VAT is analysed in the personal account rather than in the cash book.

Any business registered for VAT will report in its final accounts the **VAT-exclusive** revenues and expenses. The main exception is the VAT on business saloon cars. VAT on this type of vehicle cannot be set off against output tax, thereby increasing the full cost of such assets to the business. If a business is either exempt, or voluntarily chooses not to register for VAT, it will have to include the VAT element that it pays on its inputs, as part of its reported expenses on those items. As these businesses cannot reclaim the VAT on their inputs, the VAT becomes a cost they have to bear themselves. It is also important to distinguish between business inputs and private expenditure. If stocks of alcohol are purchased for a restaurant, and on average the retaurateur consumes 2% of this alcohol, then only 98% of the VAT on the purchases of drinks may be reclaimed.

Returning to the earlier example and the transactions entered into by Moduron Coach Tours for the quarter to June 30, how would the gross and net profit be reported for that quarter?

Trading and profit and loss account (Moduron Coach Tours) for the quarter ended June 30, 19x3

	£	£
Sales (exc VAT)		13,000
Less cost of sales (food and drink)		1,200
Gross profit		11,800
Less expenses:		
Diesel (exc VAT)	2,800	
Insurance	500	
Wages	3,000	
Road tax	1,000	
		7,300
Net profit		4,500

Note that the entries in the trading and profit and loss account are shown net of VAT. However, the VAT payable/reclaimable to or from Customs and Excise (the difference between VAT on outputs and inputs) will be shown as either a current liability or a current asset on the balance sheet. In this situation Moduron Coach Tours would have a current asset of £350 (VAT owing to them from Customs and Excise) on their balance sheet, were they to draw one up at the end of June.

The Mumbay Hotel is a holiday hotel and does not accommodate long-stay guests. Here is the trial balance as at March 31, 19x3:

	£
Revenue from residential rooms	−30,000
Revenue from commercial room hire	−10,000
Revenue from restaurant sales	−18,000
Tips freely given	−600
Cost of food, etc.	+8,000
Wages (including tips redistributed)	+15,000
Fuel and light	+4,000
Land and buildings at cost	+200,000
Depreciation to Jan 1, 19x3	−10,000
Fixtures and fittings at cost	+24,000
Depreciation to Jan 1, 19x3	−6,000
Business saloon car (new in Feb 19x3)	+12,400
Insurances	+3,000
Telephone	+2,000
Bank	−61,975
Creditors	−5,000
Purchases of consumable items	+3,000
Drawings	+15,000
Opening stock food and drink 31.3.x3	+2,500
	+147,325

Closing stocks of food as at 31.3.x3 were valued at £3,200. The balances on the VAT account and the capital account as at Jan 1 are missing, causing the failure to balance the trial balance.

It is possible to calculate the missing figures and prepare the trading and profit and loss account and balance sheet for the Mumbay Hotel for the period ending March 31, 19x3. In doing so, some of the fundamental points introduced earlier in the chapter will be reiterated. The trial balance must balance at zero as we know from earlier chapters. If we calculate the VAT account balance, it is possible to derive the balancing figure which will be the owner's capital as brought forward at the beginning of the year. Before carrying out any calculations, we need some key facts about the VAT implications for hotels:

1 All revenue including food and services provided to short-stay guests is chargeable at the standard rate. Long-stay guests (over four weeks) are not charged VAT on the accommodation proportion of their total hotel bill.
2 Room hire charges are generally exempt.
3 Food purchases for catering are at the standard rate.
4 Tips freely given are not subject to VAT, on the assumption they are kept as wages or redistributed as supplemental income to staff.
5 VAT on business cars is not recoverable as input tax.
6 Wages are not applicable.
7 Insurance is exempt.
8 Fuel, power, telephone and consumable expenses are taxable.

In our hotel example, depreciation of the fixed assets is on the following basis:

1 Land and buildings depreciate 5% on cost per annum.
2 Fixtures and fittings depreciate 25% on cost per annum.
3 Motor cars depreciate at 20% on cost per annum.

As a first step, the VAT balance at the end of the quarter will be calculated:

	£
VAT on outputs	
Revenue from guest accommodation	30,000
Revenue from restaurant sales	18,000
	48,000 × 0.175 = 8,400
Less VAT on inputs	
Catering food supplies	8,000
Fuel and light	4,000
Telephone	2,000
Consumable items	3,000
	17,000 × 0.175 = 2,975
Net VAT payable to Customs and Excise	5,425

This is the amount that the Mumbay Hotel will have to pay Customs and Excise at some time before the end of April. At the end of the quarter this amount is a credit (−) in the trial balance, and a current liability on the balance sheet.

Now that the missing VAT figure has been arrived at, it is possible to derive the opening capital figure:

	£
Discrepancy on original trial balance	147,325
Less VAT owing	5,425
Opening capital (balancing figure)	141,900

And here is the profit and loss account for the Mumbay Hotel for the quarter ended March 31, 19x3:

	£	£
Sales		58,600 (including tips)
Less costs		
Food, etc.	7,300*	
Consumable items	3,000	
Wages	15,000	
Fuel and light	4,000	
Insurance	3,000	
Telephone	2,000	
Depreciation†		
Land and buildings	2,500	
Fixtures and fittings	1,500	
Business vehicle	620	
Total expenses		38,920
Net profit		19,680

* Cost of sales of food is £2,500 + £8,000 − £3,200 = £7300.
† The depreciation for each item has been calculated for a quarter, i.e. vehicle = (£12,400 × 20%)/4 = £620.

Note also that where there is no defined product being sold, there is no need for a general trading account. Although gross profit for the restaurant will be calculated for internal purposes, in the case of a hotel, all the main expenses are subtracted from the revenue to leave only the net profit. Here is the balance sheet of the Mumbay Hotel as at March 31, 19x3:

	Cost £	Depn £	NBV £
Fixed assets			
Land and buildings	200,000	12,500	187,500
Fixtures and fittings	24,000	7,500	16,500
Vehicle	12,400	620	11,780
	236,400	20,620	215,780
Current assets			
Stocks of food, etc.		3,200	
Less current liabilities			
Creditors	5,000		
VAT payable	5,425		
Bank overdraft	61,975		
		72,400	
Net current liabilities			(69,200)
Net assets			146,580
Financed by			
Opening capital Jan 1, 19x3			141,900
Add net profit			19,680
			161,580
Less drawings			15,000
			146,580

10.6 THE MECHANICS OF VAT FOR TOUR OPERATORS AND TRAVEL AGENTS

Earlier in the chapter we covered the fundamental principles of VAT, how it is calculated, and how it is recorded in the accounts. It is now necesary to look at the special case of tour operators and travel agents, as a case study in the somewhat complex field of calculating VAT liability for this type of business. The relevant topic is the **tour operators' margin scheme.**

Businesses registered for VAT must normally account for VAT on all their outputs less the VAT on all their inputs. This is not the case for tour operators who buy travel, hotel, holiday and certain other supplies of a kind enjoyed by travellers, from a third party and resell them as principals. Under this scheme the tour operator or agent does not account for the VAT on the full selling price, but on the margin between the VAT-inclusive purchase price and the selling price. The VAT is payable to the tax authorities of the country in which the seller of the holiday is situated. If the business is a travel agent and acts solely as a booking agent, arranging a supply between two other parties, then it only has to account for VAT on the commission earned.

If the supply is in any part made up of travel (involving the conveyance of twelve or more passengers) the VAT is zero-rated in the United Kingdom. Where travel or any of the supplies listed below are involved, it is therefore important that the purchase cost and selling price of a 'package' is separated into its constituent parts, so the VAT on the margin can be calculated correctly. The following items are standard-rated supplies for margins earned on HTL packages:

- Hotel bedrooms and any other holiday accommodation
- Catering if supplied as part of a package
- Guides and couriers (except airport and resort staff)
- Admissions to theatres and places of entertainment, including museums and sporting events
- Courses, tuition, etc., and the right to attend conferences, exhibitions, etc.
- The hire of sporting equipment (e.g. ski packs) and facilities to play (e.g. green fees)
- Car parking (including parking at airports)
- Car, taxi, bicycle, boat and hang-glider hire

If the whole package is enjoyed outside the European Union, whether it includes the above items or not, then the margin is zero-rated, as are all travel costs of conveying twelve or more passengers. If the tour operator supplies the above items from its own resources, as opposed to buying them from a third party ('in-house'), the VAT on those supplies should be calculated in the normal way.

The tour operator should not include insurance premiums or other financial charges in the total sales value from which it subtracts its costs to determine the margin. Financial elements within the outputs are exempt items, so they fall outside the margin scheme.

There is a lot to digest in this section, so we will now examine the mechanics of calculating VAT for travel agents through a small case study. YFS (Young, Free and Single) Holidays buys package holidays for resale to people between 18 and 30. The following information is available for the year to June 30, 19x3:

	Cost to tour operator £	Prices charged £
* UK travel (12 or more passengers)	16,000	22,000
* EU travel	15,000	19,000
* Travel outside EU	8,000	11,000
Accommodation UK	12,000	15,000
Accommodation EU	22,000	26,000
* Accommodation outside EU	14,000	17,000
Hire of equipment	6,000	8,000
Hire of transport	10,000	12,000
Admission to places of interest	2,000	3,000
Travelling guides and couriers	4,000	4,000
** Cruise ship	9,000	11,000
*** Insurance premiums	1,000	1,800
Total		149,800

All the above amounts are exclusive of VAT.

  * Zero-rated margin supplies.
 ** Cruise ship costs are apportioned 40% travel, 60% other; therefore 60% of the cost is taxed at the standard rate.
*** Financial items are exempt and are not included in the margin scheme.

Method for calculating annual liability to VAT

Step 1: Add together all the sales of supplies (excluding exempt items)

$$£149,800 - £1,800 = £148,000$$

Step 2: Add up the VAT-inclusive cost of standard-rated margin scheme supplies

	£	VAT £	VAT INC £
Accommodation UK	12,000	2,100	14,100
Accommodation EU	22,000	3,850	25,850
Hire of equipment	6,000	1,050	7,050
Hire of transport	10,000	1,750	11,750
Admission to places of interest	2,000	350	2,350
Travelling guides and couriers	4,000	700	4,700
Cruise ship costs (9,000 × 60%)	5,400	945	6,345
Total	61,400	10,745	72,145

Step 3: Add up the cost of the zero-rated margin scheme supplies

	£
UK travel (12 or more passengers)	16,000
EU travel	15,000
Travel outside EU	8,000
Accommodation outside EU	14,000
Cruise ship costs (9,000 × 40%)	3,600
Total	56,600

Step 4: Add together the results of Steps 2 and 3

$$£72,145 + £56,600 = £128,745$$

Step 5: Calculate the total margin on the margin scheme supplies

$$\text{step 1} - \text{step 4} = £148,000 - £128,745$$
$$= £19,255$$

Step 6: Calculate the proportion of the margin represented by standard-rated margin scheme supplies

$$\text{step 5} \times (\text{step 2/step 4}) = £19,255 \times (72,145/128,745)$$
$$= £10,790$$

Step 7: Calculate the standard-rated VAT element on the margin calculated in step 6

$$£10,790 \times 7/47 = £1,607$$

This is the amount payable to Customs and Excise.

Profit
The profit made by YFS on its activities for the year can be calculated as follows:

	£
Sales	149,800
Less costs inclusive of VAT (128,745 + 1,607*)	130,352
Net profit	19,448

* The £1,607 VAT due on the margin, calculated above, is borne as an additional expense to the tour operator as this VAT is not recoverable.

SUMMARY

1 **VAT is an indirect tax, introduced as part of EU policy to move towards a system of taxation which could eventually be harmonized to minimize trading distortions between member states, while providing a central budget for carrying out EU policy.**

2 **VAT is a tax on the value added at each stage in the manufacture or provision of a product or service. Although it is collected by businesses in this value chain, VAT is borne entirely by the consumer.**

3 **There can be more than one rate of VAT, reflecting the political, economic and fiscal priorities of a nation with regard to certain types of goods and services.**

4 **The scope (goods and services subject to VAT) also depends on political, economic, and fiscal priorities.**

5 **A VAT liability or claim depends on whether or not the VAT on outputs exceeds the VAT on inputs in any tax period, and this will depend on the types of goods and services supplied.**

6 **Customs and Excise requires the completion of form VAT 100.**

7 **VAT needs to be accounted for in the double-entry system and dealt with in the final accounts.**

8 **There are specific VAT requirements for tour operators, travel agents and related businesses.**

ASSESSMENT

MULTIPLE-CHOICE QUESTIONS

Assume the VAT rate is 17.5%

Question 1
What type of tax is VAT?

A A tax on consumer expenditure, collected in stages
B A direct tax on the value of a product
C A sales tax based on a percentage of selling price
D A tax on profit incurred by each supplier in a value chain

Question 2

Which one of the following statements is untrue?

A All businesses must register for VAT unless their annual turnover is less than a certain amount, or unless they supply exempted goods and services.

B VAT paid on the inputs of a business that exclusively supplies zero-rated outputs cannot be claimed back.

C VAT at the standard rate accounts for 7/47 of the VAT-inclusive price, when the standard rate is 17.5%.

D If a business sells exclusively exempted goods and services, the VAT on any inputs at the standard rate should be included as part of the cost of those inputs when disclosed in the trading and profit and loss account.

Question 3

If the following balances were brought down at the end of a VAT tax period relating to a small seaside hotel, what would be the total amount owed to Customs and Excise at the end of that period?

	£
Revenue from bedroom accommodation (inc VAT)	23,500
Revenue from room hire for conferences	14,000
Restaurant sales (inc VAT)	8,225
Bar sales (exc VAT)	4,000
Expenses:	
Fuel and power (exc VAT)	8,000
Wages and salaries	15,000
Food costs (exc VAT)	3,000
Alcoholic drinks for bar (exc VAT)	2,400

A £6,050
B £980
C £6,055
D £3,080

Question 4

An amusement arcade which purchases its equipment on a credit basis would be recommended to use which method of dealing with its VAT liabilities, in order to improve its cash flow?

A Cash basis
B Quarterly invoice basis
C Annual accounting scheme
D Monthly accounting basis

Question 5

A tour operator's quarterly turnover is £56,000. The cost of its margin scheme supplies was £35,000 excluding VAT. Of those supplies, 20% were for supplying cruises, and 40% were UK and EU air fares; the rest were taxable at the standard rate. How much VAT is the tour operator liable for at the end of the period?

A £1,486
B £1,478
C £1,214
D £1,499

EXERCISES

Exercise 1

Circuitous Coach Tours runs passenger tours wholly within the United Kingdom. Here are the VAT-inclusive totals for the quarter ended September 30, 19x3:

	£
Total ticket sales (including food)	20,025
Total sales value of food and drink	3,525
Cost of food	2,115
Cost of diesel	2,632
Wages	4,500
Insurance	750
Road tax	1,150

And here is a blank VAT return form (VAT 100):

Value Added Tax Return for the period   (VAT 100)
01 06 x3 to 30 09 x3

Circuitous Coach Tours	Registration No	Period
Buston Depot	284 7212 54	09 x3
HAMLEY		
Warwickshire	Due date: 31 10 x3	

Your VAT Office telephone number is 01235 325175   £ p

VAT due this period on **sales** and other outputs	1	
VAT reclaimed in this period on **purchases** and other inputs	2	
Net VAT to be paid to Customs or reclaimed by you (Difference between boxes 1 and 2)	3	
Total value of **sales** and all other outputs excluding VAT. Include your box 6 figure	4	
Total value of **purchases** and all other inputs excluding VAT. Include your box 7 figure	5	
Total value of all **sales** and related services to other EC Member States	6	
Total value of all **purchases** and related services from other EC Member States	7	

Retail schemes. If you have used any of the schemes in the period covered by this return please enter the appropriate letter(s) in this box.

If you are enclosing a payment tick this box: DECLARATION by the signatory to be completed by or on behalf of the person named above.

I . . . . declare that the information given above is true and complete.

Required

Calculate the VAT payable or reclaimable by Circuitous Coach Tours for the quarter ended 30.9.x3, and complete the VAT 100 tax form.

Exercise 2

Information for the quarter ended June 30, 19x3 is available for the Puntin holiday camp, which opened for business on April 1, 19x3.

Assets and liabilities as at 1.4.x3

	£
Capital	−262,000
Fixed assets	+238,000
Stock	+12,000
Bank account	+12,000
	0

Additional information: summary of transactions

	£
Cash takings (std rate) inc VAT	29,375
Receipts from bookings (std rate) inc VAT	105,750
Paid to creditors for standard-rated supplies	12,925
Paid to creditors for zero-rated supplies	6,000
Wages and salaries	35,000
Standard-rated expenses exc VAT	25,000
Purchase invoices from creditors inc VAT:	
Standard rate	17,625
Zero rate	7,500

Depreciation is charged at 15% on cost annually. The closing stock of food and drink is valued at £8,000.

Required

(a) Prepare the ledger accounts for the Puntin holiday camp, showing the summarized entries, including the VAT account on an invoice basis.
(b) Draw up the trading and profit and loss account for the quarter ended 30.6.x3, and a balance sheet as at 30.6.x3.

Exercise 3
Here are the assets and liabilities of the Oakwell restaurant, as at the end of August 19x3:

	(£)
Capital 31.8.x3	−106,460
Land and buildings at cost	+80,000
Business car inc VAT	+14,100
Provn for depreciation (car) as at 31.8.x3	−2,820
Furniture, fittings and equipment (FFE)	+10,000
Provision for depn (FFE)	−2,500
Bank account	+2,400
Cash on hand	+300
Stocks of food and drink (as at 30.6.x3)	+12,400
VAT	−3,200
PAYE	−850
NI	−320
Debtors (credit card company)	+1,200
Creditors	−4,250
	0

The following errors were discovered after the trial balance had been prepared.

1 Food purchases from a cash and carry were omitted from the accounts completely. The tax-exclusive amount was £200.
2 Cash takings of £1,200 for restaurant meals had been entered in the sales account and cash book as £2,100; the VAT entries were also based on this incorrect entry.
3 The business car was purchased from a dealer in the last few months, with the restaurant's old vehicle offered in part-exchange. The bookkeeper had dealt correctly with all the entries connected with the disposal, except for the double entry involving the trade-in allowance. The trade-in allowance given for the old vehicle was £3,000 excluding VAT. The depreciation policy was to charge 20% on the straight-line basis, assuming a whole year's depreciation in the year of acquisition and none in the year of disposal.

Required
Amend the accounts on the basis of the above information, and prepare a corrected balance sheet as at 31.8.x3.

Exercise 4
The Caribou is an all-inclusive holiday centre providing a range of exclusive outdoor activities in Scotland. The business deals exclusively with Gaelic Holidays, a company that only supplies this holiday, and which charges an inclusive price to its clients. Gaelic Holidays sells the holiday, air fare (London to Aberdeen), the transfer service, and insurance cover as one package, via UK travel agents. The details of the arrangements are as follows:

Caribou Holidays for the year to 30.4.x3. (all exclusive of VAT)

Person-weeks sold	500
Caribou's price per week (food, accom, equipment)	£250*
Air fare per person (return)	£100
Transport costs (chauffeur transfer)	£32,000
Airport representative salaries (overheads)	£60,000
All-in package price per week	£1,000
Insurance premiums (included in all-inclusive price)	£25,000

* All standard-rated margin scheme supplies.

Required
Using the tour operators' margin scheme, calculate the VAT due from Gaelic Holidays on its supplies.

CHAPTER 11

Accounting for recreation and leisure clubs

OBJECTIVES

- Identify different types of recreation and leisure clubs.
- Distinguish between recreation and leisure clubs and commercial organizations.
- Describe the sources of income from which such clubs sustain themselves.
- Record the income generated and expenditure incurred by recreation and leisure clubs.
- Prepare the final accounts and notes for recreation and leisure clubs.

11.1 TYPES OF RECREATION AND LEISURE CLUBS

Millions of people belong to organizations that provide for their various interests, activities and general leisure needs. These organizations exist to provide the location and facilities for people who have common interests, and who want to share and exchange information and views. These organizations include sporting, social and political clubs. There are also clubs that provide a focal point for like-minded people to pursue activities such as walking, painting, photography and model building. A club offers its members an outlet to indulge their specific leisure and recreational interests in an atmosphere of mutual appreciation and affinity.

Apart from their obvious advantages, in terms of social and informational exchange, leisure clubs also give people a chance to use the specialist equipment and infrastructure on which their activities depend, items to which they might otherwise have no access. Clubs that have expensive equipment are snooker clubs, trampolining clubs, photographic clubs and DIY clubs. Clubs that provide vital infrastructure are athletics clubs, gymnastics clubs and clubs with function rooms.

This specialization of interests or activities affords the economic benefits to individuals of 'clubbing together' to provide the necessary funds with which to finance and organize their particular requirements. Some clubs depend less on the equipment or the hardware that is offered, and more on the club as a focus for social interaction. Political or social clubs offer a meeting-place for people who share common views, aspirations or circumstances, to discuss them in a supportive atmosphere. Such clubs depend for their popularity on the appeal of the surroundings and the general ambience rather than on any specific equipment. These clubs may offer a service to their members in the form of providing information through talks and lectures given by guest speakers or by members themselves. Clubs in this category include the Women's Institute, the Scout and Guide Associations, Darby and Joan clubs, clubs for ex-service personnel, self-help groups of all kinds, and working men's clubs.

11.2 THE DISTINCTION BETWEEN CLUBS AND COMMERCIAL ORGANIZATIONS

Recreation and leisure clubs are formed and managed through the cooperation of their members; they exist entirely for the benefit of their members and they belong to their members. Commercial organizations are formed in order to satisfy the needs of their customers, while offering financial rewards to their owners. The larger commercial organizations are often owned and managed by entirely different groups of individuals.

The priorities of recreation and leisure clubs are different to the priorities of commercial organizations. Although profit maximization or other commercial objectives are high on the priorities of the owners and managers of commercial organizations, providing satisfaction and meeting the needs of their members are usually the top priority of recreation and leisure clubs.

A commercial organization is usually managed by functional experts with the appropriate qualifications and experience. As the economic stakes are high in commerce, the efficient management of such organizations demands the employment of well-paid and highly skilled individuals, who have vested in them the authority to take decisions quickly and incisively. The management of clubs is more democratic and is normally undertaken on a voluntary basis by a committee, comprising members voted to their positions by the membership as a whole. Committee members may hold a position, or office, as a consequence of their occupational background, or simply because they are respected and valued as members of the club. Consequently, decisions take longer to make, and compromises often arise from the need to accommodate the views of different factions.

Although there are major distinctions between recreation and leisure clubs and their commercial counterparts, both types of organization engage in financial transactions that need to be recorded, processed and reported. The ways in which this is done will reflect the differences between the transactions and the information that is required.

11.3 SOURCES OF INCOME FOR RECREATION AND LEISURE CLUBS

All organizations engage in financial transactions and require some form of financial record keeping and control. Recreation and leisure clubs, like any other organization, require a source or sources of income from which to finance their various activities. In the long term, if sources of funds exceed the uses of funds, the survival of the organization may be threatened. From which sources may such clubs generate income?

1 Annual membership subscriptions or dues
2 Life membership subscriptions
3 Donations
4 Profits from the sale of alcoholic and other drinks
5 Profits from the sale of food
6 Profits from the sale of equipment
7 Profits from raffles, bingo and gaming machines
8 Profits from the organization of social events or entertainments
9 Income from investments

This list is by no means exhaustive, and the sources of income for clubs are limited only by the activities the clubs are willing to pursue. As most recreation and leisure clubs will acquire income from many sources, the way the financial results of such organizations are recorded and reported will need to reflect this. A commercial organization will normally have a trading and profit and loss account to indicate the gross profit made from its primary operations, and the expenditure incurred in generating this gross profit, leaving the net profit earned in the period. The financial report of the recreation and leisure club will need to indicate the income generated from different activities; this will require several trading accounts, the profits from which are reported in an overall statement. This statement is known as the income and expenditure account.

11.4 MEASURING AND REPORTING INCOME AND EXPENDITURE

Although many accounts of recreation and leisure clubs may be no more that a record of the receipts and payments made to and from the bank account, there is still a requirement to prepare formal accounts in accordance with the accounting concepts and conventions used in any other type of organization.

Many club treasurers do no more than carry out a bank reconciliation between the club's cash book and the monthly bank statement. Recording, processing and reporting the accounts of organizations involves much more than this. From the list in the previous section, the most significant is the income generated from membership subscriptions, either annual or life.

The Red Kite Hang-Gliding Club has 48 members. The annual subscription is currently £15 (£13.50 last year). The committee have decided to increase the subscription to £16 next year. The last accounting period of the club was from May 1, 19x6 to April 30, 19x7. At the beginning of the year, 12 members had paid in advance their annual subscriptions for the current year and 8 owed subscriptions for the previous year. All but one of them were eventually received by the end of the current year. By the end of the year, 10 members had failed to pay the current year's subscription and 4 members had paid in advance for next year's subscriptions. How much subscription income should the club recognize in the current financial period, and how much money was received from members during the financial period?

Annual subscriptions a/c

Ref	£	
Balances 1.5.x6:		
Subs prepaid b/d	−180.00	(12 × £15.00)
Subs in arrears b/d	+108.00	(8 × £13.50)
Bank: last year's subs	−94.50	(7 × £13.50)
Bank: this year's subs	−390.00	(26 × £15.00)
Bank: next year's subs	−64.00	(4 × £16.00)
Annual subs income and expenditure (I+E)	+720.00*	(48 × 15)
Bal c/d 30.4.x7:	+99.50	
Being balances 30 April:		
Subs prepaid b/d	−64.00	(4 × £16.00)
Subs in arrears b/d	+163.50	(10 × £15.00) + (1 × £13.50)
	+99.50	

* Regardless of how much money was actually received, the subscription income due for the year was (48 × £15).

The total cash received from members is £94.50 (for last year's subscriptions) + £390.00 (for this year's subscriptions) + £64.00 (for next year's subscriptions) = £548.50. Only £548.50 has actually been received, but under the accruals concept, the club has recognized 48 × £15 = £720 as the total subscription income for the year.

The balances on the subscription account at the end of each period will represent subscriptions owing or prepaid by members. Where subscriptions are prepaid, this is a liability from the viewpoint of the club, as at that time the club theoretically owes the money to the member. Subscriptions owing from members are effectively an asset, as they are debts that the club owns at that time.

The subscription account should be supported by full records of the number of members currently belonging to the club. In a sense this can be thought of in the same way as the debtor ledger. As an individual pays his or her subscription, this should be recorded in the individual's account. As explained in Chapter 7, there is a need to reconcile the total of the individual balances on the members' accounts with the total balances on the subscriptions account to check the accuracy of record keeping and possibly to identify errors or even fraud. In some clubs, however, this side of the record keeping is fairly primitive, and an element of trust is involved. Particularly with sports and social clubs, it is the case that members themselves are responsible for keeping their subscriptions up to date.

Life memberships

Another way of attracting subscription income is to offer life memberships. This is a method of improving the cash flow of the club and attracting loyal members to the club over the long term, while offering an attractive discount for this loyalty in comparison with the annual subscription.

The Snapshot Photographic Club offers subscriptions in two alternative ways. The annual subscription is £10, whereas a life membership is £100. In the current year there are 50 members and an additional 20 life members. Life memberships were introduced two years ago; 10 joined in the first year and another 10 last year.

During the current year 3 life members die, and 12 life members join the club. There are no outstanding subscriptions at the beginning or end of the accounting period. What alternative methods are there for accounting for these subscriptions, and what impact would they have on the recognition of subscription income for the year? Here are three options:

1 Treat all new life membership subscriptions as income for the current year.
2 Only recognize the life membership income when the member dies.
3 Allocate the income appropriately over the life of the member.

The first two methods violate the accruals concept. The income from life memberships should be recognized in the income and expenditure account as income throughout a period of a life membership, not only in the years in which that membership was received or when the member dies. An additional problem in recognizing income when the member dies is the need to be aware of the timing of these events, and the morbidity of such record keeping. Allocating the life membership income over the life of the member suffers from the disadvantage of subjectivity in estimating how long the member will survive.

The answer to this problem is to set up a standard write-down for life membership allowing income to be gradually recognized. In the Snapshot example it will be assumed the standard life membership write-down is 10% per annum applied to the opening balance plus the income received in the current year. How would the accounts be recorded in year 3?

Subscription income a/c		*Life membership fund a/c*	
Ref	£	Ref	£
Bank (annual subs)	−500	Bal b/d	−1,710*
I+E account	+500	Bank (life members)	−1,200
		I+E account	+291[†]
Balance c/d	nil	Balance c/d	−2,619

* The opening balance on the life membership account is calculated as follows. Year 1: £1,000 received from life members less 10% income recognized for that year, so

$$\text{Balance at end of year 1} = £1,000 - (£1,000 \times 10\%)$$
$$= £900$$

Year 2: the balance brought down is £900; add £1,000 received from life members less 10% income recognized during the year, so

$$\text{Balance at end of year 2} = £1,900 - (£1,900 \times 10\%)$$
$$= £1,710$$

† The life membership income recognized in the current year is

$$(\text{year 3 opening balance} + \text{new life memberships}) \times 10\% = (£1710 + £1200) \times 10\%$$
$$= £291$$

The closing balance on the life membership account represents the as yet unrecognized income from life memberships to be credited to the income and expenditure account in future periods. This mechanism of gradually writing off the account is based on the reducing-balance method when depreciating a fixed asset over its useful life (Chapter 5), except here we are attributing income instead of allocating expenditure. It is irrelevant that the three members die during the period; their original subscription will still be written off in the normal way, even after their deaths have occurred. Where there are substantial receipts of money from life memberships, it would be advisable to invest this money in an interest-bearing deposit account, the annual interest from which would then be recognized as additional income for the club in the income and expenditure account.

Other income

Apart from subscriptions, income is generated from a range of other sources. Of these, the club bar is usually the biggest contributor when such clubs are licensed. A club will usually engage in a number of activities and it will be necessary to calculate the surpluses or deficits on each of them before the final income and expenditure can be prepared.

11.5 PREPARATION OF FINAL ACCOUNTS AND NOTES

In order to prepare the final accounts and notes of recreation and leisure clubs, a comprehensive example will be used. The assets and liabilities for the Lonsdale Wining and Dining Society as at December 31, 19x6 were as follows:

	£
Land and buildings at cost less depreciation	+100,000
Fixtures and fittings at cost less depreciation	+25,000
Bank and cash	+5,000
Deposit account	+23,000
Bar stocks	+9,500
Bar creditors	−1,200
Rates prepaid	+350
Annual memberships owing from members	+1,000
Annual memberships prepaid	−400
Balance on life membership fund	−35,000
Accrued expenses:	
Stewards' wages	−250
Balance as at December 31, 19x6	−127,000*

* As you should have understood in Chapters 2 and 3, assets − liabilities = capital. In the case of a non-commercial organization, capital is known as the accumulated fund. In this case it amounts to £127,000.

The cash book of the club contains the following information:

Cash book	Payments	Receipts
Ref	£	£
Balance b/d		5,000
Bar sales		22,500
Annual subscriptions		15,000
Life memebership subs		6,500
Ticket sales:		
Wine-tasting		250
Trip to Boulogne		1,100
		50,350
Bar creditors	4,800	
Tel, elec, water	880	
Wine taster's fee	50	
Wine for tasting	220	
Rates	600	
Coach to Boulogne	120	
Ferry tickets, Boulogne	800	
Bar stewards' wages	12,000	
Bar sundry expenses	2,000	
Deposit account	6,500	
Cleaners' wages	3,500	
Cleaning materials	105	
Rebuilding cellars	20,000	
Total receipts		51,575
Balance c/d		−1,225

The following information was also available at the end of December 19x6:

	£
Bar stock	+1,850
Bar creditors	−900
Deposit account	+31,270
Rates owing	−230
Tel, elec, water prepaid	+75
Prepaid annual subscriptions	−900
Annual subscriptions owing	+400

The land and buildings are depreciated at the annual rate of 5%, and fixtures and fittings at the rate of 20% on the reducing-balance method. Nothing was withdrawn from the deposit account during the year.

The first step in assessing the financial performance of the club over the period is to calculate the income generated from its activities. The club has earned annual subscriptions over the year, and in addition has attracted new life members. The method for apportioning life membership income to the income and expenditure account is by the reducing-balance method at a rate of 10% per annum, applied to the brought-down balance and including the current year's receipts from life memberships.

Subscription income a/c		*Life membership fund a/c*	
Ref	£	Ref	£
Balances b/d:		Balance b/d	−35,000
Prepaid subs	−400	Bank (LMS)	−6,500
Accrued subs	+1,000	I+E account	+4,150**
Bank (annual subs)	−15,000		
I+E account	+13,900*	Bal c/d	−37,350
	−500		
		LMS = life membership subs	
Being balances b/d:		* Balancing figure	
Prepaid subs	−900	** Life membership income	
Accrued subs	+400	= (35,000 + 6,500) × 10%	
Total	−500		

The accounts connected with bar income will now be recorded:

Bar creditors a/c	
Ref	£
Bal b/d	−1,200
Bank – payments to creditors	+4,800
Purchases	−4,500*
Bal c/d	−900

Bar trading and profit and loss account

	£	£
Sales		22,500
Opening stock	9,500	
Purchases	4,500	
	14,000	
Closing stock	1,850	
	12,150	
Cost of sales		12,150
Gross profit c/d		10,350
Bar sundries	2,000	
Bar stewards' wages:		
12,000 – wages owing from start of year	11,750	
		13,750
Net deficit from bar sales		(3,400)

* Balancing figure

Additional costs of running the bar include the cost of bar sundries and the stewards' wages. The other activities the club were involved in during the year were the wine-tasting and the trip to Boulogne. The income from these activities is calculated by subtracting the expenditure they incurred from the revenue they generated:

Wine-tasting	£	£		*Trip to Boulogne*	£	£
Revenue		250		Revenue		1,100
Less:				Less:		
Cost of wine	220			Cost of coach	120	
Taster's fee	50			Ferry tickets	800	
		270				920
Deficit on tasting		(20)		Surplus on trip		180

The other source of income was the interest earned on the deposit account. As no withdrawals were recorded, the amount of interest can be derived in the following way:

Deposit a/c	
Ref	£
Bal b/d	+23,000
Bank a/c	+6,500
Interest a/c	+1,770*
Bal c/d	+31,270

* Balancing figure

It is now possible to prepare the income and expenditure account for the Lonsdale Wining and Dining Society (LWDS).

Income and expenditure account (LWDS) for the year ended December 31, 19x6

	£	£
Income from annual subscriptions		13,900
Income from life memberships		4,150
Total subscription income:		18,050
Surplus from the trip to Boulogne		180
Interest on deposit account		1,770
Total income:		20,000
Deficit on bar sales	3,400	
Deficit on wine-tasting	20	
Rates:		
(+ 350 prepaid at start of year + 600 paid +		
230 owing at end year)	1,180	
Tel, elec, water (880 − 75 prepaid)	805	
Cleaners' wages	3,500	
Cleaning materials	105	
Depreciation:		
Land and buildings (100,000 × 5%)	5,000	
Cellar (20,000 × 5%)	1,000	
Fixtures and fittings (25,000 × 20%)	5,000	
Total expenditure		20,010
Excess of expenditure over income		(10)

The balance sheet of the LWDS is therefore as follows:

Balance sheet (LWDS) as at December 31, 19x6

	Cost £	Depn £	NBV £
Fixed assets			
Land and buildings at cost	100,000	5,000	95,000
Cellars*	20,000	1,000	19,000
Fixtures and fittings	25,000	5,000	20,000
	145,000	11,000	134,000
Investments			
Deposit account			31,270
Current assets			
Bar stocks		1,850	
Subscriptions accrued		400	
Tel, elec, water prepaid		75	
		2,325	
Less current liabilities			
Bar creditors	900		
Prepaid subscriptions	900		
Rates owing	230		
Bank overdraft	1,225		
		3,255	

Balance sheet (LWDS) as at December 31, 19x6 (cont'd)

	Cost £	Depn £	NBV £
Net current liabilities			(930)
Net assets			164,340

Financed by

Opening accumulated fund			127,000
Add excess of expenditure over income			(10)
Life membership fund			37,350
			164,340

* As the cellars have been rebuilt, this expenditure would be classified as capital expenditure, which is recorded as a fixed asset and depreciated accordingly.

Here is an alternative way of looking at the above balance sheet, from the perspective of a recreation and leisure club:

Balance sheet (LWDS) as at December 31, 1996

	£	£	£	£
We have accumulated				
Opening accumulated fund				127,000
Less excess of expenditure over income				(10)
Life membership fund				37,350
				164,340

Of which we have sunk in fixed assets

	Cost	Depn	NBV	
Land and buildings at cost	100,000	5,000	95,000	
Cellars	20,000	1,000	19,000	
Fixtures and fittings	25,000	5,000	20,000	
	145,000	11,000	134,000	

Leaving us with working capital comprising Investments

Deposit account		31,270		
And current assets				
Bar stocks		1,850		
Subscriptions accrued		400		
Tel, elec, water prepaid		75		
		33,595		

Less current liabilities

Bar creditors	900			
Prepaid subscriptions	900			
Rates owing	230			
Bank overdraft	1,225			
		3,255		
Working capital			30,340	
Net assets				164,340

This format for the balance sheet differs from the conventional format by putting the 'financed by' section at the top, and the net assets below. It is a useful format as it reflects the nature of this type of organization and its relationship with the members it serves and to which it belongs.

SUMMARY

1 Recreation and leisure clubs play an important part in the social life of millions of individuals.

2 Recreation and leisure clubs cover all types of activities, from sports clubs to self-help groups.

3 Recreation and leisure clubs sustain themselves with income generated from a variety of sources.

4 Accounting for recreation and leisure clubs is based on traditional accounting concepts and conventions.

5 Subscription income is calculated and recorded on an annual basis and for life memberships.

6 The financial activities of recreation and leisure clubs produce deficits and surpluses that should be calculated and recorded.

7 Summarized accounting reports are prepared for recreation and leisure clubs in a way that is easy to understand and reflects the nature of the organization.

ASSESSMENT

MULTIPLE-CHOICE QUESTIONS

Question 1
Which of the following statements could be made about a recreation and leisure club?

A An organization where most transactions are non-financial
B An organization with aims that are non-commercial
C An organization where financial control is relatively unimportant
D An organization which is managed by all its members

Question 2
From which of the following would a recreation and leisure club not normally generate income for itself?

A Life membership subscriptions
B A sporting club providing the use of land to members
C Fees from non-members
D Providing food and drink

Question 3
The following balances exist on the annual subscriptions account at the beginning and end of the year:

Start of year	£	End of year	£
Owing by members	500	Owing by members	200
Prepaid by members	300	Prepaid by members	600

If there are currently 80 members on the books and the annual subscription is £15.00 per year, how much cash was received by the club during the year?

A £600
B £1,800
C £1,400
D £1,000

Question 4

Which of the following methods of accounting for life membership subscriptions accords with both the accruals concept and the prudence concept of accounting, and requires the least record keeping?

A To recognize the subscriptions received from life members as income in the income and expenditure account in the year in which it was originally received.
B To recognize the income received from life membership subs over a period of time representing an average life membership period in years.
C To recognize the subscriptions received from a life member as income only in the year in which the member's death is notified to the club.
D To calculate the annual subscription as a percentage of the life membership subscription and then use this rate with the reducing-balance method to allocate life membership income to profit on an annual basis.

Question 5

Which of the following terms used in the accounts of commercial organizations is also used in the accounts of recreation and leisure clubs?

A Profit
B Balance sheet
C Trading account
D Capital

EXERCISES

Exercise 1

The Drawfade Golf Club in Portugal ended its third year of existence as at October 31, 19x3. The club had 285 members on its books as at October 31, 19x3. Of these, 45 were life members that joined at the following times:

10 in year 19x0–19x1
15 in year 19x1–19x2
20 in year 19x2–19x3

The golf club's policy is to allocate life membership income to the income and expenditure account, adopting the reducing-balance method and using the annual subscription as a proportion of the life membership fee as the appropriate percentage write-off.

At the end of October 19x2, 12 members owed annual subscriptions from the previous year, and 8 had paid for the year to November 31, 19x3 in advance. Other details are as follows:

Subscription fees

	19x0–19x1	19x1–19x2	19x2–19x3	19x3–19x4
	Es	Es	Es	Es
Annual fee	60,000	66,000	72,000	76,000
Life membership	600,000	680,000	720,000	760,000

On October 31, 19x3, 9 ordinary members had paid in advance for the next year's annual subscription and 5 owed subscriptions from the previous year. One of these 5 still owed for the year to October 31, 19x2.

Required
Prepare the ledger accounts for both the life membership fund and the annual subscriptions.

Exercise 2
The Ovoid Rugby Club had the following balance sheet as at June 30, 19x3:

Balance sheet (Ovoid Rugby Club) as at June 30, 19x3

	Cost £	Depn £	NBV £
Fixed assets			
Clubhouse and stands	120,000	24,000	96,000
Fixtures and fittings	32,000	16,600	15,400
	152,000	40,600	111,400
Current assets			
Bar stocks		1,850	
Subscriptions in arrears		2,040	
Bank account		6,760	
		10,650	
Current liabilities			
Creditors for bar supplies	700		
Subscriptions in advance	1,235		
		1,935	
			8,715
Net assets			120,115
Financed by			
Opening accumulated fund (July 1, 19x1)			100,000
Surplus for the year to June 30, 19x2			20,115
			120,115

The receipts and payments record for the year to June 30, 19x3 was as follows:

Cash book: Ovoid Rugby Club

	£
Balance b/d	+6,760
Subs received	+17,500
Bar takings	+12,300
Bar purchases	−7,200
Bar steward's salary	−4,900
General expenses	−2,600
Maintenance	−3,750
Deposit account	−10,000
Heating and lighting	−850
Balance b/d	+7,260

Further information

The following balances were available at June 30, 19x3:

	£
Bar stocks	1,600
Subs in arrears	1,800
Subs in advance	1,450
Creditors for bar supplies	620

The club's policy is to provide for depreciation annually on fixed assets at the following rates:

Clubhouse and stands	2.5% of cost
Fixtures and fittings	10.0% of cost

The cash transferred to the deposit account was transferred three months before the year-end. The interest rate earned was 6% annually, and no withdrawals were made from the account by June 30, 19x3.

Required

Clearly showing the surplus or deficit made on the bar, prepare the annual income and expend-iture account for the Ovoid Rugby Club for the year ended June 30, 19x3, and a balance sheet as at that date.

Exercise 3

The Cantorion Choral Society has prepared the following receipts and payments statement for the year ended March 31, 19x3:

	£	£
Balance b/d		420
Receipts		
Members' subs		1,800
Donations		200
Sales of tickets		2,200
Arts Council grant		3,000
		7,620
Payments		
Secretarial exps	550	
Rent of practice hall	800	
Accompanist's salary	500	
General expenses	1,300	
Travel costs	2,200	
Sheet music	1,100	
		6,450
Balance c/d		1,170

The following valuations are also available:

	April 1, 19x2	March 31, 19x3
Subscriptions in arrears	200	120
Subscriptions in advance	50	35
Owing to suppliers of sheet music	315	195
Stocks of sheet music at cost	500	550
Arts Council grant accrued	900	750

Required

(a) Calculate the accumulated fund balance as at 1.4.x2.
(b) Prepare the income and expenditure account for Cantoris for the year ended 31.3.x3; show all workings.
(c) Compile the balance sheet for Cantoris as at 31.3.x3.

Exercise 4

Here is a list of assets and liabilities for the Gourmet Culinary Pursuits Club as at February 28, 19x3:

	£
Land and buildings at valuation	+95,000
Equipment and fittings at valuation	+15,500
Stocks of food and consumables	+800
Subscriptions owing from members	+350
Subscriptions in advance from members	−220
Life membership fund	−8,200
Insurance claim not yet settled	+730
Creditors for food and consumables	−410
Bank overdraft	−120
9% capital bond (two-year bank deposit)	+3,000
One year's interest on capital bond accrued	+270

Required

Draw up a balance sheet for the Gourmet Culinary Pursuits Club, as at December 28, 19x3, in accordance with the specific format suitable for recreational and leisure organizations.

CHAPTER 12

Accounting for multiple ownership

OBJECTIVES

- Understand the nature of a partnership agreement.
- Appropriate the profits earned by a partnership.
- Make the necessary adjustments for partnership changes.
- Dissolve a partnership and convert to a limited company.
- Recognize the distinctive features of a limited company.
- Prepare the final accounts of a limited company.
- Account for changes in corporate financial structure.

12.1 THE PARTNERSHIP AGREEMENT

Before the middle 1800s, the main way in which large amounts of finance could be raised in order to undertake major business ventures was through the collaboration of a small number of wealthy individuals. They would pool their resources in order to carry out significant commercial ventures and to share the risk associated with these undertakings. Good examples are road, bridge and canal building programmes, and overseas trading activities such as the tea and silk trade with India and China.

Since the introduction of limited companies (sections 12.5 to 12.7), partnerships as large organizations have become increasingly uncommon, but are still prevalent among small businesses, and are the predominant organizational type in certain business sectors such as the legal, medical and financial professions.

A partnership may include from two up to twenty people, and unless there is an express or implied agreement between partners, the way in which that partnership operates is governed by the 1890 Partnership Act. Partnerships are normally set up because a mutual advantage is to be gained. An example is an owner of a property with catering facilities in partnership with a trained chef. Between them they have the means to earn profits but neither could do so without the other. Another example is a top Formula One racing driver with the ability to bring the best out of a car in partnership with a team of constructors that can provide a fast car and the necessary technical and financial backup. The two parties derive mutual benefit.

Once a partnership has been agreed in principle, it is necessary to agree formally how the net profit earned from the partnership is to be shared between the partners. With a sole trader, as we have seen earlier, there is no problem. All the net profit is added to the capital of that owner on the balance sheet and that is an end to the matter. With partners, the manner in which this profit is shared should be based on the contribution that each makes to the earnings of the partnership as a whole. There are several determining factors:

1 The financial capital originally invested in the business.
2 The financial capital that is maintained by each partner in the business from period to period. This will be affected by the level of drawings made by each partner.
3 The sacrifice that each partner has made in order to become a partner, e.g. their potential earnings in an alternative position or their foregone investment opportunities. This is known as the imputed cost or the opportunity cost.
4 The specific skills or talents that are brought into the business, skills which determine the profitability of the business.
5 The physical and/or mental contribution that each partner might make to the day-to-day operations of the business.

All these factors would need to be taken into account when drawing up the partnership agreement. A partnership agreement will usually have the following components:

- Interest receivable on capital invested
- A share of the interest charged on the drawings of partners
- Salaries paid for physical or mental effort invested
- A share of the residual profit (SORP)

12.2 THE APPROPRIATION OF PROFIT

How such an agreement might work is illustrated in the following example. A skiing instructor, a farmer and a financier agree to become partners in the setting up of a dry-ski complex in a beautiful part of the British Isles. The following agreement is drawn up.

- Interest on drawings is to be charged at 12%.
- Interest of 10% is receivable on the original capital invested.
- The salary paid to the ski instructor is £15,000.
- Residual profits are to be shared in the ratio 2:2:1 (instructor: farmer: financier).

Here is the trial balance of the partnership for the first year:

Trial balance of Ski-West partnership as at December 31, 19x2

	£
Land (NBV)	+50,000
Buildings (NBV)	+90,000
Equipment (NBV)	+51,500
Bank and cash	+12,000
Creditors	−5,500
Net profit	−82,000
Capital accounts (1.1.x3):	
Instructor	−10,000
Farmer	−50,000
Financier	−100,000
Drawings:	
Instructor	+32,000
Farmer	+12,000
Total	0

As the net profit has already been derived, and as the profit and loss account of this business would be similar to that of any other business, we will start by **appropriating** (sharing) the net profit among the partners in accordance with the partnership agreement. The appropriation account is a logical development of the profit and loss account, dividing up the profits in various ways.

Appropriation account for the Ski-West partnership for the year ended December 31, 19x2

		£	£
Net profit b/d			82,000
Add interest on drawings:			
Instructor	(32,000 × 12%)	3,840	
Farmer	(12,000 × 12%)	1,440	
			5,280
			87,280
Less interest on capital:			
Instructor		1,000	
Farmer		5,000	
Financier		10,000	
			16,000
			71,280
Salaries			
Instructor			15,000
			56,280
Share of residual profits:			
Instructor		22,512	
Farmer		22,512	
Financier		11,256	
			56,280

The net profit and the interest charged on the partners' drawings has been shared between the partners in accordance with the formal partnership agreement. How are these appropriations of profit added to the capital invested by the partners?

In partnership accounting, each partner has a capital account that records their original investment in the business. This account is not adjusted for profits earned, and is only altered if the partners introduce new capital or there is a change in the partnership, such as the resignation, retirement, death or admission of a new partner. All profits earned from the partnership are credited to entirely separate accounts, known as **current accounts**. Although they are called current accounts, they actually represent capital in another form. The reason for having them is to keep a separate record of how much additional capital each partner has accumulated within the business since the business commenced.

Here are the entries that would have been made in the current accounts of the three partners for their first year of operation. Note how the entries have been obtained from the appropriation account.

Current a/c (instructor)			Current a/c (farmer)			Current a/c (financier)		
Ref		£	Ref		£	Ref		£
Bal b/d		nil	Bal b/d		nil	Bal b/d		nil
Interest		−1,000	Interest		−5,000	Interest		−10,000
Salary		−15,000	Salary		nil	Salary		nil
SORP		−22,512	SORP		−22,512	SORP		−11,256
Int on drawings		+3,840	Int on drawings		+1,440	Int on drawings		nil
Drawings		+32,000	Drawings		+12,000	Drawings		nil
Bal c/d		−2,672	Bal c/d		−14,072	Bal c/d		−21,256

As this is their first year, there are no opening balances on the current accounts. Note that the interest, salary and SORP are credited (−) to these accounts to reflect that this represents income for the partners, and is in effect owed by the business to the partners in accordance with the separate entity concept introduced in Chapter 1. The income is reduced by the drawings and the interest on the drawings. After recording these transactions, the balance sheet for the Ski-West partnership looks like this:

Balance sheet of the Ski-West partnership as at December 31, 19x2

	£	£
Fixed assets		
Land		50,000
Buildings		90,000
Equipment		51,500
		191,500
Current assets		
Bank and cash	12,000	
Current liabilities		
Creditors	5,500	
Net current assets		6,500
Net assets		198,000
Financed by		
Partners' capital accounts:		
Instructor	10,000	
Farmer	50,000	
Financier	100,000	
		160,000
Partners' current accounts:		
Instructor	2,672	
Farmer	14,072	
Financier	21,256	
		38,000
		198,000

It is apparent that the net addition to the capital of the partners is £38,000 for the year, which represents the original profit of £82,000 less the total drawings of £44,000. Note that the interest on drawings is not additional profit, but a redistribution of the profit favouring the partners who withdrew the least amount of capital from the business. In this case, as the financier made no drawings at all during the period, a net gain was made by a redistribution from the other two partners, mainly the skiing instructor.

12.3 CHANGES TO THE PARTNERSHIP

From time to time a partnership will need to change. Perhaps a partner will resign, retire or die, and they will need to be replaced; or an extra partner may be introduced. During any changes. It is very important to ensure that all partners, outgoing and incoming, are treated equitably. Two main areas cause problems:

– Fair valuation of the tangible assets of the partnership
– Fair valuation of the intangible assets of the partnership

At the end of the year, the skiing instructor wishes to leave the partnership in order to take up a business opportunity at an Alpine resort in Switzerland. The main considera-tion of the partners is to decide on the entitlement of the instructor. The way this is done is to have the assets of the partnership revalued. After the revaluation, the assets are valued as follows:

	New value £	Original book value £
Land	65,000	50,000
Buildings	95,000	90,000
Equipment	40,000	51,500
Total	200,000	191,500

The asset accounts are adjusted for these new amounts by adding or subtracting the difference between the new value and the existing book value. Their overall value has increased by £200,000 − £191,500 = £8,500.

In effect, what has happened is that the claim of all the partners has increased by this amount, therefore their capital accounts should be adjusted in order for the balance sheet to balance. But how much of the increase should be credited to the capital account of each partner? The answer is to use the existing profit-sharing ratio. The skiing instructor's capital would be increased by

$$£8,500 \times 0.4 = £3,400$$

The farmer's capital would be increased by

$$£8,500 \times 0.4 = £3,400$$

And the financier's capital would be increased by

$$£8,500 \times 0.2 = £1,700$$

Having ensured the increase in the fair value of the tangible assets has been credited to the partners, would the instructor now be happy with his or her entitlement from the business? The answer would be no, because the balance sheet fails to put a value on a whole range of intangible assets which contribute to the earning potential of the business (Chapter 5). It is worth restating which factors these might include:

1 A loyal, regular, and expanding customer base
2 The skills and attributes of the employees
3 The location of the business
4 The reputation and image of the organization

All of these factors, and many more, may mean that the business, as a going concern, is worth more than indicated by the total of the tangible net assets. During the year, the total value of the business would have increased simply because of these factors, and because the business can be expected to make profits for the owners in the foreseeable future and beyond. To take the specific circumstances of Ski-West, a regular customer base may have been built up because the employees will have impressed them with their training and interpersonal skills. They will have enjoyed negotiating the contours of the slope and the panoramic views. Finally, after they return home, these satisfied customers will relate their positive experiences to many friends and relations, continuing the cycle.

The value of such a virtuous cycle should not be underestimated. Providing excellent service, creating a positive experience for customers, will mean repeat business and will lead to higher profitability for the organization. A business that continues to pursue excellence is valuable to its owners because it is valued by its customers. But if the management of the business is not careful, the virtuous cycle may easily turn into a vicious cycle of poor service, leading to negative experiences, and ultimately to a fall-off in custom and profitability.

Given that Ski-West steadily increased its trade during the year and was on course for higher profits next year, wouldn't the skiing instructor be entitled to a share of this additional value, not represented by tangible assets? Yes, of course; the skiing instructor would want a fair share of this value, known as **goodwill**, to be determined before accepting an entitlement. How, therefore, may goodwill be ascertained? This is a major problem. Ultimately the total value of a business can only be objectively determined through sale. The value of a business can be deemed equivalent to what a potential buyer would be willing to pay for it. The skiing instructor would want to know this, without relying on subjective valuations made by professionals. Unfortunately, the valuation of goodwill within a going concern is a matter for negotiation between partners, and these negotiations may be fraught with problems.

The skiing instructor appears to have a valid claim on a share of the goodwill to which he or she has contributed. But the other partners could argue that a proportion of this goodwill was due to the instructor's involvement, and it would disappear on his or her departure. These kinds of negotiation may be very complicated and sometimes quite tricky.

Assuming that all partners agree on a figure of £35,000 for the goodwill, what would be the full entitlement of the departing partner following the valuations and negotiations?

Capital account (skiing instructor)

Ref	£
Bal b/d 31.12.93	−10,000
Transfer from current a/c	−2,672
Revaluation of assets	−3,400
Share of goodwill*	−14,000
Balance c/d	−30,072

* Goodwill = 35,000 × 0.40

The skiing instructor has an entitlement of just over £30,000, and the entitlements of the other partners would also have increased accordingly. The other partners would need to find this sum in order to pay it out, or the outgoing partner could accept a proportion in cash and the rest could be left in the business as a loan, attracting a commercial rate of interest.

The other option would be for a new partner to be sought whose contribution to the business on admission could be used to pay out the departing partner. Losing a key partner like this would normally require a replacement, or the business could not continue in its present form. We will assume that a new skiing instructor is admitted immediately, bringing in £50,000 as capital and participating in the new profit-sharing ratio (PSR) of 3:4:3 (new instructor:farmer:financier). Here are the capital accounts of the new partners following the negotiations.

Capital a/c (new instructor)		*Capital a/c (farmer)*		*Capital a/c (financier)*	
Ref	£	Ref	£	Ref	£
		Bal b/d	−50,000	Bal b/d	−100,000
		Reval	−3,400	Reval	−1,700
		Goodwill	−14,000	Goodwill	−7,000
Cash a/c	−50,000				
G/W w/off	+10,500	G/W w/off	+14,000	G/W w/off	+10,500
Bal c/d	−39,500	Bal c/d	−53,400	Bal c/d	−98,200

It is rarely acceptable accounting practice to keep a goodwill account on the balance sheet, partly out of prudence, but mainly due to the subjectivity involved. However, when the constitution of a partnership changes, it is necessary to recognize the goodwill that exists and to adjust each partner's capital account for any goodwill existing in the business at that time. The normal practice is as follows:

1 Credit (−) the goodwill inherent in the business to the **old** partners' capital accounts in their **old** PSR.
2 Debit (+) the goodwill to the **new** partners in their **new** PSR, thereby eliminating the goodwill from the accounts.

On the introduction of the new partner, the adjustment for goodwill would be to credit the existing partners in their old PSR (2:2:1) – as has already been done in order to calculate the entitlement of the departing partner – then to write off the goodwill against the capital accounts of all three new partners in the new PSR (3:4:3). Note that the capital of the farmer is not altered by the goodwill adjustment as the farmer's share of the profits has remained unchanged by the change of skiing instructor. And although the capital of the new partner is recorded as £39,500, the reality is that if the business were sold for the expected amount, the new instructor would receive the £39,500 entitlement on his or her capital account and an appropriate share of the goodwill or 'profit'. This share would be £10,500; added to the £39,500 this gives £50,000, which is the amount the new instructor had originally invested. This reflects the fact that the new instructor has not made any contribution to the goodwill inherent in the business at the time he or she was admitted.

If it is assumed that the original partner's entitlement was paid out from the £50,000 that the new instructor introduced, the new balance sheet would look like this:

Balance sheet of the Ski-West partnership as at January 1, 19x3

		£	£
Fixed assets			
Land	(revalued amount)		65,000
Buildings	(revalued amount)		95,000
Equipment	(revalued amount)		40,000
			200,000
Current assets			
Bank and cash*		31,928	
Current liabilities			
Creditors		5,500	
Net current assets			26,428
Net assets			226,428
Financed by			
Partners' capital accounts:			
New instructor		39,500	
Farmer		53,400	
Financier		98,200	
			191,100
Partners' current accounts:			
New instructor		nil	
Farmer		14,072	
Financier		21,256	
			35,328
			226,428

* Note that the bank account is the original amount plus the amount invested by the new partner less the amount paid out to the old partner, i.e. £12,000 + £50,000 − £30,072 = £31,928.

12.4 PARTNERSHIP DISSOLUTION AND CONVERSION

Having examined the accounting entries for the departure or admission of a new partner, consider the situation where the business is dissolved and all the partners have their entitlements settled. Following an acceptable offer, Ski-West was to be sold to Ski-UK PLC with immediate effect from January 1, 19x3. The agreed consideration was £300,000 for all the net assets of the partnership except cash. The procedure required to deal with the dissolution is as follows:

Step 1: transfer all asset and liability accounts except cash and capital accounts to a realization account.
Step 2: credit (−) the purchase consideration to the realization account and debit (+) the bank account.

Step 3: transfer the profit or loss on realization to the capital accounts of the partners.
Step 4: transfer the balances on the current accounts to the capital accounts.
Step 5: close off the capital accounts by transferring cash from the bank account to the capital accounts to satisfy the outstanding balances.

Steps 1,2: realization account and bank account

Realization account

Ref	£
Land	+65,000
Buildings	+95,000
Equipment	+40,000
Creditors	−5,500
Bank (cons)	−300,000
Profit on realization*	−105,500

* Note that this 'profit' on realization is not really a profit. Remember that the consideration is to buy the going concern, and that the payment is for tangible and intangible assets. The goodwill has not been separately identified here, but it was valued at £35,000. In fact, the real profit is £105,500 − £35,000 = £70,500, but in this situation it is not necessary to make the distinction.

Steps 3,4,5: capital accounts

Capital a/c (new instructor)		*Capital a/c (farmer)*		*Capital a/c (financier)*	
Ref	£	Ref	£	Ref	£
Bal b/d	−39,500	Bal b/d	−53,400	Bal b/d	−98,200
Profit on realn	−31,650	Profit on realn	−42,200	Profit on realn	−31,650
Curr a/c	nil	Curr a/c	−14,072	Curr a/c	−21,256
Bal c/d	−71,150	Bal c/d	−109,672	Bal c/d	−151,106
Bank	+71,150	Bank	+109,672	Bank	+151,106
	0		0		0

Bank account

Ref	£
Bal b/d	+31,928
Real a/c	+300,000
Cap a/c (new instructor)	71,150
Cap a/c (farmer)	−109,672
Cap a/c (financier)	−151,106
Balance c/d	0

Note that the shares of the 'profit' on realization – £31,650 (£105,500 × 0.3), £42,200 (£105,500 × 0.4) and £31,650 (£105,500 × 0.3) – are credited to the capital accounts of the appropriate partners. When the consideration is received into the bank account there is exactly enough in the bank to satisfy the claims of the partners, allowing the partnership to be finally dissolved, and closing off all accounts of the partnership. But what about the financial position of the new company? If we assume that its only asset before the purchase of Ski-West was £300,000 cash raised from issuing 300,000 one-pound shares to the general public, the balance sheet of the new company following the purchase of Ski-West would be as follows:

Balance sheet of Ski-UK PLC as at January 1, 19x3

	£	£
Fixed assets, intangibles		
Goodwill		105,500*
Fixed assets, tangibles		
Land		65,000
Buildings		95,000
Equipment		40,000
		305,500
Current assets		
Bank and cash	nil	
Current liabilities		
Creditors	5,500	
Net current liabilities		(5,500)
Net assets		300,000
Financed by		
Ordinary share capital (300,000 × £1 shares)†		300,000

* Note that the goodwill figure represents the difference between the consideration paid for the net assets acquired and their fair values. As the fair values agree with the book values of those assets, the goodwill figure agrees with the profit made by the partners on realization.
† This terminology will be explained fully in the next section.

12.5 DISTINCTIVE FEATURES OF LIMITED COMPANIES

The other type of organization which has multiple owners is the limited company. The limited company is far more common than the partnership, particularly among larger organizations. The need for large amounts of investment to finance major commercial ventures requires individuals of great wealth to collaborate and pool their resources through partnership. There was a limit, however, to the amount of capital that could be raised in this way, and the great demand for capital brought about by the Industrial Revolution required that an alternative way had to be found, in order to raise the finance needed. Two main obstacles had to be overcome:

1 To limit the financial risk to entrepreneurs
2 To encourage much greater investment in smaller sums

In response the British government passed the **Limited Liability Act** in 1855 and replaced it with the **Joint Stock Companies Act** in 1856. The first Companies Act was passed in 1862.

The 1855 Act recognized the principle of **limited liability**, which effectively meant that an individual's losses would be limited exclusively to their investment in such organizations, and they would not be expected to meet creditors' claims from private resources. This was the first statutory recognition of an organization as a separate entity, with legal rights and obligations. This principle considerably reduced the financial risk of investing in business, and encouraged more investment as a consequence. The other major feature of the limited company was the **share**. This in effect was capital divided up into small parcels which allowed the flexibility for people to invest very small or very large amounts in an enterprise, and investors were rewarded in two ways:

1 They were entitled to regular payments known as dividends if financial performance permitted.
2 The capital value of their investment, the share, would increase if the company retained a proportion of its profits within the business, and continued to trade successfully.

The opportunity to acquire a shareholding, above all, extended business investment beyond the exclusive domain of the very rich, to include a whole range of moderately well-off individuals, who had the disposable income to make such investments, however small. Both limited liability and the shareholding greatly increased the availability of finance for investment and fuelled the Industrial Revolution, which gave Britain its industrial pre-eminence in the late nineteenth century and the early twentieth century. Since 1856 there have been a number of Companies Acts which have maintained the original principles, and have introduced and amended regulations for such organizations, in the light of the industrial and commercial developments of their time. The most comprehensive revisions of the law in relation to the control, and reporting of the financial affairs of companies in recent years were embodied in the Companies Acts of 1948, 1967 and 1985.

We will now explore the difference between a company, as a business entity, and other organizations. The share capital is the total amount of the original investment made in a company by its owners. There are two main types of shareholding:

– Preference
– Ordinary

Their main characteristics are shown in Table 12.1.

The characteristics in Table 12.1 mean that the risk involved in the ownership of preference shares is less than the risk involved in the ownership of ordinary shares. On the other hand, the rewards to preference shareholders are usually more moderate. If profits are high, then after the payment of preference dividends, there will be enough to pay a substantial dividend to ordinary shareholders, leaving sufficient profits to retain for further investment in the business.

The control that a preference shareholder has over their investment is also more limited as these shares do not normally carry a vote, whereas the ordinary shareholder has certain constitutional rights within the company. The main rights include control over the management of the company through the election of **directors** who form the top layer of operational management. It is their responsibility to manage the company, and therefore the funds invested in that company, in the interests of all the investors, particularly the ordinary shareholders. This function is known as **stewardship**.

Table 12.1 Main characteristics of preference and ordinary shares

	Preference share	Ordinary share
Claim on profits and net assets	Prior*	Final
Voting rights	Rare	Common
Dividend	Fixed	Variable

* If there are adequate net profits after tax, the preference shareholders are entitled to their dividends before any profits can be made available to ordinary shareholders. Also, in law, if the company cannot meet its debts and goes into liquidation, i.e. its net assets are sold, the right to settlement goes in the following order:

1 Preferred creditors (banks, etc., who have secured loans)
2 Government authorities, e.g. VAT, Inland Revenue
3 Other lenders, creditors and trade creditors
4 The preference shareholders
5 The ordinary shareholders

Note that shareholders are last in the pecking order, and the preference shareholders have the prior claim.

The main forum for exercising shareholders' constitutional rights is the annual general meeting (AGM). The AGM is where the financial performance of the company is reported upon, questions are asked and answered, and the dividends are approved. The confirmation, re-election or otherwise of directors may also take place at the AGM, depending on the articles of the company. Shareholders may also be asked to vote on constitutional changes such as an increase in the authorized share capital of the company, or to widen the trading objectives of the company.

The company does not raise all its finance from shareholders. There may be scope to borrow funds from other sources. Companies usually do this by issuing **debentures**. Debentures are long-term loan certificates of a certain denomination such as £1, £5 or £10. These loans will attract a fixed rate of interest throughout the term of the loan. A debenture certificate will state the following items:

1 The nominal value of the certificate
2 The repayment date of the certificate
3 The date(s) and amount of the interest receivable

The extent to which the company obtains its finance from borrowings as against shareholders' funds is known as financial gearing. Gearing is an important ratio which partly influences the risk to the owners in terms of their return on investment, and the security of their investment as a whole. Financial gearing will be discussed more fully in Chapter 19.

As with partnerships, the trading and profit and loss accounts of companies are no different to those of sole traders. The differences only become apparent after net profit has been struck. These differences arise from the company's special financial structure.

12.6 THE FINAL ACCOUNTS OF LIMITED COMPANIES

To put these ideas into context, imagine the creation of a company in the coach tours and excursions business. The accounts for its first year of operation and the necessary notes and workings will also be prepared. The business is to be set up by the issue of a prospectus, which outlines its objectives and its anticipated financial performance. The company is to be financed in the following way:

	Number	Price	Interest
Preference shares	100,000	100p	7%
Ordinary shares	800,000	50p	–
Debentures (redeemable in 20x0)	80,000	100p	8%

The finance was to be used to acquire the following:

	£
Land and buildings	100,000
Coach fleet (15 vehicles)	395,000
Fuel pumps and storage tanks	60,000
Spare parts and consumables	25,000

The company commenced operations on the April 1, 19x2. The business mainly operated UK-based hotel holiday travel for several large hotel chains, but also operated some of its Super-Continental coaches in Europe on behalf of Thomas Moore Holidays. After the first year of operations, the following information was available:

Trial balance of Eurex (Super Travel) Ltd as at March 31, 19x3

	£
Ordinary share capital	–400,000
7% Preference share capital	–100,000
8% Debentures (20x0)	–80,000
Land and buildings	+100,000
Coach fleet (15 vehicles)	+405,000*
Fuel pumps and storage tanks	+60,000
Opening stocks of parts and consumables	+25,000
Cash in hand and at bank	+222,500
Debtors	+25,000
Creditors	–32,000
Sales	–510,500
Route licences	+24,100
VAT payable	–12,000
Administration expenses	+115,000
Selling and distribution expenses	+68,500
Interest paid	+3,200
Interim preference dividends paid	+5,000
Interim ordinary dividends paid	+10,000
PAYE owing for March	–1,800
Purchases of fuel and consumables	+85,000
Rental income (spare land)	–12,000
	0

* See item 5 below

The following information was also available:

1 Closing stocks of fuel and consumables were valued at £21,400.
2 At the year-end, £10,500 was owing for advertising expenses.
3 The rental income received was for the period August 1, 19x2 to July 31, 19x3.
4 Depreciation of fixed assets was to be charged as follows:
   - Land and buildings at 5% per annum on cost
   - Fuel pumps and storage tanks at 10% per annum on cost
   - Coaches at 20% per annum on cost (part-years accounted for).
5 One Sexton coach was traded in at the end of September 19x2 for £20,000 against a new continental touring coach which cost £30,000. The older coach originally cost £25,000. The only entries were to reduce the bank balance by £10,000 and to increase the fixed assets by £10,000.
6 A provision for doubtful debts of 2% of debtors was to be raised against the outstanding debtors at the year-end.
7 The route licences are granted for a ten-year period, after which they will need to be renegotiated. It is anticipated that they will be worthless when they expire.
8 Proposed dividends for the year to be approved at the AGM were as follows:
   - The remainder of the preference dividend
   - 6p per ordinary share
9 The balance of the interest payable on the debentures was to be provided for.
10 Corporation tax of £25,000 was to be provided for.

The following are the final accounts of the company prepared in accordance with the Companies Act 1985 (Format 1):

Trading, profit and loss and appropriation account for Eurex Ltd for the year ended, March 31, 19x3

	£
Sales	510,500
Cost of sales (note 1)	(176,600)
Gross profit	333,900
Selling and distribution expenses (note 2)	(79,000)
Administrative expenses (note 3)	(122,910)
Other operating income (note 4)	8,000
Interest payable and similar charges (note 5)	(6,400)
Profit on ordinary activities before tax	133,590
Taxation	(25,000)
Profit for the financial period	108,590
Dividends paid and proposed (note 7)	(65,000)
Retained profit for the financial period	43,590
Earnings per share (note 8)	12.70p

Note 1: Cost of Sales

The cost of sales comprises those expenses which can be primarily associated with the operational activity of the company. In this case those costs include the following items:

	£
1 Fuel and consumables used in providing coach travel services	
Opening stock of fuel and consumables	25,000
Purchases	85,000
	110,000
Less closing stocks on hand	21,400
	88,600
2 Depreciation on pumps and storage tanks	
$(60,000 \times 0.1)$	6,000
Depreciation on coach fleet	
$(370,000 \times 0.2) + (30,000 \times 0.1) + (25,000 \times 0.1)$	79,500
3 Loss on sale of disposed coach = proceeds* – NBV of coach	
NBV of coach = cost – depreciation	
$= 25,000 - (25,000 \times 0.1)$	
$= 22,500$	
Loss on sale $= (20,000 - 22,500)$	2,500
	176,600

* Trade-in allowance

Note 2: Selling and Distribution costs

£68,500 + advertising owing for previous quarter (£10,500) = £79,000.

Note 3: Administrative expenses

- £115,000 + depreciation on land and buildings + increase in provision for doubtful debts.
- Depreciation on land and buildings = (£100,000 × 0.05) = £5,000.
- As this is the first year of operations, the provision for doubtful debts is created at the year-end. Provision = (£25,000 × 0.02) = £500.
- The route licences are depreciated at 10% on the straight-line basis, giving (£24,100 × 0.10) = £2,410.
- Total administrative expenses = £115,000 + £5,000 + £500 + £2,410 = £122,910.

Note 4: Other operating income

The company generates additional income from the rental of spare land. This rental was paid for one year in advance from August 1, 19x2. The income attributable to the past accounting period therefore amounts to £12,000 × 2/3 = £8,000.

Note 5: Interest payable and similar charges

The debenture interest attributable to the past financial period = £80,000 × 0.08 = £6,400, of which £3,200 has been paid.

Note 6: Dividends paid and proposed

The preference shares attract a 7% fixed annual dividend. This dividend must be appropriated from profits, regardless of the dividend already paid to preferential shareholders by way of interim dividends. The ordinary dividends appropriated from the remaining profits include the interim dividends paid during the year plus any dividend proposed by the directors for approval at the AGM. Note that the proposed dividends are yet to be paid, and will therefore appear on the balance sheet as current liabilities.

	Preference dividends £	Ordinary dividends £
Interim paid	5,000	10,000
Final proposed	2,000*	48,000**
Total	7,000	58,000

$$\text{* Preference dividend proposed} = (100{,}000 \times 0.07) - 5{,}000$$
$$= 2{,}000$$
$$\text{** Ordinary dividend proposed} = 800{,}000 \times 0.06$$
$$= 48{,}000$$

Note 8: Earnings per share (EPS)

The EPS is defined as the net profit after tax available to ordinary shareholders before extraordinary items. In this case the EPS is

$$(\pounds108{,}590 - \pounds7{,}000)/800{,}000 = \pounds101{,}590/800{,}000$$
$$= \pounds0.127$$
$$= 12.7\text{p}$$

It is now highly unlikely for any expenditure to be classed as extraordinary, under the financial reporting standard FRS3.

The Balance sheet for Eurex as at 31.3.x3

	Notes	£
Fixed assets		
Intangible assets	(1)	21,690
Tangible assets	(2)	472,000
Investments		nil
		493,690
Current assets		
Stocks	(3)	21,400
Debtors	(4)	24,500
Investments		nil
Cash at bank and in hand		222,500
		268,400

	Notes	£
Creditors (amounts falling due within one year)	(5)	(138,500)
Net current assets		129,900
Total assets less current liabilities		623,590
Creditors (amounts falling due after more than one year)	(6)	80,000
Net assets		543,590
Capital and reserves		
Ordinary share capital	(7)	400,000
Preference share capital	(7)	100,000
Retained profits		43,590
		543,590

Notes to the balance sheet

Note 1

	Route licences £
Intangible fixed assets:	
Cost or valuation at 1.4.x2	24,100
Less depreciation	2,410
Cost or valuation at 31.3.x3	21,690

Note 2
Tangible fixed assets

	Land and buildings £	Coaches £	Fuel pumps and tanks £	Total £
Cost or valuation at 1.4.x2	100,000	395,000	60,000	555,000
Additions	nil	30,000	nil	30,000
Disposals	nil	(25,000)	nil	(25,000)
At 31.3.x3	100,000	400,000	60,000	560,000

	Land and buildings £	Coaches £	Fuel pumps and tanks £	Total £
Accumulated depreciation:				
At 1.4.x2	nil	nil	nil	nil
Provision for the year	5,000	79,500	6,000	90,500
Disposals	nil	(2,500)	nil	(2,500)
At 31.3.x3	5,000	77,000	6,000	88,000

	£
Note 3	
Stocks of fuel and consumables at 31.3.x3	21,400

	£
Note 4	
Trade debtors less provision	24,500
Other debtors	nil
Prepayments and accrued income	nil
	24,500

	£
Note 5	
Creditors (amounts falling due within one year):	
Trade creditors	32,000
Other creditors (advertising)	10,500
Prepaid income (rent)	4,000
Debenture interest	3,200
Proposed dividends	50,000
Taxation and social security (25,000 + 1,800 + 12,000)	38,800
(corporation tax, VAT and PAYE)	
	138,500

	£
Note 6	
Creditors (amounts falling due after more than one year):	
80,000 × 100p debentures at 8% (20x0)	80,000

	£
Note 7	
Called-up share capital, allotted and fully paid:	
Ordinary shares of 50p each	400,000
7% Preference shares of 100p each	100,000
	500,000

This report and notes are quite complicated, and require careful scrutiny to see where all the figures have come from. It is essential to work through it very thoroughly indeed, as many of the techniques and concepts introduced in earlier chapters are finally brought together here. The presentation is also important, as it complies with Format 1 of the Companies Act 1985, which is the most popular way to present the final reports of limited companies.

12.7 CORPORATE CAPITAL STRUCTURE

Finally in this chapter the capital structure of a company will be examined to see how it may be changed in various circumstances. The capital of a company can comprise investment by shareholders (preference and ordinary) and by lenders. These investors are rewarded through the payment of dividends or through interest. Ordinary shareholders in particular, but also other investors, will be indirectly rewarded by the company re-investing undistributed profits within the business. These retained profits are also known variously as unappropriated profits, profit and loss reserves, undistributed profits and revenue reserves.

Retained profits form part of the ordinary shareholders' capital, but the company as a whole benefits from the retention of funds, as future success or even survival depends on reinvestment to some extent. The other investors will benefit, as the regular payment of their rewards depend partly upon the ongoing financial performance of the business.

From time to time the company may undertake transactions to increase or change its capital structure. The main circumstances in which this might happen are as follows:

1 When additional shares or debentures are issued to raise finance.
2 When reserves are utilized to increase the number of shares in issue, for whatever reason.
3 When fixed assets are to be revalued.
4 When one company takes over another for a consideration that is greater than, or less than the fair value of its net assets.

The financial effects of these circumstances on the capital structure of a company will be explained through the following example, where each step develops upon the effects of the previous steps. Elektra Gaming and Leisure Ltd are financed by 500,000 one-pound ordinary shares and by retained profits:

Authorized share capital = £1,000,000

Profits retained within the company = £250,000

Elektra's directors wish to raise more funds in order to prepare themselves financially for a possible take-over bid
They decide that they need to issue an additional 250,000 ordinary shares. What are the implications of this plan? If these shares are to be issued on the open market, to people other than existing shareholders, the rights of the existing shareholders must be protected. The **par** or **nominal** value of the shares is £1, but what is the average net asset value of the shares?

	£		
Ordinary share capital	500,000		
Retained profits	250,000		
	750,000 / shares issued	=	750,000 / 500,000
		=	1.50

As the net assets of the company attributable to ordinary shareholders are £750,000, each share has an asset value of £1.50. It is likely that the market value of the shares would be even higher, as inherent amounts of goodwill are not included in the valuation of these net assets. Let us look at the result of issuing the additional 250,000 shares at £1 and then at £1.50.

Issue at £1.00	£		
Ordinary share capital	750,000		
Retained profits	250,000		
	1,000,000 / 750,000	=	1.33

When shares are issued at less than their net asset value, the average net asset value of the existing shares is **diluted** from £1.50 to £1.33, whereas the new shareholders make a windfall gain of 133p – 100p = 33p by buying shares which are immediately worth at least £1.33 for the £1.00 paid.

Issue at £1.50	£		
Ordinary share capital	750,000		
Revenue reserves	250,000		
Share premium	125,000		
	1,125,000 / 750,000	=	1.50

Here the average net asset value has been maintained at £1.50, so all the shareholders, existing and new, have their investment unaltered by the transaction. Note that the profit or premium on the issue of the shares, £250,000 × 0.50 = £125,000, is not added to the share capital account, but to a separate account called the **share premium account**. In effect, the share premium is part of the ordinary shareholders' capital in the same way as ordinary share capital, but it is identified separately and may be dealt with in a restricted fashion in accordance with the Companies Act 1985. It is possible, and still fair, to issue shares at less than their asset value **but only to existing shareholders**.

The consequence of this is that, although the average value of the shares is diluted, this is compensated through more shares being owned by the existing shareholders. This is known as a **rights issue**.

Elektra decide to issue shares to existing shareholders, not to attract additional cash, but in order to utilize some of the retained profits of the company
One of the main reasons for making such an issue would be to reduce the average value of the shares, making them more attractive on the open market, or to ultimately increase the number of shareholders, which may make a take-over more difficult. It will be assumed that the directors wish to issue one share for every five held by existing shareholders. This type of issue is known as a **scrip** or **bonus** issue.

Issue 1 for 5	£		
Ordinary share capital	900,000		
Retained profits	100,000		
Share premium	125,000		
	1,125,000 / 900,000	=	1.25

Note that the net assets attributable to the shareholders have not changed from £1,125,000. This is because no cash has been raised. The entries involved are to increase the ordinary share capital from £750,000 to £900,000, i.e. £750,000 + £750,000/5, and to reduce the retained profits accordingly. The overall effect is to dilute the average value of the shares from £1.50 to £1.25. But the existing owners are no worse off, as the average fall in value is compensated by their now owning 20% more shares than they did before.

Elektra decide to revalue some of their metropolitan properties in line with current prices. The valuers estimate that £200,000 can be added to the asset values of the company

The capital structure of the company changes in the following way:

Revaluation of assets	£
Ordinary share capital	900,000
Retained profits	100,000
Share premium	125,000
Revaluation reserve	200,000
	1,325,000 / 900,000 = 1.47

Note that the asset value of the company rises by £200,000. On paper the shareholders are all better off by 147p − 125p = 22p per share. It is illegal to distribute this additional wealth to shareholders because of the requirement that only **realized profits** should be capable of being distributed to shareholders. The only part of the shareholders' funds that can normally be distributed, therefore, are those profits originally declared in the profit and loss account.

Elektra finalize a deal whereby they take over the following company by issuing the rest of their authorized share capital to the shareholders of this company, where the value of these shares is agreed at £175,000

Elektra is to take over 100% of a bookmakers in a busy town. The capital structure of this company is as follows:

Better Bookie Ltd	£
Ordinary share capital (£1)	50,000
Retained profits	80,000
Revaluation reserve	20,000
Shareholders' funds	150,000

The capital of the bookmakers reflects the fair value of its net assets at the date of acquisition. Here is the capital structure of Elektra after the take-over has been finalized.

Take-over of Better Bookie (Consideration £175,000)	£
Ordinary charo capital	1,000,000
Retained profits	100,000
Share premium	200,000
Revaluation reserve	200,000
	1,500,000

The financial structure of Elektra post take-over can be explained as follows:

Ordinary share capital: the agreement involved the issue of the remainder of the authorized share capital of Elektra, 1,000,000 − 900,000 = 100,000 shares at £1 each. These shares are issued leaving the share capital at £1,000,000.

Share premium: as the shareholders of Better Bookie Ltd have accepted the shares of Elektra are worth £175,000, this figure is therefore agreed as the **consideration** being offered for Better Bookie Ltd. The difference between the nominal or par value of the shares (£100,000) and the consideration (£175,000) is regarded as the premium on the issue of these shares, £175,000 − £100,000 = £75,000. The premium is added to the previous balance (£125,000) to give a total of £200,000.

Overall the total shareholders' funds of the new enlarged company are £175,000 greater than they were before, reflecting the fact that Elektra have gained £175,000 of net assets following the acquisition. However, the fair value of the net assets of Better Bookie Ltd was agreed at £150,000, so why did Elektra pay an additional £25,000 for this company? The answer is because of **goodwill**. Elektra have estimated that those factors which represent goodwill have a value of at least £25,000 or, as rational decision makers, they wouldn't have given this price for the company.

Alternative methods of dealing with goodwill

In this case the goodwill has been purchased by another company. The accounting profession has technically accepted two alternative treatments for this 'purchased' goodwill under SSAP 22:

1 Record the purchased goodwill in the intangible fixed-assets section of the balance sheet, thereby recognizing this as part of the asset value of the business. It is recommended that this goodwill should be 'depreciated' over a relatively short period of time, normally up to a maximum of twenty years.
2 Reduce the appropriate reserves of the acquiring company by the whole amount of the goodwill. These reserves would normally be the retained profits. This method keeps the goodwill off the balance sheet, avoids the need for annual depreciation, and immediately reduces the funds of the ordinary shareholders on acquisition.

The validity of the first method versus the second method has been the source of fierce debate within the accountancy profession for many years. The weight of opinion, for sound logical reasons, is now moving towards the first method, and it is expected that a new standard on goodwill will reject the use of the second alternative.

In our example we have taken the first method, recognizing the goodwill as part of the net assets of the business. If we had adopted the second method, the capital structure of Elektra would have looked like this:

Take-over of Better Bookie (Goodwill written off)	£
Ordinary share capital	1,000,000
Retained profits	75,000
Share premium	200,000
Revaluation reserve	200,000
	1,475,000

This time we have reduced the retained profits of Elektra to £100,000 − £25,000 = £75,000, leaving the net assets of the company £25,000 less than they were under the other method. Under law it is only possible to deduct the goodwill from the reserves which are 'realizable'. This means that elimination of goodwill against reserves reduces the company's ability to distribute dividends to the shareholders in the future. On the other hand, under this alternative, there is no need to depreciate this goodwill in subsequent periods, avoiding these charges against future distributable profits available to ordinary shareholders. Finally, if it is assumed that all the circumstances were the same except that the consideration was agreed at £125,000 instead of £175,000, what would be the difference in the final capital structure?

Take-over of Better Bookie (Consideration £125,000)	£
Ordinary share capital	1,000,000
Revenue reserves	100,000
Share premium	150,000
Revaluation reserve	200,000
Capital reserve	25,000
	1,475,000

This time we need to examine the share premium and the capital reserve:

Share premium: as the agreed consideration (the perceived value of the 100,000 shares) is £25,000 more than the par or nominal value, the share premium increases to £150,000 from its pre-take-over level of £125,000.

Capital reserve: as the fair value of the net assets of Better Bookie is agreed at £150,000, and the consideration is £125,000, the shareholders of Elektra could be said to have made a windfall gain of £25,000. This is because, if the separable net assets are indeed valued at £150,000, they could immediately be sold by the acquiring company for more than their purchase price. This could seen as 'negative goodwill', but in fact it is more similar to a revaluation reserve, where the assets are recognized as being worth more than their original purchase cost. This is actually recorded as a capital reserve and forms part of the ordinary shareholders' funds. As with a revaluation reserve, this 'profit' cannot be classed as distributable until such time as the gain is ultimately realized.

SUMMARY

1 The nature of a partnership should be set out in an agreement.

2 In a partnership any profits have to be appropriated among the partners.

3 When a partner joins or leaves, any changes in the partnership need to be shown in the accounts.

4 There is a recommended procedure for dissolving a partnership.

4 Limited companies have certain features that distinguish them from other organizations.

5 Format 1 of the Companies Act 1985 is the most popular way to prepare final accounts and associated notes for limited liability companies.

6 Adjustments are required for transactions that affect the capital structure of a limited company.

ASSESSMENT

MULTIPLE-CHOICE QUESTIONS

Question 1

It is rare that a formal partnership agreement will directly recognize which one of the following factors?

A The capital originally invested by each partner in the business
B The capital currently invested by each partner in the business
C The physical/mental effort invested by each partner in the business
D The extent to which each partner withdraws wealth from the business for private purposes

Question 2

A partnership comprises two individuals who each originally invested £100,000 in a business, and they share their profits in the ratio 2:1. The original partners admit a third partner to share profits equally, introducing capital of £50,000. The three partners agree that the inherent goodwill of the business at the time of admission was £12,000. If goodwill is not to be kept in the books, which of the following amounts would reflect the correct balance on the capital account of the new partner?

A £46,000
B £42,000
C £38,000
D £54,000

Question 3

Which one of the following statements is not true with respect to limited companies?

A All shareholders of a company are considered to be its owners.
B In direct terms the dividends attributable to the preference share are the only participation that a preference shareholder has in the income created by a company.
C As a preference shareholder has priority over an ordinary shareholder with respect to participation in profits, and in the event of liquidation, a preference shareholder can be said to have more control over company affairs than an ordinary shareholder.
D The dividends payable to ordinary shareholders are decided by the directors of a company for approval by the ordinary shareholders at an AGM.

Question 4

From the following extract of the profit and loss account for Easy-Pack Catering Supplies Ltd, calculate the earnings per share (EPS) for the 1,000,000 shareholders holding ordinary £1 shares.

	£
Profit on ordinary activities before tax	140,000
Taxation	(50,000)
Profit on ordinary activities after tax	90,000
Extraordinary gains	23,500
Profit for the financial year	113,500
Preference dividends paid and proposed	(12,500)
Ordinary dividends paid and proposed	(35,000)
Profits retained	66,000

A 12.75p
B   9.00p
C 10.10p
D   7.75p

Question 5

If a company with the following capital structure makes a rights issue to existing shareholders of two shares for every three owned, for £1.20 each, by how much will the share premium account increase after the transaction?

	£
600,000 × 50p ordinary shares	300,000
Retained profits	180,000
Capital reserve	10,000
Share premium	10,000

A £280,000
B nothing
C £480,000
D £200,000

EXERCISES

Exercise 1

Charlie Chef and Barry Brewer are currently in partnership providing good food, and brewing and selling real ale in a country restaurant. The trial balance for the partnership as at December 31, 19x3 was as follows:

	£
Capital accounts	
Chef (1.1.x3)	−25,000
Brewer (1.7.x3)	−19,600
Current assets	+30,000
Current liabilities	−17,400
Fixed assets	+55,000
Net profit to 31.12.x3	−32,000
Drawings	
Chef	+4,000
Brewer	+5,000
	0

Notes

Barry Brewer was admitted to the partnership on July 1, 19x3. When he joined, he deposited £19,600 in the partnership bank account. After the preparation of the above trial balance, it has been discovered that accounting entries have not been made for the following matters agreed between the two partners when Barry Brewer was admitted:

1 Profits were assumed to have been earned in the proportion: 30% in the first six months and 70% in the last six months.
2 The valuation of the land of Charlie Chef was to be agreed at £8,000 more than recognized in the books.
3 Goodwill inherent in the restaurant was agreed at £17,000 at the time that Barry Brewer was admitted. According to best accounting practice, this goodwill is not to be recognized as an asset in the books.
4 Interest on drawings of 10% annually was to be charged on the partners' drawings.

The partnership agreement from 1.7.x3 provides for the following:

1 Interest on capital originally invested is to be credited to partners at the rate of 6% per annum.
2 Barry Brewer is to be paid a salary as a master brewer of £4,000 annually; Charlie Chef is to receive £8,000.
3 The partners are to share profits equally.

Required

(a) Prepare the capital accounts of Charlie Chef and Barry Brewer as at 1.7.x3.
(b) Prepare the partnership profit and loss appropriation account for the year ended 31.12.x3, and a balance sheet as at that date. In your workings show the current accounts of both partners.

Exercise 2

Hop, Skip and Jump, who have been in business running a fitness centre, have decided to dissolve their partnership and to sell their key fixed assets to Fittodrop Ltd. They have been sharing profits and losses 2/5, 2/5, 1/5 respectively. The balance sheet of the partnership as at April 30, 19x3 is as follows:

	Cost	Depn	NBV
	£	£	£
Fixed assets			
Premises			85,000
Equipment			35,000
Fixtures			20,000
Motor vehicles			15,000
			155,000
Current assets			
Stock (consumables)		700	
Debtors		5,000	
		5,700	
Current liabilities			
Creditors	2,000		
Bank	4,500		
		6,500	
Net current liabilities			(800)
Net assets			154,200
Financed by			
Capital accounts:			
Hop			30,000
Skip			60,000
Jump			50,000
			140,000
Current accounts:			
Hop		12,000	
Skip		8,000	
Jump		(5,800)	
			14,200
			154,200

Fittodrop Ltd agree to take over all the fixed assets except the motor vehicles for a consideration of £150,000. This is to be satisfied by the issue of £100,000 ordinary shares at a par value of £1 each, allocated to the partners in accordance with their profit-sharing ratios. The balance is to be paid by £50,000 cash.

It was agreed by the partners that Hop and Skip should take over the two motor vehicles at an agreed valuation of £6,000 each. The consumable stock was sold for £400, and the debtors were sold to a factoring agency for 80% of their book value. Creditors are paid off at their book value. The legal and incidental costs of the dissolution come to £2,400.

Required
Close off the books of the Hop, Skip and Jump partnership, showing all the entries required in the realization account, the capital accounts, the consideration account and the bank account.

Exercise 3
The Transworld travel agency has the following trial balance as at 31.12.x3:

	£
Ordinary share capital (£1 shares)	−1,200,000
Retained profits	−420,000
Balances owing from customers	+3,200,000
Balances owing to tour operators	−2,400,000
Commissions earned	−700,000
Administrative expenses	+450,000
Goodwill on purchased business	+24,000
Selling and distribution expenses	+120,000
Interim dividend paid	+20,000
Land and properties	+840,000
Fixtures and fittings (F+F)	+200,000
Provn for depreciation – F+F (1.1.x3)	−50,000
Capital reserve	−25,500
Trade creditors	−24,500
Bank account	+20,000
Revaluation reserve	−54,000
	0

The following information also needs to be taken into account:

1 The depreciation policy is 20% on the reducing balance on fixed assets.
2 Purchased goodwill is amortized over 10 years. The goodwill was connected with an acquisition of a smaller chain of travel agents two years ago.
3 The ordinary dividends proposed at the AGM were 4.50p per share.
4 The estimated corporation tax liability for the year was £19,000.

Required

(a) Prepare the profit and loss and appropriation account of the Transworld travel agency for the year ended December 31, 19x3 prepared in the abbreviated columnar format, showing the earnings per share earned for the year.
(b) Draw up the balance sheet of Transworld as at May 31, 19x3.

Exercise 4

The following balances were extracted from the books of the Northleigh Hotel as at 31.5.x3:

	£
Ordinary shares of 100p each fully paid	−100,000
8% Preference shares at 50p	−50,000
7% Debentures (£10 each)	−50,000
Fixed assets:	
Land and buildings at valuation	+260,000
Fixtures fittings and equipment (FFE) at cost	+95,000
Depn FFE as at 1.6.x2	−42,000
Stock as at 1.6.x2	+6,500
Debtors	+4,000
Creditors	−22,420
Administrative expenses	+32,000
Selling and distribution expenses	+10,200
Interest paid	+1,750
Sales	−239,390
Purchases	+87,240
Directors' emoluments	+30,000
Bank balance	+12,120
Share premium account	−10,000
Retained profits as at 1.6.x2	−25,000
	0

The following information is also available:

1 Closing stocks of food, drink and consumables were £5,500.
2 Depreciation on the fixtures, fittings and equipment is to be provided annually at the rate of 10% per annum on cost.
3 The ordinary dividends proposed for the year were 9%. The preference dividend was also proposed and approved.
4 Administration expenses accrued were established at £1,598 at the year-end. Selling and distribution expenses for advertising had been prepaid, amounting to £6,000.
5 The corporation tax liability for the year was estimated at £15,000.

The company also needs to account for the following developments during the year to 31.5.x3:

1 The land has been substantially revalued by £30,000, and this has not yet been recognized in the books.
2 During the year, the hotel took over a small bus company with the following capital structure at the time of take-over:

	£
Fixed assets (vehicles)	+50,000
Stocks	+10,000
Shares (40,000 × £1)	−40,000
Revenue reserves	−20,000

Northleigh Hotel agreed a consideration of £40,000 shares valued at £1.70 as the fair price to offer the shareholders of the bus company for their business. This major transaction had not been accounted for in the books. The company's policy is to write off purchased goodwill against the available retained profits, and to depreciate the vehicles at 20% of cost each year. A full year's depreciation is to be charged for the year to May 31, 19x3.

Required
Prepare the trading, profit and loss, and appropriation account of the Northleigh Hotel for the year ended 31.5.x3, and a balance sheet as at that date. Take into account all the additional information and incorporate the necessary adjustments. Show all your workings.

ABC Leisure Drome

Here is the trial balance of the partnership of Aldwich, Berwick and Chiswick, who own and run ABC Leisure Drome, a UK holiday camp.

	July 31, 19x3 £
Debtors for room and conference hire	12,000
Creditors	6,400
Provision for bad debts (1.8.x2)	588
Land and buildings	186,000
Fixtures and fittings	165,000
Provision for depn (1.8.x2)	45,600
Camp minibuses	30,200
Provision for depn (1.8.x2)	15,380
Stocks of food and drink (1.8.x2)	15,300
Purchases of food and drink	95,995
Sales of food and drink	140,100
PAYE	2,500
VAT (owed by ABC)	22,200
NI	750
Bad debts	581
Staff wages	136,145
Establishment expenses	54,095
Admin expenses	25,100
Deposits for bookings	16,400
Fees for accommodation	290,000
Capital accounts:	
A (1.8.x2)	120,000
B (1.8.x2)	60,000
C (1.8.x2)	60,000
Current accounts:	
A (1.8.x2)	12,000
B (1.8.x2)	4,357
C (1.8.x2)	2,200
Drawings:	
A	22,000
B	24,000
C	11,860
Bank account	20,199
	0

The previous balance sheet of this organization (as at 31.7.x2) is contained in Appendix 1 (p. 206).

The partnership agreement

The partnership agreement allows for interest on capital to be paid at a rate of 7% per annum. B and C are entitled to salaries of £12,000 and £15,000 respectively; any residual profits are to be shared among the three partners in the ratio 2:2:1 (A:B:C). Interest on drawings of 5% is to be charged against the partners' current accounts.

Matters to be taken into account at the year-end

At the end of July 19x3 establishment expenses prepaid amounted to £5,230, and accrued administration expenses totalled £3,540. During the period 1.8.x2 to 31.7.x3, a minibus was purchased for £12,000. The partners traded in another minibus against the new one, for which they received an allowance of £4,500. This minibus had originally cost the partnership £7,000 when purchased, and had a net book value (NBV) of £5,000 at the time of its disposal. No entries regarding the acquisition or disposal had been made in the accounts. The depreciation policy on minibuses is to charge 15% on the cost of each minibus over six years, with the expectation that at the end of six years the residual value of the minibuses would equal 10% of the original cost. A full year's depreciation is charged on acquisitions, but no depreciation is charged in the year of disposal. There were no other fixed-asset disposals during the year. Depreciation on fixtures is to be charged at 20% using the reducing-balance method.

The bad debt provision is to be made equivalent to 8% of debtors; these debtors are entirely comprised of unpaid balances for corporate conferences, rooms and entertainment charges. During the year, a bar steward was dismissed on reasonable suspicion that he had been stealing quantities of drink. The value of what was stolen was unknown. The normal policy of ABC is to allow normal leakage at 2% of sales, which is absorbed into the gross profit margin. Any level of loss above this level is classed as abnormal, and is separately itemized in the bars and restaurants trading account. The normal markup on all food and drink is cost plus 50%.

At the end of July 19x3, the closing stock of food and drink was valued at £13,300 (purchase invoice value). Of this, a batch of non-alcoholic bitter was approaching its sell-by date. It was decided by the partners to make this available for sale at half the normal retail price. This stock originally cost £300.

The offer

The partners were approached by an entertainments and leisure company called Blackjack Gaming Ltd, offering to pay a consideration of £350,000 for the tangible net assets of the ABC business as at 31.7.x3. Blackjack will take over all the assets and liabilities of ABC, excluding the minibuses, which Berwick was to take over at a price of £13,000, and the debtors who are to be sold for cash to a factor for £6,665. The consideration for the rest of the net assets (excluding cash), is to be paid by £150,000 cash, and the balance is to be satisfied by issuing Blackjack shares. Sixty percent of the share capital was to be in the form of Blackjack's existing one-pound ordinary shares, the balance to be a new issue of 8% one-pound preference shares. Blackjack's ordinary shares are considered to be worth £1.50 each on the open market. The partners agreed to all these terms, as long as the land and buildings of the holiday camp were valued by a chartered surveyor. The valuation for the land and buildings was assessed and agreed at £200,000.

The settlement details

When final settlement of the partners' entitlements took place, it was agreed by the partners that partners A and B should receive £60,000 each from the bank account, the remaining balance to be paid to C. A was to receive all the ordinary shares, and finally the preference shares were to be allocated in such a way as to satisfy the remaining balances on all the partners' capital accounts.

Required

As accountant for ABC Leisure Drome you are required to do the following as at July 31, 19x3:

(a) Prepare the profit and loss and appropriation account for ABC for the year ended July 31, 19x3.
(b) Prepare the updated current account balances of each partner for the year to July 31, 19x3, taking into account all the information given.
(c) Prepare a balance sheet for the partnership as at July 31, 19x3.
(d) Prepare a cash flow statement for ABC for the period to July 31, 19x3.
(e) Close off the accounts of the partners at the take-over date (1.8.x3), prepare the realization account and calculate the exact entitlement of each partner in terms of cash, ordinary share, and preference shares.

As accountant for Blackjack Gaming Ltd you should draw up a balance sheet of the company following the acquisition of ABC Leisure Drome. The net assets of Blackjack before the take-over are in Appendix 2. The policy of Blackjack is to write off any purchased goodwill against the available retained profits of the company. Any balance remaining should be shown on the balance sheet as goodwill, to be depreciated over a ten-year period.

APPENDIX 1

Assets and liabilities of ABC Leisure Drome as at August 1, 19x2

	£
Debtors for room hire	10,500
Creditors	7,350
Provn for bad debts (1.8.x2)	588
Land and buildings	173,000
Fixtures and fittings	152,000
Provn depn (1.8.x2)	45,600
Camp minibuses	30,200
Provn depn (1.8.x2)	15,380
Stocks of food and drink (1.8.x2)	15,300
PAYE	2,200
VAT (owed by ABC)	18,000

Assets and liabilities of ABC Leisure Drome as at August 1, 19x2 (cont'd)

		£
NI		800
Prepaid expenses		2,140
Accrued expenses		3,210
Capital accounts:		
A	(1.8.x2)	120,000
B	(1.8.x2)	60,000
C	(1.8.x2)	60,000
Current accounts:		
A	(1.8.x2)	12,000
B	(1.8.x2)	4,357
C	(1.8.x2)	2,200
Bank overdraft		31,455
		0

APPENDIX 2

Net assets of Blackjack Gaming Ltd before take-over of ABC as at July 31, 19x3

	£
Ordinary share capital (£1 shares)	1,500,000
Revenue reserves	368,200
Share premium account	55,000
Land and buildings at valuation	1,150,000
Cash on hand and at bank	530,000
Debtors	87,000
Vehicles at valuation	61,600
Creditors	159,500
VAT owing	25,000
Fittings and equipment at valuation	700,400
PAYE	61,200
NI	15,500
Accruals	13,000
Prepayments	9,600
Investments (shares in various companies)	120,000
Provision for taxation	23,700
Proposed dividends	37,500
Debenture loan stock (8%)	400,000
	0

CASE NOTES

This major exercise should be tackled at the end of Part 1. There is a considerable amount of work for the student. Knowledge from all chapters is tested at some point during the exercise. After the students have read the case carefully, a preliminary discussion seminar should take place to establish what is required and how it should be achieved. It is best to set out the tasks in line with what is required and to tackle them in that order. Although the tasks should be handled discretely to make them manageable, the case itself links them all together, so the students can see how various aspects of financial accounting are dealt with in a single business scenario.

What is tested

1 How to use the double-entry system. The trial balances at the beginning of the case and in the appendices are single columns that balance at zero. How to check them by assigning positive or negative signs to each item in each list to ensure the totals actually sum to zero (Chapters 2 and 3).

2 How to prepare a trading and profit and loss account and appropriation account in vertical format (Chapter 4). In preparing this statement, certain technical areas are also covered:
   - Accruals and prepayments (Chapter 4)
   - Treatment of provisions, depreciation/disposals and bad debts (Chapters 5 and 7)
   - Valuation of stocks, and treatment of normal and abnormal losses (Chapter 6)
   - PAYE and NI (Chapter 9)
   - VAT (Chapter 10)
   - Calculation of subsidiary trading accounts within a major profit and loss account (Chapter 11)
   - Partnership appropriation procedures, including the treatment of interest on drawings (Chapter 12)

3 How to complete the current accounts of partners then balance them (Chapter 12).

4 How to prepare a cash flow statement, how to recognize the difference between profit and cash flow, and the impact of the accruals concept (Chapter 8).

5 How to close off the accounts of a partnership, combining capital and current accounts, posting a realization account and satisfying the entitlements of partners from a consideration account. This exercise tests the ability to deal with goodwill, and the revaluation of tangible fixed assets (Chapter 12).

6 How to prepare a balance sheet of a limited company using vertical format and incorporating the net assets of another business (Chapters 4 and 12).

7 How to present VAT and PAYE on a balance sheet (Chapters 9 and 10).

SUGGESTED APPROACH AND SOLUTION

Compile a trading, profit/loss and appropriation account for ABC

Let us begin with the acquisition and disposal of the minibuses, which have been completely omitted from the accounts, and calculate the depreciation provision to be charged for the year. The best way to do this is to construct the necessary ledger accounts, not forgetting the £7,500 entry to the bank account.

Minibuses at cost account		Provision for depn account	
Ref	£	Ref	£
Bal b/d 1.8.x2	+30,200	Bal b/d 1.8.x2	−15,380
Bank*	+7,500	Disposals[†]	+2,000
Disposals	+4,500	P+L account[‡]	−5,280
Disposals	−7,000		
		Bal c/d 31.7.x3	−18,660
Bal b/d	+35,200		

Disposals account		
Ref	£	
Minibuses A/C	+7,000	
Provn for depn	−2,000	
Minibuses A/C	−4,500	(allowance)
Loss on disposal	+500	

* Payment of cash for new vehicle £12,000 − £4,500 (trade-in allowance on old vehicles) = £7,500.

† As the original cost of the disposed vehicle was given as £7,000, the depreciation on this vehicle must have been £2,000 for the asset to have a net book value of £5,000 when it was traded in.

‡ The depreciation charge for the year is based on 15% of the cost of vehicles held at the year-end, so £35,200 × 0.15 = £5,280.

Next we will deal with the stock adjustments. The stolen stock can only be estimated once we have arrived at the gross profit margin for the bars and retaurants.

	£	£
Sales of food and drink		140,100
Opening stock	15,300	
Purchases	95,995	
	111,295	
Less abnormal loss	1,868	
	109,427	
Less closing stock	13,225	
COS and normal losses		96,202
Gross profit		43,898
Abnormal loss		1,868
		42,030

Abnormal loss calculation

The normal gross profit percentage for food and drink is cost plus 50% or one-third of selling price. If ABC had achieved one-third of sales, gross profit should have been £140,100/3 = £46,700. They actually achieved 42,030/140,100 = 30%. Therefore, the leakage is 3.33% of sales, or £46,700 − £42,030 = £4,670, rather than the allowable 2%. Anything above 2% is to be treated as an abnormal loss. And 2% of sales is £140,100 × 0.02 = £2,802, therefore the abnormal loss is £4,670 − 2,802 = £1,898.

Although the distinction between abnormal and normal losses makes no difference to the bottom-line net profit from the bars and restaurant, the maintenance of a normal margin based on the difference between buying prices and menu prices is a good control mechanism for monitoring leakage or dishonesty. It is particularly useful when examined over a number of periods, and for comparison of bars or departments within an organization.

Valuation of closing stock

The closing stock of food and drink at cost was £13,300. Of this, non-alcoholic bitter that originally cost £300 is to be written down to half its normal retail value. As the normal price of this batch of stock would be £300 × 1.5 = £450, the reduced price or **net realizable value** (NRV) of the stock is £225. Using the concept of prudence, this stock should be valued at its cost or its net realizable value, whichever is the lower. In this case the lower figure is the NRV, so the stock should be valued at £225. Effectively we should reduce the stock valuation by £300 − £225 = £75.

The trading, profit and loss account and appropriation account for ABC Leisure Drome can now be produced.

Trading and profit and loss account and appropriation account (ABC Leisure Drome) for the year ended July 31, 19x3

	£	£
Turnover (accommodation inc deposits)		306,400
Gross profit from bars and restaurants		42,030
		348,430
Less expenses:		
Loss on disposal of minibus	500	
Increase in provision for bad debts (note 1)	372	
Bad debts	581	
Increase in provision for:		
Depreciation (fixtures) (note 2)	23,880	
Depreciation (vehicles)	5,280	
Staff wages	136,145	
Estab exps (−5,230)	48,865	
Admin exps (+3,540)	28,640	
		244,263
Net profit		104,167
Add interest on drawings (note 3)		2,893
Net profit for appropriation		107,060
Interest on capital invested:		
Aldwick (7% of £120,000)	8,400	
Berwick (7% of £60,000)	4,200	
Chiswick (7% of £60,000)	4,200	
		16,800
		90,260

Trading and profit and loss account and appropriation account (ABC Leisure Drome) for the year ended July 31, 19x3 (cont'd)

	£	£
Salaries:		
Berwick	12,000	
Chiswick	15,000	
		27,000
		63,260
Shares of residual profit:		
Aldwick (1/2)	31,630	
Berwick (1/4)	15,815	
Chiswick (1/4)	15,815	
		63,260

Note 1
The provision for doubtful debts should be equivalent to 8% of the debtors as at July 31, 19x3, i.e. £12,000 × 0.08 = £960. The current provision is £588, so the increase in the provision is £960 − £588 = £372.

Note 2
The depreciation on the fixtures is calculated by taking the cost of the fixtures, subtracting the accumulated depreciation and multiplying by 20%; this gives (£165,000 − £45,600) × 0.20 = £23,880.

Note 3
The drawings of the partners were as follows:

	£
Aldwick	22,000
Berwick	24,000
Chiswick	11,860
Chiswick	57,860 × 0.05 = 2,893 (interest)

Preparation of partners' current accounts

Next the columnar current accounts of the partners are prepared. The opening balances are obtained from the trial balance as at 31.7.x3 and the appropriation account for the period ended 31.7.x3.

Aldwick account		*Berwick account*		*Chiswick account*	
Ref	£	Ref	£	Ref	£
Bal b/d	−12,000	Bal b/d	−4,357	Bal b/d	−2,200
Int on cap	−4,200	Int on cap	−4,200	Int on cap	−8,400
Salary	nil	Salary	−12,000	Salary	−15,000
SORP	−31,630	SORP	−15,815	SORP	−15,815
Drawings	+22,000	Drawings	+24,000	Drawings	+11,860
Int draw	+1,100	Int draw	+1,200	Int draw	+593
Bal c/d	−24,730		−11,172		−28,962

Preparation of the balance sheet of ABC as at July 31, 19x3

The next step is to prepare the balance sheet of the partnership as at 31.7.x3.

Balance sheet (ABC Leisure Drome) as at July 31, 19x3

	Cost £	Depn £	NBV £
Fixed assets			
Land and buildings	186,000	nil	186,000
Fixtures and fittings	165,000	69,480	95,520
Vehicles	35,200	18,660	16,540
	386,200	64,260	298,060
Current assets			
Stocks of food and drink		13,225	
Debtors	12,000		
Less provision	960		
		11,040	
Prepayments		5,230	
Bank account (20,199 – 7,500)		12,699	
		42,194	
Less current liabilities			
Trade creditors	6,400		
Accruals	3,540		
VAT	22,200		
PAYE	2,500		
NI	750		
		35,390	
Net current assets			6,804
Net assets			304,864
Financed by			
Capital accounts:			
Aldwick	120,000		
Berwick	60,000		
Chiswick	60,000		
			240,000
Current accounts:			
Aldwick	24,730		
Berwick	11,172		
Chiswick	28,962		
			64,864
			304,864

Cash flow statement of ABC for the year to July 31, 19x3

The next step is to prepare the cash flow statement (Chapter 8). You need to use the list of assets and liabilities at the end of 19x2 (Appendix 1). It is best to start with a reconciliation of the operating profit to net cash flow from operations.

Reconciliation of operating profit to net cash flow from operating activities

	£
Operating profit (before int on drawings)	104,167
Depreciation charges	29,160
Add loss on disposal	500
Decrease in stocks	2,075
Increase in net debtors	(1,128)
Increase prepayments/reduction accruals	(2,760)
Increase in creditors inc VAT, PAYE, NI	3,500
Net cash inflow from operating activities	135,514

Now the cash flow statement itself can be prepared:

Cash flow statement (ABC Leisure Drome) for the year ended July 31, 19x3

	£	£
Net cash flow from operating activities		135,514
Returns on investments and servicing of finance		
Drawings (22,000 + 24,000 + 11,860)		(57,860)
		77,654
Taxation		nil
		77,654
Capital expenditure		
Fixed assets purchased*	(33,500)	
Proceeds from disposals	nil	
		(33,500)
Management of liquid resources		
Capital introduced	nil	
Loans raised	nil	
Loans redeemed	nil	
		nil
Increase in cash and cash equivalents		44,154[†]

* Payments to acquire fixed assets comprise £7,500 paid for the new minibus, and £13,000 each on land and buildings, fixtures and fittings.
[†] The increase in cash and cash equivalents is £31,455 + £12,699 = £44,154.

Undertake the dissolution of the ABC partnership

The next stage in this exercise is to undertake the dissolution of the partnership as at August 1, 19x3. Before this the capital accounts of the partners must be updated with the revaluation of the land and buildings at £200,000. This is a revaluation of £14,000. Each partner should be credited (−) with their share of this. Under the agreement, £7,000 should be added to A's capital account, £3,500 to B's and £3,500 to C's.

Now all the assets, including the revalued land and buildings, and the liabilities, will be transferred to a realization account. The amounts realized for these net assets will also be posted.

Realization account ABC

Ref	£
Land and buildings	+200,000
Fixtures and fittings	+95,520
Vehicles	+16,540
Stocks	+13,225
Debtors	+10,040
Prepayments	+5,230
Creditors	−6,400
Accruals	−3,540
VAT	−22,200
PAYE	− 2,500
NI	−750
Realizations	
Bank (debtors)	−6,665
Berwick cap a/c	−13,000
Blackjack a/c*	−350,000
Profit on realn	−64,500
Aldwick a/c (2)	+32,250
Berwick a/c (1)	+16,125
Chiswick a/c (1)	+16,125
	0

* The consideration was agreed at £350,000

Now the capital accounts of the partners will be dealt with. They need also to be combined with the current accounts, and finally they will be closed off from the bank account and the Blackjack (BJ) consideration account:

Aldwick account		Berwick account		Chiswick account	
Ref	£	Ref	£	Ref	£
Bal b/d	−120,000		−60,000		−60,000
Reval land	−7,000		−3,500		−3,500
Curr a/c	−24,730		−11,172		−28,962
Vehicles			+13,000		
Realn a/c	−32,250		−16,125		−16,125
	−183,980		−77,797		−108,587
Cash	+60,000		+60,000		+50,364
BJ a/c	+120,000				
BJ a/c	+3,980		+17,797		+58,223
	0		0		0

Bank account		Blackjack consideration a/c	
Ref	£	Ref	£
Bal b/d	+13,699	Realization a/c	+350,000
Debtors	+6,665	Bank (A, B, C)	−150,000
BJ a/c	+150,000	Ord shares (A)	−120,000
A cap a/c	−60,000	Pref shares (A, B, C)	−80,000
B cap a/c	−60,000		
C cap a/c	−50,364		0
	0		

Compile the amended balance sheet of Blackjack as at August 1, 19x3

The final stage is to draw up the new balance sheet of Blackjack Gaming Ltd after the acquisition of ABC Leisure Drome. The assets and liabilities taken over by Blackjack must be added to the company's own assets and liabilities. Account must also be taken of how the acquisition of these net assets was financed and how they will be incorporated into the capital structure of Blackjack. Note that the acquisition is financed by £150,000 cash, £120,000 of ordinary shares, and £80,000 of preference shares. The shares are a new issue, so they must be added to the shares already in issue. There is no problem with the preference shares, but a complication arises with regard to the ordinary shares. If each ordinary share is deemed to be worth £1.50 to the partners, the number of shares required to make £120,000 is 120,000/1.50 = 80,000. The shares should be shown as £80,000 ordinary shares at £1 par value, and the difference of £40,000 as a share premium, showing that the shares were issued at a price higher than their nominal or par value.

Net assets for Blackjack Gaming Ltd before take-over of ABC

	31.7.x3 £	Changes £
Ordinary share capital (£1 shares)	−1,500,000	−80,000
Preference shares		−80,000
Retained profits	−368,200	+71,415*
Share premium account	−55,000	−40,000
Land and buildings at valuation	+1,150,000	+200,000
Cash on hand and at bank	+530,000	−150,000
Stocks		+13,225
Debtors	+87,000	
Vehicles at valuation	+61,600	
Creditors	−159,500	−6,400
VAT owing	−25,000	−22,200
Fittings and equipment at valuation	+700,400	+95,520
PAYE	−61,200	−2,500
NI	−15,500	−750
Accruals	−13,000	−3,540
Prepayments	+9,600	+5,230
Investments (shares in various companies)	+120,000	
Provision for taxation	−23,700	
Proposed dividends	−37,500	
Debenture loan stock (8%)	−400,000	
	0	0

*Goodwill and retained profits

Goodwill is to be written off against the retained profits of the company. Goodwill is obtained by deriving the difference between the consideration paid for the partnership assets taken over, compared with their fair values (which in this case are the amended net book values). The value of the net assets taken over can be calculated as follows:

$$£304,864 + £14,000 - £16,540 - £11,040 - £12,699 = £278,585$$

This is arrived at by summing the capital and current accounts of the partners and adding the amount by which some of the fixed assets were revalued, less the value of the assets not taken over by the company, namely the vehicles, the debtors and the cash at the bank. Therefore, purchased goodwill is £350,000 – £278,585 = £71,415, which will be written off against the retained profits of the company. The Blackjack balance sheet can be amended as follows:

Balance sheet (Blackjack Gaming Ltd) as at 1.8.x3

	Cost £	Depn £	NBV £
Fixed assets			
Land and buildings	1,350,000	nil	1,350,000
Fixtures and fittings	795,920	nil	795,920
Vehicles	61,600	nil	61,600
	2,207,520	nil	2,207,520
Investments			120,000
Current assets			
Stocks		13,225	
Debtors		87,000	
Prepayments		14,830	
Bank account		380,000	
		495,055	
Current liabilities			
Creditors	165,900		
Accruals	16,540		
Proposed dividends	37,500		
Proposed tax	23,700		
VAT	47,200		
PAYE	63,700		
NI	16,250		
	370,790		
Net current assets			124,265
			2,451,785
Less 10% debentures			400,000
Net assets			2,051,785

Balance sheet (Blackjack Gaming Ltd) as at 1.8.x3 (cont'd)

	Cost £	Depn £	NBV £
Financed by			
Ordinary share capital (£1 shares)			1,580,000
8% Preference share capital (£1 shares)			80,000
Share premium			95,000
Revenue reserves			296,785
			2,051,785

PART 2

Management accounting and internal reports

CHAPTER 13

Costing a product or service

OBJECTIVES

- Distinguish between expenses and costs.
- Relate cost control to organizational structure.
- Define the three main components of cost.
- Calculate the direct material cost of a product or service.
- Calculate the direct labour cost of a product or service.
- Allocate and apportion overhead costs to a product or service.
- Calculate the total cost of a product or service where multiple products or services are produced or provided in various departments.
- Compile a product cost structure report for a product or service.

13.1 EXPENSES AND COSTS

After having read Part 1, you will have recognized that the profit of an organization as a whole is the difference between the attributable revenues that the organization generates within a financial period, less the attributable expenses incurred by that organization within the same financial period. Expenses are classified according to the types of products or services used in generating the revenues. They range from the expenditure incurred on producing or acquiring the stocks or services that are the primary revenue earner, to the expenses incurred in supporting the business organization in general. General expenses include establishment expenses, such as rent, rates, power and insurance, through to salaries, depreciation, consumables and services used, such as professional fees and interest on borrowings. In financial accounting, these expenses are aggregated and classified by generic type for reporting purposes.

In management accounting there is a need to classify expenses in a more sophisticated manner in order to help management plan and control expenditure incurred, and to provide a basis for decision making. Managers need to be able to obtain answers to the following additional questions about expenditure in order to make decisions more effectively:

1 What expenditure is incurred?
2 Who incurs the expenditure?
3 Where is the expenditure incurred?
4 When is the expenditure incurred?
5 How is the expenditure incurred?
6 Why is the expenditure incurred?

If a business is to control costs and plan expenditure appropriately, managers need to know the answers to all of the above questions, and this may not be easy. It is particularly important to find out why an expenditure is incurred, as this will indicate whether the expenditure needs to be incurred at all. Many organizations fail to do this, so they incur expenditure unnecessarily and are therefore less competitive and less profitable than they might be.

Consider certain expenses incurred in a large hotel. The first question would be, What types of expenditure are incurred? These might be

- Staff wages
- Depreciation
- Consumable materials

The second question might be, Where and on what is this expenditure incurred? Here are three possible items:

- The wages paid to staff who run the laundry, which cleans the linen and clothing of guests, therefore these **staff wage expenses** are consumed in laundry costs.
- The **depreciation expense** is created by the initial capital expenditure on bedroom furniture and fittings, and is therefore consumed in bedroom costs.
- Part of the **cleaning material expenses** is created by the need to clean dishes and cooking appliances, therefore these cleaning material expenses are consumed in kitchen costs.

The distinction between what expenditure is generated and where it is consumed is the essential difference between expenditure and cost, and is indicative of the difference between the financial accounting perspective and the management accounting perspective. Let us look at more examples from a hotel business:

Expenditure incurred on	Cost consumed within	
Wages	Reception	(overtime for staff)
Food	Kitchen	(food ingredients)
Depreciation	Bedrooms	(furniture, TV, phone)
Insurance	Swimming-pool	(accident insurance)

The financial accountant is only really concerned with the classification of financial expenditure by generic type. The management accountant will need to sub- and cross-classify these expense headings according to where the expenses are consumed. The management accountant will identify specific **costs**. And the management accountant will take the distinction one step further. For what **specific purpose** in the business are these costs consumed? Let us take the above cost classifications and classify them further:

Cost consumed	Specific cost purpose
Wages in reception	Informing, directing and charging
Food	Meal ingredients for providing meals
Depreciation of bedroom furniture	Providing comfortable seating and bedding, entertainment and clothes storage
Swimming-pool insurance premium	Covering users for potential financial loss from disability or death

Taking the consumption of costs further, who or what ultimately benefits from the consumption of these costs? It is fairly obvious that all costs are ultimately consumed by the customers, in the quantity and quality of the product or service they are willing to pay for. In the hotel, costs are incurred while satisfying a range of needs of the guests.

The importance of identifying and measuring which types of costs are incurred, and how they are related to the ultimate consumers, can be useful in making decisions about the future operations of the business. Therefore, managers must ask, are the costs incurred necessary at the current level, or even at all, in order to provide the paying customer with what they want, or what they would appreciate? The more remote the expenditure from its ultimate consumption as a cost, the more difficult it is to answer this question. That is why the origin of expenditure should, if possible, be traced all the way through to its ultimate consumption. Here is one way to subclassify certain expenses as consumed costs on a ferry. The cost centres are the column headings and the expenses are listed down the left-hand side.

	Engine room £	Bar and restaurant £	Navigation £	Domestic £	Total £
Wages	80,000	65,000	100,000	50,000	295,000
Depreciation	95,000	25,000	35,000	28,000	183,000
Materials	84,000	45,000	12,000	10,000	151,000
Total	259,000	135,000	147,000	88,000	629,000

In financial accounting, the £629,000 would be classified as wages, depreciation and materials expenses. In management accounting, those same expenses would be cross-classified according to where and for what purpose those expenses were incurred. In other words, the management accountant would analyse the expenses in terms of where they were finally consumed as costs. In fact, the management accountant would need to further subclassify the costs in each department in order to establish exactly what, who, where, when, how and why expenditure has been incurred.

13.2 COST CONTROL AND ORGANIZATIONAL STRUCTURE

The main advantage of classifying costs is to control them and to make individuals responsible for them. A business organization may consist of many individuals, or only a few. The only way they can be managed effectively is to have some form of structure and some form of command and communications system. This command and communications system can come in a variety of forms to suit organizations of different types and sizes (Fig. 13.1).

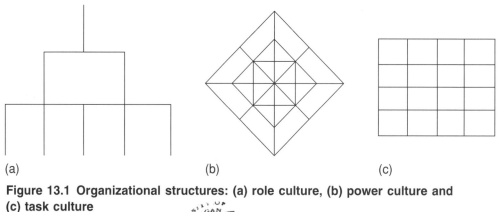

(a)   (b)   (c)

Figure 13.1 Organizational structures: (a) role culture, (b) power culture and (c) task culture

UNIVERSITY OF GLAMORGAN · PRIFYSGOL MORGANNWG · Learning Resources

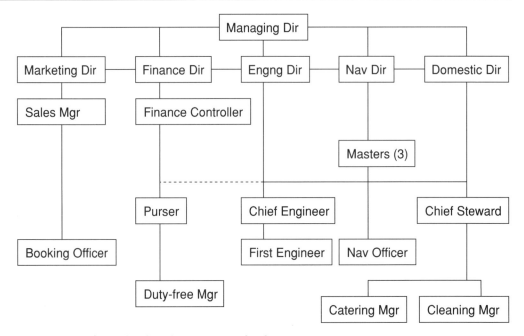

Figure 13.2 Organizational structure of a ferry company

The **role structure** is based on the concept of a bureaucracy as expounded by Max Weber in 1908 (Gerth, H.H. and Mills, C.W., eds, 1991, *From Max Weber: Essays in Sociology*, London: Routledge); it is particularly apt for a large formal organization which faces a stable environment. Here jobs are well defined and specialized, and communications and responsibilities are delineated clearly; this structure might be suitable for a vehicle-licensing centre. The **power structure**, or the 'web', is suitable for small organizations which are closely knit, where the power and communications network is concentric, and where the leader or 'spider' has direct control over all parts of the organization. Newly formed businesses often have this structure, but it is probably unsuitable after an organization reaches a certain critical size. The power structure might be appropriate in small to medium-sized hotels.

The **task or matrix** structure is best suited to an organization where management and control are on a two-dimensional plane. A good example of this would be a college of higher education, where the tasks are the courses, which are both managed administratively, and serviced by subject specialists. The course managers deal with timetabling and resource procurement and deployment, whereas subject managers manage the academic development of teaching staff, development of subject-based course material, and the procurement of learning resources on a subject basis.

The type of organization largely determines the level and scope of responsibility and control that various individuals have over costs. It is common for organizations to be structured in a way that combines the three pure structures above. In order to explain this further, Fig. 13.2 shows the organizational structure of the Channel Ferry Company, operating with three vessels from three ports.

Most of the command structure is hierarchical, but some relationships are less clear. Although the masters have direct command over navigational matters, the masters' direct control of other areas such as the engineering department, and the chief steward's catering and cleaning functions is more ambiguous. The purser is only responsible directly to his offshore superior, the financial controller, and has only an indirect line of communication with the master of the ship. However, the chief engineer, and the chief steward have dual command lines. They are responsible to their functional directors, who are probably responsible for recruitment, remuneration, training and significant capital expenditure, but more immediately responsible in day-to-day operational matters to the master of the ship, particularly so in the case of the engine room, where navigational requirements will determine engine usage. Where there is apparent dual authority, this need not lead to a conflict of interests, as long as the command lines relate to different functional areas of a department's responsibilities.

The relationship between cost control and organizational structure is very important. If a department takes responsibility for certain activities, then it should be held account-able for these activities. If we take the following classes of expenditure, who should he be held responsible for their control?

- Fuel and power costs
- Food and beverage costs
- Wages of engineering staff
- Depreciation of navigational equipment
- Cleaning costs

The answers depend upon how much responsibility or discretion the departmental managers have over the consumption of these costs. The fuel expenditure is generated by the chief engineer, who is responsible for the purchasing of diesel for the engine-room generation plants. However, the consumption of part of this power could be deemed the responsibility of the chief steward, as the power used would depend on the operational decisions taken at departmental level, such as the opening hours for the restaurant, how much cooking is to be done onboard, how many appliances will be used and for how long, etc.

If the chief engineer is responsible for staff recruitment, and for salary structures within the engine room, then the responsibility for wage costs within that department must lie with the chief engineer. If, however, each ferry's staffing levels and salary structures are centrally controlled by the engineering director, then responsibility for those costs is higher up in the organizational structure. With food and beverages, if responsibility for purchasing lies with the catering manager at the local port, and the menu is controlled at ship level, then these costs will be the sole responsibility of the catering manager report-ing to the chief steward.

Responsibility for depreciation costs of navigational equipment would depend on who had responsibility for buying the fixed assets for the bridge, and who decided on the depreciation policy. It is likely that this responsibility would lie at board level, decided upon by the engineering director, with reference to the financial director. Finally, with regard to the cleaning costs, it must be established how much responsibility the chief steward and/or their subordinates have for staffing, for purchasing of cleaning materials and for the level of their consumption. Many issues are involved in deciding where the responsibility falls for controlling costs, but if costs are to be controlled, it is important that all the responsible individuals and departments are identified and held accountable.

13.3 THE THREE MAIN COMPONENTS OF COST

The overall cost consumed in a department or business as a whole can be subclassified under three different components: **direct costs, indirect costs,** and **remote costs.** It is easiest to think of these three cost components in relation to producing a product, but they can also be applied to a service, perhaps a service in the tourism, leisure and hospitality industry. Consider the costs associated with the provision of indoor go-kart facilities.

Grand Prix Karting Ltd has set up an indoor complex on a greenfield site on an enterprise zone. The annual costs associated with the running of the operation are as follows:

- Rent and rates for land and building
- Depreciation on karts
- Wages of car handlers
- Wages of cashiers
- Wages of workshop mechanics
- Manager's salary
- Depreciation on buildings and fittings
- Fuel and consumable parts for karts
- Insurance on building
- Accident and indemnity insurance for racing
- Wages of cafe/bar staff
- Food and drinks costs

Before it is possible to classify these costs into the three main components, the main revenue-earning activities have to be identified. For a manufacturing organization this is usually clear-cut, as the revenue will be generated by selling a manufactured product or range of products. For a service business it is sometimes less clear, particularly if a range of services are carried out in the one organization, and where overlap may occur. In the above example it is fairly easy to see that the services offered are to race karts, to accommodate spectators, and to sell food and drink. We will assume that revenue is actually earned from racing and catering.

Costs directly associated with the generation of the two sources of revenue will be identified first, then costs only indirectly associated with the sources of revenue, and finally costs which are remotely associated with a specific source of revenue.

	Sources of revenue	
	Racing	Catering
Direct	Fuel and parts	Food and drink
	Handlers' wages	Catering staff wages
	Accident and indemnity insurance	
Indirect	Depreciation on karts	Telephone costs within cafe
	Wages of workshop mechanics	Cafe cleaning materials
		Metered power
Remote		Manager's salary
		Wages of cashiers
		Depreciation of buildings, etc.
		General power costs
		Rent and business rates

Deciding on whether the cost is directly or indirectly associated with the revenue-earning activity is quite difficult. Can it properly be decided that the depreciation on the karts is directly or indirectly associated, or is the decision based on judgement? One way of helping someone to make the appropriate judgement is to ask, if the activity level changed, would the costs change or **could they be changed** in response over the short term? The handlers' wages could be reduced if there were a reduction in the number of cars being raced, as less handling hours would be required immediately.

On the other hand, the depreciation charges on the karts would not be affected until the business decided to dispose of one or more of the vehicles. This decision would not be taken on a day-to-day basis, but would be considered over the longer term, once a clear trend had been established. It is, however, easier to decide which costs are remotely associated with any particular source of revenue. They are normally the establishment costs of the organization as a whole, such as rents, rates, buildings depreciation and maintenance, the salaries of the higher levels of management, and costs consumed in specialist functional areas such as accountancy, personnel and marketing. These remote costs cannot be related specifically to any revenue-earning function, only to the operation of the business as a whole.

Direct costs, indirect costs and remote costs can themselves be subdivided:

Direct costs: direct materials, direct labour, direct expenses
Indirect costs: costs which, although clearly identified with a particular revenue-earning function, are not directly determined by the level of activity within that function.
Remote costs: costs which cannot be associated closely with any particular revenue-generating function within the business, but which are incurred on behalf of the whole organization.

The direct costs are those costs, subdivided into materials, labour and expenses, that are easily associated with the revenue-generating activity, and may be directly influenced in the short term by the level of activity within a revenue-generating function. They are also known collectively as the **prime cost** of the product or service. All indirect costs are known in costing terminology as overheads, but it is possible to make the distinction between costs which, albeit indirectly, can be associated with a specific revenue-generating activity, and costs which cannot be so easily associated.

13.4 CALCULATING THE DIRECT MATERIAL COST

The calculation of the material cost of a product may be relatively straightforward or relatively complex, depending on the product or service concerned. Some products may have only one or two ingredients or components, such as a loaf of bread, or an ice-cream, where as others may have hundreds or even thousands of parts, such as an outboard motor for a powerboat. To illustrate the method for calculating the material cost in a product, consider a standard main meal served in an Angus Steakhouse. The standard ingredients and quantities are as follows:

Sirloin steak   (0.25 kilo)
Prawns   (0.125 kilo)
Avocado   (1/2)
Mixed salad   (1 carton)
Baked Potato   (one, medium size, 0.20 kilo)
Onion rings   (3 ready-battered)

These ingredients are bought in the following quantities at these prices:

Sirloin steak*   (£68 per 20-kilo box of assorted frozen cuts)
Prawns†   (£7.60 for a 5-kilo bag of frozen prawns)
Avocado   (£8.00 for a box of 25)
Mixed salad   (£12 for a case of 50)
Baked potato   (£2.50 for a 25-kilo sack)
Onion rings   (frozen bags at £2.40 for 60)

* The weight attributable to frozen water is 15%.
† The weight attributable to frozen water is 5%.

Chapter 6 introduced various methods of calculating the cost of stocks issued for production or sale. These methods included first in, first out (FIFO); last in, last out (LIFO); and the weighted average cost method (WAVCO). If a business has stocks, materials or parts which have been purchased at different prices in a period of inflation, then whichever method is used will determine the recognized cost of the materials issued, and therefore the profit earned on the sale of those products. For a review of these methods, refer back to Chapter 6.

It is possible to calculate the material cost of the above meal, assuming the ingredient stocks were all at the same price in the stores, or that they were valued at a weighted average cost. To calculate the cost per standard portion of the ingredient within the meal, the first step is to calculate how many standard portions of the ingredient can be obtained from each stock item. With the frozen provisions, begin by subtracting the water content from the gross weight of the stock item:

Sirloin steak   (20 kilos × 0.85) = 17 kilos
Prawns   (5 kilos × 0.95) = 4.75 kilos

The next step is to divide the net weight or quantity of the stock items by the standard quantity of the ingredient in each meal to ascertain the number of portions per standard stock item:

Sirloin steak   17/0.25   = 68 portions
Prawns   4.75/0.125 = 38 portions
Avocado   25/0.5   = 50 portions
Mixed salad   50/1   = 50 portions
Baked potato   25/0.20   = 125 portions
Onion rings   60/3   = 20 portions

Finally divide the cost per stock item (pence) by the number of portions to be obtained from each stock item:

Sirloin steak	6,800/68 portions	=	100p
Prawns	760/38 portions	=	20p
Avacado	800/50 portions	=	16p
Mixed salad	1,200/50 portions	=	24p
Baked potato	250/125 portions	=	2p
Onion rings	240/20 portions	=	12p
Total standard direct material cost of meal			174p

Therefore, in order to calculate the direct material cost of any product, it is necesary to establish the following information about that product:

1 Identify the ingredients, components or parts which constitute the final product or service.
2 Ascertain the quantities of each ingredient, component or part included in the final product or service.
3 Record the quantities or weights of these ingredients, components or parts in a single stock item as supplied.
4 Divide the cost of the stock item by the number of standard portions, units, or components in each stock item.

13.5 CALCULATING THE DIRECT LABOUR COST

Strictly the direct labour cost is the labour cost that is totally identifiable or consumed in the product itself. However, a restaurant doesn't sell a product on its own, it sells a complete service. We will continue with our example of the Angus Steakhouse to illustrate the calculation of direct labour costs. The following information is available:

Staff wage rates per hour	£
Chef	8.00
Assistant chefs	5.00
Washing-up staff	3.00
Waiting staff	4.00

Hours worked on a standard batch of meals		Hours
Chef	(1 person × 6 h)	6.00
Assistant chef	(3 people × 8 h)	24.00
Washing-up staff	(2 people × 4 h)	8.00
Waiting staff	(4 people × 5 h)	20.00

The number of meals served varies throughout the week, but from past experience the average numbers of meals served in a week are as follows:

Mon	Tues	Wed	Thurs	Fri	Sat	Sun	Total
40	45	60	70	120	140	85	560

The average number of meals served per standard night of the week is 560/7 = 80. Then, for any given night, we can calculate the total direct wages paid to staff directly associated with the provision of meals:

	Hours		Hourly rate	Cost £	Cost per meal* £
Chef	6.00	×	8.00	48.00	0.60
Assistant chef	24.00	×	5.00	120.00	1.50
Washing-up staff	8.00	×	3.00	24.00	0.30
Waiting staff	20.00	×	4.00	80.00	1.00
Total direct wage cost per batch of meals				272.00	3.40

* Cost per meal = cost/80

The direct labour cost in each standard meal, based on a standard night, is £3.40 per meal. The various components of that cost are distributed between the chefs' wages, serving staff wages and washing-up staff costs. The other direct cost consumed in the provision of a meal is the power cost of preparing and cooking. This can be calculated and related directly to each batch of meals, but as it may not be possible to separate the kitchen power usage from the establishment as a whole, all the power costs in this example will be included within the broad category of overheads.

A good example of a direct expense which can be directly related to a product or service is a unit-based franchise fee, a royalty or a commission. For example, a fast-food franchisee may have to pay a small percentage fee to the franchiser for every meal sold under the franchise agreement.

13.6 ALLOCATION AND APPORTIONMENT OF OVERHEAD COSTS

We will continue with the Angus Steakhouse example, and identify those costs which are defined as overheads. Looking at the rest of the costs consumed within the restaurant business, they are either indirectly associated with the main activity, providing meals, or remotely associated with it. Here are the weekly overheads:

	£
Rent	100
Rates	70
Insurance	45
Manager's salary	300
Telephone	15
Power	35
Wages for bookkeeper, clerks	107
Entertainment licence	28
	700

These expenses cannot be directly related to the provision of the food itself, except for that part of the power consumed in the kitchen, as indicated earlier. The rest of these costs are consumed within the establishment as a whole and do not depend on the level of activity. For example, if demand for meals were to rise or fall significantly, most of these costs would be unaffected in the short term. So what can be done with these costs? The total direct cost of a standard steak meal is as follows:

	£
Direct materials	1.74
Direct labour	3.40
Prime cost	5.14

The prime cost is the cost of providing a standard meal in a standard week to a customer, or is it? This depends on the purpose of costing. The purpose of costing is to identify what costs are consumed and where, in order to control and monitor them. There is, however, another possible purpose of calculating costs, and that is to use them as a guide to pricing, and to estimate the profitability of a product in advance. If this is the case, it is necessary to assign the overhead costs of the establishment to the product or service provided, in addition to the direct or prime costs. If the selling price were based on the direct cost only, the business would fail to **recover** the overhead costs incurred during the period, and would make a loss on selling the product. How then are the overhead costs assigned to the product?

The distinction between allocation and apportionment

Allocation and apportionment are traditionally used in management accounting for the assignation of overheads to departments or to products and services. Allocation usually takes place when the overhead is indirectly associated with a department, product or service, but can be objectively assigned to it, such as power costs where separately metered to a department, or where wages are for staff that exclusively work in a particular department or in one activity area. Another example is where specific insurance cover can be related to a particular activity or department, such as insurance on kitchen appliances. Where overhead costs are, to all intents and purposes, only remotely related to any one area of productive activity or any single department, the accountant has to use a measure of subjectivity in assigning the overhead on some appropriate basis. This is known as apportionment of overheads.

In the example of the steakhouse, as in many small organizations which produce a single product in one department, the only basis for assigning overheads is to assign them en bloc to the product or service provided. The average weekly overhead costs are £700. In an average week the restaurant provides 560 meals, so it is reasonable to say that £700/560 = £1.25 must be recovered per meal. This is known as the **overhead recovery rate** (ORR). The restaurant can now estimate that the full or **absorption** cost of the meal is as follows:

	£
Direct material costs	1.74
Direct labour costs	3.40
Prime cost	5.14
Overhead recovery rate per meal	1.25
Full absorption cost per meal	6.39

This full cost indicates to the management of the restaurant that if the **costs remain the same** and the **same quantity of meals are sold each week**, a price of £6.39 per meal must be charged to recover all costs. The key point here is that the full absorption cost per meal depends on an accurate estimate of the costs and the level of activity. If costs change through different purchase prices and wage rates, through menu changes or working practices, then the total cost per meal will change. It is important that estimates of costs are reliable and up to date if the profitability of the business is to be properly maintained.

The other key point is the level of activity. Assuming that all costs remain the same, but the weekly number of meals provided increases to 700 per week, what would be the full absorption cost of a standard meal?

	£
Direct material costs	1.74
Direct labour costs	3.40
Prime cost	5.14
Overhead recovery rate per meal	1.00*
Full absorption cost per meal	6.14

* The overhead recovery rate per meal is now £700/700 = £1.00 per meal.

The full cost is now £0.25 less than before, and the only reason is that the overhead costs are being 'spread' over a greater number of meals, reducing the overhead recovery rate needed from each individual meal. This is a fundamental point in management accounting and must be thoroughly understood.

13.7 CALCULATING THE TOTAL COST OF A PRODUCT IN A MULTIPRODUCT, MULTIDEPARTMENTAL BUSINESS

The allocation and apportionment of overheads needs to be calculated in a more sophisticated way if a business has more than one productive department, or if it makes a variety of products. A business is involved making harnesses of exterior fairy lights for the pub and entertainment trade. The business has two departments. The financial data based on previous experience is as follows:

	Wire crimping	Fitting
Materials		
(20 m of cable at £0.25 a cable)	£5.00	
(20 bulbs and seats at £0.35 a bulb)		£7.00
Direct labour		
Hours per harness	None	
Hours per harness		0.50
Wage rate per hour		£5.00
Machine hours per harness	0.10	
Productive capacity		
Max machine hours per month	750	
Max labour hours		6,250
Operating capacity	2/3	80%
Total overhead costs		
Indirect costs	£100,000	£120,000
Remote costs		£300,000*

* These are centralized administration, selling and distribution costs, and establishment costs for the month.

If the objective is to establish a **full cost** per harness produced, it is necessary to calculate the following:

	£
Direct material cost per harness	X
Direct labour cost per harness	X
Prime cost	X
A proportion of overhead cost per harness	X
Total absorption cost per harness	X

The direct costs are fairly simple to ascertain. It is the overheads that present the problem to accountants. The indirect costs are already allocated to each department. Indirect costs are those which can be clearly identified with a specific department or even with a product or service. These would include the wages of supervisors, departmental maintenance staff costs and metered power costs.

However, centralized or remote costs need to be apportioned to the departments on an appropriate basis. How this is done will depend on their nature. If some of these costs include canteen costs, then an appropriate basis might be the total number of staff employed in each department. Factory rent might be more appropriately based on the area of each department as a proportion of the total. The key to this is to decide what creates, consumes or **drives** the cost. Assume the centralized costs are mainly driven by the area occupied by each department:

Wire crimping area (m²)	Fitting area (m²)
20,000	12,000

The remote costs would then be apportioned to each department on this basis:

	Wire crimping £	Fitting £
Indirect costs	100,000	120,000
Remote costs*	187,500	112,500
Total overhead	287,500	232,500

* Wire crimping department: (20,000/32,000) × 300,000
  Fitting department: (12,000/32,000) × 300,000

The next step is to relate this overhead to the productive capacity of each department in an appropriate way. The reason for this is to attempt to **recover** the overhead costs in a charge made for each productive hour worked on the product. What is the **maximum** productive capacity of each department in a month?

	Wire crimping	Fitting
Labour hours		6,250
Machine hours	750	

Note that where a department is heavily automated, it is more appropriate to use machine hours as a basis for expressing productive capacity. The normal capacity of the departments is as follows:

Wire crimping	Fitting
750 h × 2/3 = 500 h	6,250 h × 0.8 = 5,000 h

If the productive hours per month are divided into the total overhead to recover per month, it gives the amount of overhead that should be charged per hour worked in each department:

Wire crimping
£287,500/500 h = £575 per machine hour worked

Fitting
£232,500/5,000 h = £46.50 per direct labour hour worked

The estimated full cost of the fairy-light harness may now be compiled, by preparing a product cost structure report:

Product cost structure (fairy-light harness)

	£	£
Direct material costs		
Wire crimping	5.00	
Fitting	7.00	
Direct labour costs		
Wire crimping	nil	
Fitting (5.00 × 0.5)	2.50	
Prime cost		14.50
Overhead costs:		
Wire crimping (575 × 0.10)	57.50	
Fitting (46.50 × 0.50)	23.25	
Total overhead cost		80.75
Total absorption cost		95.25

The management of this business would then need to add a profit loading to this full cost in order to charge a price that covers the full cost and yields an acceptable profit margin. Then the management could ascertain the total profitability of each type of product, and obtain useful information on the management and control of costs by product and by department. But these total costs are highly dependent on the accurate collection and recording of internal cost information, which requires reports and calculations from design engineers and work-study experts to ensure that the figures obtained are valid and reliable. The major area of controversy, however, is the apportionment of overheads. This is the area of greatest subjectivity, as the choice of apportionment basis, and the determination of the productive capacity of a department, are matters of pure judgement on the part of management.

The total cost calculated for a product can appear very different depending on which judgements prevail, and which methods are adopted. Following on from this, a great deal of caution must be exercised when using information from the product cost structure, particularly when it is rigidly applied as a basis for decisions on how to price a product, whether to accept an order from a customer, whether the product should be discontinued or bought in from outside. These types of decision rely on information presented and calculated in an entirely different way; it is examined more thoroughly in Chapter 15.

SUMMARY

1 **There is a difference between cost and expense.**

2 **The consumption of costs is controlled at various levels of the organizational structure.**

3 **Costs can be broken down into three main components: direct, indirect and remote.**

4 **Direct costs comprise direct materials, direct labour and direct expenses.**

5 **Indirect and remote costs are known as overheads.**

6 **Overheads are allocated and apportioned to a product or service.**

7 **A product cost structure report is prepared for a product or service.**

ASSESSMENT

MULTIPLE-CHOICE QUESTIONS

Question 1
Which one of the following statements most accurately sums up the difference between expenses and costs?

A Costs are the detailed breakdown of expenses by item.
B Costs are expenses analysed by what, who, where, when and why they are incurred by the organization.
C All costs are expenses related to productive activities.
D Expenses are payments explained by generic type, whereas costs are payments explained by location or department.

Question 2
Which one of the following costs might be outside the direct responsibility of a hotel general manager who reports to a regional director of an international chain of hotels?

A Staff costs
B Fresh food and provision costs
C Depreciation of bedroom furniture
D Theft and leakage

Question 3
Which one of the following costs might be classified as a remote cost in a pottery business?

A Cost of clay and glaze consumed
B Wages of the turning supervisor
C Broken pots and unusable clay
D Rent of factory

Question 4
What is the prime cost of providing a guided tour of a slate mine? The following costs are consumed in a month:

	£
Depreciation on the quarry cage	1,500
Wages of the cashier	440
Wages of guide (paid per tour)	720
Electricity for activated laser lighting	1,100
Royalties to actor for voice-over	30
Power used in moving quarry cage	800
Cost of candles, slates and other consumables used in demonstrations	50
Salary of centre manager	460
General insurance premiums	1,100

A £720
B £770
C £1,570
D £2,670

Question 5

A chip manufacturer for computer games has two production departments. Each department produces a games chip as the main component of a games cartridge. What would be the full cost per chip based on the following information for the last four weeks?

	Department 1 £	Department 2 £
Direct costs		
Materials	10,000	15,000
Labour	30,000	40,000
Royalties (£5,000)		
Overheads allocated and apportioned	25,000	20,000
Labour hours worked	2,000	400
Machine hours worked	400	4,000
Total chips produced	200,000	

A 47.5p
B 50.0p
C 72.5p
D 75.5p

EXERCISES

Exercise 1

A troupe of entertainers have a manager. Two of the troupe are highly skilled acrobats, the other three are dancers. The dancers are paid less per hour than the other two. The manager wishes to charge out the group for special outdoor and indoor occasions, on an hourly basis. All performances require both of the acrobats but only two of the three dancers. The information for the troupe is as follows:

	Acrobats	Dancers
Working hours per week	40	45
Minimum practising time	55%	76%
Holidays per year	2 weeks on half pay + bonus of £50 a week	2 weeks on full pay
Wage rate per hour	£15	£10
Food and accommodation allowance per week	£140	£80
Accident indemnity insurance per week	£20	£16

Required

Determine the hourly charge-out for the whole troupe while they are commissioned for entertainments if a profit of cost + 50% were required on the troupe's activity.

Exercise 2

A small business employing eight people makes professional specification wooden baseball bats. There are two productive departments, the sawing department and the shaping and finishing department. The full information is as follows:

	Sawing	Shaping and finishing
People employed	3	5
Hourly wage rate	£6.00	£7.50
Working hours per week	40	40
Paid holidays (weeks)	2	4
Christmas bonus	£60	£84
Time per bat (min)	30	48
Material cost	£1.50	£0.25

The factory works normally at full capacity, keeping unsold bats in store. Sales of bats in the month were 800 at a price of £24.95. Total overheads for the month were estimated at £8,500.

Required

(a) Calculate the full cost per bat produced.
(b) Calculate the total profit for the month.
(c) Calculate the amount and value of the closing stock.

Exercise 3

A factory making garden settees has two production centres and three service centres. The following estimates relate to June 19x3:

	Production centres		Service centres		
	A	B	1	2	3
	£000	£000	£000	£000	£000
Allocated costs	45	35	160	71	34
Productive capacity:					
Machine hours		13,355			
Labour hours	42,290	7,250			
Product information					
Material usage (m)	4.50	1.50			
Material cost per metre	£1.00	£1.50			
Labour hours per unit	2.00	0.50			
Hourly wage rate	£3.50	£5.50			
Machine hours per unit	nil	1.75			

Service centre 1 is a personnel department which services all centres; service centre 2 is a production and maintenance-only canteen; and service centre 3 is a production maintenance department. The apportionment of the allocated overhead costs from the service centres to the productive centres is to be carried out on the following basis:

	Allocation of overheads				
	A	B	1	2	3
	%	%	%	%	%
Service centre 1	55	20	0	15	10
Service centre 2	45	45	0	0	10
Service centre 3	60	40	0	0	0

Required

Calculate the full cost of producing one garden settee.

Exercise 4

A local authority has borrowed £2.0 million at an interest rate of 7% per annum and has built a leisure and sports complex. The estimated annual operating overheads are as follows:

	£000
General establishment costs exc interest	35
Chemicals for swimming-pools	6
Provisions for snack bar	20
Provisions for licensed bar	16

The centre is operated on an activity centre basis, where responsibility for certain costs and revenues lies with activity centre supervisors. Further information is as follows:

Centre number	Activity	Staff salaries £000	Capital cost £000	Estimated revenue £000	Area occupied m²
1	Pool 1	18.30	600	50	2,500
2	Pool 2	10.75	250	25	1,500
3	Gymnasium	8.10	200	25	3,000
4	Snack bar	11.35	200	80	1,500
5	Licensed bar	9.45	250	20	800
6	Admin	34.05	500	nil	700
		92.00	2,000	200	10,000

The following items have been agreed:

1 Depreciation costs for the building should be based on 10% of the capital cost of the building, apportioned between the activity centres in accordance with the capital cost per centre.
2 Interest on capital borrowed should be apportioned to activity centres on the basis of the capital cost per centre.
3 Establishment costs should be apportioned according to the area that each activity centre occupies.
4 The costs associated with administration should be allocated to activity centres 1 to 5 on the basis of the estimated revenues to be made from each centre.
5 The surplus or deficit made from the snack bar and the licensed bar is to be apportioned over activity centres 1 to 3 in line with the revenues generated from each one.

Required

(a) Prepare profit statements for centres 1 to 3, after allocating and apportioning all the direct costs, the overheads and the costs or surpluses from centres 4 to 6.
(b) Calculate the overall profitability, or otherwise, of the municipal leisure and sports centre.

CHAPTER 14

Pricing a product or service

OBJECTIVES

- **Make pricing decisions based on available cost information.**
- **Make pricing decisions based on market conditions.**
- **Make pricing decisions to optimize profit, based on cost and market information combined.**
- **Make pricing decisions in special situations.**

INTRODUCTION

Part 2 of this book is mainly about accounting for decision making, and how management accountants provide the necessary information for management to make appropriate decisions in the interest of the investors for whom they act as stewards.

Investors in business, particularly shareholders, are interested mainly in the profitability of their investment. Profitability is a function of revenue generation and cost control. Traditionally management accountants or 'cost accountants' have been primarily concerned with the second of the above functions of profit, namely the recording, measurement and control of costs. Clearly revenue generation is as important as cost control in determining profit. Indeed, compared with cost control, it can offer greater flexibility with respect to profitability in certain situations. The implications of revenue generation must therefore play an important part in the considerations of the management accountant, if the information provided to management is to be really useful. Following on from this, as revenue generation is a direct function of **price** multiplied by the **quantity** sold, the management accountant should be involved in the pricing policy of the business, along with other functional experts such as those in the marketing and sales departments.

14.1 PRICING BASED ON COST DATA

Chapter 13 analysed costs by type, whether they were directly related to productive activity or whether they were overheads. The chapter also covered how it was possible to build up a full cost for a product, absorbing both the direct costs and the overhead costs in some appropriate way, in order to ensure that all costs may be recovered. In many industries, including the tourism, leisure and hospitality sector, this full cost calculation is traditionally used as the main method of testing the viability of their business proposals.

The full cost method is primarily used in business planning, in order to ascertain if the cost structure of the business can support a price that the customer may be willing to pay, while allowing an acceptable level of profitability to those that are intending to invest in the business. This technique is known as the **cost-plus** method of pricing. It essentially involves calculating the total cost of a product or service by absorbing all costs, including overheads, and adding an 'acceptable' profit margin on top. We will now look at this method in relation to pricing hotel bedrooms. The Faroway Hotel has the following internal accounting data available for a particular year, excluding restaurant and bar data:

	£
Building and establishment costs (inc depn)	11,000
Staff costs	145,000
Direct materials	10,000
Insurances	15,000
Interest payments	12,312
Rates	5,000
Telephones, postage and entertainment licences	2,000
Total costs to recover from beds	200,312

There are a total of 30 bedrooms, 20 singles and 10 doubles. It is estimated that throughout the year they should be 70% occupied on average, the double rooms need to be 1.5 times the price of the single rooms, and a net profit of cost plus 25% is required. What price should be charged for each type of bedroom, assuming a 365-day year? These are the sort of questions a hotel proprietor would be interested in, and here is a method which logically determines a pricing policy, taking these factors into account.

Step 1
What revenue is required for the year? To cover costs and make a 25% profit requires

$$£200,312 \times 1.25 = £250,390$$

Step 2
How many beds per night are occupied on average for both types of bedroom, given a 70% occupancy rate?

$$\text{Singles} = 20 \times 0.7 = 14$$

$$\text{Doubles} = 10 \times 0.7 = 7$$

Step 3
Construct a simple relationship between the desired revenue for the year and the number of occupied rooms of both types. The required annual price for the single rooms can be denoted as P_s, and the required annual price for the double rooms as P_d. An expression can then be formulated:

$$7P_d + 14P_s = £250,390 \tag{1}$$

This means that 7 double rooms multiplied by the price of those rooms for a year plus 14 single rooms multiplied by the price of these rooms for a year, should total £250,390 in order to achieve the objective. We also know that

$$P_d = 1.5P_s \tag{2}$$

Equations (1) and (2) can be solved simultaneously in the formal way, or by simplifying equation (1) by rewriting P_d in terms of P_s. It is possible to say that

$$10.5P_s + 14P_s = £250,390$$

which means

$$24.5P_s = £250,390$$

giving the price of a single room per year as

$$£250,390/24.5 = £10,220$$

Therefore the price of a single room per night is

$$£10,220/365 = £28$$

Therefore the price of the double room per night is

$$£28 \times 1.5 = £42$$

This can be checked by examining the annual revenue:

$$(P_d \text{ per night} \times \text{occupied rooms each night} \times 365)$$
$$+ (P_s \text{ per night} \times \text{occupied rooms each night} \times 365)$$
$$= (£28 \times 14 \times 365) + (£42 \times 7 \times 365)$$
$$= £143,080 + £107,310$$
$$= £250,390$$

This technique is useful where more than one different type of product or service exists and where prices need to reflect this, and where the costs cannot be allocated or apportioned directly to bedrooms, making it difficult to produce a product or service cost structure per unit.

An oversimplification of this cost-plus method which has been used in the hotel industry for many years has been the **rule of a thousand**. This rule states that for every £1,000 spent on the construction and furnishing per room (the capital cost of buildings and furnishings), on average £1 should be charged per room. This method is supposed to take into account the prevailing operating conditions and financial structures in the average hotel. This method is seriously flawed as no room or hotel is an average, and the relationship between investment costs and prices cannot always hold true.

Like most HTL business, the hotel business is extremely cyclical in nature, and financial performance is particularly sensitive to changes in economic and social conditions. So it is safe to say that the rule of a thousand will not be valid in any meaningful way over a wide range of establishments or for any length of time. The **Hubbart formula** is a more sophisticated but still relatively crude method used in the United States by the American Hotel and Motel Association. Here is an example. The following data is available for the 40-room Wardsworth Residential Hotel in the Lake District:

	£
Ordinary share capital + reserves	162,000
£1.00 debentures (10%)	100,000
Selling and distribution costs	8,000
Administration costs	5,000
Direct costs of food and drink	12,600
Bar and restaurant staff costs	12,900
Finance costs (100,000 × 0.10)	10,000
Bedroom staff costs and indirect materials	9,100

The desired profit after tax on shareholders' funds is 15%. Taxation is estimated to be 40%. The restaurant and bars are allocated and apportioned with 30% of the administration costs. Selling and distribution costs are centralized, as are finance costs, and the desired operating profit from the bars and restaurant is the total cost + 20%. Average occupancy is expected to be 75%. The Hubbart formula might work something like this:

	£
Desired net profit on capital employed (162,000 × 15%)	24,300
Add taxation (40/60) × 24,300	16,200
Net profit before tax	40,500
Add finance costs	10,000
Net profit before interest and tax	50,500
Add selling and distribution costs	8,000
Total operating profit for whole hotel	58,500
Operating profit required from bars and restaurant	5,400
Total operating profit required from rooms	53,100
Operating costs for rooms	12,600
Annual revenue required from rooms	65,700

The operating profit based on the cost-plus method for the bars and restaurant is calculated like this:

	£
Direct costs of bars and restaurant	12,600
Allocated and apportioned overheads:	
Staff costs	12,900
Admin costs (5,000 × 0.3)	1,500
	27,000
Profit based on cost plus 20%	5,400
Revenue from bars and restaurants	32,400

The operating costs for the rooms are calculated like this:

	£
Staff costs and indirect materials	9,100
Allocated and apportioned overheads:	
Admin costs (5,000 × 0.7)	3,500
Accommodation operating costs:	12,600

If £65,700 is to be taken from (12 × 0.75) rooms in a year, i.e. 9 rooms per night for 365 days, then the required price per room per night will need to be

$$\tfrac{1}{9}(£65,700/365) = £20$$

As you can see, the Hubbart formula starts from the required rate of return on the owner's capital employed, and works back to the total revenue that needs to be generated from the accomodation.

Where a product or service cost structure is established, as in the fairy lights example of Chapter 13, it is a relatively simple matter to build a desired profit margin into the unit cost in order to reach a full cost price which will guarantee a specific level of profit. In the restaurant trade, where the major activity of the organization is providing food and beverages, pricing policies might be more crude. In this type of business the only cost that can be assigned directly to the product objectively is the direct material cost, because the direct labour costs of cooking and serving the meals would in practice be treated as an overhead. The pricing policy for such a business is to establish a direct materials cost-plus policy, in order to set a price that covers all overheads and provides an acceptable profit margin.

The following information is available for the Happy Doughnut mobile cafe. The only products sold are doughnuts and coffees. The direct material cost is 10p for each doughnut, and 5p for each coffee. Total overheads such as power, van depreciation, etc., are £5,160 per annum. The owner has invested £40,000 in the business and requires an annual rate of return of 30%. If the business is estimated to sell 600 coffees a week and 400 doughnuts, and coffees are to be sold at double the price of doughnuts, what price should be charged for each to attain the required rate of return in the year, assuming the cafe operates 52 weeks of the year?

The first step is to calculate the direct costs of the total products provided:

$$(600 \times 52) \times £0.05 + (400 \times 52) \times £0.10 = £1,560 + £2,080$$
$$= £3,640$$

The next step is to establish the required sales revenue to be generated in order to cover direct costs, overheads and profit:

$$£3,640 + £5,160 + (£40,000 \times 0.30) = £3,640 + £5,160 + £12,000$$
$$= £20,800$$

Then to find the price per item, where the price of a coffee is twice the price of a doughnut, the following expression may be constructed:

$$(600 \times 52)P_c + (400 \times 52)P_d = £20,800$$

where P_c = price of coffee
P_d = price of doughnuts

As a doughnut is half the price of a coffee, $P_d = 0.5P_c$ we can rewrite the expression in terms of P_c

$$(600 \times 52)P_c + (400 \times 52)(P_c/2) = £20,800$$

$$(31,200 + 10,400)P_c = £20,800$$

$$41,600P_c = £20,800$$

$$P_c = £0.50$$

Therefore, the price of a coffee needs to be 50p, and the price of a doughnut needs to be 25p.

Quite often in the catering business, direct costs per type of product are not even estimated on an item-by-item basis. This is often impractical, particularly for a restaurant providing a *table d'hôte* menu with a wide variety of choice. The catering industry normally charges a bill for food and drink at one sitting relating to one customer at a time. Often such a business will estimate the total number of 'covers' per period and the average value of this, as this is easily available from past till receipts and bill analysis. In this case the price charged is based on a gross profit percentage calculated in a similar way to the Hubbart formula. Here is an example.

The Upper Crust restaurant is financed by £200,000, upon which the owners require a 20% annual return. Labour and overheads are £80,000, and the total covers based on past data are 20,000 a year at an average cover price of £12. If it is assumed that demand, costs and prices for the restaurant will remain constant into the following year, an average gross profit percentage margin for this restaurant can be calculated, from which a material cost-plus policy may be obtained:

$$\text{Net profit to achieve} = £200,000 \times 0.20$$
$$= £40,000$$

$$\text{Estimated gross profit to achieve} = \text{net profit} + \text{labour and overheads}$$
$$= £40,000 + £80,000$$
$$= £120,000$$

$$\text{Anticipated sales turnover} = 20,000 \times £12$$
$$\text{(based on past data)} = £240,000$$

$$\text{Gross profit margin} = 120,000/240,000$$
$$= 50\%$$

The conclusion to be drawn from this is that, **on average**, if the desired return is to be achieved, the price of the items on a bill should be made up in the following way, perhaps best illustrated by taking a cover bill from one table during the year:

	£
Bill total exc VAT	100.00
Gross profit (50%)	50.00 (from above)
Direct material cost	50.00

Therefore, if it is to be based on direct material cost plus a percentage, the pricing policy in this case must be to charge cost + 100%, or double the material cost, to arrive at the selling price. On average, for every £50 spent on food and beverage purchases, the policy to adopt is to charge £100 to the customer, in order to reach the desired net profit. Although a simple average is useful as a guide, the single-margin approach will not take sufficient account of products and services which are very different within the same menu selection, and there may be a need to apply a mix of profit margins, taking into account other factors apart from cost alone. The influence and importance of these other factors are covered in the next section.

The cost-plus method is a good method of establishing that the price decided upon will recover all the business's costs, given that all assumptions on cost and activity levels are met, and more important, that the methods used for estimating costs and activity levels are valid and reliable.

14.2 PRICING DECISIONS BASED ON MARKET CONDITIONS

Cost-plus pricing is really a planning technique rather than an operational decision-making technique. This is because most businesses in the tourism, leisure and hospitality sector rarely rely on full cost data to decide the current price to charge for their products or services. It is usually much more important to charge the price that 'the market will bear', as it is often known. The full-cost technique can then be applied to see if this obtainable price covers the full cost of the product or service, and how much profit can be made at this price.

It is beyond the scope of this textbook to examine in detail the different types of markets in which businesses may operate. But it is important to realize that if a business is in some way providing a unique product or service, then the scope to charge a price based on cost plus a desired percentage is greater than in a market where the product or service is similar to those provided by many other suppliers. A good example of this would be to look at cafe or bar prices in a Mediterranean seaside resort, where there are a dozen or so very similar establishments within a radius of one kilometre, selling drinks and standard dishes at almost exactly the same prices, and compare this with a golf course operating on an island where no other golf courses exist. The essential difference between businesses in these two extreme types of market-place relates to the power that each business has to charge a price that it wants to charge. The business with little or no competition is known as a **price maker**, whereas the business in a very competitive and crowded market is known as a **price taker**.

Tourism, leisure and hospitality businesses can often be in situations where their pricing decisions must take adequate account of what their competitors are doing, and increasingly businesses should try to anticipate their competitors more often than they have to respond. The same goes for their approach to other key actors in the external environment, e.g. the government. Prices are probably the most significant factor affecting the quantity of products or services **demanded**. At all prices the total quantity of a product or service demanded will be determined by

- Current disposable incomes
- Taxation
- Advertising
- Fashions and tastes
- Weather
- General consumer confidence
- Demand for substitute and complementary goods and services*

* For example, if the demand for holidays in Spain increases due to price changes or due to any of the above factors, there may be a resultant change in demand for British holidays. If there is a reduction in demand for touring caravans due to price changes or any other factor, there will be a corresponding reduction in demand for holiday caravan sites.

Here are examples of pricing decisions that may be taken as a result of market conditions rather than cost pressure:

1 Increasing the price following a successful advertising campaign which creates a great deal of consumer demand.
2 Selling a price at cost or below cost to attract customers into a retail establishment, where they may be encouraged to purchase other products or services on which higher profits can be made.

3 Increasing prices or reducing prices because your direct competitors have done so, for whatever reason.

4 Increasing the price of your product because the demand for it has increased due to a reduction in the price of a good or service that complements your product. If rail travel to a seaside resort fell in price, there might be increased demand for hotel accommodation at that resort.

5 Charging higher or lower prices because the weather was affecting the demand for the tourist attraction.

There are any number of factors other than cost which can determine the pricing policy of a business, all of which relate to competitive market conditions and the prevailing economic climate. It is the duty of capable management to anticipate or at least respond quickly to developments in their business's external environment, which either pose a serious threat to the business, or which present real opportunities for that business. Stimulus for such speedy response is not likely to come from internal cost information alone.

If a business is to understand how to price its products or services appropriately, it needs to understand the demand for these goods and services at various prices and in various market conditions. Demand for a product or service is normally inversely related to the price charged for that product or service, all other things being equal. Therefore, if quantity demanded on the x-axis of a graph is plotted graphically against price on the y-axis, the resulting function is normally **downward sloping** (Fig. 14.1). The reason for this can be explained in two fundamental ways:

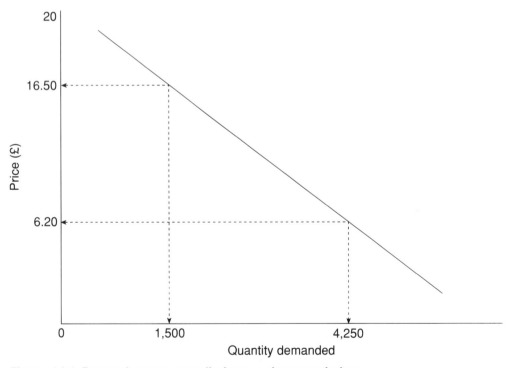

Figure 14.1 Demand curves usually have a downward slope

Income effect: if an individual has a certain level of disposable income and wants a certain product or service, a fall in the price of that product or service will mean that the same disposable income of this individual will be enough to purchase more of the product than was previously possible.

Substitution effect: as more and more of a product is consumed, the less the extra enjoyment, satisfaction or marginal utility is to be derived from consuming additional quantities of this product. Where opportunity exists to buy some other product or service which yields greater additional enjoyment or satisfaction, the less someone will be prepared to pay for more of the original product.

The extent to which the demand for a product is responsive to the price charged for that product or service is known as **the price elasticity of demand**. The price elasticity of demand for a product or service can have a significant impact and influence on pricing decisions, and the price–demand relationship of a business's products or services should be investigated by the use of appropriate market research techniques. This may be explained by considering three bus routes for which the following information is available:

Route 1

Ticket price	Passengers carried	Total sales
£5	40	£200
£7	25	£175

Route 2

Ticket price	Passengers carried	Total sales
£4.00	45	£180
£6.00	30	£180

Route 3

Ticket price	Passengers carried	Total sales
£5.50	44	£242
£6.50	38	£247

In all three cases the quantity demanded is established at two different prices. The following observations can be made:

1 On route 1 charging a higher price yields lower sales in pounds than charging the lower price.
2 On route 2 charging a higher price yields the same sales in pounds as charging the lower price.
3 On route 3 charging a higher price yields higher sales in pounds than charging the lower price.

This leads to the following conclusions:

1 The demand for tickets on route 1 is **elastic** over this range of quantities and prices.
2 The demand for tickets on route 2 is **unitary** over this range of prices.
3 The demand for tickets on route 3 is **inelastic** over this range of prices.

The definition of elasticity is as follows:

1 If the change in sales value moves in the opposite direction to the change in price, then demand over that range can be described as **elastic**.

2 If the change in sales value doesn't change between two different prices, then demand over that range can be described as **unitary**.

3 If the change in sales value moves in the same direction as the change in price, then demand over that range can be described as **inelastic**.

The extent to which these conditions hold true over the relevant range of possible prices will be a very important determinant of pricing policy. Taking the three bus routes, what are the differences in the costs of running the bus at different ticket prices and with different numbers of passengers? The answer is very little if any! If this is true, then the business can make the greatest profits by maximizing its sales revenue. If it has knowledge of the demand for its services at different ticket prices, it would maximize its profit by charging the following prices on each route:

Route 1	Route 2	Route 3
£5.00	£6.00 or £4.00	£6.50

In fact, as will be shown in the next example, the best price to charge on route 2 to maximize revenue will be somewhere between £4 and £6.

There are many non-manufacturing businesses, particularly in the tourism, leisure and hospitality industry, where a similar cost structure holds true. Here are some examples:

- Bicycle hire
- Fairground rides
- Most scheduled travel services
- Golf courses or pitch and putt
- Cinema and theatres
- Football clubs

All of these businesses have a certain cost structure which they would have to maintain in order to offer an appropriate level of service. There is relatively little scope to alter the cost structure in response to the level of demand for these services. Take the golf course. All staff, such as the professional, the steward, and the greenkeeper, would have to be paid whether or not there were a hundred or a thousand golfers a day. Given this is the situation for many service-based businesses, the main objective in pricing policy is to maximize sales revenue over a relevant range of prices and quantities demanded.

Returning to the concept of the downward-sloping demand curve, let us examine a football club with a maximum crowd capacity of 30,000 and a forthcoming Premiership game on Saturday. The data available from previous games is shown below and plotted as a graph in Fig. 14.2.

Price of ticket	Size of crowd	Gate receipts
£10	10,000	£100,000
£9	12,000	£108,000
£8	14,000	£112,000
£7	16,000	£112,000
£6	18,000	£108,000
£5	20,000	£100,000

Figure 14.3 plots the revenue function (gate receipt = ticket price × number of tickets) versus the ticket price; this produces a parabola or dome-shaped curve where the maximum revenue lies somewhere between £7 and £8. Therefore the maximum revenue

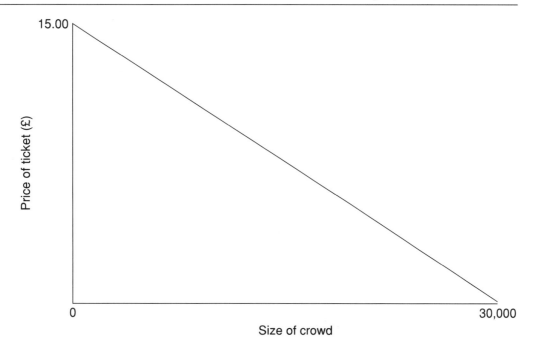

Figure 14.2 Demand schedule for football tickets

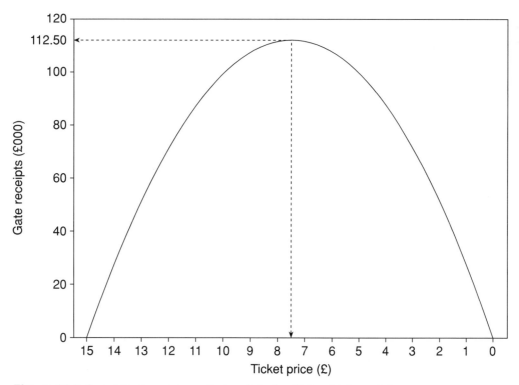

Figure 14.3 A revenue curve: gate receipts for Saturday's match

will be generated when the takings are £112,500 from a crowd of 15,000 people. The optimum ticket price to charge on a Saturday according to the market information is therefore (112,500/15,000) = £7.50 per ticket.

The demand schedule suggests the elasticity of demand between £7 and £8 is unitary. This means they are equidistant from the centreline of the curve (shown by a dotted line in Fig. 14.3), one on the upward slope and the other on the downward slope. The peak of the curve will always lie between two prices that define a range where the elasticity of demand is unitary. A price within this range will normally give a higher revenue than the price at either endpoint.

A normal downward-sloping curve will produce different revenues at different prices. For the top half of the curve, prices move in the opposite direction to total revenue, giving price elasticity over the range £15 to £7.50. Exactly halfway down the curve, at a price of £7.50, the demand becomes unitary. For the bottom half of the curve, prices move in line with total revenue, giving price inelasticity over the range £7.50 to £0.

With this information and knowing that none of their costs can be avoided with a smaller gate, the logical conclusion is for the football club management to price the tickets at £7.50 in order to maximize their profits on the day.

14.3 PRICING TO OPTIMIZE PROFIT USING COST AND MARKET INFORMATION

Before introducing a method to establish the point of profit maximization, it is necessary to examine cost behaviour. The costs incurred by a business are normally a function of time, or the scale and volume of productive output. By examining some of the following cost categories, it can be decided whether they are predominantly incurred with respect to time or with respect to output:

- Royalties
- Productivity bonus payments
- Depreciation of fixed assets
- Power
- Building insurances
- Interest on loans
- Rent
- Wages of supervisors
- Commission of sales staff
- Direct material costs

If these costs are examined over the short term (less than a year), the following costs might be expected to remain **fixed** over that period, and be determined simply by time elapsed:

- Rent
- Building insurance
- Interest on loans
- Depreciation of fixed assets

The following costs would be expected to **vary** over the short term with respect to productive output:

– Direct material costs
– Royalties
– Commission of sales staff
– Productivity bonus payments

Examining the remaining two categories of cost, it might be argued that they would depend on both time and output. Taking supervisors wages, if production varied enough over the period, there might be a periodic need to employ, train, lay off, or redeploy supervisors to manage a fluctuating workforce. This would be particularly true where the operatives were employed on a part-time or temporary basis. Over the very short term, however, this cost category might be classified as fixed.

Power would be largely fixed with respect to lighting and heating, as a minimum level of light and heat is needed in an establishment, whatever the level of output. However, if a business operates at significantly different levels of activity over a period, it is likely that the power required for productive machinery and for productive departments will vary in accordance with these activity levels.

The basic point is that all costs will vary over the long term, as businesses increase or cut back their scale of operations in response to long-term trends in the market and competitive position. For example, if a company undertakes a major investment programme, such 'fixed costs' as rent and depreciation will change to reflect the significant increase in the scale of operations. On the other hand, all costs are fixed at a single moment. The crucial factor is the timescale being considered. Decision taking is a continuous process that must be made with the most up-to-date and reliable information. If the planning of output levels occurs week by week, or even month by month, the timescale involved will influence the view that management have on the nature of the business's costs.

Costs which are fixed over the relevant timescale with respect to productive output are known as **fixed** costs. Costs which vary directly with productive output are known as **variable** costs. Note that not all costs fall neatly into these categories. The supervisors' costs would be described as **step-costs**; whereas costs which have both a fixed element and a variable element, such as utility costs (telephone or electricity), are called **part-variable costs**, or **part-fixed costs**. How all these cost categories behave in relation to productive output is depicted in Fig. 14.4.

We will now concentrate on the pure cost types, fixed and variable. The total cost of an organization can be said to be made up entirely of fixed and variable costs, despite the fact that some individual cost categories are hybrid in their behaviour, or may actually change from being one type to another over time or output level.

Before examining a method for maximizing profit, it is necessary to ask the question: Are variable costs perfectly variable over the whole possible range of productive output of a business? Economic theory, and indeed common sense, would tell us that this is not the case. There are two aspects to this.

As productive output increases, operational efficiency may increase

1 Increased amounts of labour applied to a productive process facilitates efficiency in the way the work is undertaken, through division of labour, and the extra or marginal productivity per person is increased.
2 Increased production requires the purchasing of higher quantities of direct materials. If larger orders are placed, it is possible to benefit from quantity discounts that will reduce the unit cost.

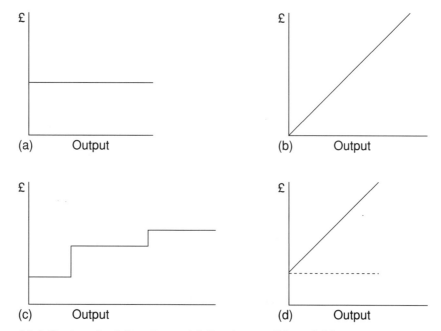

Figure 14.4 Cost–output functions: (a) fixed cost, (b) variable cost, (c) step-variable cost and (d) part-variable cost

3 As production increases, humans learn through experience to operate more efficiently.
4 As productive output increases, the scope widens to replace manual labour with equipment or machinery.

As productive output increases beyond a certain point within the present productive capacity of the business, operational efficiency may eventually decrease

1 As production rises to higher levels, there may be problems of motivation and group cohesiveness, as small teams become larger and more impersonal, and tasks become overspecialized and tedious.
2 As it is possible that learning helps to increase labour efficiency up to a point, it is possible that learning is eventually superseded by complacency and the adoption of expedient short cuts.
3 At much higher levels of production it may be necessary to commission major plant and equipment to cope with increased output, but it may not be possible to fully utilize these indivisible resources. Alternatively there may be a need to pay premium or overtime rates to operatives until such a level of output is reached where these indivisible resources can be introduced efficiently into the productive process.

The law of diminishing returns

Economic theory describes the subsequent reduction in efficiency as output rises within the short-term capacity of the firm as the **law of diminishing returns**. Economic and behavioural theory would indicate, therefore, that the linear relationship between variable costs and output does not exist in reality, and the curvilinear function shown in Fig. 14.5 would be found over a given range of output.

Fixed costs are more straightforward. If they are recognized as being fixed over a specific timescale then the fixed-cost function against productive output must be a

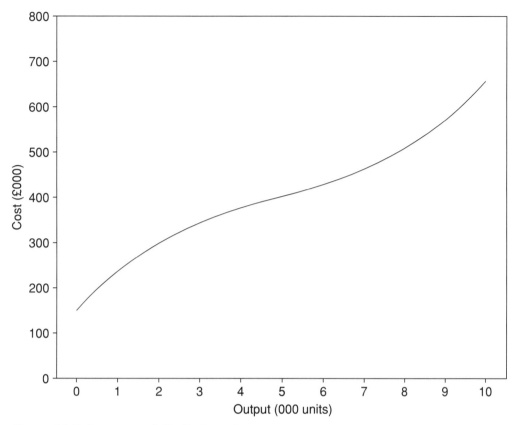

Figure 14.5 An economist's S-shaped curve

horizontal straight line over the whole range of output. If fixed costs are added to the variable costs at all levels of output, a total-cost function can be produced for the output range, as shown in Figure 14.6.

The management accountant recognizes that the total cost function will have the shape of Fig. 14.6, and acknowledges the non-linear relationship between variable costs and output. But for the sake of pragmatism, and to some extent simplicity, accountants assume that over the **relevant range** of output – from somewhat more than a zero level of production to somewhere less than the maximum short-run capacity of the business – the relationship between variable costs and output can be taken as linear. The argument is that, over this range, the relationship may on average be changing from one where the average variable costs per unit of output are falling, to one where the average variable costs per unit are rising. When the relationship is as unclear and ambigous as this, a linear average through the curve may be a reasonable compromise. It is also true to say that, as they are merely based on forecasting or extrapolation techniques, the accuracy of these cost functions leaves much to be desired.

Having examined demand and cost behaviour, and the essential distinction between fixed and variable costs, it is now possible to develop a technique for pricing to optimize profit. A travel agent (Costa-Packet) sells a specific package holiday to customers, which they buy from a holiday company at a fixed price per holiday per person. The total fixed costs of the travel agent, including rents, rates, insurance, etc., come to £5,000 per month.

Each holiday is purchased for £50 and is presently sold for £140; the demand for the holidays currently stands at 100 per month. The travel agent's market research information

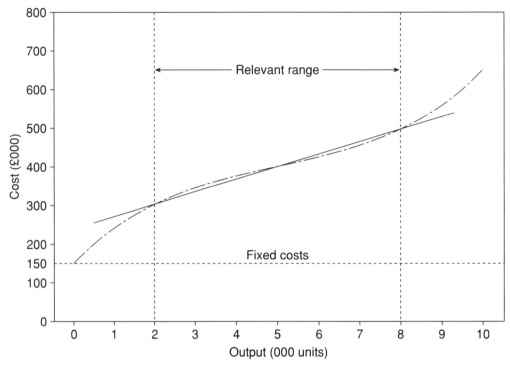

Figure 14.6 An economist's total-cost curve (–·–·–) with an accountant's best-fit line (——) within a relevant range

from ABTA reveals that, in this situation, every £20 change in price will change annual demand by 20 as follows:

Price of holiday		Monthly quantity demanded
180		60
160		80
140	present level	100
120		120
100		140
80		160

All this information can be tabulated:

Units sold	Fixed cost £	Variable cost £	Total cost £	Marginal cost £	Price £	Total revenue £	Marginal revenue £
60	5,000	3,000	8,000		180	10,800	
				1,000			2,000
80	5,000	4,000	9,000		160	12,800	
				1,000			1,200
100	5,000	5,000	10,000		140	14,000	
				1,000			400
120	5,000	6,000	11,000		120	14,400	
				1,000			−400
140	5,000	7,000	12,000		100	14,000	
				1,000			−1,200
160	5,000	8,000	13,000		80	12,800	

The columns headed marginal cost and marginal revenue represent the difference in total cost and the difference in total revenue between each level of output. Firstly, for every extra 20 holidays sold it is clear that the total cost increases by £1,000 or by £1000/20 = £50 per holiday sold. This makes sense as the travel agent pays £50 per holiday to the holiday company.

Secondly, as the price is lowered from £180 to £120, the total revenue increases, indicating price elasticity over that range. Where price elasticity exists, the marginal revenue will always be positive. Between a price of £120 and £80 the total revenue falls, indicating price inelasticity over this range. The marginal revenue over this range of quantities will be negative.

If the total revenues earned are compared with the total costs incurred at all output levels, some important information emerges:

Units sold	Total revenue (TR) £	Total cost (TC) £	Profit (TR – TC) £
60	10,800	8,000	2,800
80	12,800	9,000	3,800
100	14,000	10,000	4,000
120	14,400	11,000	3,400
140	14,000	12,000	2,000
160	12,800	13,000	–200

Notice that the point of profit maximization lies somewhere around 100 holidays, where the price charged per holiday is £140. But from this table it is not possible to be sure whether the actual point of profit maximization will be just above, just below or exactly at this point. And if the marginal cost and marginal revenue from p. 254 are compared in the output ranges below 100 units and above 100 units, what conclusion can be drawn?

In the range 60–100 units the marginal revenue exceeds the marginal cost; in the range 100–160 the marginal cost exceeds the marginal revenue. These observations lead to a fundamental rule. Here they suggest that the profit of the travel agent will continue to increase as more holidays are sold as long as one condition is satisfied:

The total revenue from selling all holidays including the extra holiday sold must be greater than the total revenue obtained from selling all holidays excluding the extra holiday sold.

The data for the travel agent can be shown graphically, and perhaps some of these ideas become clearer on a graph. Note that the point of profit maximization is indicated in two ways:

1 Where the gap between total revenue and total cost is the greatest
2 Where the marginal cost and the marginal revenue functions intersect

In order to derive the optimal selling price (where profits are maximized) it is first necessary to derive the total-cost function and the total-revenue function (Fig. 14.7). The total cost (TC) can be expressed as follows:

$$TC = f + vq$$

where f = fixed cost
v = variable cost
q = quantity sold

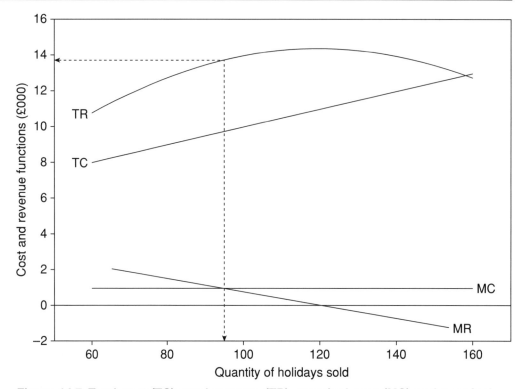

Figure 14.7 Total cost (TC), total revenue (TR), marginal cost (MC) and marginal revenue (MR) for the travel agency Costa-Packet

For the current level of holiday, 100 holidays, the total cost can be calculated as

$$TC = £5,000 + (£50 \times 100) = £10,000$$

In order to derive exactly the optimal selling price (where profits are maximized) it is necessary to establish the marginal cost (MC) and the marginal revenue (MR) functions mathematically as opposed to graphically. Profit is maximized where these functions cross, i.e. where they are equal. The marginal cost has already been established at £50. To derive an expression for the marginal revenue, the total revenue should first be calculated. This is done in two stages:

1 Derive an equation linking price to quantity.
2 Multiply the equation in step 1 by the quantity sold.

Given the demand schedule for the holidays, it is possible to say that if the price were increased to £240, no holidays at all would be sold. The reason is that for every £20/20 = £1 increase in price, one less holiday will be sold over the year. Moving from the present sales level of 100 at the price of £140, if the travel agent were to increase the price by £100, demand would fall by 100 to 0. To increase demand from 0 to 1 holiday, the price would have to be reduced by £1 to £239. Therefore, the maximum selling price attainable for a sales level of q holidays is

$$SP = £240 - £(1 \times q)$$

$$SP = £240 - £q$$

This can be tested by substituting the current selling price of £140 into the equation:

$$£140 = £240 - £q$$

$$q = 100 \quad \text{(as expected)}$$

This mathematical equation gives the slope of the demand curve for the package holidays. If it is multiplied by the quantity sold, it leads to the total revenue (TR) function:

$$TR = q(240 - q)$$
$$= 240q - q^2$$

It is now necessary to use elementary calculus to obtain a marginal revenue function from a total revenue function, as this technique enables the rate of change in revenue to be **derived** from the original TR equation. It is beyond the scope of this book to explain calculus, but the simple rule is that if we want to know the **derivative** of a polynomial function, we multiply the coefficient by the power then decrease the power by one:

$$TR = 240q - q^2$$

$$MR = 240 - 2q \quad \text{(derivative of TR)}$$

Here is an unrelated example, just to practise taking a derivative:

$$y = x^4 + 20$$

$$dy/dx = 4x^3 \quad \text{(derivative)}$$

The coefficient of x^4 is 1 and the power is 4. On taking the derivative, we multiply the coefficient by the power, $4 \times 1 = 4$, then we decrease the power by one, $4 - 1 = 3$. The constant, 20, does not affect the rate of change of the function, so it generates no term in the derivative. The conventional symbol for a derivative of y with respect to x is dy/dx.

If the MC and MR functions are combined into an equality, we obtain

$$50 = 240 - 2q$$

$$q = 95$$

This value can then be substituted into the original price equation:

$$SP = 240 - q$$
$$= 240 - 95 \quad (q = 95)$$
$$= 145$$

We can check whether this exact result does indeed produce a greater profit than selling a quantity of 100 holidays:

	£
Total revenue selling 95 holidays, 95 × £145	13,775
Total cost, £5,000 + (95 × £50)	9,750
Net profit	4,025

This means the travel agent can make £25 more profit than he could selling 100 holidays.

14.4 PRICING STRATEGIES IN SPECIAL SITUATIONS

Pricing strategies have been examined from different perspectives. Pricing determined by the internal cost structure of a business, known as cost-plus pricing, was first examined, followed by pricing strategies based on external information. The information used included an assessment of the competitive position, the economic climate, and market research data gathered on the price–quantity relationships existing for the business's products and services, and other substitute or complementary goods. Finally a logical approach for deriving an optimal price and quantity for a particular product or service was explored, based on available cost and market information.

What emerges from this is that no single strategy for pricing can be used at all times and in all situations. Business managers must be flexible in their approach to pricing, taking into account all the information that is available. Where a business is operating in a market as a price maker, such as a national lottery, then the cost-plus method may be adopted. Where a business is operating in a highly crowded and competitive market, where very similar products are offered to the customer, there may be no choice other than to charge the going rate. This might be the case for a Blackpool landlady, offering bed-and-breakfast accommodation on the promenade.

It is quite common for businesses who have spare capacity, and for whom a business opportunity presents itself, to adopt a below-full-cost pricing strategy, in order to increase overall profitability. For example, it will be assumed that following the previous market research exercise, Costa-Packet is currently selling 95 package holidays a month at £145. Therefore, the cost structure at this level of sales is as follows:

	£
Sales (95 × 145)	13,775
Variable costs (95 × 50)	4,750
	9,025
Fixed costs	5,000
Net profit	4,025

If the total cost per holiday to the travel agent is calculated, it is (£4,750 + £5,000)/95 = £102.63 approximately. If at the end of the month, a school approached the travel agent and asked for 30 package holidays, but was only willing to pay £75 each for them, would it be worth the travel agent selling them if they were still available from the holiday company at the same cost? On the face of it, as the average full cost of selling the holidays is over £100, it would not appear to be a good strategy to accept the order. But we can check this.

Profit earned by Costa-Packet selling 125 holidays in a year

	£
Sales (95 × 145)	13,775
Additional sales (30 × 75)	2,250
Total revenue	16,025
Variable costs (125 × 50)	6,250
	9,775
Fixed costs	5,000
Net profit	4,775

Contrary to what might have been expected, Costa-Packet would make additional profit of £750 as a result of accepting the extra order. What is the reason for this? The critical point is to look at the extra or marginal cost of supplying the holidays and compare it with the extra or marginal revenue to be generated from this supply. The minimum short-run price for a product or service should normally be at least equal to the variable cost, but in certain extreme situations, as part of a wider profit mix, a price might be set at a level below even this minimum short-run price. This might be done because of the known relationship between the demand for one product and another, such as the demand for a substitute or a complementary product.

Another example is a sports shop selling two complementary products such as cricket bats and balls. The current prices, variable costs and weekly demand for each are as follows:

	Bats	Balls
	£	£
Selling price	25.00	3.00
Variable cost	10.00	2.50
Demand per week	100	150

It is assumed that with a £1 reduction in price, the demand for balls will increase by 40%, and due to more customers entering the sports shop to buy balls, there will be a related increase of 20% per week in the demand for bats at the same price. If this happens, what will be the effect on total profit of reducing the price of balls by £1? Firstly it is necessary to calculate the profitability of the two products before the price reduction:

	Bats		Balls
	£		£
Sales (100 × 25)	2,500	(150 × 3)	450
Variable costs (100 × 10)	1,000	(150 × 2.50)	375
Profit before fixed costs	1,500		75

The total profit before subtracting fixed costs on the two complementary products is £1,500 + £75 = £1,575 per week. Next the profitability of the two products will be calculated following the price reduction to balls:

	Bats		Balls
	£		£
Sales (120 × 25)	3,000	(210 × 2)	420
Variable costs (120 × 10)	1,200	(210 × 2.50)	525
Profit before fixed costs	1,800	Loss	(105)

The total profit before subtracting fixed costs on the two complementary products is £1,800 − £105 = £1,695 per week. The overall profitability of both complementary products, following the change in pricing strategy, has been increased by £1,695 − £1,575 = £120. It was therefore more profitable for the sports shop to sell the balls at below variable cost, incurring a loss on the balls, because this was more than compensated by the increase in profit made due to the increased demand for bats at the same price! Note that it is not necessary or relevant to include the fixed costs incurred by the sports shop in this exercise, as it is assumed the change in pricing strategy would have no effect on the weekly fixed costs incurred by the business.

In conclusion, while it is recognized that in the short run and in special situations a particular pricing strategy may be adopted, it must be accepted that a business can only remain in business if it charges prices for its products and services which in combination produce revenues that will cover all its costs over the long run, and provide an acceptable level of return to its investors. If a business fails to achieve this, it can have no viable long-term future.

SUMMARY

1 **Price is as important, if not more important than cost in determining profit in certain circumstances.**

2 **It is possible to price services or products based on various cost-plus techniques, such as the Hubbart formula.**

3 **Market conditions and economic factors are important in pricing services and products.**

4 **Given adequate cost and revenue information, a sales price and quantity may be derived in order to maximize profit.**

5 **In special one-off situations, particular pricing strategies may be employed at the margin, where prices may be set at below cost in order to take advantage of certain business opportunities presented, or to meet short-term competitive threats.**

ASSESSMENT

MULTIPLE-CHOICE QUESTIONS

Question 1
If an hotel has total costs of £310,250 and wishes to make a profit of total cost plus 20%, which of the following prices must the hotel charge for its single rooms? There are 30 singles and 20 doubles, which are 60% occupied on average, and the price for each single room is to be 75% of the price for each double room. Assume 365 days in the year.

A £30
B £33
C £60
D £25

Question 2
Which of the following statements best describes the pricing policy that should be followed by a business in a competitive market and whose costs are all fixed in the short term?

A Set a price based on cost plus a small percentage
B Set a price that is just below its competitors' prices
C Set a price that is just above its competitors' prices
D Set a price at which revenue is maximized

Question 3

If the demand for a product over a specific range is inelastic, which of the following best defines price inelasticity?

A As price increases, quantity demanded increases
B As price increases, profit increases
C As price decreases, sales value increases
D As price changes, sales value changes in the same direction

Question 4

A £1 change in the price of green fees on a golf course causes the monthly total of visiting golfers playing rounds to change by 50. At a price of £5 the records show that 100 green fees are paid per month. What is the price that should be charged to maximize revenue from green fees?

A £5.50
B £4.20
C £3.50
D £2.20

Question 5

Which one of the following statements is not true with respect to pricing policy?

A In the long run all costs are variable, so long-term pricing strategy must aim to set prices at full cost plus an acceptable profit margin to reward investors.
B In the short term a single-product company will reduce its overall profit if it sells additional product at less than its marginal cost.
C A business facing inelastic demand between two prices should set the price at the lower price to maximize revenue.
D A company selling complementary products or services may improve its overall profitability by selling one of the complements at a price below its variable cost.

EXERCISES

Exercise 1

The Pan Gulf chain of motels in Florida, USA, is deciding on a pricing policy for its new generation of economy travel motels. All hotels will be of a uniform size and design, and all revenue is to be generated from accommodation. The costs per built unit per year are estimated as follows:

	$
Building and establishment costs (inc depn)	300,000
Staff costs	440,000
Indirect materials	4,800
Interest payments	24,000
Rates	14,560
Telephones, postage, entertainment licenses	8,400
	791,760

The total capital cost of each hotel unit to build and get ready for business is $5.0 million. The owners require a 15% return on this investment after meeting the above annual costs. The accommodation comprises three types of room, 60 singles, 40 doubles and 24 family rooms. It is anticipated that singles and doubles should achieve an average of 80% occupancy, but the family rooms only an average of 50%. The desired relative price structure is to be as follows:

Double room to be 1.5 times the price of a single room
Family room to be 2.0 times the price of a single room

Required
Calculate a price per type of room per night which will meet the overall investment requirements of the hotel owners, for each built unit. Assume a 365-day year. Show all your workings.

Exercise 2
The Devar restaurant has undertaken analysis of the past year's internal accounting records. The following information has been obtained:

	£
Total takings for the year	200,000
Average number of covers	12,000
Labour costs	29,800
Overhead costs	12,600

It is anticipated that if trade increases in line with past years' growth, a 10% increase in customers can be expected next year. It is also anticipated that general inflation of restaurant prices will be 5% in the coming year. It is expected, however, that labour and overhead costs can be maintained at their current levels. The restaurateur desires a rate of return of 20% on the capital currently invested in the business which stands at £250,000.

Required
The restaurateur wants to operate a food cost-plus pricing policy controlled by the chef, who has a day-to-day knowledge of food prices. What overall percentage should the chef add to the cost of food ingredients and drink to achieve the rate of return required by the owner?

Exercise 3
The Formidable Hotel in the Alps generates revenue from room letting and from selling food and drink in its bar and restaurant. The hotel has 20 standard rooms, which it normally operates at 75% occupancy. The following information is available.

	L000
Ordinary share capital and reserves	540,000
L2,000 debentures (8%)	120,000
Administration expenses	40,000
Selling and distribution expenses	60,000
Direct costs of food and drink	37,600
Finance costs (120,000 × 8%)	9,600
Indirect materials	
Bedroom cleaning and laundry	4,340
Bar and restaurant consumable supplies	5,000
Staff costs	
Laundry (bedroom linen) and chamber staff	34,885
Kitchen, bar and restaurant	21,000

The shareholders require a rate of return of 18% on their capital. The corporation tax rate is currently at 25%. The accommodation part of the hotel operation is to be apportioned with 60% of the administration and selling and distribution costs. The remainder is apportioned to the restaurant and bars. The expected profit margin from the sale of food and drink is based on direct cost of materials plus 200%.

Required

Prepare a statement based on the Hubbart formula which builds up to the revenue required from the rooms. From this, estimate the price per night to be charged for each standard room in the hotel, in order to meet the overall financial objectives.

Exercise 4

The Jump For Their Lives (JFTL) bunjee-jumping business earns its income by travelling to carnivals and fetes, offering opportunities for people to make sponsored jumps for charities of their choice. It has the following costs per day:

	£
Daily rental of lorry and extending platform	300
Drivers' wages for the day	150
Daily site rental cost	200
Fuel cost of moving lorry and for idling	50
Additional fuel cost of using extending platform per jump made	4

The elasticated rope needs to be replaced every 200 jumps; the cost of a replacement is £500. From analysing the prices charged by competitors, and the demand for jumps at these prices, it emerges that for every £1 change in the price, the change in demand for jumps will be two people. JFTL currently offers jumps at £32 a time, and on average there are 40 jumps per day. In any given day it is possible for 100 jumps to be made if the extending platform is used continuously.

Required

(a) Calculate the net profit made at the current price of £32 per jump.
(b) Graph the TC and TR functions of the jumping business over its possible range of jumps in a day, showing the point at which profit is maximized.
(c) Perform a mathematical calculation of the exact price to offer and the corresponding number of jumps (to the nearest round jump) in order to maximize the profitability of the business on any given day.

CHAPTER 15

Accounting for contribution

OBJECTIVES

- Compare and contrast the economist's and the accountant's view of cost and revenue behaviour against output.
- Understand break-even analysis from a graphical perspective and a mathematical perspective.
- Use contribution theory in cost–volume–profit analysis.
- Relate contribution to price in the C/S ratio.
- Use contribution theory to evaluate business alternatives.
- Apply contribution theory to decisions on product or service mix.
- Apply contribution theory to profit maximization when resources are scarce.
- Decide whether to make a product or buy it.

15.1 THE BEHAVIOUR OF COST AND REVENUE AGAINST OUTPUT

Chapter 14 showed that, in theory, variable costs may not change in exact proportion to the change in output, due to a number of economic and behavioural factors. And, in practice, the management accountant argues that a business can assume a linear relationship between variable costs and output over a relevant range of output.

Turning to revenue, Chapter 14 used two different perspectives to demonstrate that the price charged and the demand for a product or service are inversely related in most cases. First, if prices change, the relative value of the individual's current disposable income will change, allowing that individual to buy more or less of the product than before the change took place. Second, as more of a product is demanded by an individual, each subsequent consumption of the product will yield marginally less satisfaction than the previous purchase. Eventually there will come a point where, at the current price, an individual may derive more satisfaction by using their income to purchase an alternative product. The individual in this situation will only be prepared to purchase more of the original product if its price is reduced.

The accountant's view is more simplistic with regard to the relationship between quantities demanded and prices charged at those levels. The accountant will assume that the same price can be charged over a range of demand levels, i.e. that the marginal revenue of each item will remain the same as more quantities are sold. The economist normally sees price and demand moving in opposite directions, and defines the total-revenue curve as a dome shape. The accountant, on the other hand, will see the total-revenue function as an upward-sloping linear function.

Taking the accountant's side in this argument is less easy than when defending the assumption of linearity in the variable-cost function over a relevant range of output. Here are the main arguments in favour of the accountant's position:

1 Over the relevant range of output, particularly in a market where the business is not a significant player, the same price might be charged in the short term.
2 Reliable demand information is usually very difficult to obtain, so accurate estimates of demand schedules are not available. Assuming linearity may be an acceptable expedient over a reasonably narrow range.

It is fairly clear that if linearity is not to be assumed for costs and revenues, it will be extremely difficult to observe the relationships between them over a large range of productive output, and even more difficult to make reliable assessments of where profits can be maximized, or to work out the effects of taking decisions at the margin.

15.2 BREAK-EVEN ANALYSIS

Break-even quite literally means what it says; it is where the business makes neither a profit nor a loss. As profit is defined as the difference between total revenue (TR) and total costs (TC) at a specific output level, the break-even point is the output and sales level where both TR and TC are equal. Having been introduced to the graphical representations of TR and TC in Chapter 14, they can now be put together in a combined graph. Firstly we assume that the economist's view prevails and the non-linear TC and TR functions apply (Fig. 15.1).

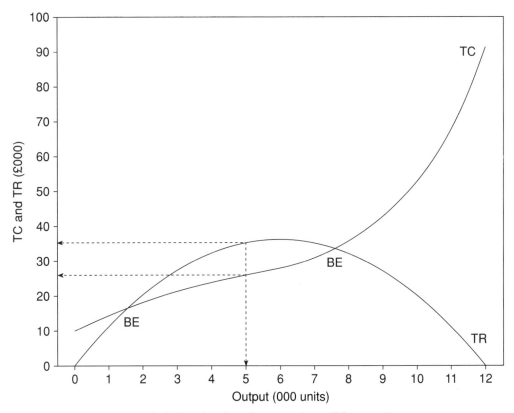

**Figure 15.1 An economist's double break-even chart: TC = total cost,
TR = total revenue and BE = break-even point**

As the TC curve is shaped like an S and the TR curve is shaped like a dome the TC and TR curves inevitably cross twice. At the points where the curves intersect, there is no profit or loss. The economist would recommend the business to operate at a level between the two break-even points, where the gap between TR and TC is the widest, i.e. the point of profit maximization.

The accountant's break-even chart is far simpler, and from now on the analysis in this chapter will be based on the assumptions of the accountant, while recognizing the short-comings of this approach.

Some entrepreneurs intend to start a mobile beach bar selling cans of ice-cold drinks at a beach in Menorca for 200 days a year. Here is the relevant information on this business:

Costs
Cost of beer cans	Pta 80
Annual beach-trading licence	Pta 40,000
Annual cost of refrigerated vehicle	Pta 200,000

Revenue
Maximum daily capacity of trike (assuming only one load per day)	200 cans
Price per can	Pta 100

This information can be presented in the form of a table:

Units sold	Price Pta	Total revenue Pta 000	VC per can Pta	VC Pta 000	FC Pta 000	TC Pta 000	Profit or loss Pta 000
0	100	0	80	0	240	240	(240)
10,000	100	1,000	80	800	240	1,040	(40)
20,000	100	2,000	80	1,600	240	1,840	160
30,000	100	3,000	80	2,400	240	2,640	360
40,000	100	4,000	80	3,200	240	3,440	560

The maximum capacity is 200 cans per load × 200 days = 40,000 cans. Figure 15.2 shows that the break-even point is at exactly 12,000 cans. The data in the table placed it somewhere between 10,000 and 20,000 cans. This information is very useful to the owners of the mobile drinks bar, as it tells them they only need to sell 12,000 of the 40,000 that it can possibly carry. The business will cover its costs, if all cans are sold, with the vehicle being 12,000/40,000 = 30% full.

If a business makes this sort of estimate of its total costs and total revenues at various levels of output, its viability can be assessed before set-up. Figure 15.2 also indicates profit or loss earned either side of the break-even point. The profit or loss at any given level of output is indicated by the distance between the TR function and the TC function. Unlike the economist, the accountant assumes the gap between TR and TC continues to widen after the break-even point, up to the productive capacity of the business. What this tells the owners of the mobile bar owner is that if they were to sell all the cans they could carry for the season, they would make a profit of Pta 560,000.

The break-even graph is also an excellent way of illustrating some key points about business. These points will be explored by identifying what changes to the lines on the graph would cause the business to reach the break-even point earlier. Here are three:

1 If the intersect of the TC line were lower down the y-axis
2 If the angle of the TC line were shallower
3 If the angle of the TR line were steeper

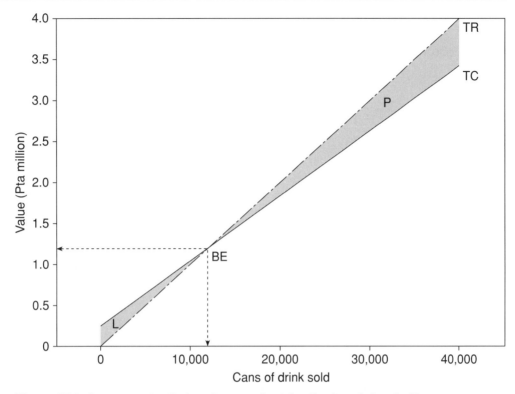

**Figure 15.2 An accountant's break-even chart for the beach bar in Menorca:
TC = total cost, TR = total revenue, BE = break-even point, P = area of profit,
L = area of loss**

If any or all of these modifications could be made to Fig. 15.2, the result would be to
reach the break-even point earlier. This would have two consequences:

1 It would reduce losses at all levels of output below the break-even point.
2 It would increase profits at all levels of output above the break-even point.

What do the three modifications to the TR and TC functions actually mean in accounting terms?

1 The intersect of the TC curve with the y-axis is determined by the fixed costs incurred
   in the financial period.
2 The angle of the TC line is determined entirely by the variable cost per unit.
3 The angle of the TR line is determined entirely by the price charged per unit.

This means that if the break-even point is to be arrived at sooner, and the relative
profitability is to be improved at all levels of output, one or all of the following must
take place:

1 Fixed costs must be reduced for the period.
2 Unit variable costs must be reduced.
3 The price must be increased.

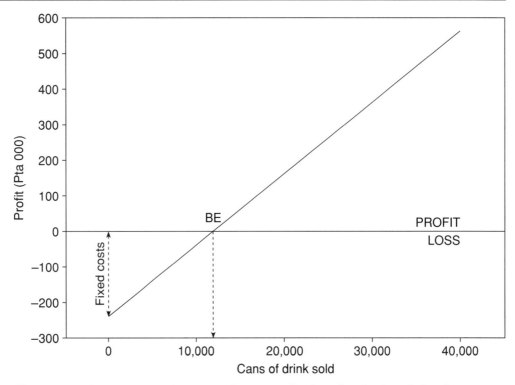

Figure 15.3 An accountant's cost–volume–profit chart for the beach bar in Menorca: BE = break-even point

The absolute profitability of the business depends on how many units are being produced and sold. (This is the volume along the x-axis at which the business is currently operating.)

The fundamental relationships between these variables and their effect on profitability are crucial for the business manager who seeks to maximize profits, so we will devote some attention to them. This analysis entirely depends on the accountant's ability to separate a business's fixed costs from its variable costs, which is not always easy or possible (Chapter 14).

The break-even information for the beach bar can be shown in a different way, which makes profit and loss easier to determine at all levels of output. Figure 15.3 shows profit and loss on the y-axis, and volume in units along the x-axis. The profitability function crosses the x-axis (zero profit) at the break-even point in units.

Although graphs are particularly clear in expressing relationships between these key variables, they are time-consuming to draw. And as the relationships are assumed to be linear, it is fairly easy to express them in the form of an equation:

$$N = pq - (f + vq)$$

where N = net profit
p = price
v = variable cost
f = fixed cost
q = sales or output

This simply says that profit is the difference between price times quantity sold, less fixed costs plus unit variable cost times quantity sold. The break-even point can be obtained by substituting $N = 0$ in the equation:

$$0 = pq - (f + vq)$$

$$pq = (f + vq)$$

If we take the example earlier where

$$p = 100$$

$$f = 240,000$$

$$v = 80$$

we can substitute these values into the equation:

$$100q = (240,000 + 80q)$$

$$20q = 240,000$$

$$q = 12,000$$

The break-even equation, $pq = (f + vq)$, can be restated more simply:

$$\text{Break-even point in units} = q = f/(p - v)$$

which can be tested with the same example:

$$q = 240,000/(100 - 80)$$
$$= 240,000/20$$
$$= 12,000$$

From now on the formula $q = f/(p - v)$ will always be used, in order to calculate the break-even point in units. The original equation, $N = pq - (f + vq)$, can be used to ask 'what if' questions with regard to any of the above variables. It can be applied to the mobile drinks vendor in the following way.

Question 1

At what sales volume would the business earn Pta 400,000 profit, assuming the same price and cost structure as before?

Answer

$$400,000 = 100q - (240,000 + 80q)$$

$$640,000 = 20q$$

$$q = 32,000$$

This can be tested to see what the profit would be:

		Pta
Sales value	(32,000 × 100)	3,200,000
Variable costs	(32,000 × 80)	2,560,000
		640,000
Fixed costs		240,000
Net profit		400,000

Question 2

What price would need to be charged to show a profit of Pta 360,000 at 30,000 cans a season?

Answer

$$360,000 = 30,000p - (240,000 + 2,400,000)$$

$$3,000,000 = 30,000p$$

$$p = 100$$

This does not need to be tested because, by referring to the data on p. 266, a price of Pta 100 does indeed yield a profit of 360,000 at sales of 30,000 cans. The advantage of the mathematical method is that it saves time in answering hypothetical questions of the 'what if' type, and gives more precise solutions than the graphical method.

15.3 CONTRIBUTION THEORY

It has been shown how the graphical method visually describes the relationships between the key variables in cost, volume and profit analysis. These relationships can be expressed in simple mathematical notation, which provides quick and accurate answers for hypothetical questions regarding the future operating strategy of a business.

The same relationships will now be approached using an accounting technique known as contribution theory. Contribution theory merely restates the mathematical relationship in a way that more readily conforms with the accountancy perspective. The technique naturally requires the separation of fixed and variable costs in assessing the performance of a business. Contribution is the difference between the selling price of a product or service, and the variable cost of producing or providing that product or service for sale. This relationship can be described on a unit basis:

Price – variable cost per unit = unit contribution

or in total terms:

Sales value – total variable costs = total contribution

The reason why the result is called a contribution is as follows. Having subtracted from the selling price the variable cost incurred in making a product or service available for sale, the difference is available to contribute towards the **fixed costs** incurred during the period. If the total contribution earned from all sales exceeds the fixed costs for the period, the surplus is known as net profit. In accounting terms, this relationship can be expressed in the form of a contribution statement.

Let us now assume that the drinks vendors in Menorca actually set up in business, that all the financial estimates were correct, and that 23,500 cans were sold.

Contribution statement (Menorca Drinks)

	Pta 000
Sales revenue (23,500 × 100)	2,350
Variable costs (23,500 × 80)	1,880
Contribution towards fixed costs	470
Fixed costs for the season	240
Net profit	230

Therefore the profit is easily calculated as the surplus contribution (over and above fixed costs) of Pta 230,000.

This information can be arrived at differently. What was the break-even point? Answer 12,000 cans, as calculated earlier. At this point, no profit is made, so the contribution exactly equals the fixed costs. Taking the additional sales beyond the break-even point, 23,500 − 12,000 = 11,500, and calculating the contribution made by these units, it can be said that all this contribution is now profit, as fixed costs have already been covered. The way to do this is to calculate the unit contribution per can, which is given by

Selling price − variable cost per unit = Pta 100 − Pta 80
= Pta 20

Multiplying 11,500 by Pta 20, we obtain the net profit of Pta 230,000, calculated earlier. Or it could be said that the total contribution, 23,500 × Pta 20 = Pta 470,000, less the fixed costs of Pta 240,000 is the net profit of Pta 230,000. Once the unit contribution has been calculated, the calculation of profit is much less time-consuming than preparing the whole contribution statement. This simple relationship is very useful for answering the types of hypothetical questions that were asked earlier in mathematical notation. Let us try two more hypothetical questions:

Question 3

If the drinks vendors were to make the same profit next season by selling only 10,000 cans, how much would they need to charge?

Answer
The key to this is to establish that the same contribution would be required to cover the same fixed costs and to make the same profit. This contribution was Pta 470,000. However, the contribution has got to come from only 10,000 cans as opposed to 23,500. The contribution required from each can sold is therefore Pta 470,000/10,000 = Pta 47. As the variable cost is still Pta 80, the price per can must now be increased to Pta 80 + Pta 47 = Pta 127. This hypothesis can be checked by preparing a full contribution statement:

Contribution statement (Menorca Drinks)

	Pta 000
Sales revenue (10,000 × 127)	1,270
Variable costs (10,000 × 80)	800
Contribution towards fixed costs	470
Fixed costs for the season	240
Net profit	230

Note that the same profit is achieved with a much lower sales revenue than before. Going back to the economic theory, we can ask a hypothetical question: if the vendors increased their price by Pta 47, would there be demand for 10,000 cans? The answer would depend on a number of factors, the most significant of which would be the level of competition the vendors might be facing, and the prices that any competitors might be charging.

Question 4

If the drinks vendors bought a megaphone for Pta 16,000 at the beginning of the second season, how many extra cans would they need to sell to make the same profit as they did in their first season, assuming they can now buy cans for Pta 75 each.

Answer
The key to this is to establish by how much the contribution would have to be increased in the following season, having incurred this additional fixed cost. Obviously, by assuming that the whole cost will be consumed in one season, the contribution will have to rise by Pta 16,000 in that season. The total contribution required will now need to be Pta 470,000 + Pta 16,000 = Pta 486,000. The new contribution per can is Pta 100 – Pta 75 = Pta 25; so if the total contribution required is divided by the unit contribution, it is possible to calculate the number of cans that the vendors need to sell, i.e. 486,000/25 = 19,440. This may now be checked by preparing the full contribution statement:

Contribution statement (Menorca Drinks)

	Pta 000
Sales revenue (19,440 × 100)	1,944
Variable costs (19,440 × 75)	1,458
Contribution towards fixed costs	486
Fixed costs for the season (+16,000)	256
Net profit	230

15.4 THE CONTRIBUTION/SALES RATIO

A useful concept is the percentage contribution made by every £1 taken as sales:

$$\frac{\text{Total contribution}}{\text{Sales revenue}} \times 100\%$$

Taking the last contribution statement, the contribution/sales ratio (C/S ratio) was (486/ 1944) × 100% = 25%. This means that for every £1 taken as sales, 25p is contributing to fixed costs and subsequently to profit. This gives a quick method of answering the question, How much sales value must be generated in order to break even? Simply calculate

$$\frac{\text{Fixed costs}}{\text{C/S ratio}} = \text{Pta } 256,000/0.25$$

$$= \text{Pta } 1,024,000$$

This can be tested by preparing a contribution statement where the sales are Pta 1,024,000:

Contribution statement (Menorca Drinks)

	Pta 000	%
Sales revenue (10,240 × 100)	1,024	100
Variable costs (10,240 × 75)	768	75
Contribution towards fixed costs	256	25
Fixed costs for the season	256	
Net profit	nil	

Sometimes, as mentioned earlier, the fixed and variable costs of a business cannot easily be identified. However, there is a method that allows them to be ascertained from total data, where information on unit cost and selling price is not available. This may be a useful technique for a business that wishes to investigate the cost–volume–profit relationship existing within its business, or for analysts who wish to evaluate a business when only financial accounting information is available.

The following information is available for the Texas burger bar:

	May $	June $
Sales	3,000	4,000
Total costs	2,000	2,500
Net profit	1,000	1,500

From this, is it possible to find out the proportion of costs which are fixed and the proportion which are variable, along with the break-even level of sales revenue? The answer is yes, if it is assumed that input and output prices have remained constant within the period. The key to this is in examining the **change between the two months**. The revenue has increased by $1,000 and the costs have changed by $500.

If the costs incurred have changed over a short period such as a month, it may be assumed that the changes are due to volume changes and are variable in nature. So the contribution made by the company on the difference between each month is $1,000 − $500 = $500; in other words, over the short term, when some costs are fixed, any change in profit is due to a change in contribution. Therefore the C/S ratio is established as being 500/1,000 = 50%, and it is therefore possible to reformulate the profit statements as contribution statements:

	May	June	
	$	$	%
Sales	3,000	4,000	100
Variable costs	1,500	2,000	50
Contribution	1,500	2,000	50
Fixed costs	500	500	
Net profit	1,000	1,500	

The break-even point in the sales revenue can be calculated as $500/0.5 = $1,000$. This sort of analysis, incorporating the simplifying assumptions made above, is useful in order to establish the vulnerability of a company to a downturn in business. From this information, if we take June as an example, sales can fall by $3,000/4,000 = 75\%$ before the company will move into losses. This information is not available from the full cost alone, and gives management a better insight into the financial position and strength of the business. This technique will be investigated further in Chapter 19.

15.5 EVALUATING BUSINESS ALTERNATIVES

Contribution theory can now be put into practice by the use of a small case study. Water Leisure Ltd is to be set up selling two products, water-skis and wet suits. The following estimated information is available:

	Water-skis		Wet suits
	£		£
Prices	140		200
Purchase cost	70		120
Commission to sales staff	20%		10%
(based on selling price)			
Estimated sales	300		400
Other estimates for the year		£	
Total staff costs, including commission		30,000	
Establishment costs		14,400	
Share capital invested		150,000	
10% debenture loan taken out		50,000	

A bulk order discount of 10% is available on skis for orders of greater than 20 pairs at a time. It is assumed initially that orders placed during the year for skis will not exceed this minimum quantity.

With this information, a contribution statement must be prepared calculating the estimated profit to be made over the first year of trading, and calculating the resulting rate of return on the share capital originally invested. In addition, the accountant of the company has been asked to attend the next board meeting of the company, prepared to answer the following four questions:

1 How much sales revenue must be generated per week from the shop (assuming 50 weeks a year) in order to break even?
2 How much sales revenue must be generated per week if the annual rate of return on capital employed is to be 20%? Assume the sales mix remains constant.

3 If the bulk order discount is to be obtained from the suppliers through less frequent ordering, how much could the price of each pair of skis be reduced if the same unit contribution is to be earned per pair sold?

4 If an advertising campaign is to be launched promoting a 15% off deal on the wet suits at the year-end, and the cost of this publicity is estimated to be £5,940, how many more wet suits must be sold to pay for the whole promotion?

First of all, the cost structure of the business should be established. All the variable costs per unit and the fixed costs for the year should be identified. It should then be possible to calculate the contribution per unit of the products.

		Water-skis	Wet suits
		£	£
Purchase price		70	120
Sales commission		28	20
Unit variable costs		98	140
Fixed costs	£		
Staff costs*	13,600		
Establishment costs	14,400		
Interest	5,000		
Total fixed costs	33,000		

*The fixed proportion of the staff costs should exclude the total commission earned by sales staff, which is classified as a variable cost. The commissions are as follows:

	Water-skis	Wet suits
	£	£
Quantity × commission		
300 × £28:	8,400	
400 × £20:		8,000

Therefore the fixed staff costs are £30,000 − (£8,400 + £8,000) = £13,600.

The contribution per product is as follows:

	Water-skis	Wet suits
	£	£
Selling price	140	200
Unit variable cost	98	140
Unit contribution	42	60

It is now possible to calculate a useful piece of information for a company with more than one product, the weighted average contribution to sales ratio, or the C/S ratio. This tells the company what percentage (on average) of its takings contributes towards fixed costs and profit. It is calculated as follows:

		£	%
Total sales	(140 × 300) + (200 × 400)	122,000	100
Total contribution	(42 × 300) + (60 × 400)	36,600	30
Variable costs		85,400	70

This means that for every £1 taken over the till, assuming a constant sales mix, 30p will be **contributed** towards fixed costs and profits. It is now possible to calculate the total contribution statement of the business for the following year:

Total contribution statement for Water Leisure Ltd

	£
Sales	122,000
Variable costs	85,400
Contribution	36,600
Fixed costs	33,000
Net profit for the year	3,600

Now that the basic analysis has been carried out, it is possible to prepare the items for the board of directors.

Item 1

How much sales revenue must be generated per week from the shop (assuming 50 weeks a year) in order to break even? The required contribution to break even is £33,000 which equals the fixed costs. As the C/S ratio is 30%, the weekly sales revenue required to break even is

$$£33,000/0.3 = £110,000/50$$
$$= £2,200$$

Item 2

How much sales revenue must be generated per week if the annual rate of return on capital employed is to be 20%? Assume the sales mix remains constant. The required contribution is £33,000 + the desired profit of £150,000 × 0.2, a total of £63,000. As the C/S ratio is 30%, the weekly sales revenue required to break even is

$$£63,000/0.3 = £210,000/50$$
$$= £4,200$$

Item 3

If the bulk order discount is to be obtained from the suppliers through less frequent ordering, how much could the price of skis be reduced if the same unit contribution is to be earned per pair sold? It is necessary to go back and look at the individual contribution of the skis, £42 per pair. How much contribution will be gained if the buying discount is obtained?

The discount is £70 × 0.10 = £7.00 per pair of skis, so all things being equal, a price reduction of £7.00 would be possible. But all things are not equal, as the sales price of the skis determines the commission level. If the price level is reduced, the commission will also be reduced. How is this accounted for?

For every £1 reduction in price, the commission will fall by 20p, therefore each £1 off the price yields only 80p less contribution. Therefore it is possible to reduce the original price by as much as £7.00/0.80 = £8.75. Starting from the previous contribution per pair of skis, which is £42, we can test this result as follows:

New unit contribution		£	£
Selling price	(140 – 8.75)		131.25
Variable cost:			
Purchase price	(70 – 7.00)	63.00	
Commission	(131.25 × 0.2)	26.25	
Unit variable cost			89.25
Unit contribution			42.00

Item 4

If an advertising campaign is to be launched, promoting a 15% off deal on the wet suits at the year-end, and the cost of this publicity is estimated to be £5,940, how many more wet suits must be sold to pay for the whole promotion? In this case a decision at the margin is being examined. If it is assumed this promotion is launched at the year-end, then it is necessary to look for additional sales on top of the normal 400 planned.

The additional contribution required to pay for this promotion is £5,940 as the campaign is pursued in order to create extra sales of wet suits. As the price of each wet suit is being reduced by 15%, the unit contribution made by each additional sale will be as follows:

New unit contribution	£	£
Selling price (200 × 0.85)		170
Variable costs:		
Purchase cost of suit	120	
Commission (170 × 0.10)	17	
Unit variable cost		137
Unit contribution		33

As the extra contribution earned from each additional sale of wet suits at the discounted price is £33, and the total additional contribution required to cover the advertising costs is £5,940, the company needs to sell at least 5,940/33 = 180 more wet suits for the promotion to be viable.

Evaluating alternative business plans without unit cost or price data

In the Water Leisure case study, the costs were analysed between variable costs and fixed costs, and unit variable costs and prices were available. Where this detailed information is not available, but total revenue, total variable costs and total fixed costs are known or can be derived, it is still possible to evaluate whether one business alternative will be more profitable than another.

Taking the summary financial data from a cut-price air ticket sales business, it is possible to evaluate three independent financial proposals for the following financial year.

Nantucket Bucket Ltd (present position)

	$
Sales revenue	850,000
Variable costs	680,000
Contribution	170,000
Fixed costs	120,000
Net profit	50,000

Proposal 1: increase the price of tickets to customers by 20%. Given the competitive climate in the American airline market, the unit sales of tickets would be expected to fall by 30%.

Proposal 2: cut the price of the tickets by 10%, which would generate 20% more ticket sales.

Proposal 3: launch an advertising campaign to increase ticket sales by 25%; this will cost $25,000.

Neither the individual ticket prices nor the unit contributions are known, but contribution theory can be used to evaluate which of the three options should be adopted. A suitable approach to this type of analysis is as follows.

Proposal 1

	Nantucket Bucket Ltd $	Price change multiplier	Unit change multiplier	New plan $
Sales revenue	850,000	1.20	0.70	714,000
Variable costs	680,000		0.70	476,000
Contribution	170,000			238,000
Fixed costs	120,000			120,000
Net profit	50,000			118,000

Note that it does not matter that unit prices and variable costs are not known. What matters is the overall change caused by the proposal. For example, if the price is increased by 20%, the total revenue will increase by 20%, but as the price increase causes a fall in demand, we have to multiply this total by 70% to recognize that not so many tickets are sold. As sales volume falls, the total variable costs of the tickets fall, due to 30% fewer tickets being required from the airlines, and this must be accounted for.

Proposal 2

	Nantucket Bucket Ltd $	Price change multiplier	Unit change multiplier	New plan $
Sales revenue	850,000	0.90	1.20	918,000
Variable costs	680,000		1.20	816,000
Contribution	170,000			102,000
Fixed costs	120,000			120,000
Net profit	50,000			(18,000)

This proposal is clearly inferior to the first one and is also inferior to continuing with the original marketing plan.

Proposal 3

	Nantucket Bucket Ltd $	Fixed cost increment	Unit change multiplier	New plan $
Sales revenue	850,000		1.25	1,062,500
Variable costs	680,000		1.25	850,000
Contribution	170,000			212,500
Fixed costs	120,000	+25,000		145,000
Net profit	50,000			67,500

In terms of profit making, this improves upon the existing plan but it is inferior to proposal 1.

15.6 CONTRIBUTION THEORY AND PRODUCT-MIX DECISIONS

Where a business produces or provides a range of products or services, it should regularly assess whether all these products are effectively contributing to the business as a whole, or whether other products may be introduced that would make a better contribution. Decisions of this sort require information on the market and on costs, so these decisions should be made with the joint cooperation of the accounting department and the marketing department. The problem with this type of evaluation is the distinction between profitability and contribution, and fundamental to this is the concept of costs that are avoidable and costs that are unavoidable.

A publisher of garden and leisure books, in its first year of operations, currently publishes three paperbacks. The financial information available on the business is as follows:

	Book A	Book B	Book C
Selling price	£2.50	£9.00	£6.00
Books sold	10,000	12,000	6,000
Material and labour costs per unit	£0.50	£0.75	£0.60
Royalties (fraction of cover price)	10%	12%	15%
Author's annual retainer	£3,000	£2,000	nil
Costs allocated and apportioned:			
Administration costs	£30,000	£30,000	£10,000
Selling and distribution costs	£15,000	£27,500	£18,400

The profitability of each book will now be calculated:

	Book A £	Book B £	Book C £	Total £
Sales revenue	25,000	108,000	36,000	169,000
Material and labour costs	(5,000)	(9,000)	(3,600)	(17,600)
Royalties	(2,500)	(12,960)	(5,400)	(20,860)
Contribution	17,500	86,040	27,000	130,540

	Book A £	Book B £	Book C £	Total £
Fixed costs:				
Author's retainer	(3,000)	(2,000)	nil	(5,000)
Administration costs*	(30,000)	(30,000)	(10,000)	(70,000)
Selling and distribution*	(15,000)	(27,500)	(18,400)	(60,900)
Net profit	(30,500)	26,540	(1,400)	(5,360)

* Fifty percent of the administration costs in each department can be saved if any book is discontinued, as plant and machinery can be sold. Forty percent of selling and distribution costs can be saved if the books are no longer advertised, distributed and discounted.

Using this information, conventional calculations based on total cost suggest that books A and C should be discontinued after the year-end review. As A makes the biggest loss, consider the effect of discontinuing A only. Assuming the sales and costs of books B and C are maintained for the next year, what would be the total profit for the publisher if book A were not published?

	Department A	Book B £	Book C £	Total £
Sales revenue		108,000	36,000	144,000
Material/labour costs	No activity	(9,000)	(3,600)	(12,600)
Royalties		(12,960)	(5,400)	(18,360)
Contribution	nil	86,040	27,000	113,040
Fixed costs:				
Author's retainer	(3,000)	(2,000)	nil	(5,000)
Administration costs	(15,000)	(30,000)	(10,000)	(55,000)
Selling and distribution	(9,000)	(27,500)	(18,400)	(54,900)
Net profit	(27,000)	26,540	(1,400)	(1,860)

To discontinue book A would be beneficial to the organization as a whole, as the total profitability of the whole business is increased by (£5,360 – £1,860) £3,500. Why is this?

By discontinuing A, the publishers lose the contribution to fixed costs that A makes, but they can save more than this through being able to avoid a proportion of the allocated costs in that department. However, certain establishment costs cannot be avoided, such as rent, business rates, administration and management salaries. These costs are shared by the organization as a whole and, to all intents and purposes, they are indivisible. The difference between the loss incurred by the publishers can be explained in the following way:

	£
Contribution lost by discontinuation of book A	(17,500)
Avoidable FC (30,000 × 0.50) + (15,000 × 0.40)	21,000
Net change in profitability	3,500

The crucial point is that net profit per product is irrelevant. If the product or service makes a contribution towards the fixed costs of the organization, removing it from the range will serve to reduce overall profit, as long as this is not outweighed by the possible savings on avoidable departmental fixed costs. When deciding on a strategy for product or service mix, the contribution made by each item should be examined, taking into account the costs that can be avoided if discontinuation takes place. If a product makes a positive contribution to fixed costs, but the fixed costs that can be saved by discontinuation outweigh this contribution, then the business should discontinue the product unless there are wider considerations. To prove this point, we will prepare the schedule under the assumption that C is discontinued and A is retained.

	Book A £	Book B £	Department C £	Total £
Sales revenue	25,000	108,000		133,000
Material costs	(5,000)	(9,000)	No activity	(14,000)
Royalties	(2,500)	(12,960)		(15,460)
Contribution	17,500	86,040	nil	103,540
Fixed costs:				
Author's retainer	(3,000)	(2,000)	nil	(5,000)
Administration costs	(30,000)	(30,000)	(5,000)	(65,000)
Selling and dist costs	(15,000)	(27,500)	(11,040)	(53,540)
Net profit	(30,500)	26,540	(16,040)	(20,000)

This time the avoidable fixed costs are subtracted from the overheads of department C. The reduction in profitability caused by discontinuing book C, as compared with keeping all three books, is £20,000 – £5,360 = £14,640. That is to say, the publishers would be worse off by £14,640 if they discontinued C, despite the fact that book C was an accounting loss-maker. This is explained in the following way:

	£
Contribution lost by discontinuation of book C	(27,000)
Avoidable FC (10,000 × 0.50) + (18,400 × 0.40)	12,360
Net change in total profitability	(14,640)

Clearly the best decision for the publishers would be to discontinue A, but to keep C, which would mean that the business would make an overall profit of £1,140, as already calculated.

To conclude, a product or service should normally be discontinued if the following criteria apply:

1 It does not make a contribution to fixed costs.
2 The avoidable fixed costs to be saved by discontinuing the product or service outweigh the contribution made by that product or service.
3 If a product or service can be introduced that produces a greater contribution to the organization than the product facing discontinuation, assuming no impact on fixed costs.

The last of these criteria introduces the economic concept of **opportunity cost**. The opportunity cost involves looking at alternative uses for the facilities and resources utilized by an individual product within a range. Could these resources be used more profitably by producing or providing another product? This would involve the business taking into account the contribution that the new product would make in comparison with the original product. This contribution should also include any fixed-cost savings that could be made in producing the new product compared with producing the original product.

Opportunity cost is an economic concept. What it means is that the cost of utilizing resources in their present manner should include the benefits foregone by not using them for their next best alternative. The following simple example may explain the idea further.

A chef is employed by a hotel for £12,000 a year, and has £20,000 in the building society earning 10% per annum. The chef decides to set up a restaurant business, using the savings and leaving the job at the hotel. The estimated revenues are £80,000, and the annual costs are estimated to be £67,000. Should the chef become self-employed?

On the face of it, as the business is projecting an annual net profit of £13,000, it would seem a viable proposition. However, the projections do not include the opportunities foregone by going into this business, as opposed to keeping the job, and keeping the money in the building society. In order to set up the business, the chef has had to give up the salary of £12,000 and the interest of £20,000 × 0.10 = £2,000, a total of £14,000. This is known as the opportunity cost of the current use of resources.

The opportunity cost should be included with the other estimated costs of the enterprise. If they are, the projected profit becomes a projected loss of £1,000, and the chef would be advised to remain employed. The notion of opportunity cost will be examined further when considering contribution theory for scarce resources.

15.7 PROFIT MAXIMIZATION WHERE RESOURCES ARE LIMITED

It should be evident that unit product or service contribution, not unit net profit, is the critical factor when it comes to evaluating total profitability within a multiproduct or multiservice business. It is not that profit and contribution are in some way contradictory or incompatible. They are not. If contribution is maximized then so is profit; or if contribution is not adequate to cover fixed assets, then at least losses will be minimized. This is because contribution is a better measure of relative performance when it comes to shared facilities and resources. Chapter 13 explained how the apportionment of shared costs is an arbitrary process, and the resulting full-cost structure of an individual product or service will vary according to the method for apportioning remote costs.

Contribution is a more objective measure of an individual product's relative performance within a multiproduct business, because variable costs are implicitly **product-specific or service-specific at unit level**. If sales can be identified by product or service directly, and variable costs can be similarly identified, the difference between them, known as the contribution, is also specific to a product or service. If this is the case, then contribution is the only way in which the relative financial performance of an individual product or service should be compared with another.

In the short run, most businesses are constrained in their available production or service capacity. But theoretically there are no such constraints in the long run. The short-run constraints are listed in Table 15.1. Where there are constraints of this type, management must decide, in the light of these constraints, which products or services to produce or provide. The way in which they do this is to ask: which one of our products or services produces the greatest contribution to the business per pound sterling/gallon/metre/hour/square metre/kilo/seat/sale/order of the scarce resource utilized?

Table 15.1 Short-run constraints on production or service capacity

Limit	Example
Within the organisation	
Limit on space	Seats in a theatre
Limit on plant and equipment	Capacity of kiln in a pottery
Outside in the environment	
Limit on supply of materials	Sea bass for restaurant
Limit on skilled staff	Jockeys for racehorses
Statutory limits on output	Milk quotas
Limits on demand	All products and services

It does not matter how the constraint is measured. The key issue is which of the products or services that can be made or provided makes the best use of the limited resource in contributing to the fixed costs and profits of the organization as a whole.

Consider a very simple example. An agency has two comedians available to it for one night. It has to pay each comedian £100 for a nightly performance. The only booking available for this particular night is at the West Hill Social Club. The club is prepared to pay the agency £180 for comedian A and £200 for comedian B.

Clearly the agency has to make a choice between using comedian A or B. The constraint in this situation is effective demand for the service that is offered. If two venues were available for that night, they would offer both comedians a date, as long as the booking charge exceeded the comedians' nightly fees, i.e. as long as a contribution was made on each booking. In this case, as only one can be used, and as both comedians have the same variable cost, the agent would use B, as the price charged for B is higher.

Here is a more comprehensive example. A horse-racing syndicate has four horses and four registered jockeys. The following information is available on these horses for a particular day's racing:

	Ascot	Bangor	Chester	Doncaster
Horse	1	2	3	4
Entry fee	£1,200	£500	£200	£600
Travel and incidentals	£50	£90	£120	£60
Jockey's fee	£100	£100	£100	£100
Prize money, win only:	£32,500	£6,000	£9,600	£7,000
Betting odds	12–1	2–1	5–1	5–2

Of the entry fee, various proportions are asked for as deposits before a horse can be officially entered. The balance is paid at the track on the day, if the horse is running.

	Ascot	Bangor	Chester	Doncaster
Deposit on entry fee	50%	20%	30%	0%

The syndicate had intended running all four horses, but on the morning of the day itself, one of the jockeys was beginning a three-day ban for whip abuse and was not available to ride. Which horse should the trainer not run, of the four available to race on that day? This problem involves two considerations with regard to contribution: (a) probability and (b) avoidable costs. The contributions that each horse can make to the syndicate's fixed costs and profit are as follows:

	Horse 1 £	Horse 2 £	Horse 3 £	Horse 4 £
Prize money (£/odds)	2,500	2,000	1,600	2,000
Entry fee to pay	(600)	(400)	(140)	(600)
Jockey's fee	(100)	(100)	(100)	(100)
Travel, etc.	(50)	(90)	(120)	(60)
Contribution	1,750	1,410	1,240	1,240

Note that in a two-horse race, for example, where both horses are known to have identical chances to win, with the bookmaker requiring only to breakeven, odds of 1–1 (evens) should theoretically be offered on each horse. This would mean that the monies paid out to the backers of the winning horse would be exactly met from the stakes placed by backers of the losing horse. Therefore, evens is the same as a probability of 1/2, and 5–2 is the same as a probability of 2/7. In the case of horse 1, if the prize money offered for a win is £32,500 and the odds are 12–1, the horse has a probability of 1/13 of winning that amount, so based on probability, the prize money obtainable is £32,500/13 = £2,500.

The only part of the entry fee that should be included in the schedule as a variable or avoidable cost, is that part of the entry fee that is still to be paid, i.e. the fee that can still be saved by not running the horse. The deposit already paid is irrelevant to the decision about which horse should now be withdrawn.

The limiting factor is the availability of the jockeys. Horses 1 and 2 both provide more contribution per jockey than horses 3 and 4. The owning syndicate would be indifferent as to whether they would withdraw the horse at Chester or the horse at Doncaster from a purely financial viewpoint, as they would mean the loss of identical contributions. The final decision may have to be based on factors not yet reflected in the betting odds, such as the condition of the ground, etc., or on qualitative factors such as whether a horse needs a run or not, or even on the personal preferences of the jockeys.

Constraints with multiple products or services

If a business produces or provides more than one product or service, and several constraints limit the maximum possible output of that business, a technique known as **linear programming** may be used. This technique can help management decide on the optimal plan in order to maximize the contribution earned by the business in a given period.

Suppose a souvenir manufacturer makes two aluminium ornaments for the tourist trade in Paris; the Eiffel and the Dame. The information on their production is given below:

	Eiffel	Dame
Contribution per unit	FFr 10	FFr 10
Labour time per product	12 min	8 min
Aluminium	600 g	1,000 g

There are constraints on the amount of labour that is available in the month, and on the amount of aluminium:

Labour available per month   200 h (1 h = 60 min)
Aluminium available   1,200 kg (1 kg = 1,000 g)

The optimum production plan for the business can be plotted on a graph to find the greatest contribution. First it is necessary to convert the information into equations. The objective is to maximize

$$10e + 10d \text{ (contribution)}$$

where

$$e = \text{number of Eiffels produced}$$

$$d = \text{number of Dames produced}$$

subject to the constraints

$$12e + 8d = (200 \times 60) \text{ (labour constraint)}$$

$$600e + 1,000d = (1,200 \times 1,000) \text{ (material constraint)}$$

So what would be the maximum number of Eiffels that could be made within the labour constraint if no Dames were produced? The answer is

$$12,000/12 = 1,000$$

How many Dames could be made if no Eiffels were produced? The answer is

$$12,000/8 = 1,500$$

The line of constraint can be graphed by joining these two points on a graph plotting the maximum possible quantities of e and d along the x and y axes (Fig. 15.4).

Using the same method, it is possible to calculate the coordinates needed for the aluminium constraint. How many Eiffels could be made from the available aluminium if no Dames were produced? The answer is

$$1,200,000/600 = 2,000$$

How many Dames could be made from the available aluminium if no Eiffels were produced? The answer is

$$1,200,000/1,000 = 1,200$$

It is possible to graph these constraints, which will limit possible combinations of outputs for Eiffels and Dames within the month. Any point which lies within the limits of both constraint lines, the **feasible region**, will indicate a possible production plan (i.e. anywhere in the region of the graph within the boundaries of the critical constraint lines and the x and y axes).

With both products making a contribution, the optimal position will lie at an extreme point somewhere on the limit of the feasible region, but where exactly? At any point on the graph, it is possible to draw an isocontribution line (a line connecting combinations of d and e which will yield equal contribution). The equation of this line is derived from the objective function $10d + 10e$, already shown. As the unit contributions from both products are identical, the contribution line will form an equilateral triangle wherever it

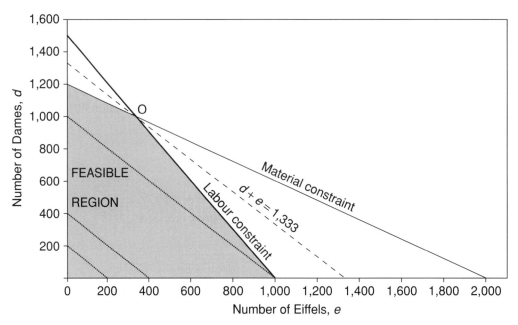

Figure 15.4 Linear programming: the three dotted lines are isocontribution lines with the equation 10d + 10e = c, where c = total contribution

is plotted on the graph. That is to say, the angle between the contribution line and each axis will be 45°, assuming appropriate scaling. Had the unit contributions been different for each product, the gradient of the contribution line would have been different. The optimal solution can therefore be found graphically by plotting the contribution line $10d + 10e = C$ as far as it can go from the origin of the graph, while still remaining in contact with the feasible region at some point. To do this, draw an arbitrary isocontribution line L and lay a ruler on top of it. Keeping the ruler parallel with line L, move it through the feasible region towards the lines of constraint and away from the origin. Just before the entire length of the ruler leaves the feasible region there will be the optimum solution to $10d + 10e = c$.

If the optimal solution were to be calculated mathematically, it would involve the use of simultaneous equations. By referring to Fig. 15.4 the optimum has been found at the point where both constraints cross, or where the values of each separate equation coincide. The equation of the labour constraint is

$$12e + 8d = 12,000 \qquad (1)$$

and the equation of the aluminium constraint is

$$600e + 1,000d = 1,200,000 \qquad (2)$$

Multiplying equation (1) by −50 and writing it above equation (2) gives

$$-600e - 400d = -600,000 \qquad -50 \times (1)$$

$$600e + 1,000d = 1,200,000 \qquad (2)$$

Adding them together gives

$$-600e - 400d = -600,000$$

$$600e + 1,000d = 1,200,000$$

$$600d = 600,000$$

$$d = 1,000$$

Substituting this into equation (1) gives

$$12e + (8 \times 1,000) = 12,000$$

$$12e = 4,000$$

$$e = 333 \qquad \text{(to the nearest unit)}$$

This means the maximum contribution that can be earned by the company in the following month is by making 1,000 Dames and 333 Eiffels:

	FFr
1,000 × FFr 10	10,000
333 × FFr 10	3,330
	13,330

15.8 MAKE-OR-BUY DECISIONS

Where a business has a limited ability to produce or provide all the products for which there is a demand, it may be possible to satisfy this demand by subcontracting part of the productive capacity, or through buying in the shortfall in output. The choice between producing or purchasing is the subject of this section.

One of the most important choices that faces a business is whether to make a product or whether to buy it in. In the souvenir example it might pay the manufacturer to buy in additional materials and additional labour time from another source, as long as the combined cost of doing so is below the additional contribution of FFr 10 to be gained by producing and selling additional Dames and/or Eiffels. In fact, if these products were available in completed form from a wholesaler at below FFr 10, it would be more profitable to satisfy surplus demand through buying in the completed product from that source.

Although the tourism, leisure and hospitality industry is mainly service-based, some sectors are involved in manufacture, usually with respect to food products. A crucial strategic issue here is that the cost structure of the company is determined directly by the type of policy pursued. It is now necessary to return to the crucial distinction between fixed costs and variable costs. If a business manufactures its own products, it will need to incur variable costs and fixed costs in order to make the product available. If the business buys in the equivalent product from a supplier, a higher proportion of the costs will be variable.

Two companies will now be compared. One is a restaurant which makes its own food on the premises, the other is a restaurant that purchases in ready-made meals. In all other respects their businesses are identical.

	Home-made £	Ready-made £
Sales revenue for year	105,000	105,000
Variable costs	35,000	70,000
Contribution	70,000	35,000
Fixed costs	45,000	10,000
Net profit	25,000	25,000

Both restaurants make a profit of £25,000 per year. Does it matter that they have different cost structures? From a strategic management perspective, the cost structure does matter in that if a general change in the demand for restaurant food takes place, the effects on these businesses will be different.

Scenario 1: Sales revenue increases from the original level by 30%

It is necessary to multiply both the sales revenue and the total variable costs for each organization by 1.30 to find the new profit level. Fixed costs are unaffected.

	Home-made £	Ready-made £
Sales revenue for year	136,500	136,500
Variable costs	45,500	91,000
Contribution	91,000	45,500
Fixed costs	45,000	10,000
Net profit	46,000	35,500

The organization with the greater dependence on fixed costs benefits more from the increase in demand than the organization with a greater dependence on variable costs.

Scenario 2: Sales revenue falls from the original level by 30%

It is necessary to multiply both the sales revenue and the total variable costs for each organization by 0.70 to find the new profit level. Fixed costs are unaffected.

	Home-made £	Ready-made £
Sales revenue for year	73,500	73,500
Variable costs	24,500	49,000
Contribution	49,000	24,500
Fixed costs	45,000	10,000
Net profit	4,000	14,500

This time the organization with the greater dependence on fixed costs is relatively worse off than the other organization. In fact, if the fall in revenue were a little more than 30%, the Home-made Restaurant would move into a loss situation.

Many businesses in the tourism, leisure and hospitality sector have a similar cost structure to the Home-made Restaurant, such as airlines, railways, hotels, leisure centres, golf
courses and a whole host of amenities which are available for the general public. These
businesses are therefore vulnerable to falls in demand for their services and they are very
badly affected by a general economic downturn.

The reason that a business produces for itself, rather than buying in initially, is to
get a cost advantage over the competition. This is simply a case of comparing the **full
absorption cost per unit** of making the product with the current purchase price of the
equivalent product. If the full cost of producing is less than the cost of buying in, the
decision may be taken to produce.

However, a business may need to review its policy on make or buy. If there is a downturn in demand, the full cost of the produced product will rise in comparison with the
bought-in price, simply because fixed costs are being spread over fewer units. A business
in this situation may be tempted to stop production and start buying in, if a saving can
be made. This would only be sensible if it could immediately avoid incurring at least
some of its fixed costs. In reality, as many of these costs are shared with other facilities,
there may not be scope to make the required savings, and other costs may be unavoidable in the short term. Assume the Home-made Restaurant is about to review its policy
on make or buy. It is established that of the fixed costs currently incurred, £30,000 can
be saved immediately if production of food is discontinued. The following unit cost and
price information can be assumed for both businesses if they decided to manufacture for
themselves.

	Home-made £
Price of meal	15.00
Unit variable cost per meal	5.00
Purchase price of equivalent bought-in meal	10.00*

* Equal to the price paid by Ready-made for its meals.

Would the Home-made Restaurant be better off if it decided to buy in meals rather than
continue to produce, having seen a downturn in business of 30%?

		Home-made £
Total sales	(4,900* × 15)	73,500
Variable costs	(4,900* × 10)	49,000
Contribution		24,500
Fixed costs		15,000
Net profit		9,500

* 4,900 = (73,500 ÷ 15)

In this situation it does seem more profitable to move from production to a buying-in
policy, as the profit can be increased from £4,000 to £9,500. Would the decision be the
same if the review had taken place following a 30% increase in business?

		Home-made £
Total sales	(9,100* × 15)	136,500
Variable costs	(9,100* × 10)	91,000
Contribution		45,500
Fixed costs		15,000
Net profit		30,500

* 9,100 = (136,500 ÷ 15)

In this situation it is clear that the restaurant would be better off maintaining its production facilities, as the profit made was originally £46,000.

The financial implications of cost structures and the effect of changes in the level of demand will be further discussed in Chapter 19, which describes how to evaluate a business's vulnerability to failure. Also, note how the decisions here were purely quantitative; they took no account of other issues that may influence the make-or-buy decision. Here are some of them.

Strategic considerations on make or buy

Is there a substitute?
It may not be possible to buy in an equivalent product if the product is unique, and the business is the sole supplier in the market. An ice-cream parlour that sells ice-cream made from a special recipe, handed down from generation to generation, will not be able to buy the equivalent product, only a similar and possibly inferior version.

Is the alternative source reliable and of the appropriate quality?
If there is an available source of materials, components or finished products, the purchasing business should ensure the source is reliable in terms of availability and quality.

Are adequate resources available?
If the financial evaluation of the make-or-buy choice comes down in favour of making, it is important to check that adequate resources are available; if not, a financially sound policy may still be unfeasible. The first consideration must be whether the financial capital that would be required can be obtained in order to acquire the fixed assets upon which the manufacturing process depends? This would certainly be a considerable amount if the business were to be set up on a greenfield site. This would involve examining the sources of finance available. Can adequate funds be raised from shareholders, from lenders or from government agencies? From the operational standpoint, are the direct materials required for producing the product available? Are the skilled staff available? Is it possible to purchase the necessary plant and equipment?

SUMMARY

1 **Accountants and economists take different views of cost and revenue behaviour.**

2 **The break-even point can be can calculated by several methods: graphical, mathematical and the contribution method.**

3 Contribution theory is a quick way to evaluate business proposals and alternatives from a financial perspective.

4 Contribution theory can be applied to the financial evaluation of product and service mix.

5 Contribution theory can be applied to profit maximization where there are limits on activity.

6 Contribution theory can be applied to the financial evaluation of a make-or-buy policy.

ASSESSMENT

MULTIPLE-CHOICE QUESTIONS

Question 1
If a business wants to increase the rate at which total contribution increases at all levels of sales volume, which one of the following decisions will produce the required result?

A Increase price
B Reduce fixed costs
C Increase unit variable costs
D Increase sales volume

Question 2
A hotel has 40 standard rooms. The variable costs of letting a room for the night are £5 for cleaning and washing laundry and for replacing consumables. The standard price per room is £30, and the total monthly fixed costs are £15,000. What proportion of occupancy would be required in order to make a monthly profit of £5,000? Assume 30 days in the month.

A 1/2
B 1/6
C 2/3
D 1/3

Question 3
A restaurant has the following cost structure:

	£
Sales	100,000
Variable costs	60,000
Contribution	40,000
Fixed costs	20,000
Net profit	20,000

Which of the following alternatives would produce the worst profit?

A Increase price by 20%, which would produce a fall in demand of 10%
B Do nothing
C Buy a machine that will increase annual fixed costs by £10,000, but which will reduce unit variable costs by 20%
D Reduce the price by 10% and spend £10,000 on advertising, producing a 20% increase in sales volume

Question 4

If a travel agent is deciding between cutting product A or product B from its range of holiday packages, what would be the overall effect on profit of cutting one rather than the other?

	Package A	Package B	Package C
Sales	5,000	6,000	8,000
Variable costs	5,500	4,000	6,000
Contribution	(500)	2,000	2,000
Fixed costs allocated and apportioned*	2,000	3,500	1,000
Net profit or loss	(2,500)	(1,500)	1,000

A No difference either way
B An overall difference of £1,500
C An overall difference of £500
D An overall difference of £2,500

* Assume none of the fixed costs are avoidable.

Question 5

The popular Chiltern Hotel always operates at 100% capacity and offers three types of bedroom. The information on the rooms is as follows:

	Family	Double	Single
Number of rooms available per night	100	100	100
Price per room per day	£40	£30	£21
Cleaning time per room	1.0 h	45 min	30 min
Daily cost of laundry and consumables	£10	£6	£4

Due to a shortage of cleaning staff on one particular day, the number of available cleaning hours is only 200. The fixed costs of the hotel, including all staff wages and salaries, are £4,250 per day. Given the shortage of cleaning staff means that not all rooms can be made available, what is the maximum profit that can be earned from the hotel?

A £6,350
B £2,034
C £2,100
D £2,000

EXERCISES

Exercise 1

The senior management accountant of Roux Ski, Geneva, is asked to advise the board of directors on a production and sales plan for their ski-pants factory in Lyon for the following month. Here is the cost information available for the four-week period to July 31, 19x3 based on a normal production plan:

	SwFr
Direct and indirect labour (40% variable)	300,000
Direct and indirect materials (2/3 variable)	570,000
Rent	30,000
Machine costs including depreciation (10% variable)	100,000
Sales and distribution costs (25% variable)	40,000
Finance costs	80,000
	1,120,000

These costs are based on the factory operating at 80% capacity, which means producing 5,200 pairs of ski pants a month, and selling them at SwFr 250 a pair. Two plans are being considered by the board:

1 Increase the price to SwFr 300 and sell 4,000 pairs.
2 Reduce the price to SwFr 220 and increase the sales to 7,500 pairs per month.

The second option involves exceeding the normal capacity of the factory, and this can be overcome by doing one of the following:

(a) Purchasing a new industrial sewing-machine and hiring two extra staff for a total additional monthly fixed cost of SwFr 95,000.
(b) Subcontracting the additional work to Laisserfaire Ltd, buying in the equivalent product for SwFr 200 a pair.

Required

(a) Calculate the break-even point under the original plan, and under plan 1.
(b) Calculate the profit under all the alternatives.

Exercise 2

The Oversea Hotel has the following financial information from its last summer season, which lasted 12 weeks:

	£	£
Sales revenue		
An average of 25 guests for 12 weeks at £60 a week		18,000
Bar sales at an average of £15 per guest per week		4,500
		22,500
Costs		
Food (variable)	6,000	
Cost of drink (variable)	2,250	
Cleaning materials (20% variable)	1,500	
Salaries (fixed)	5,000	
Heat and light (50% variable)	2,800	
Advertising (fixed)	4,500	
Entertainment (fixed)	950	
		23,000
Net loss		500

The hotel proprietor was not happy with the loss incurred last year, and expects the same commercial conditions to prevail for the coming season. The proprietor asks for suggestions to improve the performance of the hotel and receives the following ideas:

1 The proprietor's son suggests increasing the weekly price of accommodation by 15%, but will produce an estimated fall in bookings of 10%.
2 The proprietor's spouse suggests that more entertainment should be provided. It is estimated this would have the effect of increasing the weekly bookings by 20%, only achievable perhaps by doubling the weekly costs of entertainment, and increasing the advertising spend by £1,000.
3 The proprietor's daughter suggests that cheaper food and smaller portions could achieve a 40% reduction in the food bill per person.
4 The proprietor's mother suggests that the price of drinks should be reduced to generate more income from that side of the business. A 10% reduction in the price of beer would generate a 50% increase in the volume of drink sold.

Required

(a) Evaluate each of the four suggestions. Which would be the most profitable suggestion? Or would the hotel be better off by staying as it is?
(b) What are the non-financial considerations that the proprietor of the hotel might wish to take into account when considering the desirability of each alternative?

Exercise 3

The directors of Holly Tours Ltd are reviewing the profitability of their four holiday packages and considering the potential effect of alternative ways to vary the product mix. The company accountant has given the board of directors the following information:

	Total £	A £	B £	C £	D £
Sales	125,200	20,000	36,000	25,200	44,000
Cost of tours	88,550	9,500	14,114	27,936	37,000
Gross profit	36,650	10,500	21,886	(2,736)	7,000
Operating expenses	23,944	3,900	5,952	5,652	8,440
Net profit or loss	12,706	6,600	15,934	(8,388)	(1,440)
Holidays sold		100	120	180	200
Price per package		£200	£300	£140	£220

The costs of tours from holiday companies are directly proportional to the number sold. There are some additional variable operating expenses per holiday sold:

A	B	C	D
£23.40	£25.00	£20.00	£24.00

The rest of the operating expenses are fixed and cover staff salaries, administration and establishment costs.

Required

(a) Evaluate each of the four proposals on the agenda for the next board meeting. Your evaluation should calculate the change in projected net profit figure of Holly Tours under each of these four proposals, as against the no-change option:
   – Discontinue package C, with no consequential change in sales of the other packages.
   – Discontinue packages D and C, with no consequential change in the sales of the other two packages.
   – Discontinue C and increase the price of D to £264 with an expected drop in the sales of D to 150.
   – Launch a post-Christmas advertising campaign costing £1,000 which would increase the sales volume of all packages by 10%.
(b) Write a short memo to the finance director outlining your recommendation. Explain why discontinuing products which make net losses on an individual basis may not always improve the profitability of the business as a whole. And outline other factors that should be taken into account before ultimately deciding on a plan for the business.

Exercise 4

A wedding-cake shop makes two types of cake:

	Cake 1	Cake 2
	£	£
Price	25.00	30.00
Ingredients	(2.00)	(3.00)
Labour cost per cake	(10.00)	(15.00)
Unit contribution	13.00	12.00
Fixed costs per year	1,000	1,500
Demand for cakes per year	500	300

The cakes are made by one cook who works 50 weeks a year for 30 hours a week. The cook is paid on a per-cake basis, and the time taken to make and bake a cake is as follows:

Cake 1	Cake 2
2 h	2.5 h

Required

(a) Calculate whether all the cakes can be made to meet the present demand. If there is a resource constraint to overcome, which cake should take priority with regard to utilizing this limited resource? Which cake production should be cut back and by how much?

(b) An option exists to purchase all of cake 1 or cake 2, or to cease production altogether and buy in all requirements from another source. The buying-in prices are as follows:

Cake 1	Cake 2
£15.00	£20.00

To cease production of either or both cakes would involve an immediate 25% saving on the allocated and apportioned fixed costs per product. Given this option, compare the profitability of producing all cakes as against buying in all cakes. What would be the best overall plan for the business from the viewpoint of profitability?

CHAPTER 16

Planning and budgeting

OBJECTIVES

- Understand that organizations should have strategic objectives determined by environmental influences and internal resource constraints.
- Determine an annual planning cycle with reference to the longer-term strategic plan.
- Obtain the data from which detailed individual budgets can be prepared.
- Construct a cash budget for the business.
- Prepare the master budget for the whole organization.
- Recognize the human behavioural implications inherent in preparing, negotiating, implementing and controlling the budgetary cycle.

INTRODUCTION

To plan is to act now to influence or determine some future event. A simple example is when a car driver looks in the mirror before making a manoeuvre. If the road is clear, the manoeuvre may be successfully undertaken. If no preparatory action precedes the ultimate action, the success of this action may not be guaranteed. Another example is the run-up of the long-jumper in an athletics competition. The ultimate objective is to land further up the sandpit than any of the other competitors in the event. This is achieved by landing as far up the jumping board as possible without crossing the line, at enough velocity, with as much power, to gain enough height, to spring as far forward up the sandpit as possible. The approach requires the athlete to focus intently on the jumping board at the end of the run, to ensure their rate of acceleration up the run and their length of stride are appropriate for the correct leg to hit the board at just the right point with enough impact.

The long-jumper must therefore continuously evaluate progress along the run in relation to the objective, taking appropriate corrective action should a mismatch develop between the required stride pattern and the current position in relation to the jumping board. If a mismatch does develop, taking no action will result in a no-jump if the board limit is exceeded, or in a short weak jump if the take-off is made prematurely. If the corrective action is too much or too late, the run will falter through excessive stretching for the jumping board, or through having to include an extra step.

This example includes all three elements for successful achievement of objectives:

Planning: where we want to be sometime in the future.
Feedback: assessing where we are now in relation to where we should be now.
Control: reappraising how, if it is still possible, our original objective may still be achieved.

Planning takes place over different timescales. The success of planning depends on the recognition of the interdependence between planning on these different levels. Take a school pupil of age 16 about to sit examinations. The pupil may have decided on a long-term career in hotel management. This will determine the ultimate vocational qualification required for entry to this career path. This in turn will determine the academic qualifications needed over the next few months to gain entry to an appropriate course, or its prerequisite. These requirements will therefore determine the immediate priorities for the forthcoming revision programme, and will determine the specific examination techniques and approach.

The overall planning cycle is therefore a top-down process, as the long-term objective(s) should determine the shorter-term behaviour and operations of the individual or the organization, which lead to the eventual achievement of the objective(s). From a control perspective, what is done from minute to minute, hour by hour, and day to day will have a direct influence on the outcome of longer-term plans. For the long-term objectives to be fulfilled, it is important that control is exercised in the short term, otherwise the place where individuals or organizations end up will not match where they want to be.

Long-term plans therefore need to be supported by short-term operational objectives which steer an individual or an organization to its desired goals. It is important from a control perspective that frequent feedback takes place, recognizing the gap between where the individual or organization wants to be and where it currently is, and allowing corrective action to be taken as soon as possible. The planning cycle is shown in Fig. 16.1.

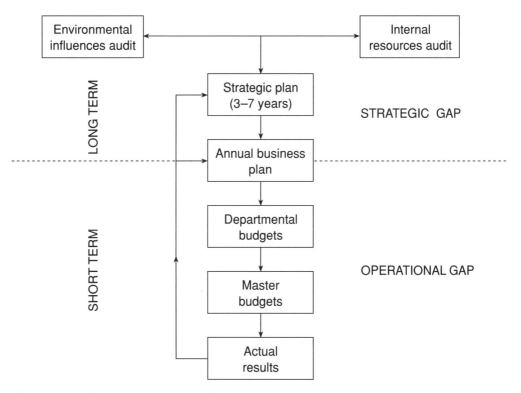

Figure 16.1 The planning and budgetary cycle

16.1 STRATEGIC PLANNING

As individuals need to identify a purpose to their existence, a meaning to their lives, and a broad direction to follow, so do organizations. This is partly because organizations consist of individuals who have their own personal needs, ambitions and aspirations, but mainly because an organization exists to provide a focus that coordinates and integrates these individual requirements towards a common purpose.

Individuals primarily require an income to meet their physiological needs, but there is also a psychological need to be occupied and stimulated, a need for social interaction, a need for power, a need for authority, a need for respect from others, and a need for self-respect and self-fulfilment. The organization is where most of an individual's needs are satisfied, whether that organization is a family, an educational establishment, a club or a business. The organization cannot operate successfully or be manageable unless it acts as a vehicle to satisfy individual needs and motivations, through the pursuit of common goals and objectives with which all members can identify.

A business organization is formed and exists in order to create wealth, initially for the investors that create and perpetuate it, but also to provide wealth for other groups of people, or stakeholders, such as employees, lenders and the government, who contribute to that organization. In order to continue creating wealth, the organization must take advantage of opportunities which present themselves, while averting potential threats to its position or existence. It must do this by making the best use of the resources available to it.

The strategic plan emerges from two distinct but interdependent audits:

1 Audit of external environmental influences
2 Audit of internal resources

Firstly an organization must decide what business it wishes to get into, and needs to re-appraise this periodically in the light of external and internal developments. The decision on what products or services to produce or provide should be based on the prevailing environmental influences and the resources available. In the tourism, leisure and hospitality industry, the environmental influences might include the following:

Exchange rates: affecting the numbers of foreign tourists, and their disposable holiday expenditure levels.
VAT and other tax changes: extending the scope of VAT to include books and magazines.
Demographics: a more physically active and well-off middle-aged group (empty-nesters), or a bulge in people at the age of 18–24, who enjoy low-price singles holidays.
Sociocultural values: the growth of the keep-fit exercise culture; the growth of healthy eating habits.
Government policy: relaxation of border controls and duties on imported products since 1993.
Business competition: the number and type of restaurants or tourist attractions in a given resort.

All these factors may influence the strategic direction of an organization and could influence the products or services that it might decide to produce and provide. This audit would need to be carried out regularly, as the environmental influences will change continuously, as a consequence of political, economic, technological and social trends.

However, if opportunities or threats present themselves in the environment, the business's response to this will be constrained by the resources available to it. An organization therefore, needs to audit its own physical resources and examine its own strengths and weaknesses. An internal resource audit might include the following items:

Examination of financial resources: are the required financial resources available, or can they be obtained? Can the boxing promoter afford the prefight advertising and promotional hype? Can the leisure centre obtain the finance to build the required complex, and sustain it for long enough to move into profit?

Examination of physical capacity: size of buildings, capacity of equipment and machinery. How many products can be made? How many customers can be accommodated? What should be the number of lanes in a bowling alley, the number of berths on a ship, the number of seats in a cinema, the number of tables in a restaurant?

Examination of human capability: are there enough of the right kind of employees to support the intended activity? Have the chefs got the necessary skills and experience to prepare meals of a certain standard? Are the actors convincing enough to hold an audience? Is the comedian funny? Can the band draw enough to fill the venue? Are the circus members adaptable enough to carry out a range of duties, from tent erecting to juggling?

By comparing the environmental influences (opportunities and threats), and the resource limitations (strengths and weaknesses), a strategic plan can be put together, setting the organization on a course it is able to follow, in the hope of reaching specific goals at the end. There could be a wide selection of strategic plans to suit the circumstances of a whole range of businesses in a variety of sectors. This type of audit is known as strengths, weaknesses, opportunities and threats (SWOT) analysis. Businesses can decide on long-term targets for profitability, sales volume, exports, or a specific market share, but in generic terms the number of strategies can be reduced to three main types:

- Cost leadership
- Differentiation
- Focus

These strategies revolve around gaining competitive advantage over existing and potential competitors by respectively:

Operating more economically: providing the same outputs from fewer inputs and providing better value for the customer.

Operating more effectively: providing more of what a customer specifically wants in terms of quality and service. This strategy sets the business apart from its competition by providing something different for the customer.

Operating more efficiently: using resources to focus exactly on a particular segment of a wider market, by specifically targeting the narrowly defined needs of a smaller but distinctive group of customers, by providing something special for the customer.

From now on the whole planning process will be explained using a comprehensive example. A hotel chain, which owns a number of traditional luxury hotels, has been particularly hit by a prolonged downturn in demand for this kind of accommodation. In response to a deteriorating financial position, the strategic planning committee, comprising the active board members of the company, carries out a SWOT analysis. The environmental influence audit throws up the following items:

1 Economic growth is not expected to increase significantly in the short to medium term.
2 The pound is expected to weaken against the new European currency, the euro.
3 Relaxation of immigration controls has led to increasing numbers of migrant workers moving around Europe to find employment, particularly in the skilled and professional sectors of the employment market.
4 A decline in hotel based corporate conferences has gradually taken place, as more and more companies use computer conferencing.
5 Interest rates will remain well below 10% for the foreseeable future.

And the internal resources audit has revealed these items:

1 A buyer is available to purchase three of the company's existing traditional hotel sites.
2 Suitable sites are available to the company in the appropriate places.
3 The management of the hotel has vast experience in setting up and running hotels.
4 The IT director of the company has considerable experience in the areas of smart card technology and cashless vending.

From the results of this SWOT analysis, the company decides to set up a chain of modern motels in major centres in south-east England, as high-quality, cashless, self-service holiday and business accommodation. The motels are to be functional, smart and immaculately clean, offering high-quality food, drink and accommodation. The low costs of running the hotels are to be achieved by inexpensive but stylish construction and fittings, with minimal staffing requirements. The target markets are holidaying tourists, particularly from mainland Europe, company representatives and agents, and migrant workers, particularly in the skilled and professional sectors. The generic strategy of the company is to follow a **cost leadership** strategy within the overnight motel/hotel sector, while providing the convenience, and comfort of ensuite rooms, containing TV/satellite and video facilities, and food and drink from electronic vending machines.

Staff requirements are negligible as key swipe-cards are dispensed from a machine in the hotel lobby, operated through a credit/debit card system. The swipe-card is then used by the guest to gain access from the lobby into the hotel, to enter the room, and to obtain items from the vending machines. The only staff employed apart from a maintenance team, are 'room refreshment' staff who clean, change linen and restock vending machines to predetermined levels on a daily basis.

Having carried out the SWOT analysis, the company directors decide to set up the Travel Inn chain of motels, with a plan to build one every year for the next five years. The following information is available on the company's plans. There will be 20 single and 10 double rooms per motel. The projected average occupation rate after the initial six-month launch period is expected to be 70%. The capital cost of £750,000 is to be 50% financed by an 8% debenture loan, and 50% by ordinary share capital. The plan for the next six months is as follows:

	Jan	Feb	March	April	May	June
Finance raised						
Construction phase						
Percent complete	30%	50%	100%			
				Hotel opens		
Occupation rates				30%	50%	60%

Room prices based on market research have been initially set at £35 per night for singles, and £50 per night for doubles. On average 10% of the rooms are estimated to be taken up by corporate guests whose companies settle statements on a monthly basis. Vending machines are expected to generate £10 and £16 per occupied night per single and double room, respectively. The estimated profit margin on both food and drink is 40% on the sales value. Suppliers of food and drink are paid monthly in arrears. At the end of any month, 10% of the average monthly stock requirement is expected to be on hand either in the vending machines or in storage.

Other variable costs for the hotel are estimated at £5 for a single room and £7 for a double room. These costs include laundry costs, costs of consumable items, and the staff wages of the room refreshment staff used per occupied night. Centralized fixed costs are as follows:

Depreciation	6% annually of the total capital cost with effect from 1 April
Interest	payable monthly in advance at 8% of the coupon value of the debenture (all finance raised on January 1)
Maintenance	£1,000 per calender month from April 1
Light and heat	£800 per calender month from April 1
Head-office costs	£36,000 per year incurred evenly from January 1, allocated specifically to the new development

16.2 THE ANNUAL PLANNING CYCLE

After the strategic plan has determined the broad objectives, the organization's budgetary planning committee is then charged with the responsibility of putting into detailed form the short-term financial implications of following the strategic plan. This involves collecting data from various sources and asking responsible individuals to compile programmes or budgets of activity and expenditure, which can be integrated into an overall master budget (Fig. 16.2).

The budgets are usually prepared in a particular sequence and in this example the sequence might be as follows:

1 Sales budget (accommodation and food and drink)
2 Debtor budget (corporate business)
3 Stock budget (food and drink for vending machines)
4 Creditor budget (for food and drink supplies)
5 Fixed-expenses budget
6 Fixed-assets budget (expenditure on, and depreciation of fixed assets)
7 Cash budget (estimate of monthly receipts and payments)

and the master budgets:

8 Forecast trading and profit and loss account
9 Forecast balance sheet

Before the detailed work of preparing these specific budgets is undertaken, it is necessary to establish broadly whether an adequate rate of return may be generated for the owners of the business after meeting all other commitments. This needs to be established for a normal year, when occupancy rates may have stabilized, and where the hotel has all its rooms available throughout. The budgetary committee would need to make an overall

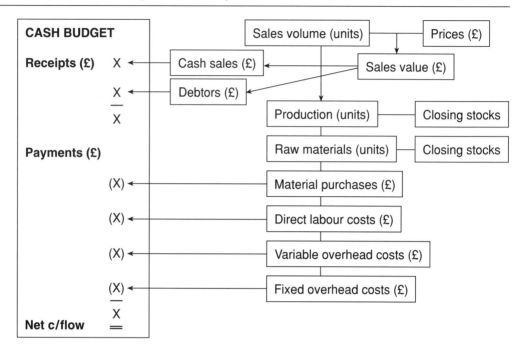

Figure 16.2 Integration of budgets

estimate of this normal level of profit per hotel, before they could take the decision whether to invest in the first place, or whether a revision of the strategic plan might be necessary.

The normal annual plan would reveal the following revenue from room letting:

$$[(20 \times £35) + (10 \times £50)] \times 365 \times 0.7 = £306,600$$

From food and drinks the revenue would be

$$[(20 \times £10) + (10 \times £16)] \times 365 \times 0.7 = £91,980$$

which amounts to 30% of the room-letting revenue.

The variable costs of food and drink are

$$£91,980 \times 0.4 = £36,792$$

and the other variable costs are

$$[(20 \times £5) + (10 \times £7)] \times 365 \times 0.7 = £43,435$$

The annual fixed costs are as follows:

Interest	(£750,000 × 0.5) × 0.08	=	£30,000
Depreciation	(£750,000 × 0.06)	=	£45,000
Maintenance	(£1,000 × 12)	=	£12,000
Light and heat	(£800 × 12)	=	£ 9,600
Head-office (HO) costs allocated for this unit		=	£36,000

With this data it is now possible to prepare a budget contribution statement for Travel Inn for one hotel in a normal year:

Annual contribution budget (Travel Inn)

	£
Total revenue (306,600 + 91,980)	398,580
Variable costs (36,792 + 43,435)	80,227
Contribution to fixed costs:	318,353
Fixed costs (30,000 + 45,000 + 12,000 + 9,600 + 36,000)	132,600
Budgeted annual profit	185,793

If the budgeted annual net profit is divided by the share capital invested by the shareholders, an approximate annual rate of return on the investment may be calculated. This gives a 185,793/375,000 = 49.53% rate of return to ordinary shareholders, with one hotel fully operational, which would seem to be a very healthy overall performance. If the rate of return had been unacceptable to the owners or the management, they would have needed to investigate options for changing some part of the plan in order to reach the required rate of return. Two questions might be asked about a plan that does not meet requirements.

Can revenues be increased in any way?

Here are some possible methods and the questions they raise:

1 Raising the price of rooms and vending machine stocks, but what about the effect on demand?
2 Increasing demand through advertising, but how effective is it likely to be at the cost?
3 Providing additional services for the customer, but would customers be willing to pay more for these?

Can costs be reduced in any way?

Here are some possible methods and the questions they raise:

1 Reducing the capital cost of construction and fitting, or will this materially reduce the quality of the accommodation provided, or the room capacity of the motel?
2 Buying vending-machine stocks from a cheaper supplier, but what about product quality and continuity of supplies?
3 Lowering the wage rates of room refreshment staff, but what about the effect on staff turnover, recruitment and general staff attitudes?
4 Reducing power costs by the introduction of timing devices and by reducing the ambient temperature on the central-heating thermostat, or would this have an adverse effect on customer satisfaction and ultimately on demand?
5 Seeking an alternative and cheaper dry-cleaning contractor, but what about the quality and reliability of the alternative?
6 Changing the depreciation rate, or would this contradict accounting conventions?
7 Reducing maintenance costs, or will this store up greater costs for the future?
8 Seeking an alternative and cheaper source of finance to replace the 8% debenture loan stock, but will this finance be forthcoming?

These questions should be asked by the planning committee, and answers should be sought from sources both within and outside the organization. If these changes can be made, and incorporated into the plan, then the required rate of return may be achieved. This process is essentially an iterative one where the budget planning committee sets the annual plan and then makes amendments to it in order to satisfy strategic requirements, and meet organisational and environmental constraints. At the end of this process an outline plan will emerge, from which the detailed budgets may be constructed.

16.3 PREPARING INDIVIDUAL BUDGETS

If the original plan was accepted, the detailed budgets for the next six months could then be compiled:

Sales budget (1)

	Jan £	Feb £	March £	April £	May £	June £
Room revenue				10,950	18,250	21,900
Food, etc (30% of room revenue)				3,285	5,475	6,570

Revenue from rooms is estimated approximately using the total room revenue projected at the normal 70% occupation. If the annual revenue at 70% is calculated per month, we have £306,600/12 = £25,550. Taking the estimated occupancy rates for April, May and June, it is possible to derive the planned monthly revenues for those months:

$$\text{April revenue} = £25,550 \times 3/7 = £10,950$$

$$\text{May revenue} = £25,550 \times 5/7 = £18,250$$

$$\text{June revenue} = £25,550 \times 6/7 = £21,900$$

Debtor budget (2)

	Jan £	Feb £	March £	April £	May £	June £
Opening debtors				nil	1,423	2,373
Sales, from (1)				14,235	23,725	28,470
				14,235	25,148	30,843
Receipts				12,812	22,775	27,996
Closing debtors				1,423	2,373	2,847

Receipts = 90% of the current month's sales revenues + 10% of the previous month's revenue, attributable to corporate customers.

Stock budget, food and drink (3)

	Jan £	Feb £	March £	April £	May £	June £
Opening stock				nil	131	219
Purchases				1,445	2,278	2,672
				1,445	2,409	2,891
Stock used (revenue × 0.4)				1,314	2,190	2,628
Closing stock				131	219	263

In the first month of operations the amount of stock purchased needs to be 110% of the monthly requirement. As 10% of each month's stock requirement is to be left on hand at the end of each month, it is possible to establish stock requirements from suppliers every month.

Creditor budget, food and drink (4)

	Jan £	Feb £	March £	April £	May £	June £
Opening creditors				nil	1,445	2,278
Purchases from (3)				1,445	2,278	2,672
				1,445	3,723	4,950
Payments				nil	1,445	2,278
Closing creditors				1,445	2,278	2,672

Fixed-expenses budget (5)

	Jan £	Feb £	March £	April £	May £	June £
Interest	2,500	2,500	2,500	2,500	2,500	2,500
Maintenance	1,000	1,000	1,000	1,000	1,000	1,000
Power	800	800	800	800	800	800
HO expenses	3,000	3,000	3,000	3,000	3,000	3,000
Depreciation	nil	nil	nil	3,750	3,750	3,750
Total	7,300	7,300	7,300	11,050	11,050	11,050

The monthly depreciation is

$$(£750,000 \times 0.06)/12 = £3,750$$

Fixed-assets budget (6)

	Jan £	Feb £	March £	April £	May £	June £
F assets b/d	nil	225,000	375,000	750,000	746,250	742,500
Expenditure	225,000	150,000	375,000	nil	nil	nil
	225,000	375,000	375,000	750,000	746,250	742,500
Depreciation, from (5)	nil	nil	nil	3,750	3,750	3,750
F assets c/d	225,000	375,000	750,000	746,250	742,500	738,750

16.4 CASH BUDGETS

Having prepared all the individual budgets, it is time to prepare a cash budget, which collates the cash flows from all the activities of the business and determines the projected cash position of the business at the end of every month. The cash flows can be obtained from the other individual budgets.

Cash budget (7)

	Jan £	Feb £	March £	April £	May £	June £
Receipts						
Shares	375,000					
Debentures	375,000					
Receipts (1)				12,812	22,775	27,996
Total	750,000			12,812	22,775	27,996
Payments						
Creditors (4)					1,445	2,278
Variable costs				1,551	2,585	3,102
Capital expenses (6)	225,000	150,000	375,000			
Interest (5)	2,500	2,500	2,500	2,500	2,500	2,500
Maintenance (5)				1,000	1,000	1,000
Power (5)				800	800	800
Fixed costs (5) (Head office)	3,000	3,000	3,000	3,000	3,000	3,000
Total	230,500	155,500	380,500	8,851	11,330	12,680
Opening bal	nil	519,500	364,000	(16,500)	(12,539)	(1,094)
(+) Receipts	750,000			12,812	22,775	27,996
	750,000	519,500	364,000	(3,688)	10,236	26,902
(−) Payments	230,500	155,500	380,500	8,851	11,330	12,680
Closing bal	519,500	364,000	(16,500)	(12,539)	(1,094)	14,222

The variable costs are (£43,435/12) × (monthly occupancy percentage/70)

16.5 MASTER BUDGETS

Forecast trading and profit and loss account (8)

After preparing all the individual budgets and the summary cash flow forecast, it is necessary to determine what will be the overall forecast profit or loss for the period under examination. Finally it is possible to assess the projected financial position of the business at the end of the period.

Forecast trading and profit and loss account for Travel Inn for the six months to September 30, 19x7

	Budgets	£	£
Total sales	(1)		66,430
Opening stock (food + drink)	(3)	nil	
Purchases	(3)	6,395	
		6,395	
Less closing stock	(3)	263	
		6,132	
Add variable costs	(7)	7,238	
Cost of sales			13,370
Gross profit			53,060
Less fixed expenses:	(5)		
Interest		15,000	
Maintenance		3,000	
Power		2,400	
Depreciation		11,250	
HO allocated expenses		18,000	
			49,650
Net profit			3,410

Forecast balance sheet (9)

Forecast balance sheet for Travel Inn as at September 30, 19x7

	Budgets	£	£	£
Fixed assets				
Buildings and fittings	(6)	750,000	11,250	738,750
Current assets				
Stock	(3)		263	
Debtors	(2)		2,847	
Bank	(8)		14,222	
			17,332	
Current liabilities				
Creditors (food + drink)	(4)		2,672	

Forecast balance sheet for Travel Inn as at September 30, 19x7 (cont'd)

Budgets	£	£	£
			14,660
Net current assets			
Less long-term liabilities			753,410
375,000 × £1			
debentures (8%)			375,000
Net assets			378,410
Financed by			
Ordinary share capital			
(375,000 × £1 shares)			375,000
Retained loss	(8)		3,410
			378,410

The business therefore projects how much profit or loss will be made for the period, and what the business's assets and liabilities will be at the end of that period.

The planning cycle then continues. The actual results will be compared with these forecasts, the differences investigated and a new plan put together for the next planning period in order to achieve the planned profit. Businesses should identify any 'operational gap' (Fig. 16.1) on a monthly basis so that the periodic plan may be adhered to. This will involve fine tuning to budgets on a monthly basis. Revised budgets may be required from the business's different departments, showing the latest expected revenues and costs, and their timings. If these forecast budgets reveal that the periodic profit objective may not be met, then corrective action will need to be taken. This will involve amending the budget with the assistance of departmental managers, or if this is not possible, the annual plan may need to be departed from.

16.6 BEHAVIOURAL ASPECTS OF PLANNING AND BUDGETING

Planning and budgeting is a complex process, as there are many budgets from all parts of the organization to compile and integrate. There exists the logistical problem of getting all the information required and putting it together within the required timescale. What is more important about plans and budgets, however, is their reliability, validity and attainability. Is the information gathered accurate, and will the plans be achieved? The answers to these questions rely to a great extent on the integrity and motivation of the individuals involved in the process. It must therefore be recognized that the setting of budgets is a negotiating process upon which the ambitions, hopes and fears of individuals depend, hence the whole process is a subjective balancing act where conflict between individual and organizational objectives must be minimized.

The first problem area is strategic planning. Have the internal and external audits been carried out correctly, or have the results been interpreted appropriately? For example, if the business is looking at the economic environment and competitive position, is the situation understood correctly, and can future events be predicted with sufficient certainty?

Some individuals have a strategic vision, based on their own drive and ambition, and their perception of the world. This vision is sometimes so focused that threats to the organization or specific opportunities may be missed. These individuals' strategic vision can change to tunnel vision or myopia unless they are aware that information must be verified and interpreted, the external environment changes very quickly, and their own personal judgement is not infallible.

At the annual planning level, the human aspects to take into account are whether the targets are too demanding or not demanding enough. The critical factor is motivation. People need targets, else they operate in an aimless and feckless way, as if in a vacuum. A salesperson selling timeshare holidays would not be so aggressive and determined if a commission were not earned for every deal, or unless a minimum number had to be sold in a specified period. The individual is motivated by rewards but also by fear of failure.

Rewards can be monetary, but inner satisfaction can sometimes motivate more than money. Professional people can get more motivated by the prospect of creative achievement, or by gaining the respect of colleagues than by simply getting paid more. Any targets must therefore be **attainable** and **demanding**. But remember that one person's impossible target is another person's easy target, depending on the aptitude, attitude and ability of the individuals. An individual will fail to be motivated if targets are impossible or facile, but also through a combination of these two aspects:

1 A target is too difficult to achieve in relation to the satisfaction to be gained from achieving it.
2 A target is not worth achieving because failing to do so brings relatively little dissatisfaction or punishment, perhaps none.

The level of satisfaction or dissatisfaction to be got from achieving or failing to achieve a target will also vary from individual to individual. It will depend on the type of employee, on social status and on all sorts of other complex psychological factors. If employees are not motivated by the rewards of achieving a target, they will not perform; nor will they perform if sanctions for failure are insignificant. The danger is that unless the individual is involved, or participates directly in the planning and target-setting process, the targets are more likely to be thought of as threats rather than inducements. Unreliable information may then be submitted, creating 'slack' during the budgeting process.

An example is a sports products representative being given an annual sales target by line to be achieved without commission. The slack is created by selling up to target and holding over orders towards the end of the month, delaying their processing and delivery into the following month. The disadvantage of this is that, although the representative is motivated to produce up to target levels, any further sales are not rewarded. The danger is that if the targets are too difficult, the representative will not be motivated to achieve them; but if they are too easy, they will encourage stock-outs through delaying order processing for which there is demand, losing immediate sales and possibly the loyalty of disappointed customers. A possible solution to this is to provide a commission on sales beyond target levels, thereby motivating the representative to carry on selling beyond the base targets. The danger is that the representative may be motivated to order excessively, and could damage relationships with customers as a result.

This example of slack creation can be adapted to any budget situation: in the sales department, in the restaurant, in the clerical office, even at board level. Wherever incentives and sanctions are used to modify behaviour, humans develop ingenious solutions to subvert them, possibly to the detriment of the organization as a whole.

The motivation of a manager needs to be appropriate to the degree of discretion they have within the business to control their department's activity. One of the greatest demotivators is being held responsible for outcomes over which one has little control. Managers are commonly held responsible in the following ways:

– By cost centre
– By profit centre
– By investment centre

The cost centre is where the manager is held responsible for the controllable costs of a department. A cost centre can be identified if the following criteria are adhered to:

1 If the manager controls both the acquisition and consumption of services and their costs.
2 If the manager significantly influences the consumption of costs.
3 If the manager significantly influences the behaviour of other individuals who have responsibility for the consumption of costs.

The problem with this type of control mechanism is the lack of incentive for managers to cut expenditure beneath the upper limit. The natural reaction is for a manager who hasn't spent up to budget by the end of the relevant period to do so without regard to the wider business interest, but merely because a significant underspend will trigger a downward adjustment to that target in the next budgetary cycle.

Profit centres are where responsibility for the creation of revenue and the control of costs are devolved to a department or individual. If the profit centre is 'genuine', where the manager has real control over sales volume and pricing as well as costs, the manager will be given a profit target to achieve by cost cutting, revenue generation or a combination of the two. How this is done will largely depend on the latitude that exists to achieve profit by one method or the other, and indeed on the personality of the manager. Where such responsibility is vested in a department or individual, motivation to achieve may be intrinsic to those individuals, and is normally less dependent on financial reward than on professional integrity or pride. An example of a profit centre is a hotel that completely devolves the management of its coffee shop to an individual or team, merely requiring an on-target achievement of profit within a specified period of time.

The danger of having 'pseudo' profit centres, where the manager is not really in control of the revenue generated or the costs incurred, lies in the manager taking decisions that improve profit in the department but not the overall profit of the business as a whole. Known as goal 'incongruence', this is often the case where a department shares fixed costs with another department and these costs are allocated or apportioned on some arbitrary basis. If the department then calculates unit profit on the basis of reallocating and apportioning these costs to individual products or services, there may be a danger that the products creating the highest profit will not be those generating the greatest contribution to the business as a whole. Where genuine latitude exists for generating revenues, and control over costs is limited to variable costs, such as purchasing food and drink in a cafe, the department is best assessed on the basis of contribution and might be better described as a contribution centre.

An investment centre is where responsibility is one step more devolved than within a profit centre. Here the manager is responsible for producing an acceptable rate of return for the investment made in their department or division. In reality this type of centre needs to be an autonomous division or company within a wider group. Perhaps a newspaper business within a wider group might be required to produce an annual rate of return on capital invested of 15%. The latitude here is that this rate of return depends on three separate factors:

- Revenue generation
- Cost control
- Financial capital invested

The newspaper could reach its required rate of return by increasing its circulation, its advertising revenue or its cover price. It could also achieve its target by cutting operating costs through reducing the workforce or sharing distribution facilities with another paper. Otherwise it could reduce the capital invested in the newspaper by selling off surplus fixed assets, e.g. replacing a printworks with cheaper desktop technology. The proceeds could be used to redeem loans or to buy back shares. As managers in this situation have a high degree of discretion, they will be motivated simply by being in control, and having a target which can be achieved in several different ways.

It is important therefore that the planning and budgetary cycle is not seen merely as a mechanical exercise, where a strategic plan is decided and detailed budgets are constructed which lead towards this overall plan. Planning and budgeting are heavily dependent on people, and must always take account of their aims, objectives, fears, suspicions and fallacies, as well as how they are motivated.

Managers of business organizations should set strategic objectives which reflect a rational assessment of the environment in which the business is operating and how this might change in the future. This involves an assessment of the organization's capabilities to deal with the opportunities and threats which may present themselves. The budgetary process which underpins the strategic plan should take adequate account of the attitudes and interests of the people that have to set and implement these budgets. The budgets should provide a clear framework for individuals to perform against. Targets should be challenging, attainable and rewarding. The process of setting targets should involve the active participation of responsible individuals, and individuals should only be held accountable for meeting targets in areas over which adequate control of performance can be achieved.

SUMMARY

1 **Planning is the process of using available information to set objectives, and deciding how they might be achieved within resource constraints.**

2 **Strategic objectives are long-term objectives of a broad nature, which must be supported by an annual planning cycle. The outcome of the annual plan should be evaluated with reference to the strategic plan, in order to establish any strategic gap which may have developed.**

3 **The annual plan comprises detailed budgetary information from all parts of the organization, which must be integrated so it can form the basis of the master budget and be used to forecast the profit or loss for a period, along with the financial position at the end of a period.**

4 **The planning and budgetary process operates within the constraints of human behaviour. All plans and budgets should firmly acknowledge the aspirations, fears and abilities of individuals.**

ASSESSMENT

MULTIPLE-CHOICE QUESTIONS

Question 1
In which order should the following elements of planning be undertaken in order to move towards a feasible plan?

1 Set objectives
2 Review objectives
3 Select alternatives
4 Identify constraints

A 1, 4, 3, 2
B 4, 3, 1, 2
C 2, 4, 3, 1
D 3, 1, 4, 2

Question 2
Which one of the following could best be described as a focus strategy?

A Concentrating on supplying low-cost, high-quality, strongly branded fast foods
B Providing no-smoking pubs
C Establishing betting shops licensed to sell alcoholic drinks that are open in the evening
D Providing a radio service through the medium of Gaelic

Question 3
A hotel requires a rate of return of 15% per annum on an investment of £200,000. The hotel has 20 rooms costing £25 per night, and total annual costs of £100,000 to meet. It currently has an occupancy rate of 70%. Assuming a 360-day year, and assuming that the planning committee want to achieve at least the target rate of return, which one of the following options would not satisfy the planning requirement?

A Increase advertising by £10,000 a year, adding £10,000 to annual costs, which will raise occupancy to 75%
B Cut annual costs by £10,000 by making some staff part-time only
C Increase the price to £30, causing occupancy to fall to 60%
D Drop the price to £20 a night, causing occupancy to increase to 90%

Question 4
A new sports shop business had £5,000 in the bank at the beginning of January and no stocks. The stocks purchased in the first month cost £10,000, and for the next two months the owner bought 1.25 times the amount of stock that he sold in the previous month. Sales in the first three months were £12,000, £15,000 and £19,500. The average gross profit margin was cost plus 50%. Monthly overheads were £2,500. How much cash was in the bank at the end of March. Purchases and sales are 100% for cash.

A £(1,375)
B £11,500
C £4,500
D £15,125

Question 5

Which one of the following would be best suited to cost-centre status within a hotel, where only staff recruitment and deployment are the responsibility of the hotel general manager?

A Restaurant
B Reception
C Domestic cleaning and laundry department
D Bar

EXERCISES

Exercise 1

Birmingham United football club had been relegated to the third division. Its crowds had been declining seriously and the players had become demotivated; the fans were baying for blood and the club's bank account was overdrawn by £150,000. The chairman convened an emergency board meeting immediately after the end of the season. He opened the meeting like this: 'This proud club is now at the crossroads. We can, as a club, muddle on as we are, unrealistically hoping to get promoted next year while risking foreclosure by the bank, who as you know are sharpening their knives for us. We can, on the other hand, stop the rot and make a stand by doing something positive to ensure a bright future for ourselves, the players and above all the fans. I hope you agree that the former option is tantamount to committing football suicide, and the gravity of the situation in my opinion requires immediate action. In view of this I have the following plan which I would like the board to consider and to support.' The main elements of the chairman's plan were as follows:

1 Immediately to sell their star player, Mark Gascoigne, for £200,000, which as a single player transaction would probably see a reduction in their gates by 15% from the start of the new season, as compared to the previous season.
2 To buy Ray Keen for £250,000 from a competing club in readiness for the fifth home game in the new season and the FA Cup competition. This would increase gates on average by 30% over the level of attendance achieved in the first four home games following the departure of Gascoigne during the closed season.
3 During the closed season, to build a family enclosure at a cost of £20,000, but expected to bring in £6,000 of extra gate receipts for each home game.
4 To refurbish and restock the supporters' shop and club at a cost of £21,500. This is expected to increase the net income from the club by 25% over the following season.
5 To sack the present manager and give the job to the club coach, which would save the club half the old manager's salary over a whole season.

Other facts

The average gate receipts per week in the previous season were £45,000 for every home game. There are roughly 28 home games to be played in the year, assuming a cup run of two home fixtures in each of the two major domestic cup tournaments, in addition to the normal league programme.

The players wages last season were to be £25,000 per week for 42 weeks in a season. Of this, Gascoigne's wages were £5,000 a week, and Keen's will be £7,000 a week from the eighth week, when he is to be transferred. Birmingham United have also agreed to pay Keen a commission of 10% of the transfer price as an initial payment. All other players' wages are expected to stay the same. The old manager's salary was £3,000 a week.

Net cash income from the supporters' club and shop were £2,500 a week during the season. The £3,000 of total establishment expenses to be paid each week mainly comprised rent and rates to the local authority for the use of the ground, but they also included the costs of training apprentices, running the reserve team and paying the groundstaff. These expenses are paid for all 42 weeks in a season, whether the club plays home or away. The policing bill per home game was estimated at £1,500 a game.

Required
Evaluate the chairman's five-point plan. How much will Birmingham United have in their bank account at the last week of the new season if everything turns out as expected? Demonstrate this by preparing a single-column cash budget for the new season. Show your workings, clearly explaining the origin of all receipts and payments anticipated to and from the club's bank account during the season.

Exercise 2
On December 31, 19x3 the assets and liabilities of Leisure Books Ltd, a bookseller specializing in non-fiction books were as follows:

	Assets		Liabilities
	£		£
Shop fittings (NBV)	37,516	Share capital	100,000
Stocks of books	45,000	Creditors	35,000
Debtors	37,500	Proposed dividends	7,500
Cash at bank	22,484		

The following transactions are anticipated for the next three months:

	Credit sales	Cash sales	Credit purchases	Cash purchases
	£	£	£	£
January	37,500	35,000	30,000	5,000
February	45,000	12,500	28,750	2,500
March	50,000	30,000	33,750	2,500

Additional information

1 Cash wages per month are £2,500.
2 Other establishment expenses are £3,000 a month paid as incurred.
3 Postage and packing is to be 8% of credit sales, and paid on despatch and delivery to credit customers in the month of sale.
4 Debtors pay in the month following the sale of books.
5 Creditors are paid in the month following purchase.
6 Shop fittings are to be purchased in January. This will cost £15,000 and will be paid for in three equal monthly instalments; the final payment will be made on March 31, 19x4.
7 The old shelving, which originally cost £10,000, was already four years old at the end of December and is expected to fetch £1,500 when sold during January.
8 Depreciation on all shop fittings is based on the reducing-balance method using an annual rate of 20%, and is charged against the accounts on an annual basis.
9 The proposed dividends will be paid 50% in February and 50% in April.
10 On March 31, 19x4 a sum of £50,000 is to be transferred from the business current account to a deposit account.
11 The gross profit made on all books is cost plus 50%.

Required

(a) Work out a cash budget for January, February and March 19x4.
(b) Prepare a forecast trading and profit and loss account for the period Jan 1 to March 31, 19x4.
(c) Draw up a forecast balance sheet as at March 31, 19x4.

Exercise 3

Leasing a property from the council, a retired catering lecturer is to open a restaurant called The College Grill on March 1, 19x3. The cost of the lease is £20,000, of which 80% is acquired in the form of a long-term loan from the bank, on which 12% interest is payable in arrears on the last day of the month in which the interest accrues. The ex-lecturer will also deposit the lump sum from his or her retirement pension in a business bank account. This amounts to £10,000. The lease acquired is for 10 years, and the annual ground rent of £4,000 is payable quarterly in advance, starting from March 1.

Catering equipment costing £9,000 will be purchased on the first day; it is expected to have a life of 10 years before needing to be replaced. Initial investment is also required in a stock of crockery and cutlery estimated to cost £2,000. It is expected that with losses and breakages this stock will need to be topped up monthly at a rate of 5% starting from April.

Wages are expected to cost £2,500 a month, including the ex-lecturer's National Insurance contributions. The ex-lecturer's drawings are expected to be £1,500 a month. The pricing policy for the restaurant is cost plus 40% of sales. All sales are for cash and the monthly figures are as follows:

	Sales £
March	4,200
April	4,900
May	6,300

All stocks of food and drink are paid for by cash and obtained from the local cash and carry. The initial stock of food and drink is to be £2,100, purchased and paid for on March 1. It is anticipated that £500 will be the value of freezer stocks, non-perishable stocks and drinks held at the end of each month.

Business rates payable are £400 a month, and all other expenses will come to £300 in March, but are expected to rise by 10% each month thereafter. The bank manager has agreed that in the short term the ex-lecturer's overdraft requirement will be honoured.

Required

Prepare a cash flow forecast for The College Grill for March, April and May, clearly indicating to the bank manager the maximum amount required as an overdraft during these first critical months.

Exercise 4

Paul Bracewell had been unemployed for three months. During this time he had been planning to set up a business retailing ice-cream and snacks. Bracewell was willing to invest his £25,000 redundancy money. He enrolled on an enterprise allowance scheme and received £80 per week for income support with effect from April 1, 19x4. Following extensive market research, he aimed to purchase a Transit-derived snack vehicle, with which he would sell a special ice-cream made by a company in Devon, based on a recipe handed down to the managing director from her great grandmother, a farmer's wife. Bracewell also planned to sell snacks and drinks.

Bracewell's strategy

1 To sell a premium 'home-made' ice-cream with accompanying snacks and drinks at popular shows and rallies in the west of England.
2 To book pitches at 24 such events (on each weekend) during the summer months (April through to September), and to work as employee for his father, a coal merchant, for 24 weeks in the winter.

Tactics to be employed

1 To purchase, convert and paint a Transit van in order to sell his products. The cost of this is estimated at £10,000. Depreciation on this vehicle is expected to be 15% on cost per year.
2 To purchase fittings and equipment costing £3,000, including ice-cream and cone dispenser, and a refrigerated display unit. The depreciation on these items is expected to be 25% on cost each year.
3 To advertise his special ice-cream in the local paper before each show at a cost of £75 per show attended.
4 To invest in a prominent, professionally painted display hoarding, advertising the ice-cream as 'Sweethams' dairy churn ice-cream – a taste of Devon'; this will cost £250. He expects that he will need to replace it every season.
5 To price his products as follows:

Ice-cream £1.00 per tub or cone
Crisps 25p a pack
Lemonade 35p a can

The anticipated purchases and sales patterns during the first season were estimated as follows. On average Bracewell expected to sell 1,000 cones or tubs per event, 1,200 packets of crisps and 1,500 cans of fizzy drinks. Bracewell expected to have 20% of his crisp and drink purchases in the first month unsold at the end of the month. He expected this level of stock to remain constant for the next five months. He would merely go to the cash and carry, and top up to the required amount before each event. As ice-cream is a perishable product which needs to be very fresh, Bracewell did not expect to have any left at the end of any event.

The profit margin on each of his products is as follows:

	Mark-up
Ice-cream	100%
Crisps	25%
Drinks	40%

As an additional overhead, as far as the ice-cream is concerned, a royalty of 10p per tub or cone is payable to Sweethams for every item sold. As far as Sweethams are concerned, they expect to receive their royalties in the month following the sales being made, and they expect to be paid for the supplies they make to Bracewell two months after Bracewell takes delivery. The crisps and lemonade are purchased in the local cash and carry, and must be paid for immediately.

Other business expenses

Bracewell expects to pay on average £500 per pitch at each event. An assistant is to be employed to help dispense the ice-cream, snacks and drinks. The wage will be £80 each weekend.

Petrol costs vary from week to week, depending on the location. The first three months involve more extensive travel, estimated at £40 per week. In the last three months this cost is expected to fall to £25 a week.

Bracewell's insurance and motor recovery insurance are all paid in July. The total comes to £430. Car tax of £150 for the year is due in April. Drawings are anticipated to be £200 per week during the summer.

Required

Prepare all the necessary budgets for this enterprise, for the first season, from April to September inclusive. Also prepare the forecast trading and profit and loss account for this period, and a balance sheet as at the last day of September.

CHAPTER 17

Standard costing and flexible budgeting

OBJECTIVES

- Recognize that performance must be monitored against plans and budgets.
- Identify significant variances between performance and budgets, and locate where responsibility lies.
- Construct a flexible budget.
- Describe a standard costing system.
- Calculate the major variances within a standard costing system.
- Reconcile actual profit with standard profit by producing a profit reconciliation statement.
- Prepare a variance analysis report and recommend possible alternative courses of action.

17.1 MONITORING PERFORMANCE AGAINST PLANS AND BUDGETS

Chapter 16 showed that businesses need to plan and budget for their future activities if their objectives are to be achieved. Planning and budgeting are not enough, however, and it is necessary to monitor progress against the planned outcomes in order to establish any significant differences, and to permit corrective action to take place. This means that performance must be regularly assessed, differences identified, and plans revised.

Although the ultimate objectives may not change, the way in which they are to be achieved may be very different and might make additional demands on resources than originally anticipated. Consider the navigation of a ship. The original objective is to get to a particular port 200 miles due north of the present port by a specific time. As long as the ship keeps to this course, checking the position will merely reveal how many more miles remain to be covered at the same heading, and how much longer the journey will take. However, if we assume the ship actually sails 107 miles NNE (Fig. 17.1), and a new position is taken, how does this affect things?

The result of this course is that the ship now has 107 miles left to travel, and the new heading must be NNW. Supposing the ship successfully follows the new heading and arrives at its destination on time, it could be said that the journey was accomplished in two stages, that the ship didn't follow the route originally intended at any point, that it travelled 14 miles more than was originally intended, and at a higher average speed than originally planned. The additional mileage and the average speed could have been reduced if a position had been taken earlier, and corrective action initiated at that point. Now suppose that no position is taken until after 214 miles have been covered; then the ship will be 76 miles away from its destination, and its new heading will need to be due

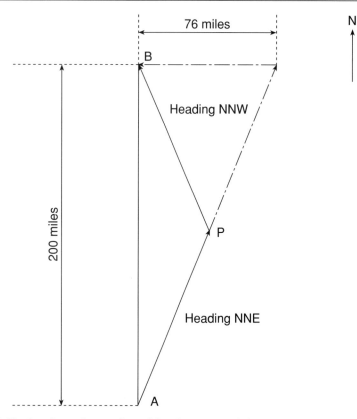

Figure 17.1 Navigation of a cruise ship: A = port of departure, B = port of destination, P = position after 107 miles on heading NNE

west. What's more, it will be too late to make up the time. In this situation the whole journey involves travelling an extra 90 miles.

The moral of the story is, monitor the current position against the original plan as often as possible. Failure to do so may mean that plans need to be revised drastically in order to meet the original objectives, and considerably more resources may be required. And if the extra resources are not available, the original objective will be impossible to achieve.

Furthermore, it is important to ascertain why the wrong decision was taken in the first place. In the navigation example, the captain should ask about the reliability of the ship's navigation equipment, its steering equipment and the competence of relevant staff.

In a business situation this means that individual budgets prepared on a monthly basis should be compared with actual performance on a monthly basis to establish significant differences, and explore in detail their possible causes.

A sports equipment retailer has anticipated sales of £4,000 for the next three months (March, April, May), and actually achieves sales of £4,500, £3,000 and £2,500. The manager of the shop may then ask the following questions:

1 Would the extra sales in the first month have been even greater if stock levels had permitted?

2 Were the extra sales in the first month merely caused by a change in the timing of demand. That is to say, were there any commercial or economic reasons why demand

in the first month may have included anticipated demand brought forward from the second month?

3 Was the reduction in sales in the second month connected with the increase in sales in the first month or was the difference entirely unrelated?

4 Why are the sales continuing to decline in the third month, and does this reflect a worrying trend about the shop itself, or changing conditions in its environment?

Changes in demand for specific products or lines within an overall range can be caused in several ways, as first indicated in Chapter 14. Here are some possible reasons:

Prices/availability of products at shop: were there any promotional offers on certain products which ceased at the end of the first month? Were certain products unavailable from suppliers during the month? These factors may involve substitute or complementary products, e.g. the price of cricket bats and pads, or the availability of one brand of trainer as against another. Were these products sold out at any time during the first month, and at what point?

Prices/availability of products with competitors: were there promotional offers in the second and third months on key product lines, substitutes and complements offered by competitors?

A change in the weather: this might cause the sales of certain items to change significantly, either upwards or downwards.

A change in general styles or fashions: this might cause a surge or drop in demand for certain products.

A first step to answering these questions is to make a stock check at the end of the month to observe which lines have significantly under- or oversold. To check this, the stock levels and monthly sales patterns of these lines need to be analysed.

It may be discovered that the difference between the budgeted sales and actual sales is an even difference over a whole range of products, not due to changes in certain key products. If this is the case, the following possible explanations may need to be examined:

Change in competitive environment: a new competitor or competitors may have entered or left the market, affecting market share for all products.

Change in general economic circumstances of the customer base: this may be caused by national or local government tax changes, a change in interest rates, or a significant change in the employment situation both nationally and locally.

A general change in attitudes and life styles: this is normally a longer-term phenomenon, but it can be the cause of general changes in demand for a whole group of products. An example might be a trend to keep-fit and exercising.

A change in the service being offered by the shop itself: are the sales staff doing their work properly? Are customers being dealt with promptly and courteously? Are products available when customers want them, and are they being merchandized to good effect?

An investigation of all the differences between what was expected and what happened is essential to controlling the financial progress of the business. This must be done at all levels of the business. In the sports shop example we were investigating differences between expected and actual sales, but this analysis must also be carried out for all parts of the business. Consider stock purchasing. Were all types and quantities of stock purchased, and at what prices? Were the same overheads incurred as originally anticipated? Were the rent for the shop, the staff costs, and the lighting, heating and telephone bills as expected? Have interest rates changed, causing borrowing costs to be different, or have insurance premiums exceeded expectations? Or even, have shoplifting and other stock losses been at the same rate as originally allowed for? These differences must all be identified and, if possible, thoroughly explained. They must then be acted upon.

17.2 RESPONSIBILITY FOR VARIANCES

In budgeting language, a difference is known as a variance. From now on, specific differences between budgeted and actual performance will be called **variances**. For the sports equipment retailer of section 17.1 we can describe the differences between actual and budgeted sales as follows:

	March £	April £	May £
Budgeted sales	4,000	4,000	4,000
Actual sales	4,500	3,000	2,500
Variance	500 (F)	1,000 (A)	1,500 (A)

Where the variance represents a difference that would (all other things being equal) increase profits, it is known as a **favourable** variance. Where the variance represents a difference that would (all other things being equal) reduce profits, it is known as an **adverse** variance. Where revenues exceed expectations, they are represented by favourable variances; where costs exceed expectations, they are represented by adverse variances.

To further explore how the principal variances are identified and explained, consider a strawberry-and-cream stall and its financial performance over a week. Here are the budgets for the following week; no stocks are left at the end of any week.

Sales budget	Qty	Price	£
Punnets	750	90p	675
Cartons	600	55p	330
			1,005

Purchases budget	Qty	Price	£
Punnets	750	50p	375
Cartons	600	35p	210
			585

Overheads budget			£
Rent			35
Staff costs			80
			115

Budgeted profit and loss account

	£
Sales	1,005
Cost of sales	585
Budgeted gross profit	420
Fixed overheads	115
Budgeted net profit	305

Following the week's business, the actual results are as follows:

Actual sales	Qty	Price	£
Punnets	750	98p	735
Cartons	650	54p	351
			1,086

Actual purchases	Qty	Price	£
Punnets	760	50p	380
Cartons	660	40p	264
			644

Actual overheads			£
Rent			40
Staff costs			100
			140

Actual profit and loss account	£
Sales	1,086
Cost of sales	644
Gross profit	442
Fixed overheads	140
Actual net profit	302

During the week the strawberry-and-cream business has generated only slightly less profits than originally planned, as there is a slight adverse variance of £3.00. It is not enough to identify merely the profit variance. It is what causes the profit variance that is important. Profit is a function of revenues less attributable expenses. It is possible that a negligible profit variance could be hiding significant variances on both revenues and costs. In a sense, the profit variance may be seen as the tip of the iceberg, so in order to be fully informed, it is necessary to investigate below the water-line. In order to make a further investigation of the variances and their origins, the week's results will be examined in more detail. A simple variance tree is shown in Fig. 17.2.

Notice that, although the profit variance is insignificant, it hides significant variances in both total costs and total sales, which all but cancel each other out. The sales revenue variance is favourable, but the cost variance is adverse and should be further investigated. The cause of the variance may be something that the business can do something about, which may allow profits to be improved in the future. Even a significantly favourable variance should be investigated, to find out what it is that the business is doing right, or to establish whether the original budgeted level was inappropriate or unrealistic. The sales revenue variance is analysed in more detail in Fig. 17.3. Its favourable aspect was mostly contributed by sales of strawberries (in punnets).

The total cost variance is further broken down in Fig. 17.4. It is made up of the variance between the budgeted cost of sales and the actual cost of sales, and the variance between the budgeted overheads and the actual overheads. In Fig. 17.4 the cost-of-sales variance is further subdivided between the variance on the cost of sales of the punnets, which is negligible, and the more significant variance on the cartons of cream.

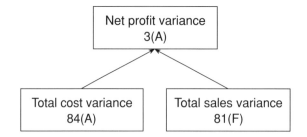

Figure 17.2 A simple variance tree

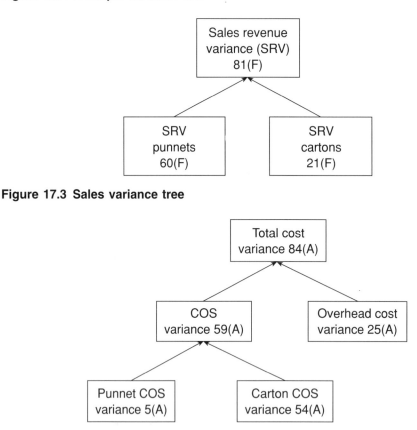

Figure 17.3 Sales variance tree

Figure 17.4 Cost variance tree

This example is a very simple illustration of how the identification of a variance between budgeted and actual profit can be further investigated, and how the underlying causes of a variance may be ascertained. It allows the business to pinpoint where and why these variances arise, in order that remedies may be attempted.

These sales revenues and cost variances can be further subdivided in order to locate their specific causes. Let us look in more depth at the sales revenue variance. It is either going to be caused by a difference in the actual price charged as against the budgeted price, or caused by a difference in the number of units sold as against the budget, or by a combination of both.

In this example the main sales revenue variance consists of the sales revenue variances on each product. Further investigation of the sales revenue variances on the strawberries would reveal they have been caused entirely by the fact that 750 punnets were sold at 8p more than was budgeted for, so the variance is explained by $750 \times £0.08 = £60(F)$. As there was no difference between the actual number sold against the budgeted sales, the price variance of £60 fully explains the sales revenue variance on the strawberries. All such variances can be similarly broken down and pinpointed to specific causes like this; a technique for calculating them systematically will be covered in greater detail later in this chapter.

It should now be clear that if actual results are compared against budgeted performance in all areas, variances may be isolated and their root causes investigated. By calculating these variances, it is possible to identify which departments and therefore which individuals are responsible, if any, and to take the appropriate remedial action.

To avoid erroneous judgements, variances between budgets and actual results must be seen in context. It is important that variances should be used for controlling performance and for motivating individuals. Management must be careful not to hold individuals or departments responsible for variances over which they have no direct control, or conflict may build up, and the real causes of problems will not be addressed.

17.3 FLEXIBLE BUDGETS

Any business comprises a variety of different functions. These functions are interdependent to a greater or lesser degree, so the performance achieved in one department may directly affect the performance of another. The performance of one department, or the lack of it, may create constraints on the ability of other departments to perform. Taking as an example a chain of sandwich bars selling filled French rolls, it is possible to identify some areas of interdependence:

1 The preparation department produces fewer filled rolls than the demand, by specific type.
2 Purchases of rolls or various fillings are inadequate to meet the needs of the preparation department.
3 Quality control allows an excessive amount of substandard rolls to be offered to customers, who subsequently return them.
4 Personnel recruits staff who cannot prepare or serve at the required rate of productivity.
5 Cleaning staff fail to clean away after previous customers, making the eating area unattractive and unappealing to prospective customers.
6 Preparation staff place the wrong amounts of filling in the rolls.

These situations illustrate problems which have implications for other functions within the business, making the root cause of any variances difficult to trace. It may be necessary to follow an investigative trail from the identified variance back to the originating variance. If it is discovered there is a favourable variance between the actual cost of the filled rolls sold and the budgeted cost, this might have been caused by any of the following:

1 Lower production level due to shortage of materials
2 Slower preparation of rolls due to inefficient staff
3 The cost of rolls or fillings being lower than expected
4 Preparation staff underfilling rolls

The interdependence of variances between the major functions of a business can be taken into account through flexible budgeting. An example is a children's slide manufacturer which has produced a master budget based on estimates for the next month:

Estimated sales	1,000 units	Estimated price	£100
Variable costs			
Materials:		Fixed costs:	
Slide	£15	Rent	£2,000
Frame	£25	Staff costs	£30,000
Labour:		Depreciation	£8,000
Slide	£4	Power	£5,000
Frame	£5	Indirect materials	£2,500

During the month, the actual sales of the slides came to 800, but all other factors remained unchanged. The actual results are now compared against the budget:

	Budgeted contribution	Actual contribution	Variance
	£	£	£
Sales	100,000	80,000	20,000(A)
Variable costs	49,000	39,200	9,800(F)
Contribution	51,000	40,800	10,200(A)
Fixed costs	47,500	47,500	nil
Net profit	3,500	(6,700)	10,200(A)

Notice that the variance in the unfavourable sales revenue is caused by the fact that 200 fewer children's slides were sold than originally budgeted for. This variance should be investigated in order to discover its cause. Was it caused by a lower demand for the slide, or was it because the production department couldn't produce any more? Looking at the favourable variable cost variance, would the management of the business be right to congratulate the production department for their efficient performance over the period? Of course not! The only reason that the variable costs have fallen is because 200 fewer slides were produced, so the material costs in the slides and frames were saved, as were the variable labour costs associated with assembling each unit. It is therefore important that any business takes into account the level of its actual activity and compares it with a **flexed budget** which takes this new level of activity into account.

The whole adverse profit variance of £10,200 is fully explained by multiplying the shortfall in production and sales by the standard unit contribution expected for each slide £200 × (100 − 49) = £10,200. This is because the only reason for a difference in profit to be reported is that fewer slides were sold. This variance is known as the sales volume contribution variance. If the original budget had been flexed to 800 units, there would have been no variances to report, although the sales volume variance would need to be investigated.

Taking the same example and giving actual results as follows, it is possible to identify more meaningful variances upon which management can act.

Actual sales	800 units	Estimated price		£90
Variable costs				
Materials:		Fixed costs:		
Slide	£12	Rent		£2,000
Frame	£28	Staff costs		£32,000
Labour:		Depreciation		£6,000
Slide	£3.50	Power		£4,000
Frame	£6	Indirect materials		£2,800

	Flexible budget	Actual result	Variance
	£	£	£
Sales	80,000	72,000	8,000(A)
Variable costs	39,200	39,600	400(A)
Contribution	40,800	32,400	8,400(A)
Fixed costs	47,500	46,800	700(F)
Net profit	(6,700)	(14,400)	7,700(A)

All of these variances are meaningful as they represent differences between the actual figures and the flexed budget at the same level of activity. It is now possible to say that these variances have been caused by operational factors both within and outside the control of the business, not simply by a difference in the general level of activity. Here are some examples:

- The sales revenue variance is entirely due to the slide being sold for £90 as opposed to £100.
- The variable cost variance is a combination of the different material purchase costs of the components and the different rates paid to the direct labour assembling them.
- The fixed costs are caused by changes in the prices of services or staff salary rates, or by a change in the level of consumption of these costs, or both.

The overall net profit variance is therefore a combination of all the above variances, and the sales volume contribution variance is caused by selling greater or smaller numbers of units than the standard set. These individual variances can now be investigated and the reasons for them identified.

17.4 A STANDARD COSTING SYSTEM

A standard is a specified quantity or monetary amount that has been estimated with reference to past experience and the future expectations of efficiency levels, productivity and prices. Product or service costs can be estimated by ascertaining the amount of material, if applicable, and direct labour spent on each unit. This might be determined by observing what quantity of material is used in a product, and at what price it may be purchased. It will also involve estimating how long a particular type of direct employee spends on various aspects of making the product or providing the service, along with the various wage rates for each type of labour involved. Setting of standards is a subjective process, as the idea of an acceptable or desired standard will vary from manager to subordinate, and from individual to individual.

The advantage of ascertaining a standard cost for a product or activity is that it makes planning and budgeting easier, and it avoids the problem of completely reformulating budgets every period. Standards also provide a controlling mechanism where behaviour is modified through motivation and appraisal. Standard costing and budgeting are completely interlinked, and the differences between the budgets based on predetermined standards and the actual outcome of operational activities is the framework upon which variance analysis depends. Standard costing allows management to locate operational problems, where significant, and is therefore a system that identifies problems by exception. Standard costing is best applied to manufacturing concerns where many products are produced and their components are numerous.

Businesses in tourism, leisure and hospitality rarely use standard costing, although it may have applications in certain sectors such as fast-food retailing, where a uniform product or service is provided, and where a high volume of activity is taking place in controlled circumstances.

To demonstrate how a standard costing system may be applied to aid the planning and control of a business, consider the case of the Kaiserburger fast-food franchise, which operates to the following predetermined standards:

Product	Ingredients	Cooking time
K burger	One brown bun, one 250 g burger	3.0 min
Standard wage rate	£3.00 per hour	
Standard power costs (oven units)	£1.20 per hour	
Standard cost of ingredients		
100 brown buns	£5.00	
80 × 250 g burgers	£12.80	
Standard burger sales		6,000 units at £0.80 per unit
Standard fixed establishment costs		£2,000 per week

The standard cost of a burger is as follows:

		£
Materials		
Burger (250 g) 12.80/80		0.16
Brown bun 5.00/100		0.05
Labour		
(3.00/60) × 3		0.15*
Power		
(1.20/60) × 3		0.06*
Total standard variable cost per unit		0.42

* The direct labour only cook burgers and they are paid to tend the oven, therefore the oven and labour time are equivalent. All other labour costs are classified as fixed costs.

As the standard price of each burger is £0.80, the standard unit contribution per burger is 80p − 42p = 38p. If the standard profit to be earned in the following week were calculated, making and selling 6,000 burgers, the results would be as follows:

	£	£
Sales (K burger)		4,800
Materials:		
Burgers	960	
Brown buns	300	
Labour	900	
Power costs	360	
Standard variable costs		2,520
Standard contribution		2,280
Fixed costs		2,000
Standard net profit		280

At the end of the month, the actual information was as follows:

		£	£	
Sales	(8,000 units)		6,000	Price £0.75
Materials:				
Burgers	(8,400 burgers)	1,512		Cost £0.18
Brown buns	(8,200 buns)	328		Cost £0.04
Labour	(380 h)	1,254		Hourly rate £3.30
Power costs	(380 h)	342		Hourly rate £0.90
Variable costs			3,436	
Contribution			2,564	
Fixed costs			1,600	
Actual net profit			964	

The variances will now be calculated, in order to explain the difference between the actual performance and the standard performance. The first step is to flex the standard budget to the actual volume of burgers produced and sold, in order to discover the variances that we can validly relate to the responsibility areas of specific individuals or departments. This is done by multiplying the unit standards by the actual volume produced and sold:

	Flexed budget		Actual result		Variance
	£	£	£	£	£
Sales (K burger)		6,400		6,000	400(A)
Materials:					
Burgers	1,280		1,512		232(A)
Brown buns	400		328		72(F)
Labour	1,200		1,254		54(A)
Power costs	480		342		138(F)
Standard variable costs		3,360		3,436	
Standard contribution		3,040		2,564	476(A)
Fixed costs		2,000		1,600	400(F)
Net profit		1,040		964	76(A)

17.5 CALCULATION OF INDIVIDUAL VARIANCES

Having flexed the standard budget and compared it with the actual results for the week, it is now necessary to identify all the variances that comprise the difference between the flexed budget profit and the actual profit earned. Variance calculation is best carried out in a systematic way, and from now on each variance will be dealt with by explaining it, calculating it and giving possible reasons for it.

Variance 1: Sales volume contribution variance

Explanation
This is the part of the profit variance caused by selling either greater or fewer units than the standard. This means that, all other things being equal, the business will have earned a higher or lower contribution than the standard contribution simply due to the difference in sales volume and for no other reason. This variance is simply the difference between the standard profit at the standard volume of sales less the standard profit based on the actual volume of units sold.

How calculated
The sales volume contribution variance is calculated by determining the difference between the volume of units actually sold and the standard volume, multiplied by the unit contribution earned per unit:

$$\text{Unit contribution} \times (\text{actual sales} - \text{standard sales}) = £0.38 \times (8,000 - 6,000)$$
$$= £760(A)$$

Possible causes
A sales volume variance may be caused by the direct marketing efforts of the business, through price changes, promotional and advertising expenditure, changes in distribution policies, or by environmental factors such as the marketing efforts of competitors, or general economic and fiscal conditions.

Variance 2: Sales price variance

Explanation
This is the variance caused by selling the actual volume sold, at a higher or lower price than the standard price originally set.

How calculated
The sales price variance is calculated by taking the actual volume of units sold and multiplying it by the difference between the standard price and the actual price:

$$\text{Actual sales} \times (\text{standard price} - \text{actual price}) = 8,000 \times (£0.75 - £0.80)$$
$$= £400(A)$$

Possible causes

This variance directly determines the sales volume variance; the reason is that, all other things being equal, price changes have an effect on the quantity demanded, as explained in Chapter 14. The price changes may be caused by an overall policy decision to change prices across the board; or where sales are made through intermediaries, discounts may be offered for taking higher-volume orders, or temporary special offers may be made as part of a promotional campaign.

Variance 3: Material cost variance

Explanation

This variance is the difference between the expected cost of the materials used at the volume of production achieved, and the actual cost of the materials used. It can be divided into two subvariances. Firstly, the difference will be caused by buying the actual amount of materials at prices which differ from the standard price, and secondly by using more or less of the materials than was originally budgeted for.

Subvariance 3a: Material price variance

Explanation

This variance is caused by a difference between the actual price and the standard price of the material purchased in the period.

How calculated

The subvariance is calculated by taking the actual quantity purchased and multiplying it by the difference between the standard purchase price per unit of quantity and the actual price:

$$\text{Actual quantity used} \times (\text{standard cost} - \text{actual cost})$$

For the burgers it is

$$8,400 \times (£0.16 - £0.18) = £168(A)$$

shown in Fig. 17.5a. For the buns it is

$$8,200 \times (£0.05 - £0.04) = £82(F)$$

This indicates that the buns were bought at a penny cheaper than budgeted for (Fig. 17.5b).

Possible causes

The main cause of a material price variance may be beyond the control of an organization. If the price of supplies increases, it may be the result of a policy decision made by an external organization. There may be scope to negotiate, or to find available alternatives, and to this extent the purchasing department could be held partly responsible.

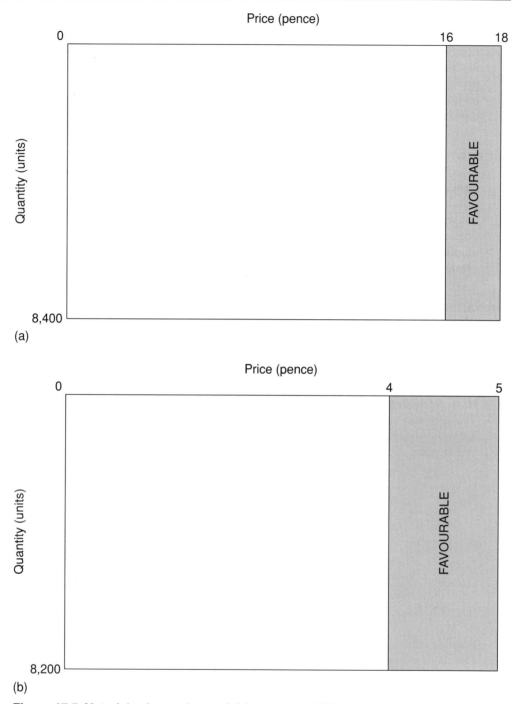

Figure 17.5 Material price variance: (a) burgers and (b) buns

Subvariance 3b: Material usage variance

Explanation
This variance is caused by the organization using more or less of a material than was set in the standard.

How calculated
The material usage variance is calculated by multiplying the standard cost per unit of the material by the difference between the quantity actually used and the standard quantity that should have been used to make the actual output:

Standard cost per unit × (actual usage − standard usage)

For the burgers it is

£0.16 × (8,000 − 8,400) = £64(A)

because 400 more burgers were used than the budgeted amount (Fig. 17.6a). For the buns it is

£0.05 × (8,000 − 8,200) = £10(A)

indicating that more buns were used than the budgeted amount (Fig. 17.6b).

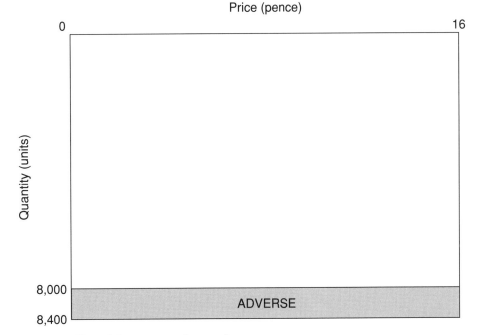

Figure 17.6a Material usage variance: burgers

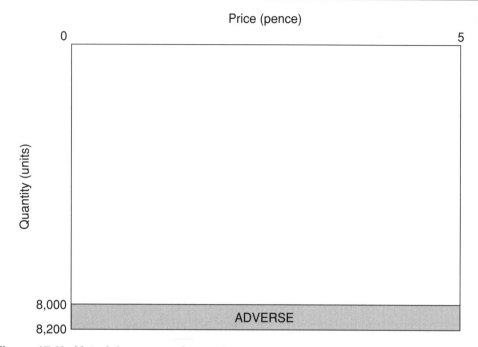

Figure 17.6b Material usage variance: buns

Possible causes
Here are the major causes of usage variances on materials:

1 Purchase of inferior or superior quality materials may affect the wastage rates. The quality of the purchases may be linked to the price paid for the supplies, so there may be an inverse relationship between the material price and usage variance.
2 The level of wastage may be affected by efficient or inefficient labour. Burgers may be wasted by overcooking them, dropping them or otherwise spoiling them. If burgers are overcooked, there may be a relationship between the material usage variance and the labour efficiency ratio (subvariance 4b), and with a favourable labour rate variance (subvariance 4a).
3 Leakage through staff dishonesty. This could arise through staff consuming goods themselves, giving them to customers or taking them home.

Variance 4: Labour cost variance

Explanation
This variance is caused by the difference between the expected cost of labour at the actual volume produced and the actual labour costs incurred at that level of output. As with the material cost variance, the labour cost variance is divided into two subvariances.

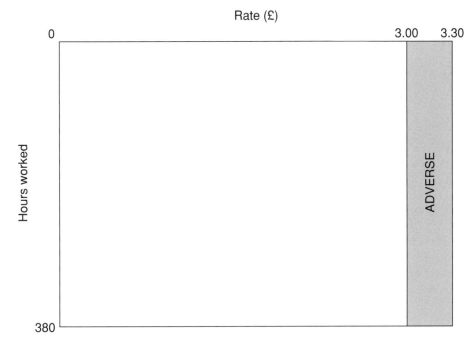

Figure 17.7 Labour rate variance

Subvariance 4a: Labour rate variance

Explanation
This variance is the result of paying the direct labour at a higher or lower wage rate than the standard rate (Fig. 17.7).

How calculated
This variance is calculated by multiplying the actual number of hours worked by the difference between the standard wage rate and the actual wage rate.

$$\text{Actual hours worked} \times (\text{standard wage rate} - \text{actual wage rate})$$
$$= 380\,\text{h} \times (£3.00 - £3.30)$$
$$= £114(\text{A})$$

Possible causes
This variance is caused by paying staff at a higher or lower rate for the following reasons:

1 An unexpected wage rate deal may have been agreed.
2 Overtime may have been worked at premium rates. This may also be evidenced by the labour efficiency variance (subvariance 4b).
3 Casual staff may have been recruited on a part-time basis that were paid at a lower rate, and for whom the National Insurance rate is lower.

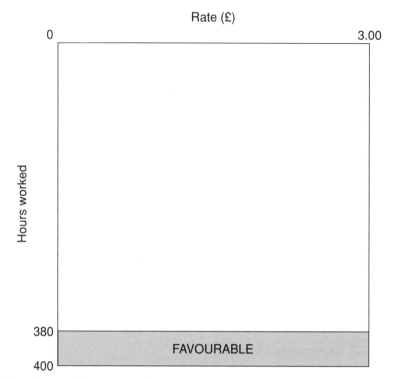

Figure 17.8 Labour efficiency variance

Subvariance 4b: Labour efficiency variance

Explanation
This variance is the result of fewer labour hours being worked to produce or provide the product or service than was originally budgeted for (Fig. 17.8).

How calculated
This variance is calculated by taking the standard rate per hour and multiplying it by the difference between the budgeted hours estimated at the actual level of output and the actual hours worked:

> Standard wage rate per hour × (standard hours − actual hours)
> = £3.00 × (400 h − 380 h)
> = £60(F)

Possible causes
The labour efficiency variance can be caused by employees performing either better or worse than expected through different capabilities, skills and experience. These differences may be caused by varying levels of motivation, due to factors including rates of pay and working conditions. This variance may be connected with the labour rate variance. The variance may be caused by non-standard training and supervision, and

unexpected industrial relations difficulties and tensions. The variance might also be caused by varying material quality, which may affect the time taken to produce or provide the product. If the burgers are slightly bigger than standard, then their cooking times may be longer. In this situation there will be a direct link with the variable overhead efficiency variance.

Variance 5: Variable overhead cost variance

Explanation
This variance is caused by the difference between the expected cost of power at the actual volume produced and the actual power costs incurred at that level of output. As with variances 3 and 4, the variable overhead cost variance is divided into two subvariances.

Subvariance 5a: Variable overhead expenditure variance

Explanation
This variance is caused by the variable overheads costing more per hour than was budgeted for. Two factors are relevant:

1 The price of power per unit purchased may differ from the standard price.
2 The consumption per hour of the machinery or equipment may differ from the standard consumption. This might be caused by technical or human factors.

In this example the variable overhead expenditure variance is not subdivided into these categories.

How calculated
The variable overhead expenditure variance (Fig. 17.9) is calculated by taking the difference between the standard power cost of the machine hours used against the actual power cost incurred:

$$\text{Actual hours} \times (\text{standard hourly power cost} - \text{actual hourly cost})$$
$$= 380\,\text{h} \times (£1.20 - £0.90)$$
$$= £114(\text{F})$$

Possible causes
This variance is either caused by the actual unit price of power being different to the standard unit price, or due to the oven consuming more or less power per hour than was expected, or a combination of both. If prices differed from the standard price, then this would be outside the control power of the business. However, if the variance were in any way caused by working practices, such as running the oven too hot or not hot enough, then this could be considered the responsibility of the operator. This variance may be linked to labour efficiency, because if the oven temperature were not standard, it is reasonable to expect that the standard cooking times would vary accordingly.

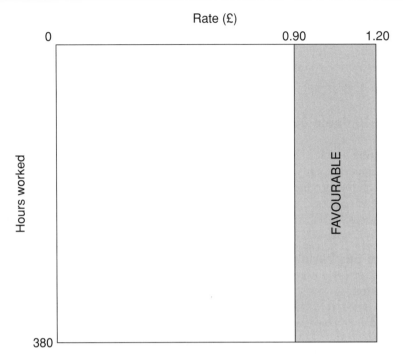

Figure 17.9 Variable overhead expenditure variance

Subvariance 5b: Variable overhead efficiency variance

Explanation
This variance is directly linked to the labour efficiency variance. It is the difference in variable overhead cost due to working greater or fewer hours on the machinery than was expected. If direct labour hours are spent on operating the ovens, then the labour hours and machine hours will be the same, assuming the equipment is in continual use, and there is no idle time.

How calculated
This variance is calculated by taking the difference between the standard and actual hours worked on the equipment and multiplying it by the standard hourly power cost (Fig. 17.10). The difference between actual hours and standard hours will be the same as for the labour efficiency variance (subvariance 4b).

> Standard power cost per hour × (standard hours − actual hours)
> = £1.20 × (400 h − 380 h)
> = £24(F)

Possible causes
This variance is caused by the same factors as were indicated for subvariance 4b. If the direct labour force is working efficiently and saving production time, it will also be saving the fuel cost per hour at the standard rate multiplied by the hours saved. Note how this variance may directly affect the expenditure variance (subvariance 5a), and may be caused by running the equipment at a non-standard temperature or a non-standard power output level.

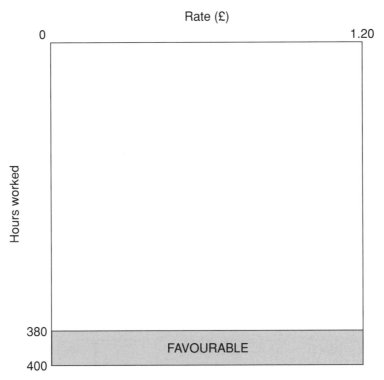

Figure 17.10 Variable overhead efficiency variance

Variance 6: Fixed overhead expenditure variance

Explanation
This variance is simply the difference between what was spent on fixed overheads and the amount budgeted for.

How calculated
The variance is calculated by taking each separate fixed overhead expense category and comparing the standard cost with the cost actually incurred. In a large organization these variances will be numerous and will need to be analysed by department or responsibility centre.

Standard fixed overhead costs – actual fixed overhead costs = £2,000 – £1,600
= £400(F)

Possible causes
These variances can be caused by price changes if the fixed costs are bought-in goods or services. For example, the lighting costs of the burger bar will depend to some extent on the unit cost of the power as supplied, and this may be outside the control of the business. However, the variance may also be caused by under- or overconsuming these costs compared with the standard cost. If too many lights are left on for long periods, or not switched off where possible, then costs may be higher than standard. The level of consumption of fixed overheads may well be within the control of an individual or department, so responsibility for these variances will rest at individual cost centres.

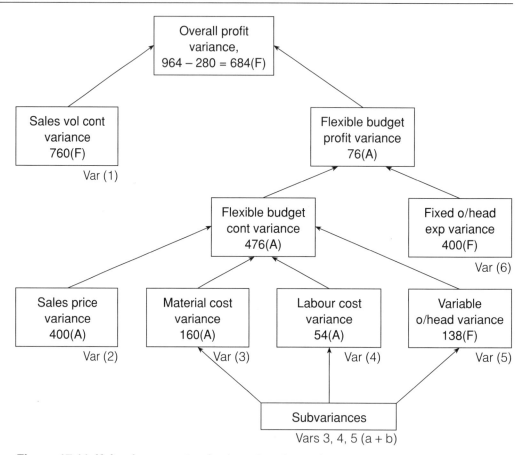

Figure 17.11 Kaiserburger: standard cost variance tree

Total variance

The total of variances 1 to 6 fully accounts for the difference between the budgeted standard profit for the period at 6,000 units, and the actual profit earned at 8,000 units.

The interrelationships between all these variances are depicted schematically in Fig. 17.11. It depicts the build-up of the subvariances to the main variances (2 to 5), which explains the overall variance between the flexible budget contribution and the actual contribution earned at the output level of 8,000 burgers. Combined with the fixed overhead expenditure variance, this variance makes up the flexible budget profit variance. Finally, this variance and the sales volume contribution variance, caused simply by selling greater or fewer units than standard, fully explain the overall profit variance.

17.6 THE PROFIT RECONCILIATION STATEMENT

The variances can be brought together in a statement that reconciles standard profit with the actual profit reported. This statement can be laid out in the following format:

Kaiserburger profit reconciliation statement

	Variance	£	£	£
Standard net profit				280
Sales volume contribution variance	(1)	760(F)		
Sales price variance	(2)		400(A)	
Material price variance:	(3a)			
Burgers			168(A)	
Buns		82(F)		
Material usage variance:	(3b)			
Burgers			64(A)	
Buns			10(A)	
Labour rate variance	(4a)		114(A)	
Labour efficiency variance	(4b)	60(F)		
Variable overhead expenditure variance	(5a)	114(F)		
Variable overhead efficiency variance	(5b)	24(F)		
Fixed overhead expenditure variance	(6)	400(F)		
Total variance		1,440(F)	756(A)	
Net variance				684(F)
Actual net profit				964

How does this statement help management to control the business and keep it on its planned course? It identifies all the variances and indicates the significant ones. Any significant variances should be investigated, both favourable and adverse.

17.7 THE VARIANCE ANALYSIS REPORT

The variances can be explained in relation to cause, effect and responsibility. This type of report can then be used as a basis for taking remedial action to keep the business planning cycle on course towards its longer-term objectives. It is now possible to analyse the significant variances of Kaiserburger with a view to identifying problems and possible remedial action.

Variances 1 and 2: Sales volume contribution and sales price variances

The favourable sales volume variance is significant in that one-third more burgers were sold than planned. The reasons need to be fully investigated by the marketing and sales department. It would seem that the adverse price variance of £400 had a significant influence, as price elasticity of demand is a key factor in determining sales volumes. However, there may be other marketing variables that may have had an influence, such as advertising and promotion, and the marketing activities of competitors.

Variance 3: Material cost variances

The burgers have cost more than planned. Is this due to factors out of the purchasing department's control, or was this a conscious decision in order to improve the quality of the burger? It may be that the wastage levels have fallen as a result. Comparisons with previous periods may confirm this. The buns have cost less than standard. Is this a consequence of good buying or is there a quality trade-off involved? The usage variance for the burgers is much more significant than for the buns. Does this indicate wastage or possibly theft? Here again comparisons with previous periods may be helpful.

Variance 4: Labour cost variance

There is a significant adverse wage rate variance. Was this due to overtime working or another reason? Perhaps the company had to make use of an employment agency to cover for absent staff, for which they had to pay higher rates of pay. The efficiency variance is favourable, indicating that fewer than the standard hours were worked, even though the rates paid per hour were higher. This may indicate that the staff are well motivated, or that the standard is not demanding enough.

Variance 5: Variable overhead cost variance

The expenditure variance is significantly favourable, indicating that fuel prices are lower than expected, or the oven is working or being operated more efficiently than standard. Is this because the staff are working efficiently or are customers getting undercooked burgers? This may be revealed in future periods by the sales volume contribution variances, as dissatisfied customers bring back less repeat business and spread the bad news to others. The variable overhead efficiency variance is favourable in line with the labour efficiency variance, as would be expected.

Variance 6: Fixed overhead expenditure variance

There is a significantly favourable fixed overhead expenditure variance of £400. This variance would need to be subdivided into its constituent expenditure categories to identify where exactly these variances originated and who precisely was responsible, if anyone. Perhaps some of these standards may need to be revised downwards.

Out of the above analysis would come recommendations on how these variances could be avoided or exploited. For example, the success of the marketing mix would be assessed and developed. The unfavourable burger price variance should be investigated. If it was simply that a bigger burger had been purchased, this might pay off in increased customer satisfaction, and may well result in more favourable sales volume contribution variances in future periods. On the other hand, it might be necessary to seek an alternative supplier. The adverse labour rate variance should also be investigated, and working rostas altered to reduce overtime working, or reduce the dependency on recruitment agency staff at times when the business is short-staffed.

SUMMARY

1 **Actual performance should be frequently monitored against budgeted performance.**

2 **Specific differences known as variances may be identified between actual and budgeted levels of performance.**

3 **Budgets need to be flexed to take into account the interdependence of performance between key functions of a business, and in order to correctly isolate meaningful performance variances.**

4 **A standard costing system allows management to locate operational problems; it has a number of important characteristics.**

5 **It is possible to calculate specific variances that explain the difference between standard and actual profit.**

6 **There is a recommended way to prepare a profit reconciliation statement.**

7 **Variance analysis reports are examined to find significant variances, which are interpreted to make recommendations for the future.**

ASSESSMENT

MULTIPLE-CHOICE QUESTIONS

Question 1
Standard costing is best described in which one of the following ways?

A A budgetary system based on estimates of costs, revenues, and activity levels, as decided by management, which will ensure that long-term aims are achieved.

B A system of fixed budgets which can be used repeatedly without having to reformulate them every month.

C A planning and control system that provides agreed targets against which performance can be measured, and that allows significant differences to be identified and acted upon.

D A planning device which can help the business improve its financial performance through continuous comparison of performance against agreed targets.

Question 2
A tour operator budgets for 200 customers in the following month for a holiday package that sells at £300, but which costs the tour operator £260 from the holiday company. If the monthly fixed costs are £4,500 and only 175 customers actually purchase the holiday, what is the flexible budget contribution variance for the month, assuming the actual price is £280 and the cost is £250?

A £1,000(A)
B £1,750(A)
C £2,750(A)
D £1,000(F)

Question 3
If an ice-cream retailer measures the ice-cream material cost variance of the business for a month, and identifies an adverse variance, which pair of circumstances could not have been the cause?

A Ice-cream prices higher than standard
   Usage lower than standard
B Ice-cream prices higher than standard
   Usage higher than standard
C Ice-cream prices lower than standard
   Usage lower than standard
D Ice-cream prices lower than standard
   Usage higher than standard

Question 4

From the following list of variances, if the overall net profit variance for the year was £400(F), which one of the answers gives the correct sales volume contribution variance?

	£
Material cost variance	200(F)
Labour cost variance	800(A)
Variable overhead cost variance	400(F)
Sales price variance	900(F)
Fixed overhead expenditure variance	800(A)

A   500(F)
B 1,900(F)
C   500(A)
D   100(A)

Question 5

If a hotel serving meals experiences a favourable labour efficiency variance in its kitchen, which one of the following variances could not be regarded as consistent with this finding?

A An adverse labour rate variance
B A favourable material usage variance
C A favourable wage rate variance
D A favourable sales volume contribution variance

EXERCISES

Exercise 1

Aural Fransen of Holland, a company wholesaling Dutch cheese, buys in complete rounds from a farming cooperative and divides them into smaller pieces. It then shrink-wraps and labels them, specifically for the UK hotel and catering export market. The following information is available for the business, which normally produces 200,000 units a month.

	Fl
Direct wage cost per unit	1.20
Direct materials	2.50
Variable overhead	0.50

Fixed overheads are Fl 120,000 per month, and semivariable overheads are allowed for at a rate of Fl 0.80 per unit above a base figure of Fl 80,000 per month. For May the actual output was 160,000 units and the actual costs were as follows:

	Fl 000
Wages	168
Materials	424
Variable overhead	96
Semivariable overhead	208
(Fixed element)	92
Fixed overhead	110

Required

Prepare a flexible budget comparison of actual performance against standard performance for the company during May, identifying the main cost variances which have occurred.

Exercise 2

The Auto-donut is a coin-operated unit which automatically cooks and dispenses doughnut rings while the customer waits. The prospective owner is undertaking trials pending a decision on whether to purchase the unit outright or not. The manufacturer's specifications or standards are as follows:

	£
Sales per month 10,000 × £0.50	5,000
Power per 100 doughnuts (10 kWh × 0.10)	1.00
Dough per 100 doughnuts (2 kg × 1.20)	2.40
Sugar per 100 doughnuts (1.5 kg × 1.40)	2.10
Rental per month	3,000

After the end of the month, the actual results from Auto-donut were summarized as follows:

	£
Takings	4,500
Cost of dough used	210 for 200 kg
Cost of sugar used	198 at £1.65 per kg
Power cost	126 at £0.12 per kWh
Rental per month	3,000

Required

(a) Calculate the following variances:
   – Sales volume and price variances
   – Material price and usage variances for both materials
   – Power rate and efficiency variance
(b) Prepare a profit reconciliation statement reconciling the standard net profit to be made from the unit in a month against the actual profit earned.
(c) Write a brief statement to say whether the prospective buyer should purchase the doughnut dispenser, giving reasons one way or another, referring to the profit reconciliation statement prepared in part (b).

Exercise 3

The following summary variances for the previous month have been obtained by a national brewer from a small local competitor:

	£
Labour efficiency variance (grain house)	400(F)
Material price variance (sugar)	113(A)
Labour cost variance (wort vats)	24(A)
Material cost variance (grain)	21(A)
Sales volume variance (bitter)	nil
Fixed overhead expenditure variance	154(A)
Material usage variance (sugar)	102(F)
Variable overhead cost variance	94(A)
Material usage variance (water)	200(A)
Sales volume variance (mild)	175(F)
Labour rate variance (grain house)	125(A)
Sales price variance (mild)	210(F)
Material price variance (water)	50(F)
Sales price variance (bitter)	62(A)

Required

Derive the actual monthly profit this brewery made last month, if their budgeted profit for the month was £4,210.

Exercise 4

Beetle Juice Ltd supply a scarlet food colouring to the wholesale catering trade. Its budgeted monthly output is 10,000 litres, and the standard cost per 100 litres is as follows:

Material	250 kg costing £0.50 per kg
Labour	4 h at £6.25 per hour
Overhead	£5,000

The standard selling price is £2.50 per litre can. During the week ended April 26, 19x4 the output of Beetle Juice was 9,860 litres, all of which was sold; the invoiced value was £26,129. The material input was 24,720 kg, which cost £13,596. Production employees booked 380 hours to the process and were paid £2,451. Overheads actually totalled £5,250 for the week.

Required

(a) Prepare a profit reconciliation statement incorporating the variances which can be obtained from the available information.
(b) Put forward real business reasons for some of the variances, and why some might cause or be caused by others.

CHAPTER 18

Accounting for capital investment decisions

OBJECTIVES

- Identify the long-term objectives of business, and how investors need to be rewarded.
- Define capital investment.
- Collect the data that is necessary in order that rational investment decisions may be taken.
- Evaluate capital investment projects by several methods using a simple comparative example.
- Examine the validity and shortcomings of the available methods of choosing between alternative projects.
- Recognize the qualitative factors involved in the capital investment decision.

18.1 THE LONG-TERM OBJECTIVES OF A BUSINESS

The commercial business enterprise may have several overall objectives. A business in the hospitality, tourism and leisure (HTL) industry should have as its primary aim the satisfaction, pleasure and enjoyment of its customers. But interconnected with this, the business must aim to financially reward those providing the service or services that the customer eventually benefits from. For example, there should be a minimum return for the owners to provide capital; for lenders to make loans; for landlords to supply land, buildings or equipment; and for labour to invest mental and physical effort. The satisfaction of the customer is the means by which all of this is achieved.

Chapter 12 first introduced the concept of **opportunity cost**. This is the notion that, included in the cost of any investment, must be the cost of benefits foregone by making a particular investment decision rather than the next best alternative. If potential shareholders in a leisure venture are to provide their capital, the return on their investment must be at least equivalent, if not better than they could get elsewhere, perhaps by investing their money in a building society at a fixed rate. If financial investment is necessary to create and maintain a business, it follows that a primary objective of business is to provide an acceptable rate of return for those investors, else they may not be forthcoming or they could withdraw their backing. However, to achieve this objective, a business must meet operational objectives such as satisfying its customers and rewarding its workforce.

18.2 CAPITAL INVESTMENT

Chapter 2 explained the distinction between capital and revenue expenditure, and how they bring financial or other benefits to the business in future periods. If a business is to take decisions to invest in a major fixed asset, it is important that any such decision meets its overall commercial interests. Although the primary commercial interest of a business must be to provide an acceptable return to its owners or shareholders, the decision also needs to be acceptable to other investors such as lenders, the workforce, the government, and to the community at large.

What types of fixed-asset investment decisions may face owners, directors or managers of HTL businesses? Here are some typical examples:

1 Whether or not to invest in a new deep-fryer.
2 Whether to charter or purchase an aircraft.
3 Whether to rent or buy a pleasure boat.
4 Which packed meal should be launched.
5 Whether to purchase an automatic glass-washer in a pub, or to employ additional staff.

These types of decision are determined at the margin, by whether one alternative or another best satisfies the financial objectives of the business. The following sections explain these financial objectives, what they are or what they should be, and how the alternatives may be evaluated most effectively.

18.3 COLLECTING DATA FOR PROJECT EVALUATION

The information required to take decisions on capital investment projects depends on the financial objectives of the organization. These objectives will normally depend on the financial requirements of the owners, and will involve asking the following questions:

1 How much net profit will the project earn over its life?
2 Will the project provide an average rate of return on the investment that exceeds the minimum acceptable rate of return required by the owners?
3 How quickly will the investment pay for itself?
4 Will the investment provide a cash surplus over its lifetime, taking into account rates of return which can be obtained in the next best alternative investment?

If these and similar questions are to be answered, it is necessary to collect data about the implications of undertaking such investment projects. What data is required?

1 The capital cost of the initial investment.
2 The amount of additional revenues associated with the project, and their timing.
3 Savings on revenue expenditure that are possible through investment in the project, and when they arise.
4 The required rate of return as decided by owners or managers.
5 The opportunity cost of investing in the next best alternative to the project under evaluation, if different from item 4.

Obtaining this data is the responsibility of the budgeting department, or a subcommittee of it, possibly called a capital budgeting committee. As some capital expenditure projects can be substantial, decisions on projects over a certain level may have to be ratified by senior or top management. Part of the budgeting committee's responsibilities is to evaluate alternative ways of achieving the long-term objectives of the business. This will involve examining exceptional opportunities for capital expansion that will affect the scale of operations, in addition to overseeing the annual plan based on normal operating capacity. The first step in the evaluation of a new investment is to estimate the initial outlay involved in going ahead. The capital cost of the investment will be obtained by asking for tenders, or estimates from suppliers and contractors.

During the life of the project, estimates will need to be made of the additional revenues that may be generated by the investment, along with their timings. This might begin with an estimate of the additional output of a fixed-asset investment, when the output can be sold, in what quantities and at what price. This information may need to be sought from experts in production and in sales and marketing. It is also necessary to carefully estimate the additional revenue expenditure involved in operating the equipment or plant, or the possible cost savings that may be gained as compared with the alternatives. For example, if catering equipment were purchased, what possible savings could be made on fuel and labour? What would be the cost of running the equipment with respect to materials, labour, fuel and maintenance? Technical expertise, involving the study of product specifications, and testing may be required.

It would also be necessary to know the rate of return required by long-term investors. This may be arrived at by determining the quantity, type and cost of finance invested in the business. How much of the funds of the business are borrowed, and at what rate of interest? How much of the funds have been invested by shareholders, and what minimum return on capital will they accept? Answering these questions helps to establish a cost of capital that any additional capital investment must satisfy in order to make these investors wealthier.

Alternatively it may be necessary to establish the rate of return to be obtained on the next best alternative investment available to the business and its investors. This might involve undertaking the same data collection and estimation exercise for available alternative projects, or at least establishing a rate of return that could be obtained in a secure investment such as a bank or building society.

18.4 EVALUATING CAPITAL INVESTMENT PROJECTS

In order to explain each method of capital investment appraisal, and how they may produce different results, a single investment situation will be used as an example. It assumes there is no inflation. A small airline with one aircraft, capacity 150 passengers, is considering two alternative methods of meeting increased demand for its services:

1 To purchase two aircraft of the same type for $8 million each.
2 To purchase one aircraft, a jumbo jet, for $12 million.

The capital investment committee of the airline are asked by the budget committee to investigate which of these alternatives is best for the shareholders of the company. Collected data and estimates for the next four years have led to the following summary:

		Two aircraft $000	Jumbo jet $000
Year 0	Initial outlay	−16,000	−12,000
Year 1	Extra sales revenue	+7,000	+4,000
	Additional expenses	−3,000	−2,000
Year 2	Extra sales revenue	+7,000	+10,000
	Additional expenses	−2,000	−2,000
Year 3	Extra sales revenue	+8,000	+6,000
	Additional expenses	−3,000	−6,000
Year 4	Extra sales revenue	+8,000	+8,000
	Additional expenses	−2,000	−2,000

All planes are depreciated on a four-year straight-line basis, and both options are expected to have a $4 million residual value at the end of their useful economic lives. Note that the additional expenses exclude depreciation charges on the planes.

Method 1: Lifetime cash surplus method

This is the simplest and most basic way of comparing the investments. The way this is done is to add together all the cash receipts throughout the life of the project and then to subtract all the cash payments for expenses throughout the same period.

	Two aircraft $000	Jumbo jet $000
Total cash receipts (years 1–4)	30,000	28,000
Total cash payments (years 1–4)	−26,000	−24,000
Net cash surplus	4,000	4,000

From this crude computation it appears the airline would be willing to accept both the projects as they would, over their lives, generate $4 million additional net cash inflows to the business. If, however, only one project could be accepted, the airline would be indifferent as to which one.

Method 2: Accounting rate of return

This method accords with the conventions of financial accounting. It uses the average net profit earned throughout the investment divided by the average capital invested in the project throughout its life. The concept underlying this approach is to calculate a rate of return earned by the project over its entire life, and to compare this for alternative projects. The accounting rate of return (ARR) is calculated in the following way:

$$\text{ARR} = \frac{\text{Estimated average net profits} \times 100}{\text{Estimated average investment}}$$

The ARR will be calculated for both alternatives facing the airline company:

	Two aircraft $000	Jumbo jet $000
Total revenues (years 1–4)	30,000	28,000
Total expenses, exc depn (years 1–4)	−10,000	−12,000
Depn (cost − residual value)	−12,000	−8,000
Net profit	8,000	8,000
Average annual net profit	2,000	2,000

The estimated average investment for each project is as follows. The average value is the average value of each investment during the life of the project.

	Two aircraft $000	Jumbo jet $000
Original investment	16,000	12,000
Residual value	4,000	4,000
	20,000	16,000
$\dfrac{\text{Average value}}{2}$	10,000	8,000
Average ARR	$\dfrac{2,000 \times 100}{10,000} = 20.00\%$	$\dfrac{2,000 \times 100}{8,000} = 25.00\%$

What can be concluded from this method of appraisal is that both projects could in theory be accepted, as both achieve a positive rate of return on investment. However, this rate of return must be compared with the desired ARR for the business as a whole, or the opportunity rate of return, before either project would be accepted. Facing a choice between the two, and assuming that 25% is an acceptable rate of return, the jumbo jet would be purchased. This alternative reveals the higher rate of return on capital employed, even though the average annual net profits yielded by the projects are equal in absolute terms.

Method 3: Payback method

This method discriminates between capital projects on the basis of which pays back the original investment in the shortest time. It involves estimating the net cash flows from the projects and measuring the exact period between the original investment and the moment at which cumulative net cash inflows exactly equal the original investment. Here are the net cash flows from each project:

		Two aircraft $000	Jumbo jet $000
Year 0	Initial outlay	−16,000	−12,000
Year 1	Net cash flow	+4,000	+2,000
Year 2	Net cash flow	+5,000	+8,000
Year 3	Net cash flow	+5,000	nil
Year 4	Net cash flow	+6,000	+6,000

Here both projects have exactly the same payback period. The investments in both cases pay for themselves in three years and four months, assuming a constant cash flow throughout each year:

$$3 + (16{,}000 - 14{,}000)/6{,}000 \qquad 3 + (12{,}000 - 10{,}000)/6{,}000$$
$$= 3.33 \qquad\qquad\qquad\qquad = 3.33$$

From this method of appraisal, the business would be indifferent as to which investment to undertake. Both projects show remarkably fast payback periods, which would normally be quite satisfactory for most businesses.

Method 4: Discounted cash fund method

This method is more commonly known as the discounted cash flow or net present value method. It is the most sophisticated of the capital investment appraisal methods. The method takes into account that money earned today has a greater value than money earned tomorrow. The reason for this is that money received sooner can be reinvested sooner in the next best alternative investment, and will earn a greater return for the investor. This concept, known as the **time value of money**, is best illustrated by the use of a very simple example.

The owner of a caravan site in a desirable location is deciding whether to charge caravanners £200 per season, or to offer a three-year contract at £600, where the fee is payable at the beginning of the first season and may be renewed at the beginning of the fourth.

	£	£
Three-year contract	600	
Year 1: Annual fee		200
Year 2: Annual fee		200
Year 3: Annual fee		200

From a purely cash perspective, the site owner would be indifferent as to whether to accept £600 at the beginning or £200 per season over three seasons. Common sense would indicate, however, that anybody would prefer to take the £600 in advance rather than collect it in instalments. Firstly, accepting the three-year contract ensures a certainty of revenue for the three years as the money is in the bag. Secondly, the site owner has the choice of consuming this sum as he or she wishes, and sooner than if the fees were collected annually.

The main reason for having the cash earlier is so it can be put to work or invested for longer. The single sum and the annual instalments can both be invested to earn interest, but all things being equal, the single sum can grow larger. Assume the site owner can invest the caravan site fee in a building society earning 10% per annum, calculated annually in advance on the opening balance each year. It is possible to calculate how much will accumulate in the account if the whole fee is invested and there is no other money in the account.

	Three-year fee
	£
Original sum	600
Year 1 interest (600 × 0.10)	60
Sum at beginning year 2	660
Year 2 interest (660 × 0.10)	66
Sum at beginning year three	726
Year 3 interest (726 × 0.10)	72.6
Sum at end of year 3	798.6 (compounded cash fund)

The site owner will have nearly £800 by the end of the third year if he invests the whole sum for three years. Now suppose instead that the site owner had invested the annual instalments, what would be the value of this compounded cash fund?

	Annual fee
	£
First instalment	200
Year 1 interest (200 × 0.10)	20
Sum at end of year 1 b/d	220
Add second instalment	200
Sum at beginning of year 2	420
Year 2 interest (420 × 0.10)	42
Sum at end of year 2 b/d	462
Add third instalment	200
Sum at beginning of year 3	662
Year 3 interest (662 × 0.10)	66.2
Sum at end of third year b/d	728.2 (compounded cash fund)

The site owner will only have £728.20 at the end of the three years if the cash is received in annual instalments. Therefore the earlier the cash inflows are received, the better off the recipient will be. This is only true if there is an alternative investment opportunity in which to reinvest surplus cash flows.

The compounded cash fund (CCF) of a sum P invested today may be expressed as an equation:

$$\text{CCF of } P = P(1 + i)^n$$

where P = principal invested
i = interest rate per period as a decimal
n = number of periods invested

In the caravan example, the CCF of the £600 received at the beginning of the first year could be expressed as

$$\text{CCF of £600} = £600 \times (1 + 0.10)^3$$
$$= £798.60$$

After calculating the CCF, it is also possible to look at things from the opposite perspective. This is achieved by calculating the amount that needs to be *invested now* in order for it to become £1 at some time in the future. This is known as the discounted value of a CCF, or the **discounted cash fund** (DCF).

In the caravan example, what sum would need to be invested now for it to be worth £798.60 in three years time? The answer to this is £600 as already known. Therefore at an interest rate of 10%, £600 is the DCF of a CCF of £798.60 available after three years. How then is the DCF of £600 derived from the CCF of £798.60?

$$\text{If} \quad £600 \times (1 + 0.10)^3 = £798.60$$

$$\text{then} \quad 600 = 798.60/(1 + 0.10)^3 \quad \text{or} \quad 798.60 \times 1/(1 + 0.10)^3$$

$$\text{therefore} \quad \text{DCF of } £798.60 = 798.60 \times 1/(1 + 0.10)^3$$
$$= £600$$

The multiplier in the DCF equation, $1/(1 + 0.10)^3$, is the reciprocal of the multiplier in the CCF equation, $(1 + 0.10)^3$. In plain terms this means that if the CCF of £1 is required, in say two years at a rate of 10%, the following calculation must be made:

$$£1 \times (1.1)^2 = £1.21$$

And if the DCF is required of £1 received after two years' investment at 10%, the following calculation must be made:

$$£1 \times 1/1.21 = £0.826$$

These factors can be easily generated using a calculator, or from referring to tables; see the appendix at the end of this chapter.

With a calculator, compounding and discounting factors can be generated using the y^x key or the $1/x$ key. Different calculators work in different ways, so it may be necessary to consult the instructions, or experiment a little. With most calculators, the necessary factors may be calculated in the following rather crude way.

To generate the compound factors

1 Key in $(1 + i)$, e.g. 1.1 where $i = 0.1$ (10%). This is effectively the compound factor at the end of the first period.
2 Press the × key either once or twice, depending on the type of calculator, then press the = key.
3 The factor displayed after pressing the = key is the compound factor at the end of the second period. By continuing to press the = key, the compound factors from the third period onwards will be generated.

Question
What is the CCF of £300 invested at 7% for six years?

Type 1.07 into the calculator and press the × key once or twice, then press the = key five times:

$$1.07 \quad \times \quad = (5 \text{ times}) \qquad \text{calculator reads } 1.50$$

Therefore the CCF of £300 in six years at this rate is

$$£300 \times 1.50 = £450$$

To generate the discount factors

1 Key in $(1 + i)$, e.g. 1.1 where $i = 0.1$ (10%).
2 Press the ÷ key once or twice, depending on the type of calculator, then press the = key once or twice.
3 The factor displayed after pressing the = key once or twice is the discount factor at the end of the first period. By continuing to press the = key, the discount factors from the second period onwards will be generated.

Question

What is the DCF of £450 received after six years' investment at 7%?

Type 1.07 into the calculator, press the ÷ key once or twice, then press the = key six or seven times, depending on the calculator being used:

$$1.07 \quad ÷ \quad = (6 \text{ or } 7 \text{ times}) \quad \text{calculator reads } 0.666$$

Therefore the DCF of £450 after six years at 7% is

$$£450 \times 0.666 = £300$$

which is consistent with the answer to the first question.

Returning to the aircraft investment decision, in order to evaluate it methodically, set out the figures in the following way:

	Discount factor (D)	Two aircraft (T) $000	T × D $000	Jumbo jet (J) $000	J × D $000
Year 0	1.000	−16,000	−16,000	−12,000	−12,000
Year 1	0.909	+4,000	+3,636	+2,000	+1,818
Year 2	0.826	+5,000	+4,130	+8,000	+6,608
Year 3	0.751	+5,000	+3,755	nil	nil
Year 4	0.683	+6,000	+4,098	+6,000	+4,098
			−381		+524

For the reasons explained earlier, cash flows in later periods are not as valuable as those in earlier periods. Using a calculator, the appropriate discount factors have been generated for each of the four years at an investment rate of 10%. This rate can be assumed to be the opportunity rate of interest available to the aircraft company on surplus funds; it is also known as the **cost of capital**. Section 18.1 explained that investment in a business needs to be rewarded. Clearly, if these rewards are to be available for owners and lenders after meeting the requirements of labour, then a minimum rate of return should be forthcoming from a project before it is undertaken.

What this means is that at an alternative interest rate of 10%, it would not be worthwhile for the airline company to invest in two smaller aircraft, as the present value of the future net cash flows doesn't match the initial investment. However, it would be worthwhile to invest in the jumbo jet, as $524,000 more cash can be generated from making this investment rather than by doing nothing.

Another way of looking at it is to say that if the airline company were to invest its original outlay of $16 million on the two smaller aircraft in an alternative investment at 10%, the compounded cash amount at the end of the four years would be more than could be accumulated if the annual net cash flows from the project were similarly reinvested. If, however, this analysis were carried out for the other alternative, the airline company would find itself better off by purchasing the jumbo jet.

Assuming an appropriate discount rate, it is possible to draw two overall conclusions about project evaluation:

1 If the DCF of all net cash flows from a project, including the initial outlay is **positive**, then the project should be **accepted**.
2 If the DCF of all net cash flows from a project, including the initial outlay is **negative** then the project should be **rejected**.

Under this method the airline company is therefore recommended to accept the project involving the purchase of the jumbo jet, and to reject the project involving the purchase of the smaller planes. This would be the case even if the company had available to it the financial resources to undertake both projects.

For certain projects it is difficult to associate revenues with the capital expenditure itself. Consider an industrial dishwasher in a large commercial restaurant. The investment is not considered as a potential revenue generator, but as a potential cost saver. A cash-saving investment is just as important to the business as a cash-generating investment, for both determine the net cash funds available to reinvest at any particular time. The following estimates have been made by the management of the Pisces restaurant:

		£	£
Initial outlay on commercial dishwasher			5,000
Annual cost savings			
Labour and breakages	(year 1)	1,000	
Labour and breakages	(year 2)	2,000	
Labour and breakages	(year 3)	2,500	
Proceeds from sale of dishwasher (year 4)		1,000	

The opportunity rate of investment is 10%. And the DCFs from the cash flows are as follows:

	£		Discount factor		£
Initial outlay	5,000	×	1.000	=	(5,000)
Annual savings	1,000	×	0.909	=	909
Annual savings	2,000	×	0.826	=	1,652
Annual savings	2,500	×	0.751	=	1,877
Proceeds from disposal	1,000	×	0.683	=	683
					+121

It would seem that it is worthwhile investing in the equipment because the DCF of the savings exceeds the original investment. This is not a significant difference, and caution should be taken not to make a hard and fast decision without looking at other factors.

Some situations require capital expenditure programmes for statutory, social or other reasons. For example, soccer clubs having to convert their grounds to all-seater stadiums, or a perfume manufacturer investing in electronic testing as opposed to animal testing. Where there are alternative ways of making this expenditure, the business should decide between projects on the basis of selecting the project which has the lowest negative DCF, as discounted at the cost of capital or some other suitable rate of interest.

18.5 PROS AND CONS OF THE FOUR METHODS

Having examined the mechanics of the various methods of capital investment appraisal, we return to the airline example and examine what conclusion a management team would draw from the findings. The findings can be summarized as follows:

	Two aircraft	Jumbo jet
Lifetime cash surplus	$+4m	$+4m
ARR	20%	25%
Payback	3.33 years	3.33 years
DCF	$-381,000	$+524,000

Under the first and third method, no distinction would be made between the projects, but it is likely that either project would be accepted. Under the second method, the jumbo jet would be preferred, and both might be acceptable if the target rate of return required was under 20%. Under the DCF method, however, the option to buy the two planes would be rejected, on the grounds that the company would be better off reinvesting the capital cost in an alternative investment attracting 10%. The theoretical validity of each of the four methods will now be critically evaluated.

The lifetime cash surplus method

The simplest method of evaluating projects is to look at the lifetime cash surplus or deficit. The advantages of this method are its simplicity and objectivity. Objectivity comes from the fact there is no need to arbitrarily allocate revenues and expenditure against each other. All that is necessary is to aggregate cash inflows (or cash savings) and cash outflows, and compare them. The estimation of cash flows is subjective to some extent, as is any type of estimation or budgeting procedure.

The disadvantage of the method lies in the fact it doesn't discriminate between early cash flows and later cash flows. Nor does the method take into account the amount of capital employed in the project and the project lifetime.

Advantages

1 Simple
2 Objective

Disadvantages

1 Doesn't discriminate between early cash flows and later cash flows.
2 No account taken of the capital invested in the project.
3 No account taken of the project lifetime.

The accounting rate of return method

This method is traditionally popular as it emerges from financial accounting practice. It is consistent with the concepts and conventions of financial accounting, because it uses the information prepared for reporting purposes. It recognizes profits as the difference between allocated revenues and allocated revenue expenditure, not the net cash flow. It also recognizes return in relation to the value of what has been invested, giving a rate of return for the project which is conceptually easy to understand, and which can be used to make comparisons. The disadvantage of this is that allocated revenues and expenses can be subjective or arbitrary, and recognized profit in a financial period will depend on the accounting policies followed.

A big problem is the allocation of capital costs over the life of the project. This is determined by accounting judgements on which depreciation method should be adopted, and what the estimated residual value of the fixed asset will be at the end of the project lifetime. This depreciation problem affects the objectivity of the evaluation in two ways. Firstly, annual depreciation charges may be inappropriate, distorting reported net profits. Secondly, as the depreciation policy determines the average value of the investment, this will also distort the average rate of return arrived at.

The major disadvantage, however, is that the method ignores strict cash flows and their timings, in accordance with the accruals concept. This is a fundamental weakness, as it is only cash that can be reinvested, not profits. For example, when a business generates credit sales against which expenditure is charged, these revenues cannot be reinvested until the debts are actually settled, which may be in a future financial period, or even worse, not at all.

Advantages

1 Intuitively easy to understand from an accounting perspective.
2 Attempts to relate financial return to the amount of capital invested, in order to make reasonable comparisons between projects of different sizes.

Disadvantages

1 Too subjective, and suffers from the criticisms levelled at financial accounting reports.
2 Doesn't recognize cash flows, so it ignores the concept that cash flows are reinvested, not reported profits.
3 Doesn't recognize the length of the project or the advantage of receiving cash earlier rather than later.

Payback method

This method has the advantage of being easy to understand, and being an intuitively attractive way of appraising an investment, How quickly can I get my money back? It is also widely used in industry. Its main theoretical advantage lies in its implicit conservatism, because in the crudest possible way, it takes some account of the timing of cash flows. However, within the payback period, the payback method ignores the timing of cash flows. On the other hand, it suffers from the drawback that it ignores cash flows after the payback period. This is a criticism which may be defended on the grounds that the further into the future the estimates go, the less reliable and valuable they will be.

Advantages

1 Easily understood and intuitively logical.
2 A prudent way of appraising an investment.
3 Takes a crude account of the timing of cash flows.

Disadvantages

1 Takes no account of the timing of cash flows within the payback period.
2 Ignores all cash flows after the payback period, which may be substantial in long-term investments.

Discounted cash fund method

This method is more sophisticated as an approach to capital investment appraisal but is based on the clear assumption that the main objective of a business entity is to maximize the wealth of its owners. However, as a method it is intuitively more difficult to comprehend. The main advantage of the method is it takes into account two fundamentally related economic concepts, opportunity cost and the time value of money.

The opportunity cost concept states that the cost or price of investing in one opportunity is to forego the opportunity to invest in the next best alternative. What this means is that, when evaluating a capital project, it is necessary to ensure it at least provides a return equivalent to making some alternative decision, or doing nothing. Stemming from this is the notion that surplus cash flows should be reinvested in the next best alternative, and the sooner they are reinvested the greater will be the eventual compounded cash fund at the end of the project.

The main disadvantage of applying these concepts is the uncertainty of the opportunity cost at various stages throughout the life of the project. The assessment of opportunity cost must in theory be carried out continuously, by evaluating prevailing alternatives. Implicitly this cannot be undertaken in advance, as future opportunities may well be unknown. In practice a notional minimum interest rate or cost of capital may be used, based on the financial structure of the business, or even on a deposit rate in a secure investment. But using a notional fixed interest rate to reflect this opportunity cost may be criticized as being naive.

Advantages

1 Based on the single and clear assumption that a business's primary objective is maximization of the owner's wealth.
2 Takes into account fundamentally important economic concepts.

Disadvantages

1 Complex to understand.
2 Opportunity cost is difficult to assess, therefore using a single discounting rate for the life of a project may be subjective at best and naive at worst.

18.6 QUALITATIVE FACTORS IN CAPITAL INVESTMENT DECISIONS

What emerges from this chapter so far is that there are no perfect methods of deciding, in a pedantic manner, the correct choice between investment projects. Certain methods are fundamentally flawed in theoretical terms and may be rejected on these grounds. All methods suffer from the irrevocable truth that what lies in the future is uncertain. Whichever method is used, its findings can only be as reliable as the data originally collected, and on the validity of the assumptions made.

Many business people faced with decisions to accept or reject projects, based on conflicting findings or marginal outcomes, may in bewilderment turn to their own intuition or gut feelings. In these situations qualitative judgements should prevail, and possible long-term, strategic or perhaps ethical considerations may outweigh the purely financial findings.

This leads back to the question, What are the fundamental objectives of a business? If it is accepted that one of the major objectives of a business is to maximize the wealth of shareholders, it may be argued that to use DCF as an investment appraisal technique is consistent in the short term. But what other considerations are there?

There may be requirements on businesses by their investors to pursue non-financial objectives such as quality or ethical ideals. Examples of these non-financial objectives may include the following:

Environmental objectives: pollution control modifications.
Maintenance of a minimum service level to a community: keeping open a rural railway line.
Maintenance of minimum working conditions for employees: provision of cleaner, lighter working areas, staff facilities and social clubs; or paying a minimum wage.
Improving safety standards for customers: all-seater football stadiums.
Pursuit of a political ethos: a newspaper refusing to run a particular type of exclusive story or an editorial.
Ethical values: not investing in projects which go against religious or social beliefs, e.g. investing in countries which exploit workers, or in products or services which are produced, obtained or provided in an undesirable manner. More specific examples are the avoidance of sacrilegious activities, tobacco investments, racial exploitation, animal exploitation, intrusive photos taken by paparazzi.

Other objectives of business or investors may involve longer-term financial considerations that don't have explicit financial implications in the short term. For example, a hotel chain is considering the purchase of a bus and coach operator, in order to diversify its operations and to reduce its travelling overhead expenses. The hotel chain is faced with buying one of two similarly sized companies. The data gathered on the two companies indicates the expected net cash flows that may be generated by each alternative acquisition. It is calculated that neither gives a positive DCF over the foreseeable future. What should be done?

Financially these findings suggest the hotel company should not take over either company. But there may be other considerations perhaps without short-term financial consequences but with important long-term consequences:

The competitive environment: is there a risk that the two companies may merge or in some way combine, and increase the travel prices charged to the hotel company. On the other hand, would the take-over of one bus company allow the opportunity for the hotel chain to make a further bid for the other company at some later stage?

Risk diversification: by not investing in a different business sector, will the hotel company leave itself exposed to a greater risk if a specific downturn takes place in the hotel business for any reason?

Cost structure: as the bus company is a capital-intensive business and the hotel business relatively labour-intensive, are the future cost structures going to be affected by such factors as employment policy or union power?

Changes in fashions and values: is the domestic hotel business facing a reduction in demand, due to an increase in the demand for foreign holidays, which will in turn produce an increase in demand for bus travel? Are roads becoming so crowded that people will prefer to travel by public transport on package holidays, rather than by car to a wider choice of hotel locations?

Tax changes: is there a possibility that changes in VAT rates for hotel accommodation and bus travel may affect the relative demand for such services in the future?

Of course there may be several longer-term strategic or qualitative factors that will override short-term financial considerations. What is important to recognize is that certain interests in an organization may be short term, such as the dividend or interest requirements of shareholders and lenders, the career aspirations of senior managers, or the pay and working conditions of the workers. However, in order to ensure its longer-term success or even to secure its ultimate survival, decisions need to be taken in the long-term interest of the organization in its community, which may sometimes conflict with the short-term rules discussed in this chapter.

SUMMARY

1 **Rules for capital investment decisions must be based upon the objectives of the business and those who invest in it.**

2 **Capital investment, as opposed to revenue expenditure, will have implications for the business and those who invest in it for several financial periods.**

3 **Capital investment methods depend in the first instance on collecting reliable data about the implications of the available investment options.**

4 **There are several methods for appraising capital investment projects.**

5 **The different methods of appraising capital investment projects all have advantages and disadvantages.**

6 **Businesses, managers and owners may need to take a longer-term view of investment decisions; this may sometimes mean taking decisions which conflict with rational short-term rules.**

ASSESSMENT

MULTIPLE-CHOICE QUESTIONS

Question 1

Which one of the following statements is true with respect to a business's overall objectives?

A If an existing business meets the objective of satisfying its customers, the adequate reward of its investors must follow.

B The ultimate objective of a business is to ensure adequate rewards for those who invest in the business.

C The satisfaction of the customers and the adequate reward to investors in the business are objectives which depend on each other.

D The ultimate aim of an existing business should be the satisfaction of its customers.

Question 2

Which one of the following would only be required if the DCF method were being used for discriminating between two alternative capital investment projects?

A The cost of capital discount rate

B The cost of the initial capital investment

C The net profit earned on the project

D All cash flows generated and incurred on the project

Question 3

An hotel is considering investing in an indoor heated swimming-pool. The financial information is as follows:

1 Initial cost £100,000, with a four-year life and no residual value

2 Net cash inflows each year are £25,000 for four years

3 Cost of capital to be covered is 8%

Under which one of the following methods would the hotel management be reluctant to make this investment, if the only requirement of the project were to cover costs over its useful life?

A None of them

B Discounted cash flow

C Accounting rate of return

D Payback

Question 4

Which one of the following methods of appraisal ignores the timing of cash flows between a business and its capital investment project?

A Lifetime cash surplus method

B Accounting rate of return method

C Payback method

D Discounted cash flow method

Question 5

Which of the following is the odd one out and why?

A Investment in social facilities
B Investment in environmental improvements
C Investment in training facilities
D Investment in new information technology

EXERCISES

Exercise 1

A caravan park owner is deciding on a pricing strategy for letting caravans on the site. The present annual storage and rental charge is £600 in advance. Under consideration is the option to offer a five-year deal to campers, payable as a one-off fee in advance. The next best alternative investment for the site owner is a one-year capital bond yielding 11% interest, which the owner can keep renewing at the same rate of interest.

Required

How much should the owner charge for the five-year rental to be as well off as renting sites annually at £600 a year?

Exercise 2

An investor is interested in buying one of two small travel agencies each up for sale at a price of £50,000. Five years ago each had a market value of £30,000. Here is the financial information for the last five years:

	Agency 1 (commissions) £	Agency 2 (commissions) £
Year 1	20,000	22,000
Year 2	24,000	26,000
Year 3	28,000	26,000
Year 4	28,000	29,000
Year 5	30,000	27,000

The annual overheads of each business are identical at £10,000. There is no way of knowing what the future cash flows of these agencies will be, so the investor has to use the available historical information as a guide to future financial performance.

Required

If it is assumed the prevailing opportunity rate of interest has remained steady at 9% and is likely to do so for the foreseeable future, which travel agency, if any, should the investor purchase, or would it make no difference which they chose? Make your decision using the following methods:

(a) Lifetime net cash surplus
(b) ARR
(c) Payback
(d) DCF

Exercise 3

A restaurant is considering whether to sack its present chef in order to employ a new chef who presently works for the competing restaurant in the same street. The financial implications have been estimated as follows:

	£
Redundancy money to old chef	2,000
Annual salary of old chef	10,000
Annual salary of new chef	15,000

Net cash flows (£) from sales of meals:

	Year 1	Year 2	Year 3	Year 4
Old chef cooking	20,000	18,000	15,000	13,000
New chef cooking	18,000	20,000	23,000	25,000

Required

What should the restaurant owner do, keep the old chef or hire the new chef? Use the DCF technique to make your assessment. What other considerations might be pertinent to this decision, which might make you reject the original finding? Use an interest rate of 10%.

Exercise 4

A coach company is considering whether to buy a new coach, to keep its old one or to 'buy' a new coach under a hire-purchase agreement. Here are the financial implications of these three options:

	Keep old vehicle £	Buy new coach £	Hire new coach £
Year 1			
(Coach price/deposit)		−27,000	−5,000
Instalments			−8,000
Repair and servicing	−2,000		−400
Ticket sales	+8,000	+10,000	+10,000
Fuel and spares	−3,000	−2,000	−2,000
Year 2			
Instalments			−8,000
Repair and servicing	−2,500		−400
Ticket sales	+7,000	+12,000	+12,000
Fuel and spares	−3,500	−2,500	−2,500
Year 3			
Instalments			−8,000
Repair and servicing	−3,500		−400
Ticket sales	+6,000	+11,000	+11,000
Fuel and spares	−3,500	−2,500	−2,500
Value of coach	+2,000	+10,000	+10,000

Required

Using the DCF method, determine which option should be taken, assuming for simplicity that either coach would be sold at the end of the third year. Assume a rate of interest of 8%.

APPENDIX: PRESENT VALUE (PV) AND FUTURE VALUE (FV) OF ONE POUND

	i = 0.05		i = 0.06		i = 0.07		i = 0.08		i = 0.09		i = 0.10		i = 0.11		i = 0.12	
	PV	FV	PV	FV	PV	FV	PV	FV	PV	FV	PV	FV	PV	FV	PV	FV
1	0.952	1.050	0.943	1.060	0.935	1.070	0.926	1.080	0.917	1.090	0.909	1.100	0.901	1.110	0.893	1.120
2	0.907	1.103	0.890	1.124	0.873	1.145	0.857	1.166	0.842	1.188	0.826	1.210	0.812	1.232	0.797	1.254
3	0.864	1.158	0.840	1.191	0.816	1.225	0.794	1.260	0.772	1.295	0.751	1.331	0.731	1.368	0.796	1.256
4	0.823	1.216	0.792	1.262	0.763	1.311	0.735	1.360	0.708	1.412	0.683	1.464	0.659	1.518	0.795	1.257
5	0.784	1.276	0.747	1.338	0.713	1.403	0.681	1.469	0.650	1.539	0.621	1.611	0.593	1.685	0.794	1.259
6	0.746	1.340	0.705	1.419	0.666	1.501	0.630	1.587	0.596	1.677	0.564	1.772	0.535	1.870	0.793	1.260
7	0.711	1.407	0.665	1.504	0.623	1.606	0.583	1.714	0.547	1.828	0.513	1.949	0.482	2.076	0.792	1.262
8	0.677	1.477	0.627	1.594	0.582	1.718	0.540	1.851	0.502	1.993	0.467	2.144	0.434	2.305	0.791	1.263
9	0.645	1.551	0.592	1.689	0.544	1.838	0.500	1.999	0.460	2.172	0.424	2.358	0.391	2.558	0.791	1.265
10	0.614	1.629	0.558	1.791	0.508	1.967	0.463	2.159	0.422	2.367	0.386	2.594	0.352	2.839	0.790	1.266

Future value = $(1 + i)n$

Present value = $\dfrac{1}{\text{Future value}}$

where i = annual interest rate
n = number of periods

INTEGRATIVE CASE STUDY 2: MANAGEMENT ACCOUNTING

The Riverslade Villas development

THE ANNOUNCEMENT OF A NEW DEVELOPMENT

The directors of Osbourne Developments Ltd were called to a hurriedly arranged meeting by their managing director, Jimmy Callagher. He opened the meeting by saying, 'Thank you for your attendance at such short notice. Gentlemen, Osbourne has been in business now for twenty years. It started off in a humble enough way: buying, improving and selling domestic properties within urban areas. It is my belief that the market is now right, and so are our finances, for us to look at developing properties for retirement and holidays.

'I am assured by the marketing department that, with an ageing population and its increased affluence, properties in this sector, particularly in the better holiday resorts, will be highly sought after. I am also convinced that, with the weather expected to improve in the UK, the demand for UK holiday flats to buy, rent or timeshare will also pick up over the next few years. Bearing all this in mind, I want you to have a look at the following proposals, relating to the land we have just purchased at Riverslade Cliffs. I also wish to give you notice of a formal board meeting in three weeks' time when a detailed analysis of these proposals will be presented by our financial director, Richard Claymore.'

After the meeting, Jim Callagher grabbed Richard halfway down the corridor, and thrust an A4 wallet into his hand. 'Dick, here's the stuff I got from the marketing and costing department. Please look at it carefully. I want an evaluation of these options using a five-year planning horizon. Remember that if we decide to rent, we will sell the whole operation at the end of the fifth year. I don't mean for us to be glorified landlords! You have been trained as a management accountant, and I expect you to make a strong recommendation to us at that meeting, on which direction we should take. The company is relying on you to make the right choice; we want to start work as soon as we can. Good luck.'

Richard looked anxiously at the contents of the wallet. It was now his responsibility to familiarize himself with the information and make recommendations based on his accounting knowledge.

THE CONTENTS OF THE WALLET

The company is intending to build flats on its newly acquired land, overlooking a picturesque bay at a popular seaside resort. Two types of flat will be built, one-bedroomed and two-bedroomed. The idea is to build 40 one-bedroomed flats and 20 two-bedroomed flats. The options for earning revenue over the four years, following completion of the development, are (1) to sell the flats outright, (2) to rent out individual flats for four years then sell the whole complex as a going concern, or (3) to sell the flats on a timeshare basis.

The land cost £200,000. Before it was purchased, Osbourne opened a project bank account with a cheque for £1 million from its main business bank account, and supplemented by a three-year debenture loan of £500,000 at an annual interest rate of 9%. The loan is to be repaid in full at the end of the third year.

Building the flats is estimated to take exactly one year. The construction costs are estimated as follows:

	£
Building materials	250,000
Fixtures and fittings	450,000
Direct labour costs	400,000
Overheads	400,000
	1,500,000

And here are the estimated revenues per type of flat under each option:

	One bedroom £	Two bedrooms £
Selling price	Full cost per flat + 50%	
Rental per week	75	90
Permanent timeshare	1,800	2,000
(for two weeks, payable in full at time of sale)		

From the time that the flats are completed, it is envisaged that under any of these options, their take-up rate will be as follows:

	Purchase	Rental	Timeshare
Take-up rate by the end of the second year	80%	70%	60%

The take-up rate is expected to grow constantly over the first two years under any option, then the occupancy rate will remain fixed at that level.

The volume of the building will be apportioned between the types of flat:

	One bedroom	Two bedrooms
Percentage of total volume	60%	40%

The fixture and fitting costs for each type of flat is proportional to its area and depends on nothing else. The areas for the two types are as follows:

	One bedroom	Two bedrooms
Area	40 m²	80 m²

Under the options to sell (timeshare and outright), the maintenance costs will fall as the flats are taken up. Maintenance and security costs for all rented flats are expected to be £10.00 per square metre per annum. Maintenance costs for unoccupied flats are expected to be £7.00 per square metre per annum.

Under the rental option, it is expected that the whole complex may be sold at the end of the fifth year for £1.75 million, a valuation based on the areas occupied by the two types of flat.

Under the selling options, the residual value or 'unexpired' construction costs, including the cost of fixtures and fittings, is to be based on the proportion of each part of the building complex that remains unsold at the end of the fifth year. Assume these flats could be sold for this amount at the end of the fifth year, in keeping with best accounting practice.

The present cost of capital for Osbourne is estimated to be 7%, and this is expected to remain the same for the next five years. For simplicity, assume the original construction costs take place at the start of the first year and all subsequent cash inflows and outflows occur on the final day of each year.

Required for the presentation

(a) Find the total profit to be made from both types of flat over the five-year period, under each of the options.
(b) Prepare annual cash budgets for the development under each of the three options.
(c) Calculate the break-even percentage occupancy for selling outright and for selling timeshares. Assume all flats are sold at the start of the second year.
(d) Decide on the best alternative to adopt under
  – Payback
  – NPV

CASE NOTES

This major exercise should be tackled at the end of Part 2. Specific areas of knowledge from most of its chapters are drawn upon and tested at some point during the series of tasks. After the students have read the case carefully, a preliminary discussion seminar should take place to establish what is required and how it should be achieved. It is best to set out the tasks in line with what is required and to tackle them in that order. Although the tasks should be handled discretely to make them manageable, the case itself links them all together, so the students can see how various aspects of management accounting theory apply to a single business scenario.

What is tested

1 How to calculate the costs of products which share resources; how to allocate and apportion costs (Chapter 13).
2 How to price products or services under the cost-plus method (Chapters 13 and 14).
3 How to treat fixed and variable costs and how to calculate break-even points in terms of occupancy (Chapter 15).
4 How to prepare budgets from data (Chapter 16).
5 How to appraise capital investment proposals under the main methods available (Chapter 18).

SUGGESTED APPROACH AND SOLUTION

To tackle the tasks in the order required at the end of the case, it is recommended to begin by calculating the costs per type of flat.

Find the total profit under each of the options

This is best approached by allocating and apportioning costs of construction, maintenance and security to each section of the overall complex. We will identify the three options as follows:

– Option 1 is selling outright.
– Option 2 is renting.
– Option 3 is timeshare.

This is done by setting up a matrix of the total cost of constructing and maintaining the flats over the five-year period:

		One bedroom £	Two bedrooms £	Total £
Construction costs				
Cost of land	(note 1)	100,000	100,000	200,000
Direct materials	(note 2)	150,000	100,000	250,000
Direct labour	(note 2)	240,000	160,000	400,000
Overheads	(note 2)	240,000	160,000	400,000
Fixtures + fittings	(note 3)	225,000	225,000	450,000
Interest costs	(note 4)	81,000	54,000	135,000
Maintenance + security				
Option 1	(note 5)	17,920	17,920	35,840
Option 2	(note 5)	54,960	54,960	109,920
Option 3	(note 5)	26,640	26,640	53,280

Note 1
The cost of the land is to be apportioned on the basis of area taken up by each type of flat. This is calculated by multiplying the area per type of flat by the number of flats to be constructed:

$$(40 \times 40) + (20 \times 80) = 3,200 \text{ m}^2$$

The land cost of £200,000 is apportioned to the two types of flat as follows:

One bedroom
$$\frac{40 \times 40}{3,200} = 50\%$$

Two bedrooms
$$\frac{20 \times 80}{3,200} = 50\%$$

Each type of flat is apportioned 50% of the land cost, which is £200,000 × 0.50 = £100,000.

Note 2
The direct materials, labour and overheads are apportioned on the basis of the volume of the building occupied by each type of flat. The apportioned direct material costs for the one-bedroomed flats are

$$£250,000 \times 0.60 = £150,000$$

Note 3

The fixture and fitting costs are apportioned on the basis of the area that each type of flat occupies. So the apportioned fixture and fitting costs for the two-bedroomed flats are

$$[(20 \times 80)/3{,}200] \times £450{,}000 = £225{,}000$$

Note 4

The interest on the debenture loan is apportioned to each type of flat on the basis of volume. For one-bedroomed flats the interest costs for three years are

$$(£500{,}000 \times 0.09) \times 3 \times 0.60 = £81{,}000$$

Note 5

The maintenance and security cost for the development is rather more complicated, as it depends on the chosen option and the occupancy level for each year of the four-year period following construction. It is best calculated by preparing a four-year maintenance and security cost matrix by type of flat and available options:

	Vacant or occupied*	Year 2 £	Year 3 £	Year 4 £	Year 5 £	Total £
Option 1						
One bedroom	V	8,960	4,480	2,240	2,240	17,920
Two bedrooms	V	8,960	4,480	2,240	2,240	17,920
						35,840
Option 2						
One bedroom	O	2,800	8,400	11,200	11,200	33,600
	V	9,240	5,320	3,360	3,360	21,280
Two bedrooms	O	2,800	8,400	11,200	11,200	33,600
	V	9,240	5,320	3,360	3,360	21,280
						109,760
Option 3						
One bedroom	V	9,520	6,160	4,480	4,480	26,640
Two bedrooms	V	9,520	6,160	4,480	4,480	26,640
						53,280

* V = vacant, O = occupied

These figures are based on the mean occupancy of each type of flat during each year. Under both selling options, the maintenance and security cost is saved as the properties are sold. This cost is therefore calculated by taking the unoccupied area of each sector and multiplying it by the appropriate rate. As both flats occupy the same area, they will have the same annual cost.

It is also important to calculate for each year the **mean occupancy rate** that prevails. Consider the rental option. If 70% of the flats are expected to be rented by the end of year 3, 35% would have been rented by the end of year 2 (assuming a constant take-up rate). However, the mean occupancy rate in each year would be as follows:

Year 2	Year 3
$\frac{1}{2}(0.35 + 0) = 0.175$	$\frac{1}{2}(0.70 + 0.35) = 0.525$

The maintenance and security cost of two-bedroomed flats could then be calculated as follows:

	Year 2	Year 3
Occupied	20 × 0.175 × 80 × 10	20 × 0.525 × 80 × 10
Unoccupied	20 × 0.825 × 80 × 7	20 × 0.475 × 80 × 7

The number 20 is the number of two-bedroomed flats, 0.175 is the mean occupied proportion in year 2, 80 is the area in square metres of a two-bedroomed flat, and 10 is the estimated maintenance and security cost in pounds per square metre of rented, occupied flat. Work through the costs carefully for all flats, checking where the figures have come from. We are now in a position to derive a total cost per type of flat:

	One bedroom £	Two bedrooms £	Total £
Cost of land	100,000	100,000	200,000
Direct materials	150,000	100,000	250,000
Direct labour	240,000	160,000	400,000
Overheads	240,000	160,000	400,000
Fixtures + fittings	225,000	225,000	450,000
Interest costs	81,000	54,000	135,000
	1,036,000	799,000	1,835,000
Maintenance + security			
Option 1	17,920	17,920	35,840
Option 2	54,960	54,960	109,920
Option 3	26,640	26,640	53,280

However, there remains a residual value for these flats under each of the options. We must subtract this residual value from the costs in order to calculate the 'expired' costs apportioned over the five-year period.

Under option 1, as 20% of the flats are unsold at the end of year 5, and assuming that at some point these flats can be sold for more than they cost to build, the residual value of each type of flat is equivalent to 20% of the allocated and apportioned construction costs, including interest. Therefore the expired costs of the flats under this option are as follows:

$$\text{One bedroom: } £1,036,000 \times 0.80 = £828,800$$

$$\text{Two bedrooms: } £799,000 \times 0.80 = £639,200$$

$$\text{Total residual value} = (£1,036,000 + £799,000) \times 0.20$$
$$= £367,000$$

Under option 2, as the rented flats are to be sold at the end of year 5, and the valuation placed on them is based on the area occupied by each type of flat, the estimated selling price of £1.75 million should be apportioned to each type of flat on the following basis:

	One bedroom	Two bedrooms
	1,600/3,200 = 50%	1,600/3,200 = 50%

Therefore the valuation at the end of year 5 is the same for both types of flat:

$$£1,750,000 \times 0.50 = £875,000$$

Therefore the 'expired' construction costs excluding interest for each type of flat are as follows:

$$\text{One bedroom: } (£828,800 - £875,000) = £-46,200$$

$$\text{Two bedrooms: } (£639,200 - £875,000) = £-235,800$$

The costs of these flats are more than covered by their estimated residual values, which effectively means they appreciate over the relevant period.

Under option 3, as 40% of the flats are unsold at the end of year 5, and assuming that at some point these flats can be sold for more than they cost to build, the residual value of each type of flat is equivalent to 40% of the allocated and apportioned construction costs, including interest. Therefore the expired costs of the flats under this option are as follows:

$$\text{One bedroom: } £1,036,000 \times 0.60 = £621,600$$

$$\text{Two bedrooms: } £799,000 \times 0.60 = £479,400$$

$$\text{Total residual value} = (£1,036,000 + £799,000) \times 0.40$$
$$= £734,000$$

We will now calculate the total revenue to be earned from each type of flat under each option.

	One bedroom £	Two bedrooms £	Total £
Option 1	1,243,200	958,800	2,202,000
Option 2	327,600	196,560	524,160
Option 3	1,123,200	624,000	1,747,200

Option 1

Add 50% to the total cost of sold flats; for the one-bedroomed flats it is

$$£828,800 \times 1.50 = £1,243,200$$

The selling price per flat can then be calculated:

$$\text{One bedroom: } £1,243,200/32 = £38,850$$

$$\text{Two bedrooms: } £958,800/16 = £59,925$$

Option 2

As the take-up rate of the rental was 0 at the beginning of year 2 and 70% at the beginning of year 4, for the first two years of renting, rent was effectively collected from 70% of the flats for one year overall. For the next two years of renting, rent was collected from 70% of the flats. Therefore, the total rent collected from the one-bedroomed flats is

$$40 \times 0.7 \times £75 \times 52 \times 3 = £327,600$$

Option 3

Multiply the total number of fortnights sold per year by their selling price. For the two-bedroomed flats this is

$$20 \times 0.60 \times 26 \times £2,000 = £624,000$$

Now there is enough data to provide the board meeting with its first piece of information. The profitabilities of both types of flat under all three options are as follows:

	One bedroom £	Two bedrooms £	Total £
Option 1	396,480	301,680	698,160
Option 2	318,840	377,400	696,240
Option 3	474,960	117,960	592,920

Each profitability is obtained by subtracting from the expected revenue the expired cost of the flats and the relevant maintenance and security cost calculated earlier. From this analysis it would seem that Osbourne Developments can make more profit by selling the flats, and the greatest profit comes from the one-bedroomed flats.

Prepare annual cash budgets for the three alternatives

The second task is to prepare annual cash budgets for the five-year period, including the year of construction. The previous task has already provided all the necessary information in some shape or form.

Annual cash budget for option 1 (selling flats outright)

	Year 1 £	Year 2 £	Year 3 £	Year 4 £	Year 5 £
Receipts					
Sales of flats*	nil	1,101,000	1,101,000		367,000
	nil	1,101,000	1,101,000		367,000
Payments					
Constn costs	1,700,000				
Interest	45,000	45,000	45,000		
Sec + maint		17,920	8,960	4,480	4,480
Loan repay			500,000		
	1,745,000	62,920	553,960	4,480	4,480
Opening bal	1,500,000	(245,000)	793,080	1,340,120	1,335,640
Add receipts	nil	1,101,000	1,101,000	nil	367,000
	1,500,000	856,000	1,894,080	1,340,120	1,702,640
Less payments	1,745,000	62,920	553,960	4,480	4,480
Closing bal	(245,000)	793,080	1,340,120	1,335,640	1,698,160

* Sales of flats are constant over the first two years of operations, so half the revenue is earned in each of the two years.

Annual cash budget for option 2 (renting flats)

	Year 1 £	Year 2 £	Year 3 £	Year 4 £	Year 5 £
Receipts					
Renting flats*		43,680	131,040	174,720	174,720
Disposal					1,750,000
	nil	43,680	131,040	174,720	1,924,720
Payments					
Constn costs	1,700,000				
Interest	45,000	45,000	45,000		
Sec + maint		24,080	27,440	29,120	29,120
Loan repay			500,000		
	1,745,000	69,080	572,440	29,120	29,120
Opening bal	1,500,000	(245,000)	(270,400)	(711,800)	(566,200)
Add receipts	nil	43,680	131,040	174,720	1,924,720
	1,500,000	(201,320)	(139,360)	(537,080)	1,358,520
Less payments	1,745,000	69,080	572,440	29,120	29,120
Closing bal	(245,000)	(270,400)	(711,800)	(566,200)	1,329,400

* Renting flats
Year 1: Both flats (17.5% × weekly rental × 52) £43,680
Year 2: Both flats (52.5% × weekly rental × 52) £131,040
Year 3: Both flats (70.0% × weekly rental × 52) £174,720
Year 4: Both flats (70.0% × weekly rental × 52) £174,720

Annual cash budget for option 3 (timeshares)

	Year 1 £	Year 2 £	Year 3 £	Year 4 £	Year 5 £
Receipts					
Selling TS*		873,600	873,600		734,000
		873,600	873,600		734,000
Payments					
Constn costs	1,700,000				
Interest	45,000	45,000	45,000		
Sec + maint		19,040	12,320	8,960	8,960
Loan repay			500,000		
	1,745,000	64,040	557,320	8,960	8,960
Opening bal	1,500,000	(245,000)	564,560	880,840	871,880
Add receipts	nil	873,600	873,600	nil	734,000
	1,500,000	628,600	1,438,160	880,840	1,605,880
Less payments	1,745,000	64,040	557,320	8,960	8,960
Closing bal	(245,000)	564,560	880,840	871,880	1,596,920

* Sales of timeshares are constant over the first two years of operations, so half the revenue is earned in each of the two years.

Calculate the break-even percentage occupancy under options 1 and 3

This task involves an understanding of the behaviour of costs over output and with time. First of all, the fixed costs for each type of flat need to be totalled. We have done this earlier:

	One bedroom £	Two bedrooms £
Fixed costs	1,036,000	799,000

To the fixed costs we need to add the maintenance and security (M+S) cost when all the flats are unoccupied:

	One bedroom £	Two bedrooms £
Unoccupied	280	560
Occupied	nil	nil

This is calculated by multiplying the rate per square metre by the total area per type of flat over four years:

$$(£280 \times 40 \times 4) = (£560 \times 20 \times 4) = £44,800$$

The total fixed and semivariable costs are as follows:

	One bedroom £	Two bedrooms £
Fixed costs	1,036,000	799,000
M+S (unoccupied)	44,800	44,800
	1,080,800	843,800

The break-even (BE) point is the number of each type of flat which needs to be sold to cover total costs exactly. This can be expressed in the following way:

$$BE = \frac{\text{Fixed costs}}{\text{Contribution per flat}}$$

The contribution made by each flat depends on the price per flat, or in the case of renting it depends on the annual rent from the flat. The contribution is also affected by the effect of changes in the maintenance and security cost. Begin with the selling price.

Option 1
The selling prices per flat are as follows:

	One bedroom £	Two bedrooms £
Prices	38,850	59,925
Total savings on M+S (4 × 280) or (4 × 560)	1,120	2,240
Total contribution	39,970	62,165
Break-even number of flats	$\frac{1,080,800}{39,970} = 27$	$\frac{843,800}{62,165} = 13.6$
As a percentage of the total built	27/40 = 67.5%	13.6/20 = 68%

Under option 1 the development company must try to occupy at least two-thirds of its flats. This is because in practice these flats are not sold immediately, and fewer savings on maintenance and security will be made as a consequence.

Option 3

	One bedroom £	Two bedrooms £
Prices		
(26 × 1,800) or (26 × 2,000)	46,800	52,000
Total savings on M+S		
(4 × 280) or (4 × 560)	1,120	2,240
Total contribution	47,920	54,240
Break-even number of flats	$\dfrac{1,080,000}{47,920} = 22.5$	$\dfrac{843,800}{54,240} = 15.5$
As a percentage of the total built	22.5/40 = 56.25%	15.5/20 = 77.5%

Under option 3 the development company must try to sell more than three-quarters of the two-bedroomed flats. On the other hand, only up to 60% of the one-bedroomed flats need to be sold to cover the costs allocated and apportioned to that part of the complex.

This difference in break-even occupancy between the two options may be attributed to the price differential in the timeshare flats between the one-bedroomed flats and the two-bedroomed flats, as against the differential on the conventionally sold flats.

Find the best option under payback then under NPV

Using the information from the annual cash budgets, we will tabulate the annual net cash flows under all three options:

	Option 1 £	Option 2 £	Option 3 £
Year 1			
Outflow	1,745,000	1,745,000	1,745,000
Inflow	nil	nil	nil
Net cash flow	(1,745,000)	(1,745,000)	(1,745,000)
Year 2			
Outflow	62,920	69,080	64,040
Inflow	1,101,000	43,680	873,600
Net cash flow	1,038,080	(25,400)	809,560
Year 3			
Outflow	553,960	572,440	557,320
Inflow	1,101,000	131,040	873,600
Net cash flow	547,040	(441,400)	316,280
Year 4			
Outflow	4,480	29,120	8,960
Inflow	nil	174,720	nil
Net cash flow	(4,480)	145,600	(8,960)

	Option 1 £	Option 2 £	Option 3 £
Year 5			
Outflow	4,480	29,120	8,960
Inflow	367,000	1,924,720	734,000
Net cash flow	362,520	1,895,600	725,040

Payback

Under all three options, the initial outlay is £1,745,000:

Cash flows	Option 1 £	Option 2 £	Option 3 £
Year 1	−1,745,000	−1,745,000	−1,745,000
Year 2	+1,038,080	−25,400	+809,560
Cum CF	−706,920	−1,770,400	−935,440
Year 3	+547,040	−441,400	+316,280
Cum CF	−159,880	−2,221,800	−619,160
Year 4	−4,480	+145,600	−8,960
Cum CF	−164,360	−2,066,200	−628,120
Year 5	+362,520	+1,895,600	+725,040
Cum CF	+198,160	−170,600	+96,920

This schedule indicates that both options 1 and 3 pay back between 4 and 5 years. Option 1 pays back in

$$4 \text{ years} + 164{,}360/362{,}520 \text{ years} = 4.45 \text{ years}$$

Option 2 doesn't pay back at all. Option 3 pays back in

$$4 \text{ years} + 628{,}120/725{,}040 \text{ years} = 4.87 \text{ years}$$

Therefore, under the payback method, the option to sell outright is the best option.

It is obvious that option 1 gives us the highest NPV too, as under option 1, cash inflows are received earlier. Option 2 is known not to be viable, so the NPVs of options 1 and 3 will be compared to come to a final recommendation:

	Option 1 £	Discount factor	NPV £	Option 3 £	Discount factor	NPV £
Year 1	−1,745,000	1.00	(1,745,000)	−1,745,000	1.00	(1,745,000)
Year 2	+1,038,080	0.93	965,414	+809,560	0.93	752,891
Year 3	+547,040	0.87	475,925	+316,280	0.87	275,164
Year 4	−4,480	0.82	(3,674)	−8,960	0.82	(7,347)
Year 5	+362,520	0.76	275,515	+725,040	0.76	551,030
NPV of option			(31,820)			(173,262)

Therefore, using the NPV method and utilizing the 7% rate for the cost of capital to Osbourne Developments, Richard Claymore would have to recommend to the board of directors not to develop the land in any of the ways contained in the wallet, based on the available estimates.

PART 3

Financial assessment and analysis

CHAPTER 19

Interpretation and assessment of financial information

OBJECTIVES

- Understand the concept of ratio analysis and its role in comparative analysis.
- Recognize the fundamental relationship between the gross profit margin ratio, the expenses/sales ratio and the net profit margin ratio.
- Define and calculate the three primary ratios which explain how well a business is utilizing its resources to generate revenue and profit.
- Define and measure profitability in terms of who invests in a business.
- Understand the concept of liquidity and calculate the main short-term liquidity ratios.
- Calculate the major working capital efficiency ratios and other efficiency ratios.
- Recognize the impact of capital structure on risk and return to shareholders.
- Calculate efficiency ratios in the hotel sector.
- Utilise cost–volume–profit ratios to assess the financial risk and opportunity facing a business.
- Define the productivity of a business in terms of the value that a business adds, and define and calculate the main value-added ratios.
- Recognize the weaknesses and drawbacks of ratio analysis as a method of assessing business performance.

INTRODUCTION

The first two parts of this book were concerned with the preparation of financial information. Part 1 involved the collection, processing and reporting of financial information for internal records and for external users. Part 2 involved the preparation of financial information in order to facilitate planning, control and decision making. A further accounting function is financial assessment and analysis. It involves examining and analysing the information that is already available, in order to understand the business conditions that underlie this information. Assessment and analysis have several purposes:

1 To investigate the financial performance of a business in two principal areas:
  - Generation of revenue
  - Control of costs
2 To see how well a business is able to meet its current obligations.
3 To see how efficiently the business is managing its working capital in the following areas:
  - Stock control
  - Credit control
  - Cash management

4 To examine how the capital structure of a business influences the potential risk and return to shareholders.

5 To look at the influence of cost and contribution structure on the potential risk and return to shareholders.

6 To see how much a business depends on the various contributors to its net output, and how its contributors are rewarded.

This chapter will consider these issues and show how the ideas of Parts 1 and 2 relate to financial assessment and analysis. The purpose is to understand why a business is performing in a particular way, and possibly to make recommendations for improvement, or to provide investors with appropriate information for their investment decisions.

19.1 RATIOS AND COMPARATIVE ANALYSIS

Absolute numbers are of limited usefulness. Consider two companies, A and B, in different sectors of the hospitality, tourism and leisure (HTL) industry. Exactly what type of businesses they are is as yet a mystery. Let us see if enough evidence can be gathered to solve this mystery. How long will it take you to make an educated guess? Their net profits for the year were as follows:

	Company A £	Company B £
Net profit	5,000	50,000

It is obvious that company B makes more profit, but which company is more profitable? The answer to this lies in relating profit to something else, such as the size of the company, the total sales it generates, or to how much capital is invested in it. In other words, we make an assessment or a judgement based on making some sort of comparison. Further information enables some useful comparisons to be made:

	Company A £	Company B £
Net profit	5,000	50,000
Sales	100,000	250,000
Share capital and reserves	50,000	200,000

If net profit is related to sales, an assessment can be made of which company generates the most net profit per £1 received from customers:

	Company A £	Company B £
Net profit ––––––– × 100% Sales	5,000 ––––––– × 100% 100,000	50,000 ––––––– × 100% 250,000
Percentage	5%	20%

By expressing the comparison or **ratio** as a percentage, company A generates 5p profit per £1 taken as sales, and company B generates 20p profit per £1 taken as sales. Net profit will now be expressed in terms of the amount of capital which has been invested by the owners in each company:

	Company A	Company B
	£	£
Net profit	5,000	50,000
	$\dfrac{5,000}{50,000} \times 100\%$	$\dfrac{50,000}{200,000} \times 100\%$
Capital invested	50,000	200,000
Percentage	10	25

Here company A generates 10p profit for every £1 invested by its owners, and company B generates 25p per £1 invested. This is also known as **return on capital employed** (ROCE). Ratios are useful in two main ways:

1 To make interbusiness comparisons
2 To make temporal comparisons

First, ratios are an extremely useful way of making meaningful comparisons between companies, as demonstrated above. Ratios have advantages over absolute numbers as they help to compare the performance of businesses of different sizes and types. They are particularly useful where businesses in the same industrial sector are compared against each other and differences isolated. Second, ratios are useful for observing trends in performance. For example, if the net profit/capital invested ratio had been calculated for the two companies in the previous year, any change in the ratios could have been observed and conclusions drawn.

19.2 GROSS AND NET PROFIT MARGINS

Continuing with companies A and B, their gross profits for the year were as follows:

	Company A	Company B
	£	£
Gross profit	40,000	150,000

The relative profitability of the two companies can now be examined. It is possible to compare the gross profit with the sales generated and to make some observations:

	Company A	Company B
	£	£
Gross profit margin	$\dfrac{40,000}{100,000} \times 100\% = 40\%$	$\dfrac{150,000}{250,000} \times 100\% = 60\%$

This ratio indicates what proportion of the sales value remains to cover expenses after the cost of sales has been deducted. The cost of sales might include production costs if the business is a manufacturer, food costs if a restaurant, or the cost of stocks purchased if a retailer. The gross profit margin is affected by two variables:

1 The price of the product or service sold
2 The cost of the product or service produced or provided

The gross profit margin is a useful indicator of the primary operating efficiency of the company. It can indicate the effectiveness of the business's marketing policy through the price that can be obtained for its products or service, and it can indicate the efficiency of the business in producing, procuring or providing those products or services. It is a valuable indicator for making comparisons between businesses.

The gross profit margins of two businesses within the same market sector are likely to be similar, as in most cases both the prices and costs are likely to fall within a narrow range. Where any significant differences are observed, they would be the result of a difference in marketing strategy, or due to the business having obtained, produced or provided the product or service at a different cost. An example is a comparison between two food retailers: a high-value low-volume specialist outlet selling a wide variety of foods, and a high-volume discount food operation selling a narrow range of food lines. The gross profit margin of the discount food retailer is likely to be much lower than the margin of the specialist retailer.

The gross profit margin would be expected to remain stable over time, despite changes in the volume of sales, as prices in relation to costs would probably not change significantly. Where gross margins do change from period to period, the reasons for this would need to be investigated. Here are some possibilities:

Change in pricing strategy: offering discounts.
Change in cost of product or service: new cheaper supplier, a change in production method, or bulk-buying discounts.
Change in product mix: deletion or addition of lines with radically different cost and price structures.

In the example, company B has a very much higher gross profit margin than company A, which suggests these businesses do not operate within the same industry sector. Looking again at the net profit margin, what can be concluded?

	Company A	Company B
Net profit margin	5%	20%

Company B reveals the highest margin. The difference between the gross and net profit margins is accounted for by the expenses or the overheads that each business incurs in carrying out its business. The profit and loss expenses are as follows:

	Company A £	Company B £
Gross profit	40,000	150,000
Net profit	5,000	50,000
Expenses and overheads	35,000	100,000

The two companies may be compared from the viewpoint of their expenses as a percentage of sales:

Company A £	Company B £
$\dfrac{35,000}{100,000} \times 100\% = 35\%$	$\dfrac{100,000}{250,000} \times 100\% = 40\%$

This demonstrates that, although the cost of sales as a percentage of sales of each company is very different, the other expenses as a percentage of sales are broadly similar. Company B's expenses account for a slightly greater proportion of its sales value than is the case with company A. This ratio indicates the degree to which a company is burdened with overheads such as establishment costs, administrative expenses, and selling and distribution costs. Businesses in different sectors are likely to vary significantly in this respect. If a car-hire company were compared with a caravan retailer, their ratios would reveal considerable differences.

The car-hire company's expenses/sales ratio would be very high as the overheads involved in such a venture would be large. The depreciation of the vehicles would probably be its greatest single overhead classification. On the other hand, the caravan retailer would have a very high cost of sales in terms of the purchase cost of the caravans, but in comparison would have low overheads, such as the expenses involved in operating from a Portakabin or office with very few sales and administration staff.

Chapter 13 introduced the distinction between fixed and variable costs. This distinction is highly relevant in the analysis of gross and net profit margins. The gross profit margin is not likely to vary over time or with respect to sales volume. This is because the cost of sales is mainly a variable cost, particularly in the retailing sector. It is also likely to be variable in the food catering sector, as the cost of sales usually includes only food ingredient costs. What this means is that if sales increase, these costs will increase proportionally. This is not true with respect to overhead costs.

These costs are largely fixed and they depend on time not activity level. Rents, rates, insurance and salaries will not normally rise significantly as sales revenue increases. This means that a business which is expanding within the short term is likely to see a net profit margin that increases with volume. This is because fixed expenses will account for an ever smaller proportion of sales value as the volume of activity increases. If a rise in this ratio is observed, then the reasons should be investigated.

19.3 PRIMARY PERFORMANCE RATIOS

When examining the financial performance of a business, there is a need to examine how well it is utilizing its resources in comparison with other businesses, and also to observe trends in performance over several financial periods. Three main ratios help with this analysis:

1 Net profit/sales (section 19.2)
2 Net profit/capital invested by owners
3 Sales/capital invested by owners (asset/turnover)

These three ratios are related by the following equation:

$$\frac{\text{Net profit}}{\text{Capital invested}} = \frac{\text{Net profit}}{\text{Sales}} \times \frac{\text{Sales}}{\text{Capital invested}}$$

This can be demonstrated by taking the ratios for company A and company B and substituting them into the equation:

Company A

$$\frac{£\,5{,}000}{50{,}000} = \frac{£\,5{,}000}{100{,}000} \times \frac{£\,100{,}000}{50{,}000}$$

$$0.10 = 0.05 \times 2.00$$

Company B

$$\frac{£\,50{,}000}{200{,}000} = \frac{£\,50{,}000}{250{,}000} \times \frac{£\,250{,}000}{200{,}000}$$

$$0.25 = 0.20 \times 1.25$$

The analysis of these ratios will indicate how effectively each company utilizes the funds available to it. Company A utilizes its long-term capital much more intensively than company B, as it produces £2 of sales value for every £1 invested by the owners, as compared to £1.25 produced by B. However, company B is much more effective in generating profit from its sales than company A. Company B is therefore incurring relatively lower expenses than company A in generating its sales, so it can be described as more efficient in this sense.

In order to improve the profit available to the owners as a proportion of the amount invested, a business must strive to improve either or both the net profit margin and the sales as a proportion of capital invested. This can be done by increasing sales value, and the proportion of it that remains after expenses have been incurred. This can be achieved by improving marketing and sales effectiveness, and by controlling expenditure.

19.4 RETURN ON CAPITAL EMPLOYED (ROCE)

The amount of profit that a business has left over after meeting all its costs is in theory available to the owners. In order to assess the profitability of a business, this profit should be expressed as a proportion of the amount currently invested by the owners. This proportion is important for making meaningful comparisons with alternative investment opportunities, either in other businesses or in safe investments such as a bank or building society. Ordinary shareholders in a business would expect to obtain a significantly higher rate of return on their capital employed than would be available in a safer investment opportunity. The capital structure of companies A and B are as follows:

	Company A £	Company B £
Shareholders' funds	50,000	200,000
10% Debentures	100,000	100,000

Both companies are partly financed by a fixed-interest loan which attracts 10% interest per year. If this 10% return available to long-term lenders is compared to the return available to the shareholders, it appears that the shareholders in company A would be dissatisfied with their return of 10% as their investment in the company inevitably carries more risk than the loan. However, it also appears that the return of 25% available to the shareholders of company B would be acceptable to them in comparative terms.

In overall terms we can calculate the rate of return available to all long-term investors. This is known as the **management efficiency ratio**. It is calculated in the following way:

$$\frac{\text{Net profit before interest and taxation (NPBIT)}}{\text{Long-term funds invested in the business as a whole}} \times 100\%$$

This indicates the weighted average return generated by the business for all its long-term investors, both owners and lenders. Here are the management efficiency ratios of companies A and B:

Company A
£
$$\frac{5,000 + 10,000}{50,000 + 100,000} \times 100\% = 10\%$$

Company B
£
$$\frac{50,000 + 10,000}{200,000 + 100,000} \times 100\% = 20\%$$

The weighted average return to long-term investors in company A is 10%. This is because both types of investor obtain a 10% return on their investment. But in the case of company B, the lower rate of return (10%) available to lenders in comparison with the 25% available to owners, dilutes the weighted average down to 20%. In effect, this ratio gives the basic **weighted average cost of capital (WACC)** of the company, a concept that was introduced for capital investment appraisal in Chapter 18.

The extent to which the WACC is diluted is determined by the extent to which the business depends for its finance on loan capital in relation to owners' capital. We will explore the further significance of this relationship in section 19.7.

19.5 LIQUIDITY RATIOS

Financial performance and profitability have now been considered. It is also important to examine the liquidity of a business. That is, to establish how effectively a business can meet its short-term obligations. This is achieved by comparing the current assets of the business with its current liabilities. Looking at companies A and B, their liquidities are as follows:

	Company A £	Company B £
Current assets		
Stock	3,000	50,000
Debtors	16,000	nil
Cash	5,000	nil
Current liabilities		
Creditors	24,000	nil
Bank overdraft	nil	10,000

Liquidity is determined by the amount of working capital available within the business. This is defined as current assets minus current liabilities. The most important liquidity ratio is the **current ratio**, which is current assets/current liabilities (CA/CL). It is not expressed as a percentage but as a proportion. The current ratios for companies A and B are as follows:

	Company A £	Company B £
$\dfrac{CA}{CL}$	$\dfrac{24,000}{24,000} = 1.00$	$\dfrac{50,000}{10,000} = 5.00$

This ratio reveals a considerable difference between the two companies. Company B is five times more liquid than company A. Company A can only just cover its obligations to creditors in the short term, yet company B can cover its obligation to the bank five times over.

Although company A would be less vulnerable if its ratio were higher, it can be argued that to have a ratio that is too high indicates inefficiency, in that too much working capital is available. Careful examination of current assets to see which of them are excessive might indicate problems like these:

Excessive stock levels: indicating poor stock control or a decline in sales volume.
Excessive debtors: indicating poor credit control and an increasing risk of bad debts.
Excessive cash or near-cash equivalents: indicating a lack of suitable investment opportunities in capital projects.

Stock is the only current asset of company B. Is this level of stock too high, or is stock essential to the company's business? As stock is the least liquid of the current assets, prudence requires that liquidity is considered in another way. If current assets **excluding stock** are compared with current liabilities, the result is a more cautious assessment of liquidity. This ratio is known as the **quick ratio** or the **acid test ratio**, and is calculated as follows:

$$\frac{\text{Current assets less stock}}{\text{Current liabilities}}$$

The quick ratios for companies A and B are as follows:

Company A
£
$$\frac{24{,}000 - 3{,}000}{24{,}000} = 0.875$$

Company B
£
$$\frac{50{,}000 - 50{,}000}{10{,}000} = 0$$

The quick ratio indicates that company A has a considerably better liquidity and company B is dangerously insolvent.

19.6 WORKING CAPITAL EFFICIENCY RATIOS

Having assessed the overall liquidity of the two companies, it is necessary to establish how efficiently they manage their working capital. The first element to examine is stock control.

Stock turnover ratio

The way that stock control is assessed is to calculate a rate of stock turnover. This is achieved by dividing the average stockholding by the cost of sales in the financial period concerned. To take a very simple example, if a fish retailer carries a day's stock and receives a £100 delivery every day of the year, the stock turnover is obviously 1 day, but this is calculated in the following way:

$$\frac{\text{Average stock holding}}{\text{Annual cost of sales}} \times 365 = \frac{100 \times 365}{36{,}500}$$
$$= 1 \text{ day}$$

From the information obtained earlier, the stock turnover ratio of the two companies can be calculated as follows:

	Company A £	Company B £
Stock on hand	3,000	50,000
Cost of sales (sales – gross profit)	60,000	100,000
Stock turnover ratio	$\dfrac{3{,}000}{60{,}000} \times 365$	$\dfrac{50{,}000}{100{,}000} \times 365$
	= 18.25 days	= 182.5 days

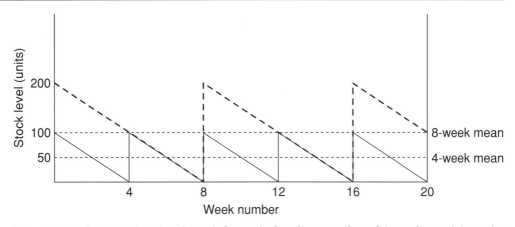

Figure 19.1 Average levels of stock for ordering frequencies of 8 weeks and 4 weeks

The stock turnover ratio can also be described as the number of times that the average quantity of stock held is sold per financial period. This is calculated for the two companies as follows:

Company A	Company B
£	£
$\dfrac{60{,}000}{3{,}000} = 20$	$\dfrac{100{,}000}{50{,}000} = 2$

These ratios indicate the entirely different stockholding policies of the two companies. Company A holds only two to three weeks stock, and company B holds stock for six months. This is a major indication of the contrast between their types of business. One word of caution: it is important that the identified stock level is representative of the average stock held within the business throughout the financial period. Many businesses in the HTL industry are cyclical, so the date of the balance sheet will partly determine the stock level.

Observing trends in the stock turnover ratio can indicate how stock is being controlled and managed. A lengthening turnover cycle can indicate two things:

1 A slowdown in sales volume while order sizes and frequency are maintained at previous levels.
2 An increase in the stockholding due to increasing order quantities, or through a reduction in the frequency of orders, while sales remain constant.

Increasing the size of orders may be in response to volume discounts or in anticipation of an imminent price rise. The effect of changing the order frequency on average stock levels and the stock turnover ratio is illustrated in Fig. 19.1. Stock levels depend on the type of business engaged in, governed by the needs of the business and to some extent by the service from suppliers. Generally the size and frequency of orders influence the costs of the stocks in two opposing ways:

1 The greater the stock order, the smaller the unit cost; this is due to volume discounts. The reorder costs will also be smaller because orders will be placed less often.
2 The greater the stock level, the greater the carrying costs, including

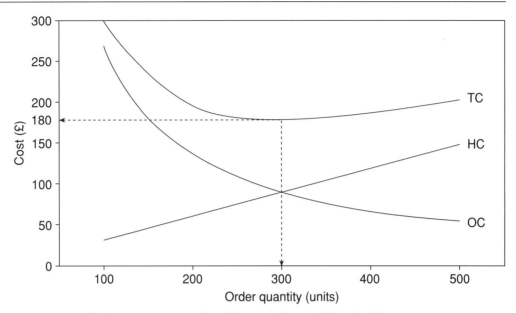

Figure 19.2 Optimal order quantity: TC = total cost, HC = holding cost, OC = reorder cost

- Storage and handling, storeroom costs, insurance
- Opportunity rate of interest on the finance tied up in the stocks
- Obsolescence and damage

As a business orders higher quantities, it will obtain a lower unit price per unit. As order levels get larger, the savings as a proportion of the total order cost will continuously fall until the cheapest rate is reached, after which further cost savings cannot be made. At the same time, the ordering costs and holding costs per unit will increase as the stock levels carried get ever higher.

The relationship between these costs is illustrated in Fig. 19.2. At a certain point, the average unit total cost of holding stocks is minimized. This is because, up to this point the savings due to volume discounts and lower order costs outweigh the carrying costs. Beyond a certain point however, the holding costs will drive the total unit cost per item upwards. Logically a business should attempt to order the quantity which produces the lowest average cost per unit. The economic order quantity can be calculated from this equation:

$$EOQ = (2UC/H)^{1/2}$$

where U = periodic usage of stock in units
C = reorder cost per order
H = holding cost per unit

If a business makes and uses 2,700 units per year, the reorder cost per order is £10 and the holding cost per unit is 60p per unit, the EOQ will be

$$\left(\frac{2 \times 2,700 \times 10}{0.60}\right)^{1/2} = 300$$

Therefore, the business would be better off ordering 300 units each time, which in this example represents a stock turnover of $300 \times (365/2{,}700)$ = nearly 41 days or nine times per year.

It is generally accepted now that the advantages of bulk ordering are far outweighed in practice by the holding costs, particularly due to the time value of money, and many businesses are reducing their stock turnover cycles dramatically. An extreme form of stock management is known as just-in-time (JIT), and was originally introduced by the Japanese. Supplies are ordered day to day, even hour to hour, so they meet the exact needs of the business in each area. This method heavily depends on having tight control over suppliers.

Debtor turnover ratio

The next working capital efficiency ratio to examine is the debtor turnover ratio. This ratio indicates how quickly a business is collecting its debts from customers. It is calculated as follows:

$$\frac{\text{Average debtors}}{\text{Credit sales}} \times 365$$

The debtor turnover ratio will be determined by two factors:

1 The proportion of total sales revenue which is on credit
2 The length of time debtors take to pay their debts

If a business is in retailing, the proportion of sales that are on credit will be minimal or non-existent. If a business is further down the value chain, such as a wholesaler or manufacturer, the proportion of credit sales to total sales will be much higher. The debtor turnover ratios for A and B are as follows:

Company A
£
$$\frac{16{,}000}{100{,}000} \times 365 = 58.4 \text{ days}$$

Company B
£
$$\frac{\text{nil}}{200{,}000} \times 365 = \text{nil}$$

This ratio indicates that, on average, company A collects its debts once every two months and company B sells exclusively for cash. For company A the proportion of the total sales on credit is not given, so the debtor turnover ratio combines the effect of cash sales and credit sales. If the credit sales alone were used as the denominator, the turnover ratio would naturally be greater.

This ratio indicates the inherently different nature of the two types of business. Observing trends in this ratio over time will indicate possible problems with credit control. Lengthening of the debtor turnover ratio may indicate that the business is extending more credit to its customers, or that on average these customers are taking longer to settle their debts. The importance of credit control was mentioned in Chapter 7, along with methods that encourage customers to pay earlier. These include offering discounts for prompt payment, operating an ageing debtor schedule, putting dubious customers on a pro-forma invoice, and generally tightening up on reminder and debt retrieval systems.

Sometimes a business may find it beneficial or even crucial to factor out its debts, in order to get cash in quickly. Factoring is where a debt recovery agency offers 90% or less of the face value of the debts to the client company. Where a business is extending more credit, this may not indicate any serious problems, indeed it may be a necessary policy in order to improve sales turnover. But note that the higher the level of debtors, the greater the likelihood of incurring bad debts, and the greater the need to make larger provisions against them.

Creditor turnover ratio

The opposite of the debtor turnover ratio is the creditor turnover ratio. This indicates the extent to which a business is depending on credit for the financing of its supplies, and the length of time it takes for a business to settle its debts to suppliers. The creditor turnover ratio is calculated as follows:

$$\frac{\text{Average creditors}}{\text{Credit purchases}} \times 365$$

As with the debtor turnover ratio, if the extent to which purchases are made on credit is not known, the turnover ratio will be a weighted average of both credit and cash purchases. A further problem also presents itself. As only the cost of sales is known, and the stock levels at both the beginning and end of the year are not known, purchases for the year cannot be derived. In this situation a constant stock level will be assumed, so the cost of sales may be used as a surrogate for purchases. The creditor turnover ratios for A and B are as follows:

Company A	Company B
£	£
$\frac{24{,}000}{60{,}000} \times 365 = 146$ days	$\frac{\text{nil}}{100{,}000} \times 365 = \text{nil}$

The average length of time that company A takes to pay its creditors is nearly five months, whereas company B pays for its purchases on a purely cash basis. This is further evidence that A and B are operating in different ways to each other.

The 146-day turnover cycle operated by company A may suggest it is experiencing liquidity problems, as confirmed by the current ratio calculated in section 19.5. The trend in this ratio over time will provide evidence of whether the credit period being taken is lengthening or contracting. Although businesses should, in principle, attempt to delay payment in order to improve their own liquidity, there can be problems with alienating suppliers in this way, who may react by refusing further credit facilities. The power balance between supplier and customer will largely dictate the extent to which the credit period is extended. A supplier with a unique product, or a prominent position in the market deserves to be treated with commercial respect. Also, from an ethical point of view, suppliers should be paid within a reasonable period of time, as their cash flow might be heavily dependent on a few very large customers. And for these businesses, punctual payment is the key to survival.

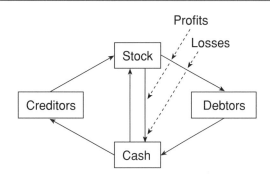

Figure 19.3 The working capital cycle

The cash operating cycle

The working capital ratios calculated earlier can be combined in a way that will indicate the average length of time a business has to wait before it collects the cash it has used during the trading cycle (Fig. 19.3).

The trading cycle involves stocks or services being sold, debts being recognized, then being settled, and the money that is collected from debtors or cash sales being used to buy stocks or services directly, or to settle debts to suppliers, and so the cycle continues. It can be thought of as a water-wheel that continuously turns.

The cash flow is the water that drives the wheel round. The more water that flows around the system, the more quickly the wheel will turn. The shorter the lengths of time between various stages in the operating cycle, i.e. the shorter the diameter of the wheel, the more often it will revolve, and the more frequent are the opportunities to recycle the cash generated.

Very often a small, rapidly-spinning wheel can generate as much cash flow as a large, slowly turning wheel. The larger wheel also needs a greater amount of water to keep it turning, hence there is a greater risk of the wheel stopping through a temporary shortage of flow. This is as true for a business as it is for a water-mill.

As a successful business should generate more cash than it uses from operations, there must be a way of utilizing any excess build-up of cash on capital expenditure. This may involve investing in capital projects or reducing long-term liabilities. If a business doesn't do this, there will be a wasteful build-up of cash, indicating a lack of investment opportunities or a management which is ignoring them.

In purely business terms, the cash position will improve if the following changes take place:

1 Sales volume is increased.
2 Stock is ordered more often.
3 A higher proportion of sales are for cash.
4 Debtors are encouraged to pay more promptly.
5 Payments to creditors are delayed as much as possible, but without damaging trading relations and jeopardizing supply.

The cash operating cycle is the period of time the business has to wait on average in order to collect cash after it has spent it. It can be calculated in the following way:

Cash operating cycle (days) = stock turnover + debtor turnover – creditor turnover

We will now calculate the cash operating cycle period for companies A and B:

	Stock T/O		Debtor T/O		Creditor T/O		
Company A	18.25	+	58.4	–	146	=	−69.35
Company B	182.5	+	zero	–	zero	=	182.50

What emerges from this is that company A has a negative cash operating cycle. This means that, in effect, A is financing its working capital from suppliers funds. Company A has a relatively short 2–3 week stock turnover cycle, a two month debtor cycle, but a five-month creditor cycle, which means it uses other people's money for over two months in a normal trading cycle.

This can be very healthy for the business if it is an ongoing and acceptable situation to suppliers. On the other hand, if the creditors are being kept waiting because the business is unable to meet its commitments, it could indicate serious liquidity problems. That is why it is unwise to look at ratios in isolation. We must refer to related ratios to confirm or contradict any findings.

A negative cash operating cycle is quite common with cash-based businesses in the HTL sector. Such businesses will either turn over their stocks quickly or won't carry any; they will sell largely for cash or even collect cash in advance through ticket sales; and they will probably settle their suppliers' accounts on at least a monthly basis.

Company B has its cash out of circulation for six months. This is entirely due to the fact that its stocks sell on average twice a year. All transactions are cash-based.

What types of business are companies A and B? Have you made up your mind yet? Company A is a wholesale supplier of individual portions of packed milk, sugar and jam for the hotel trade. Company B is a retailer of antiques. The evidence is as follows.

Company A

1 Sales profit margin is only 5% as this is a low-margin high-volume business.
2 Overheads as a percentage of sales are quite high due to the considerable establishment costs and the sales and distribution costs of a wholesale business.
3 Stock turnover is less than a month, as would be expected with fresh foods or items which sell in high volumes.
4 A substantial proportion of its sales are credit sales, as might be expected with a non-retailing business.
5 It has a negative cash operating cycle as it turns over its stock and collects its cash more quickly than it pays its suppliers.

Company B

1 Gross profit margin is very high, as would be expected where furniture is acquired cheaply and considerable value is added by restoration or repair.
2 Stock turnover of six months indicates a low-volume high-value business.
3 No credit purchases, as would be expected in a business where cash purchasing is the norm.
4 No credit sales, as would be expected in a retail business.

Can you produce any other evidence?

19.7 EFFICIENCY RATIOS FOR THE HOTEL INDUSTRY

The hotel industry in particular can be assessed fairly well using efficiency ratios of one kind or another. The main efficiency areas are as follows:

1 Occupancy rates
2 Labour cost as a percentage of sales
3 Overheads as a percentage of revenue
4 Food spend per guest or per room

Occupancy rates

Occupancy rates can be measured in the following ways:

$$\frac{\text{Rooms occupied}}{\text{Rooms available}} \times 100\%$$

$$\frac{\text{People registered as guests}}{\text{Number possible to accommodate}} \times 100\%$$

$$\frac{\text{Actual sales from rooms}}{\text{Potential revenue from rooms}} \times 100\%$$

$$\frac{\text{Room-nights occupied in period}}{\text{Bookings made in period}} \times 100\%$$

The last of these ratios measures the extent to which the hotel is accommodating short-term or longer-term guests. If the ratio came to 1 then all guests would have booked for one night only.

All of these ratios measure in one way or another the extent to which the hotel is utilizing its resources. If a hotel is in the luxury sector of the market, as opposed to the economy sector, then lower occupancy rates might be expected. However, it is the trends that are important, and seasonal fluctuations must be taken into account.

Labour cost as a percentage of sales

$$\frac{\text{Total staff costs}}{\text{Total revenue}} \times 100$$

This indicates the extent to which the revenue of the hotel is being absorbed by staff costs. An adverse trend in this is usually a result of a decline in business, whereas labour costs would normally remain fixed. It is necessary therefore to periodically assess whether the numbers of staff are still required at the hours worked to meet the needs of the customers. If necessary, staff should be laid off or have their hours reduced accordingly. Again it would be expected that a luxury hotel would have a higher ratio than an economy hotel because a higher level of service would be expected and provided.

Overhead costs as a percentage of sales

$$\frac{\text{Total overheads}}{\text{Total revenue}} \times 100$$

This indicates the extent of all overheads, including such establishment costs as rent, rates, power, insurance and labour, as a fraction of the total revenue. These costs are largely fixed in the short term, but it is possible to make savings, if necessary, to reduce costs when demand falls. Key areas where savings can be made are in the consumption of energy, such as reviewing the central heating system, increasing insulation, and reducing waste of energy in non-service areas.

Food spend per guest or per room

This could be calculated in several ways:

$$\frac{\text{Food and drink spend in a period}}{\text{Guests registered in a period}} \times 100$$

$$\frac{\text{Food and drink spend in a period}}{\text{Rooms occupied per period}} \times 100$$

This is a useful way of assessing the consumption patterns of guests and whether they are changing over time. Significant movement could be due to changes in the following factors:

- The type of clientele and their disposable income
- The quality of the food and service being offered
- The price and type of food offered

Any of these factors need to be investigated and menu changes should be made if required, or a change in advertising policy may be warranted.

19.8 CAPITAL STRUCTURE AND THE RISK–RETURN RELATIONSHIP

The return available to investors is generally governed by the rule: The greater the risk the greater the potential return. This is true for investors in business, as was indicated in Chapter 12. Long-term loans attract the lowest average rate of return, reflecting their relative security. Of the owners' investments in a business, preference shares will attract the next best rate of return, because preference shareholders have a prior claim on business profits over ordinary shareholders.

In order to explain the relationship between potential risk and return, we will examine the effect of capital structure on the return available to ordinary shareholders. Net profit available to ordinary shareholders is the profit remaining after interest and tax have been paid. The greater the extent to which the business is financed by long-term borrowing which attracts fixed interest payments, the higher the annual profits must be in order to cover this commitment. The extent to which the business is financed by debt capital is known as **financial gearing**.

The effect of financial gearing on risk and return will be explained by examining two identical hotel businesses. We will imagine these businesses have identical hotels in identical trading conditions within identical markets. The only difference is how they are financially geared.

	Hotel High-Gear £	Hotel Low-Gear £
Shareholders' funds	100,000	200,000
10% Debentures	200,000	100,000
Total long-term funds	300,000	300,000

The gearing ratio is expressed in the following ways:

$$\frac{\text{Long-term debt}}{\text{Shareholders' funds}} \times 100\% \qquad \frac{\text{Long-term debt}}{\text{Long-term debt + shareholders' funds}} \times 100\%$$

Using the second of these two ratios, the hotels are geared as follows:

	Hotel High-Gear £	Hotel Low-Gear £
Long-term debt	200,000	100,000
Long-term debt + shareholders' funds	$\dfrac{200,000}{300,000} \times 100\% = 66\%$	$\dfrac{100,000}{300,000} \times 100\% = 33\%$

Hotel High-Gear is twice as dependent on debt for its financing than Hotel Low-Gear. The net profit earned by each company before interest and tax was as follows:

	Hotel High-Gear £	Hotel Low-Gear £
	30,000	30,000
Less interest	20,000	10,000
Net profit available to shareholders	10,000	20,000
Return on shareholders' capital invested	10%	10%

How would these rates of return be affected assuming that profits before interest and tax were

– Double what they were in the year
– Half what they were in the year

Double profits

	Hotel High-Gear £	Hotel Low-Gear £
	60,000	60,000
Less interest	20,000	10,000
Net profit available to shareholders	40,000	50,000
Return on shareholders' capital invested	40%	25%

Now the rate of return to Hotel High-Gear's shareholders is superior to that obtained by the shareholders of Hotel Low-Gear. The more highly geared company shows the greater scope to improve its return to shareholders when the business climate is improving. The

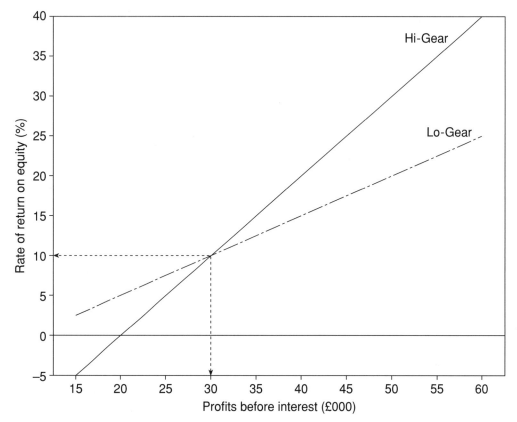

Figure 19.4 The effect of gearing on rates of return

reason for this is that, once the interest is covered, all the remaining profit is shared among relatively fewer shares.

Half profits	Hotel High-Gear	Hotel Low-Gear
	£	£
	15,000	15,000
Less interest	20,000	10,000
Net profit available to shareholders	(5,000)	5,000
Return on shareholders' capital invested	−5%	5%

In this situation, when the fortune of both companies has taken a dramatic decline, Hotel High-Gear's shareholders have seen their profits disappear, and a loss incurred. Hotel Low-Gear, on the other hand, still yields a positive return to its shareholders, and would still show a return to these shareholders if profits fell by a further one-third or 33.33%. This indicates that shareholders in the low-geared business are less vulnerable to a downturn in trading fortunes than those in the high-geared company.

Shareholders who wish to maximize their returns when trading conditions are favourable should invest in high-geared companies, and should then switch their capital into low-geared companies as trading conditions deteriorate. Figure 19.4 graphs the effect of financial gearing on returns to shareholders.

Interest cover ratio

The variability of shareholder returns in relation to financial gearing can also be expressed in terms of how many times the profits before interest and tax (BIT) would cover the fixed interest commitment. This is known as the interest cover ratio:

$$\frac{\text{Net profit BIT}}{\text{Interest payable}}$$

The higher this ratio, the less vulnerable are the shareholders to a downturn in profits. The interest cover ratio for both hotels in both the good and the poor years are shown below:

Good year	Hotel High-Gear £	Hotel Low-Gear £
Net profit BIT	60,000	60,000
Interest payable	20,000	10,000
Interest cover	3 times	6 times

Hotel High-Gear is covering its interest commitment six times, which is usually an acceptable cover ratio. Hotel Low-Gear's ratio of three times does indicate some vulnerability to a downturn in business, as we can see:

Poor year	Hotel High-Gear £	Hotel Low-Gear £
Net profit BIT	15,000	15,000
Interest payable	20,000	10,000
Interest cover	0.75 times	1.5 times

Hotel High-Gear's net profit BIT is not covering its interest payments, and is therefore showing a negative rate of return to shareholders. On the other hand, Hotel Low-Gear is still covering its annual interest commitment by $1\frac{1}{2}$ times. This ratio simply restates the effect of gearing on return to ordinary shareholders from a different perspective.

19.9 COST–VOLUME–PROFIT RATIOS

Chapter 15 introduced the relationship between cost, volume and profit. Where a business can separate its variable costs from its fixed costs, certain ratios may be calculated that can indicate a business's potential for profitability and its vulnerability to loss making. In order to explain the value of this analysis, the break-even chart is useful; it can be described using an example.

The Back-chat employment agency supplies after-dinner speakers and employs ten celebrities, all of whom command a nightly fee of £200. Customers who want after-dinner speakers are indifferent as to which celebrity they will book. Each celebrity is available for 300 nights in a year. At present only 1,500 celebrity nights are booked per annum. The agency charges a commission of 20% on the gross fee and has annual fixed overheads of £50,000 to cover. The break-even point is calculated arithmetically as

$$\frac{\text{Annual fixed costs}}{\text{Contribution per celebrity night}}$$

The contribution that each celebrity night makes towards fixed costs is the commission earned from the booking. In every case this is £40 per night, therefore the break-even point is

$$\frac{50{,}000}{40.00} = 1{,}250 \text{ celebrity nights}$$

How does this information help the managers or the investors in the business to assess its financial performance or vulnerability? It may be useful in the following ways:

1 It indicates how far bookings may drop before losses are incurred.
2 It indicates what potential there is to accommodate additional demand.
3 It can indicate to a new business the scope it has for making profits with respect to its budgeted activity level and planned capacity.
4 It can indicate the volatility of earnings in general, should the level of demand change.

Vulnerability to a downturn in business can be assessed by determining how many bookings could be lost before reaching the break-even point. This can be expressed as a ratio.

Margin of safety

The margin of safety is calculated as follows:

$$\frac{\text{Current annual sales volume} - \text{break even sales volume}}{\text{Current annual sales volume}} \times 100\%$$

Sales can mean sales volume of products, bookings, seats sold, or any type of service demanded. The ratio can also be calculated in value terms:

$$\frac{\text{Current annual sales value} - \text{break-even sales value}}{\text{Current annual sales value}} \times 100\%$$

These ratios measure the 'cushion' that a business has to absorb a fall in sales before losses are incurred, as a percentage of present sales volume or value.

In volume terms, the margin of safety of the Back-chat agency is

$$\frac{1{,}500 - 1{,}250}{1{,}500} \times 100\% = 16.66\%$$

indicating that bookings may fall by up to 16.66% from their present level before losses are incurred. This information is extremely useful to an investor as it expresses the level of exposure to risk faced by the business during a slowdown in demand.

The potential for profitability that the business is presented with may also be assessed. This is achieved by referring to the short-run maximum capacity of the business, without incurring further capital expenditure. Sometimes known as the **margin of opportunity**, it can be calculated as follows:

$$\frac{\text{Short-run capacity} - \text{present sales volume}}{\text{Present sales volume}} \times 100\%$$

This ratio indicates by what percentage the sales or bookings could be increased in the short term if the demand existed. The margin of opportunity for the Back-chat agency is

$$\frac{3,000 - 1,500}{1,500} \times 100\% = 100\%$$

This indicates that the the business has the capacity to double its bookings if the demand for these additional bookings existed. Margin of opportunity is useful as it gives an indication of the scope that a business has to improve its activity levels under favourable conditions or with appropriate marketing.

Suppose a restaurant business is operating at 100% capacity, there is no point in reducing prices, or promoting the restaurant through advertising, as in the short run no additional demand could be met. On the other hand, if a business has a break-even point at 20% capacity, and is currently operating at 15% capacity, the margin of opportunity is such that alternative marketing strategies to increase demand might well be adopted to improve the overall business position.

The margin of opportunity can be looked at in another way. If a business plan is being prepared for a new restaurant, it should look at the break-even point in relation to its maximum short-term capacity. This capacity might usefully be measured in terms of available seats or tables multiplied by the turnover per day. If a restaurant budgets to sell covers at a price averaging £40, 40% food costs with fixed costs of £97,200 per annum, the break-even point would be $97,200/(40 - 16) = 4,050$ covers per annum. If the annual capacity of the restaurant is 6,000 per annum, then the margin of opportunity for the new business might be expressed in the following way:

$$\frac{\text{Maximum short-run capacity} - \text{break-even point}}{\text{Maximum short-run capacity}} \times 100\%$$

Inserting the figures, we obtain

$$\frac{6,000 - 4,050}{6,000} \times 100\% = 32.5\%$$

This indicates that the business only has the margin of opportunity to make profits at the upper one-third of its capacity, or if it operates at two-thirds capacity or above. This type of assessment indicates the scope that the business has to be profitable. The margin seems rather too narrow.

Chapter 15 introduced the way in which vulnerability is assessed with respect to a downturn. Two restaurants were examined: one heavily dependent on fixed costs and the other heavily dependent on variable costs. The break-even charts of the restaurants will be examined from the original information in Chapter 15:

	Home-made £	Ready-made £
Sales revenue for year	105,000	105,000
Variable costs	35,000	70,000
Contribution	70,000	35,000
Fixed costs	45,000	10,000
Net profit	25,000	25,000

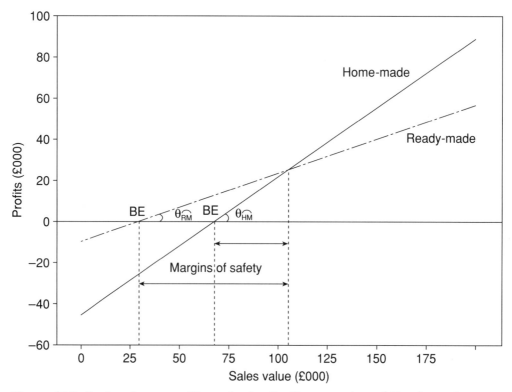

Figure 19.5 Cost–volume–profit graphs for the Home-made and Ready-made restaurants: BE = break-even point

At this level of sales both restaurants make the same net profit. It was originally found that the restaurant which was most heavily burdened by fixed costs made greater profits than the other, if demand increased and all other things remained equal. On the other hand, the restaurant with most fixed costs would fare much worse than the other restaurant if there was a fall in demand. The effects of this are shown in Fig. 19.5.

Notice how angle of incidence $\theta_{\widehat{HM}}$ for the Home-made Restaurant is much greater than angle of incidence $\theta_{\widehat{RM}}$ for the Ready-made Restaurant. The **angle of incidence** indicates the volatility of a business's profitability as against sales volume or value. It therefore indicates the profit potential of a business but also its vulnerability to losses. This is very similar to the notion of capital gearing, as examined in the previous section. The higher the ratio of fixed costs to variable costs, the greater the volatility of the returns to shareholders, all other things being equal.

What determines the angle of incidence? It is the angle between the TR line and the TC line on an accountant's break-even chart (Fig. 15.2). The gradient of the TR line is determined by prices of products or services, and the gradient of the TC line is determined by the variable costs of those products or services. The difference between sales price and variable cost is known as contribution. Therefore, the angle of incidence is determined by the average contribution that a business earns on its products or services. Where a business produces or provides a number of products or services, the angle of incidence should be measured in terms of overall contribution as a percentage of sales.

As already discussed in Chapter 15, this is the **contribution/sales ratio** and is calculated in the following way:

$$\frac{\text{Contribution}}{\text{Sales value}} \times 100\%$$

The higher the contribution/sales ratio, the more volatile the earnings against sales volume. The vulnerability of a business to losses would also depend on how far above the break-even point the business was operating, its **margin of safety**. If both ratios are used in combination, a very good assessment of the business opportunity and vulnerability can be made. Let us do this for the two restaurants:

	Home-made	Ready-made
Contribution/sales ratio:	$\frac{70,000}{105,000} \times 100\% = 66.66\%$	$\frac{35,000}{105,000} \times 100\% = 33.33\%$

The Home-made Restaurant has double the ratio of the Ready-made Restaurant. The margin of safety in terms of sales value can also be calculated:

$$\frac{\text{Current annual sales value} - \text{break-even sales value}}{\text{Current annual sales value}} \times 100\%$$

The break-even sales value can be calculated using the contribution/sales (C/S) ratio. The relevant question is: What sales value in pounds is needed to cover the fixed costs exactly? And the answer is

$$\text{Sales value} \times \text{C/S ratio} = \text{fixed costs}$$

$$\text{Sales value} = \frac{\text{Fixed costs}}{\text{C/S ratio}}$$

For each restaurant the break-even sales value is as follows:

	Home-made	Ready-made
	$\frac{£45,000}{0.66} = £67,500$	$\frac{£10,000}{0.33} = £30,000$
Margin of safety $=$	$\frac{105,000 - 67,500}{105,000} \times 100\% = 35.71\%$	$\frac{105,000 - 30,000}{105,000} \times 100\% = 71.42\%$

Therefore, the Home-made Restaurant is twice as volatile in terms of its C/S ratio, and has only half the margin of safety of the Ready-made Restaurant. Although the two restaurants make exactly the same net profit at the current level of takings, it is possible to make the following assessment:

1 The riskiest investment is the Home-made Restaurant as it has half the margin of safety.
2 The best investment for potential return is the Home-made Restaurant as it achieves double the C/S ratio.

19.10 VALUE-ADDED RATIOS

The concept of value added

Financial performance will now be looked at from a wider perspective, by examining some additional financial ratios. Up until now the predominant concern has been with the returns available to the owners of the business, and the business's ability to meet its commitments to lenders.

Chapter 1 introduced the concepts of wealth and income. Although an accounting book examines income or wealth from the perspective of the owners or the shareholders, wealth is created for and by a range of economic units within an economy. The individual, the firm and the government are all economic units interacting with each other, exchanging services and products to their mutual benefit.

The wealth created in an economy can be subclassified as

- Wages and salaries
- Interest
- Rents
- Taxes
- Dividends

These items are distributed by the economic unit in which wealth is created, and are received by those economic units that contribute or invest in some way towards that wealth-creating process.

Here are the contributors and beneficiaries of wealth creation within an economic unit:

Employees: providing physical and mental effort.
Lenders: providing temporary financial capital.
Landlords: providing temporary physical capital.
Government: providing the infrastructure to underpin the wealth creation process, such as roads, education and health care.
Owners: providing permanent financial capital.

If the total income or wealth created in an economy is to be calculated, it is first necessary to look at the economic performance of each and every economic unit. The difference between how much a business pays for the goods and services it sells, and how much it sells them for, is described as the **value added** or **net output** of that economic unit; therefore

Value added = sales − bought-in goods and services

The value added by an economic unit can be defined as 'the increase in market value resulting in the alteration of form, location or the availability of a product or service, excluding the cost of bought out goods and services' (ICMA, 1974, *Terminology of Management and Financial Accounting*). This definition highlights the fact that value can be added by providing a service, just as it can by making a physical product. This therefore means that as much value can be added by a business providing a currency exchange service to tourists as by a hotel making high-class cordon bleu food for its exclusive restaurant.

The value added by an economic unit is variously shared as income among those that have invested or contributed to the value-adding process in some way, so **value added = income**. What is physically received as income must therefore be equivalent to what is physically spent by the entity generating the wealth in the first place, so **income =**

expenditure. Excluded from the equation is expenditure on bought-in goods and services that are later to be sold; this is because these **intermediate sales** include the wealth created by other businesses. Inclusion of intermediate sales in the income calculation would lead to double counting. Within an economy it is true to say that

Value added = income = expenditure

This equation underpins the calculation of income, output and expenditure for an individual company or an entire trading bloc. To explain how value added can be expressed in an alternative format for reporting individual business performance, consider a small German holiday company. The summary for the financial period is as follows:

Baden Holiday Company (monthly summary)

	DM
Sales (holiday packages)	200,000
Cost of holidays	100,000
Interest on loans	12,000
Rent of property	8,000
Staff wages and salaries	42,000
Depreciation	4,000
Taxation	8,000
Dividends	16,000
Retained profits	10,000

The holiday company adds value which is the difference between the price of the holidays as sold to customers (via travel agents), and what they cost the holiday company to purchase. The remaining amount is then applied in various proportions to those parties who have contributed to the business in some way, including the government. What is left is retained within the business as depreciation provisions, or as retained earnings. These retained amounts are used for reinvestment in the business for replacement and expansion. In order to show the contrast between the value-added statement and the conventional profit and loss statement, the information will be prepared in both formats;

Profit and loss account

	DM	DM
Sales		200,000
Cost of sales		100,000
Gross profit		100,000
Less expenses:		
Staff wages	42,000	
Interest	12,000	
Depreciation	4,000	
Rent	8,000	
		66,000
Net profit before tax		34,000
Taxation		8,000
Net profit after tax		26,000
Dividends		16,000
Retained profits for the year		10,000

Value-added statement

	DM	%
Sales	200,000	
Bought-in goods and services	100,000	
Value added	100,000	100
Applied as follows:		
To pay employees		
Wages, pensions, and fringe benefits	42,000	42
To pay providers of financial capital		
Interest on loans and financial leases	12,000	12
Dividends	16,000	16
To pay providers of physical capital		
Rents and operating leases	8,000	8
To pay government		
Taxation	8,000	8
For maintenance and expansion of fixed assets		
Depreciation	4,000	4
Retained profits	10,000	10
Value added	100,000	100

Under this format (adapted from the Corporate Report, 1975) depreciation is included as an application of value added. Depreciation does not constitute a transfer of value, it is an accounting allocation of the original cost against revenues, to reflect the usage of fixed assets. Depreciation, therefore, *should not be included as part of value added* as it doesn't represent income to any group of individuals. Retained profits do not represent a transfer of value, but they can be legitimately regarded as the income of the owners, even though the income is retained within the business.

The reason that the depreciation component of **gross value added** is shown as an application of value added is because it may provide a useful ratio with which to assess business performance, and it may indicate something about the cost structure of the business. Let us now look at some of the value-added ratios that can be calculated. The main value-added ratios are those which are an integral part of the value-added statement.

Staff costs/value added

This ratio indicates the level of staff productivity within a business. It indicates how much per £1 of value added was consumed in labour costs. If the ratio is inverted, i.e. **value added/payroll costs**, it indicates how much value added is generated per £1 spent on labour. This ratio can indicate either the extent to which the business is labour-intensive, or the extent to which the business is inefficient in its use of staff. One would expect a leisure centre to have a low staff costs/VA ratio, as the value is added mainly by the facilities and equipment. On the other hand, the labour costs of an agency for performing artists would be very high indeed.

Interest/value added

This ratio indicates the extent to which value has been added from borrowed funds. The higher the gearing of a company, the greater the interest as a proportion of the value added. The problem is that, in certain industries such as hotels and other businesses in the HTL sector, the interest on loans raised to acquire or build properties is treated not as an expense but as part of the capital cost of acquiring the fixed asset. Known as the capitalization of interest, it can impair the reliability of this ratio.

Dividends/value added

This ratio indicates the extent to which value is added from shareholders' funds, and also the proportion of shareholders' income that is distributed. The lower its gearing and the smaller its retained profits, the higher a company's dividends/value added ratio. This ratio can indicate a short-term policy of satisfying shareholders in order to maintain the share price if the business is a quoted limited company.

Rents and operating leases/value added

This ratio indicates the extent to which the fixed assets utilized within a business have been rented or leased on a rental basis. This will depend on how the business acquires any fixed assets, and it may be influenced by the business cash flow position or changes in taxation. Examined in conjunction with the depreciation/value added ratio, it can help to indicate the ongoing commitment of the business to fixed-asset investment. But separately the two ratios may be misleading.

Taxation/value added

This ratio indicates the proportion of value added which is charged as taxation during each financial period. Any changes in this ratio over time may be due to changes in government fiscal policy. If there are no major fiscal changes between periods, the ratio should remain reasonably stable. However, if a business undergoes a major change in size or structure, or is marginal in terms of being classified as small, medium or large, it may move into a lower or higher band of corporation tax and significantly alter its ratio. Any significant variation may also be due to tax efficiency in general.

Depreciation/value added

This ratio indicates the extent to which a business uses purchased fixed assets and the rate at which the original cost of these assets is allocated against the revenues of different periods. The business has a choice of whether to invest in fixed assets by renting or by purchasing outright. The ratio will change over time and from business to business; it depends on the fixed-asset aquisition policy, the labour intensity and the depreciation policy. For example, the British Airports Authority (BAA) changed its depreciation policy on runways from 23.5 years to 100 years in 1991. This type of major change in allocation policy can make a considerable difference to this ratio without reflecting any difference in the underlying investment policy of the business.

Retained profits/value added

This ratio indicates the extent to which profits are retained as against distributed. As the retained earnings and depreciation are the only categories of value added (VA) which represent undistributed funds as opposed to distributed funds, a further ratio may be derived:

$$\frac{\text{Undistributed VA}}{\text{Total VA}}$$

The higher the figure for this ratio, the greater the reinvestment of the value added. And this suggests a business is investing more in its future than in meeting short-term commitments and objectives.

19.11 OTHER VALUE-ADDED RATIOS

Operating profit/value added

This ratio is similar to the management efficiency ratio explained in section 19.4. It measures the ability of a business to provide profit for its financial investors only. A comparison of this ratio over time or between companies can indicate the efficiency with which the management are generating returns for the long-term financial investors in the business. The ratio can be improved by increasing revenues or reducing costs, including staff costs. A bureau de change could improve its operating profit/value added ratio by purchasing an automatic change dispenser, borrowing £250,000 and making some currency receptionists redundant.

Capital employed/value added

This ratio indicates the extent to which the value added is generated by the capital employed within a business – its long-term funds. The nature of the business has a big effect on the size of the ratio. A ski school in the Alps would have an extremely low ratio, as there would be relatively little fixed-asset investment and not much stock. The value is added by the knowledge and experience of the skiing instructors, which would not be valued on a balance sheet. This is related directly to the question of goodwill. If the business is significantly supported by unrecorded intangible assets, the capital employed/value added ratio will be understated. On the other hand, a hotel depends heavily on tangible fixed assets in the form of buildings, equipment and amenities; it would have a much higher ratio.

Sales/value added

This ratio directly indicates how much value is being added to the bought-in goods and services. It is an extremely useful ratio as it can indicate the type of business being assessed, whereabouts in its value chain it may be operating, and to what extent it is vulnerable to changes in business conditions.

Consider two extremes. A speciality restaurant operating from an exclusive location, using top chefs who provide food from raw ingredients, will have a low sales/value added ratio. The value is largely added by the skill and effort of the kitchen staff, who are converting relatively low-cost ingredients into expensive and desirable meals. On the other hand, a major wholesaler of ready-made meals for pubs and restaurants, selling high volumes of stock at low margins, will have a comparatively high ratio.

The speciality restaurant is also more at risk from a downturn in business, as most of its costs are likely to be fixed (section 19.9) and it would not be able to reduce them by much if demand fell. The wholesaler, however, can respond to a change in demand simply by increasing or cutting its orders from the manufacturer, and if necessary, it could start dealing in an entirely different commodity. This makes the wholesaler less vulnerable and more adaptable to the changing conditions of the market.

19.12 WEAKNESSES OF RATIO ANALYSIS

Historical perspective

The main limitation of ratio analysis is the historical basis of financial reports. Ratios are calculated from information about activities which have taken place in the past, and this information may have been superseded by newer and more relevant data. There is also the problem of rising prices. Many ratios include capital employed or total assets, both significantly determined by non-monetary items such as fixed assets and stock. If these items are old and their values outdated, while sales and revenue expenditure are measured in current terms, the result of the ratio may be misleading. For example, profit BIT/ capital employed may appear to be improving dramatically during a period of rising prices, whereas in reality there may be a more moderate improvement or even none at all. In this situation the real rise in profits would be difficult to separate from the increase due to general inflation.

Misleading comparisons

Some ratios will be affected when a business changes an accounting policy or makes some change to accountancy practice between periods, such as changing a basis for depreciation. The change will be due to methods of accounting, not necessarily economic factors. Even more difficult to compare are two businesses in the same sector but with entirely different accounting methods. Any comparisons between them are likely to be unreliable unless the notes to the accounts are carefully scrutinized, and even then some anomalies may not be indicated.

Distortions by one-off transactions

Ratios may indicate significant changes that give cause for concern or optimism, but the reasons for these changes should be thoroughly investigated. For example, a hotel business shows a dramatic reduction in its liquidity from one period to the next. The immediate assumption might be that occupancy rates have fallen dramatically, but further examination of the balance sheet may indicate that the business has either paid off a loan or purchased more fixed assets, such as installing a luxury indoor swimming complex. Knowing that certain one-off transactions are a deliberate policy of the management may put a different interpretation on the calculated ratios. Other one-off transactions that may cause dramatic changes are acquisitions or disposals of other businesses, major bad debts, redundancy programmes, reorganisation costs and R&D spending.

Cyclical changes during a financial period

Balance sheets are normally prepared at a regular point during the calendar year. Businesses in the HTL sector are normally seasonal, so the timing of their balance sheets may determine the results of certain ratios. Take two ice-cream parlours, one with a year-end in December and the other with a year-end in June. A comparison between them is likely to be highly misleading unless some seasonal adjustment is made; for example, the stock, creditors and cash balances are likely to be very different, affecting the calculation of all liquidity and efficiency ratios.

One-dimensional picture

Ratios encourage assessors to be one-dimensional in their assessment of a business. They can engender a false sense of well-being, or they can cause undue gloom and pessimism. Put two figures together, compare them and out churns the ratio. Is it greater than the equivalent ratio in the previous period or for the equivalent business in the same period? Assessment of a business cannot be carried out by slavish adherence to the results of individual ratios without understanding the origins and reasons for the figures that were used. Ratios may indicate changes but they cannot explain them. This is a matter of interpretation by the assessor, and often the indications given by calculating one ratio may be confirmed or contradicted by examining another related ratio. For example, if a stock turnover ratio and a debtor turnover ratio are slowing dramatically, will this cause a shortage of cash to develop, and is this confirmed by observing the movement on the cash balances or in the quick ratio?

SUMMARY

1 **Comparative assessments of businesses require a form of analysis that uses ratios in order to allow relative judgements, both between businesses and over several periods.**

2 **The performance of a business may be assessed in several different ways:**

- **Profitability**
- **Liquidity**
- **Efficiency**
- **Vulnerability**

3 **Assessment of business performance or status can be widened beyond the interests of the long-term financial investors. This can be achieved by observing the shares that contributing parties receive of the total value added by a business.**

4 **Although they are useful, ratios do have weaknesses and should be treated with caution.**

ASSESSMENT

MULTIPLE-CHOICE QUESTIONS

Question 1
Which of the following businesses has the greatest net profit margin?

		Sales	COS	Expenses
		£	£	£
A	Company A	100,000	60,000	30,000
B	Company B	150,000	100,000	20,000
C	Company C	80,000	30,000	10,000
D	Company D	200,000	100,000	90,000

Question 2
Which one of the following decisions would not have any effect on the net profit/long-term capital employed ratio, all other things being equal?

A Increasing the sales price
B Paying off a long-term loan with cash on hand
C Reducing fixed costs in a reorganisation
D Raising an overdraft to purchase fixed assets

Question 3
A, B, C and D are an hotel, a boxing promoter, a fitness centre and a cut-price supermarket, not necessarily in that order. Which one of these businesses is the boxing promoter? Make your selection using the following primary ratios:

	NP/cap employed	=	NP/sales	×	Sales/cap employed
A	1/10		1/20		2/1
B	1/2		1/40		20/1
C	1/5		1/5		1/1
D	1/2		1/1		1/2

Question 4
Which one of the following strategies would not reduce the cash operating cycle of a retail business?

A Moving from weekly ordering to daily ordering
B Offering greater credit facilities to customers
C Delaying payments to creditors
D Increasing the advertising and promotional budget

Question 5
The Mermaid Hotel has 50 rooms. On average they are 60% occupied during the year. The number of bookings in the year totalled 7,300. Total direct costs of food and drink supplied in the year came to £137,970 and the rate of gross profit to selling price of food and drink averaged 40% throughout the year. Which of the following is the correct figure for the average food and drink bill per room-night for the year?

A £31.50
B £21.00
C £7.56
D £5.04

Question 6
Two hotel chains are financed by long-term capital totalling £4.5 million. Chain A is financed by £1.5 million in shareholders' funds and £3 million in 10% debentures. Chain B is financed by £3 million in shareholders' funds and £1.5 million in 10% debentures. Both companies provide a net rate of return of 20% for their shareholders in the current year. What would be the percentage difference in the net rates of return available to the shareholders of A and B if the profits of both chains, before interest, were double their present level?

A 15%
B 25%
C 0%
D 50%

Question 7

The Santos restaurant has 30 tables, and only serves evening meals. From past information, a table is normally used 4 times in an evening and an average of 2 people eat together. The average price per cover is £15 and the gross profit margin (price – food costs) is 40%. Fixed costs are £120,000 a year. Assuming a 250-day year, what proportion of the capacity of the restaurant needs to be utilized, on average throughout the year, for the restaurant to break even?

A 1/2
B 1/3
C 1/4
D 1/5

Question 8

Which of the four hotels makes the highest contribution towards its overall fixed costs?

	Hotel A	Hotel B	Hotel C	Hotel D
Margin of safety	0.20	0.33	0.50	0.25
Contribution/Sales	0.30	0.25	0.20	0.25
Break-even value	£40,000	£30,000	£25,000	£42,000

A Hotel A
B Hotel B
C Hotel C
D Hotel D

Question 9

The Designer sandwich bar generated an annual turnover of £120,000; made a gross profit mark-up on materials of 50%; paid wages of £11,000, power costs of £4,000, interest of £2,000, rent of £5,000; charged £3,000 depreciation; and retained half of the rest in the business. The other half was taken as drawings. What proportion of the value added by the sandwich bar was distributed?

A 0.50
B 0.75
C 0.25
D 0.70

Question 10

Which of these four plans is the odd one out with respect to its effect on the value added/sales ratio of a restaurant?

A Buy in prepacked soups rather than make in-house
B Reduce the wages of the kitchen staff
C Increase the menu prices
D Cut power costs by saving on electricity

EXERCISES

Exercise 1

The following information is provided about three companies: a small independent steelmaker, a chain of grocery stores and a luxury hotel. Extracts from their accounts are reproduced below.

Profit and loss extracts

	Company A £	Company B £	Company C £
Turnover/revenue	3,029,000	1,556,000	206,000
Net profit	45,000	67,000	43,000

Summarized balance sheets

	Company A £	Company B £	Company C £
Fixed assets at NBV	257,000	1,094,000	806,000
Stock	236,000	241,000	5,000
Debtors	9,000	201,000	nil
Other assets	66,000	286,000	26,000
Total assets	568,000	1,822,000	837,000
Financed by			
Shareholders' funds	320,000	1,200,000	410,000
Long-term liabilities	64,000	321,000	415,000
Current liabilities	184,000	301,000	12,000
Total liabilities	568,000	1,822,000	837,000

Required

(a) Calculate the following accounting ratios for each of the three companies:
  - Net profit percentage
  - Return on shareholders' funds
  - Current ratio
  - Acid test ratio
  - Debtor turnover ratio
  - Gearing ratio
(b) Match A, B, C with the steelmaker, the grocery chain and the hotel. Briefly explain your choice using clues obtained from calculating the ratios, and from examining the accounting information provided.

Exercise 2

Elena Limited is a supplier of fresh provisions to the hotel sector. Here are extracts from its accounts for the past three years:

	19x1 £000	19x2 £000	19x3 £000
Credit sales	1900	2100	2200
Less cost of sales:			
Opening stock	3	5	4
Purchases	1200	1300	1700
	1203	1305	1704
Closing stock	5	3	8
Cost of sales	1198	1302	1696
Gross profit	702	798	504
Trade debtors	70	100	150
Trade creditors	100	150	300

Required

(a) Calculate the following ratios for the last two years:
 - Gross profit margin
 - Stock turnover ratio
 - Debtor turnover ratio
 - Creditor turnover ratio
 - Length of the cash operating cycle (days)

(b) Assess the performance of Elena Limited in managing its working capital over the past two years, making reference to the calculated ratios.

Exercise 3

Here is an incomplete balance sheet for a company selling children's puzzles and games:

Balance sheet of Jigsaw Bits Ltd as at December 31, 19x3

	Cost £	Depn £	NBV £
Fixed assets			
Equipment and fittings			161,000
Current assets			
Stock		n/a	
Debtors		n/a	
Bank		n/a	
		n/a	
Current liabilities		n/a	
Trade creditors	n/a		
Proposed dividends	n/a		
Proposed taxation	7,000		
		n/a	
Net current assets			n/a
			n/a
Creditors: amounts falling due in more than one year			
10% Debentures			n/a
Net assets			n/a
Financed by			
Ordinary share capital (£1.00 shares)			100,000
Retained profits c/f	22,500		
Retained profits this year	n/a		
			n/a
			n/a

Additional information

1 Earnings per share = 12.5p
2 Dividends proposed = 4.0%
3 Current assets as a percentage of fixed assets = 45%
4 Net profit before tax as a percentage of sales = 10%
5 Gross profit as a percentage of sales = 30%
6 Debtor turnover ratio = 73 days
7 Stock turnover ratio = 10 times
8 Quick ratio (acid test ratio) = 1.2

Required

Complete the balance sheet using the available information.

Exercise 4

Here are the value-added statements of two companies in the HTL sector. One is a ferry company which owns three seagoing ferries, the other is a travel agency which rents five city-centre offices in prime locations.

Value-added statement

	Company X £000	%	Company Y £000	%
Sales	300		1,600	
Bought-in goods and services	60		1,400	
Value added	240	100	200	100
Applied as follows:				
To pay employees				
Wages, pensions, and fringe benefits	96	40	110	55
To pay providers of financial capital				
Interest on loans and financial leases	36	15	10	5
Dividends	24	10	14	7
To pay providers of physical capital				
Rents and operating leases	nil	0	30	15
To pay government				
Taxation	24	10	12	6
For maintenance and expansion of fixed assets				
Depreciation	48	20	8	4
Retained profits	12	5	16	8
Value added	240	100	200	100

Required

(a) Produce three pieces of evidence to indicate which company is the ferry company and which is the travel agency.
(b) Select value-added ratios that might be useful as evidence to assess the performance, productivity and structure of both companies.

Question 5

Forty Towers is a luxury hotel in deepest Dorset. For the last 30 days the following internal financial and other information is available to the directors of the Forty chain of hotels in Europe.

	Twin beds		Single beds
No of rooms in hotel	300		50
No of rooms available	220		36
Total revenue in period		£600,000	
Payroll costs		£120,000	
No of guests in period		3,500	
No of employees		375	
Cost of food and drink		£25,000	
Cost of cleaning materials		£6,000	
Total cost of laundering		£24,000	

Other information
Listed daily rate for rooms:

Twins   £120
Single   £75

Average length of stay per guest = 1.75 days

Required

(a) Mr Basil Forty, the chairman, wants the following ratios to be calculated:

- Bed utilization rate = $\dfrac{\text{Total guest nights}}{\text{Bed nights available}} \times 100\%$

- Revenue per room-day
- Cost per guest-day
- Monthly cost per employee
- Average contribution per room per month (all payroll and laundry costs are variable)

- Revenue potential earned = $\dfrac{\text{Revenue earned}}{\text{Potential revenue earned}} \times 100\%$

   (potential revenue is the revenue from available rooms)

(b) The six ratios for the chain as a whole are as follows:

Bed utilization rate	65.4%
Revenue per room-day	£45.23
Cost per guest-day	£18.50
Monthly cost per employee	£350
Average contribution per room per month	£955
Revenue potential earned	82%

Compare these figures with the values calculated in part (a) then draw some conclusions.

CHAPTER 20

Spreadsheet applications in accounting

OBJECTIVES

- Execute a variety of accounting tasks using a spreadsheet.
- Appreciate the value of spreadsheets for undertaking routine tasks in accounting and as an aid to decision making.
- Use the common commands and functions of a generic spreadsheet package.

20.1 THE VALUE OF SPREADSHEETS

For over a decade now, spreadsheets have increasingly been used by accountants and managers; they have several advantages:

1 Time saved in making tedious and lengthy calculations
2 More sophisticated data analysis and decision making
3 Ease of handling and better presentation

The main reasons that spreadsheets have become the essential tool of many accountants and managers is that they are easy to use and they do not require language-based programming knowledge. However, the type of logical thought processes that are essential in programming are also necessary in spreadsheet model building, if the maximum benefits are to be obtained from their use. The sophistication with which models are constructed can be developed as the spreadsheet user becomes more and more familiar with the commands and functions of the package that he or she is currently using.

This chapter aims to give the reader a number of tasks using the knowledge acquired in this text, tasks which will develop a familiarization with spreadsheet usage, and offer an appreciation of the real power of these packages. It is hoped this will provide a basis for further development work on spreadsheets.

There are several spreadsheet packages available at present, so it is not possible to deal with all the differences between them. However, the basic commands and functions of spreadsheets are fairly common to most packages. This chapter will only require knowledge of the most common commands and functions, and the models within each task may be built quite easily on any of the main packages. Specific step-by-step instructions will not be given; they should be contained in the user manual and the help menus.

20.2 COMMON COMMANDS AND FUNCTIONS

To use any common spreadsheet, the program is normally loaded via the Windows environment by selecting the relevant icon with a mouse pointer. If a DOS-based system is being used, the spreadsheet may be loaded by typing the relevant `.exe command` at the C> prompt. Once loaded, the spreadsheet will display a blank screen bordered by letters and numbers. Under modern Windows versions, tool-bars displaying icons for the main commands and functions may be seen. The columns are labelled A,B,C, etc., and the rows are labelled 1,2,3, etc. The cursor is a highlighted cell which can be moved up or down using the arrow keys or using **PgUp** and **PgDn**. Mouse-based systems allow the user to select the cell with the mouse pointer (normally a cross). The cell is a coordinate of the rows and columns. For example, if the **Home** key is pressed, the cursor will move to the top left-hand cell of the screen. This cell or coordinate is called cell A1. The cursor can be moved around the screen or around the spreadsheet very quickly by using the location key **F5**. If this function key is pressed, it asks for the desired cell location. After typing in the cell address that is required, i.e. Z1,000 (1,000 rows down and 26 columns across the sheet), the cursor will move to that cell immediately. To input information at a cell reference, it is possible to type in text labels for headings or descriptions, to enter numbers or to input formulae. To amend any data entered in a cell, it is necessary to double-click with a mouse on the highlighted cell, or go into the edit mode by pressing the **F2** function key.

The real power of the spreadsheet for the accountant comes from its ability to process numbers and to manipulate them, and its ability to be used flexibly in order to carry out repetitive tasks. The following skills will need to be developed in this chapter:

1 Entering text, numbers and formulae
2 Changing column widths
3 Summing a range of cells
4 Copying a range of cells
7 Cell referencing
8 Graphing

20.3 TASK 1: PREPARING THE FINAL ACCOUNTS OF A THEATRE

Here is the trial balance of the Gielier Theatre in London as at December 31, 19x6:

	£
Share capital, 100,000 × £1 ordinary shares	45,000
Profits retained	20,000
Debtors (credit cards)	8,000
Creditors (performers)	4,000
Fixtures and fittings	120,000
Rent	5,000
Wages	60,000
Credit sales	50,000
Cash sales	80,000
Cost of performers	50,000
Profits from bar and food	12,000
Provision for depn on fixtures	25,000
Stocks of food and drink 31.12.x4	2,000
Bank account overdraft	9,000

Notes

1 Provision for depreciation is 15% on cost per annum.
2 Rent paid was for the period Jan 1, 19x4 to Aug 30, 19x7.
3 Wages owing at the year-end were £3,000.
4 Dividends proposed for the year were decided at 7% per share.

To set up the spreadsheet model select cell A1 and enter the following heading as text:

Trial balance (Gielier Theatre, London) 31.12.x6

and click on **Enter**. It is recommended to widen column A substantially to allow the text headings to be entered comfortably without running into column B. With mouse-based systems this is most easily achieved by placing the mouse pointer on the line between the A and B columns on the top border and dragging the cell width to the right as far as required.

It is then necessary to enter the first account name, share capital, on the trial balance in cell A3. Keep going down, typing in the account names until cell A16 is reached. Next go to C3 and start entering the values as given above. Remember that the positive/negative notation is being used for the ledger accounts as it is very useful in spreadsheet work. Assets and expenses should be recorded as positive numbers and liabilities and income as negatives. The £ signs are entered in B2, C2 and C3, and then centred.

Having done all this, the initial part of the spreadsheet will look like Spreadsheet 1a. The next stage is to deal with the adjustments and prepare an extended trial balance. This is shown in Spreadsheet 1a. Five additional headings have been added at rows A17:A21 as compared to Spreadsheet 1a. These are the rows which accommodate the adjustments. Note that the total of columns B3:B21, C3:C21 and D3:D21 are summed in row 23. This is achieved by placing the mouse pointer on B23 then using the sum function icon if available, or by typing =sum(B3:B21). This sums the contents of the cells in the denoted range. As all liabilities and income have been entered as negatives, and all assets and expenses as positives, the accuracy of the double entry will be confirmed if a zero is displayed in cell C18.

Spreadsheet 1a

	A	B	C	D
1	Trial balance (Gielier Theatre, London) 31.12.x6			
2		(£)	(£)	(£)
3	Share capital	-45000		
4	Profits retained	-20000		
5	Debtors	8000		
6	Creditors	-4000		
7	Fixtures/fittings	120000		
8	Rent	5000		
9	Wages	60000		
10	Credit sales	-50000		
11	Cash sales	-80000		
12	Cost of performers	50000		
13	Profits, bar/food	-12000		
14	Depn provn on F/F	-25000		
15	Food and drink 31.12.x6	2000		
16	Bank overdraft	-9000		

Spreadsheet 1a (cont.)

	A	B	C	D
1	Trial balance (Gielier Theatre, London) 31.12.x6			
2		(£)	(£)	(£)
3	Share capital	-45000		=sum(B3:C3)
4	Profits retained	-20000		=sum(B4:C4)
5	Debtors	8000		=sum(B5:C5)
6	Creditors	-4000		=sum(B6:C6)
7	Fixtures/fittings	120000		=sum(B7:C7)
8	Rent	5000	-2000	=sum(B8:C8)
9	Wages	60000	3000	=sum(B9:C9)
10	Credit sales	-50000		=sum(B10:C10)
11	Cash sales	-80000		=sum(B11:C11)
12	Cost of performers	50000		=sum(B12:C12)
13	Profits, bar/food	-12000		=sum(B13:C13)
14	Depn provn on F/F	-25000	-18000	=sum(B14:C14)
15	Food and drink 31.12.x6	2000		=sum(B15:C15)
16	Bank overdraft	-9000		=sum(B16:C16)
17	Dividends expense		7000	=sum(B17:C17)
18	Depreciation expense		18000	=sum(B18:C18)
19	Prepayments		2000	=sum(B19:C19)
20	Accruals		-3000	=sum(B20:C20)
21	Dividends proposed		-7000	=sum(B21:C21)
22		----------	----------	----------
23		=sum(B3:B21)	=sum(C3:C21)	=sum(D3:D21)
24		==========	==========	==========

The sum formula can also be entered in cells C23 and D23 in the same way, or much more quickly by copying the contents of cell B23 relatively into cells C23 and D23. Relative copying means that if a cell reference formula is copied to another location, the spreadsheet software will change the coordinates automatically to operate on the new range of cells. This can be done by using the mouse pointer to drag the cell cursor across from the original cell to cover the two destination cells. Note that in order to get the final column of the extended trial balance, the contents of columns B and C are summed in column D. Once the sum formula has been entered in cell D3, the contents of this cell may be copied relatively to the whole range of cells D4:D21. This completes the data table that can be used for the final accounts. How this is done is shown in Spreadsheets 1b and 1c.

No values are entered in this part of the spreadsheet. All cell contents are formulae which refer to other cells. These formulae mainly refer to the cells in the top left-hand corner of the spreadsheet, where the extended trial balance data was entered. Formulae must always be preceded with an arithmetical operator (usually =, - or +). Note that the sales have been entered as =-(10+11). This is because there are two categories of sales and they were originally situated in the two cells D10 and D11. This demonstrates a fundamental rule in spreadsheet model building:

Never enter a value in a cell, if that value is elsewhere in the spreadsheet – always use the cell reference containing the original value.

Spreadsheet 1b

	F	G	H	I
	Profit and loss account (Gielier Theatre, London) 31.12.x6			
2		(£)	(£)	
3	Sales		=-(D10+D11)	
4	Cost of performers		=D12	
5			----------	
6	GROSS PROFIT		=H3-H4	
7	Add profit from bar, etc.		=-D13	
8			----------	
9			=H6+H7	
10	Depreciation	=D18		
11	Rent	=D8		
12	Wages	=D9		
13		- - -		
14			=sum(G10:G12)	
15			----------	
16	NET PROFIT		=H9-H14	
16	Dividends proposed		=D17	
17			----------	
18	Retained profits for the year		=H16-H17	
19	Retained profits b/f		=-D4	
20			----------	
21	RETAINED PROFITS c/f		=H18+H19	
23			==========	

The sales are preceded by a negative sign because they are shown as a negative in the trial balance. It is not desirable to display figures in the final accounts as negatives. To display a negative value as a positive, the formula is immediately preceded with a negative sign (two negatives make a positive). This has also been carried out in cells H7 (profit from bar, etc.) and H18 (retained profits b/f). The balance sheet is shown in Spreadsheet 1c.

To make headings appear in bold-face or underlined, or in different fonts, most spreadsheet packages have capabilities for altering type style and font size. Note that the liabilities are entered with negatives preceding the cell reference, ensuring the amounts are displayed as positives in the balance sheet.

This model is now complete. If the trading and profit and loss account and balance sheet were to be prepared in the following year, it would only be necessary to re-enter the balances from the ledger accounts in the trial balance and make the appropriate adjustments. From then on, nothing else would need to be done, as the final accounts all work from the cell references in the trial balance section of the spreadsheet. Wherever there are formulae, there is no need to enter data. The more sophisticated the spreadsheet, the fewer values need to be entered, and the less work for the user.

That completes the first spreadsheet model, but there is one final point. The most annoying thing is to overtype a spreadsheet formula. The whole spreadsheet will break down if this happens, so protect any formulae to avoid this inconvenience.

Spreadsheet 1c

	K	L	M	N
1	Balance Sheet (Gielier Theatre, London) as at 31.12.x6			
2		(£)	(£)	(£)
3	**Fixed assets:**	Cost	Depn	NBV
4	Fixtures + Fittings	=D7	=-D14	=L4-M4
5				
6	**Current assets:**			
7	Stock		=D15	
8	Debtors		=D5	
9	Prepayments		=D19	
10			----------	
11			=sum(M7:M9)	
12	**Current liabilities:**			
13	Creditors	=-D6		
14	Accruals	=-D20		
15	Proposed divs	=-D21		
16	Bank overdraft	=-D16		
17		-----		
18			=sum(L13:L16)	
19			----------	
20	NET CURRENT ASSETS:			=M11-M18
21				-------
22	NET ASSETS			=N4+N20
23				======
24	Financed by:			
25	Ordinary share capital			=-D3
26	Retained profits			=H22
27				-------
28				=N25+N26
29				======

20.4 TASK 2: PREPARING A PRODUCT COST STRUCTURE

Eden Garden Products produce two concrete mouldings: Leo the lion and Trixie the pixie. The details on their costs and other necessary information are given in Spreadsheet 2a. To display numbers as currency in certain cells, it is necessary to format them in the required currency style, by using the format command or selecting the currency style icon. The basic data table required in order to compile a product cost structure is now in place. Moving to the right of this area, it is possible to construct the model for the task. This is shown in Spreadsheet 2b. Note that the formulae in cells G6:G9 and H6:H9 represent the apportioned costs. For example, consider the rent.

The total rent amount in cell E11 is multiplied by the area that department B occupies as a proportion of the total area of the factory, i.e. =C20/E20. Therefore, putting the formula together gives =E11*(C20/E20). The subjective aspect here is the choice of basis upon which to apportion the particular overhead. The least clear-cut would seem to be the selling and administration costs. On what basis should they be allocated? It

Spreadsheet 2a

	A	B	C	D	E
1	Data table:		Leo	Trixie	
2	____		____	____	
3	Material usage in kilos		0.50	0.30	
4	Cost per kilo		£0.10	£0.20	
5	Labour usage in hours		0.10	0.05	
6	Labour rate per hour		£5.00	£5.00	
7	Royalties per icon		£0.12	£0.18	
8					
9	Overheads:		Dept A	Dept B	TOTAL
10			(£)	(£)	
11	Rent per year				10000
12	Supervisors' salaries		12000	14000	
13	Depreciation, plant and equip		1600	2000	
14	Power		8000	6000	
15	Canteen costs				15000
16	Selling and admin costs				36000
17	Establishment costs				24000
18	Productive hours per month		800	1000	=C18+D18
19	People employed		4	6	=C19+D19
20	Area (square metres)		60	40	=C20+D20

Spreadsheet 2b

	F	G	H	I
1	Overhead allocation and apportionment:			
2		Dept A	Dept B	TOTAL
3	Supervisors' salaries	=C12	=D12	=G3+H3
4	Depn, plant and equip	=C13	=D13	=G4+H4
5	Power	=C14	=D14	=G5+H5
6	Rent	=E11*(C20/E20)	=E11*(D20/E20)	=G6+H6
7	Canteen	=E15*(C19/E19)	=E15*(D19/E19)	=G7+H7
8	Selling/admin	=E16*(C18/E18)	=E16*(D18/E18)	=G8+H8
9	Establishment	=E17*(C20/E20)	=E17*(D20/E20)	=G9+H9
10		------------	------------	---------
11	TOTALS:	=sum(G3:G9)	=sum(H3:H9)	=sum(I3:I9)
12	Icons produced:	Leo	Trixie	
13	Hours/time per mould	=C18/C5	=D18/D5	
14				
15	ORR per icon:	=G11/G13	=H11/H13	

depends on what determines these costs. Is it area, people, production units, production hours or some other basis? This example uses the productive hours worked per month within each department.

The model may now be completed by producing a product cost structure for the two mouldings of Eden Garden Products. This is shown in Spreadsheet 2c. When this task is finished, it is possible to try different variables in the data table. How would the product cost structure of the Trixie change if the following were changed?

Spreadsheet 2c

	F	G	H	I	J
17	**Product cost structure report:**				
18			Leo		Trixie
19		(£)	(£)	(£)	(£)
20	Direct materials	=C3*C4		=D3*D4	
21	Direct labour	=C5*C6		=D5*D6	
22	Royalties	=C7		=D7	
23		-----		-----	
24	PRIME COST/UNIT		=sum(G20:G22)		=sum(I20:I22)
25	Overhead costs:				
26	ORR per unit		=G15		=H15
27			------		------
28	**TOTAL UNIT PRODUCT COST:**		=H24+H26		=J24+J26
29			======		======

1 Material cost per unit increased to 40p per kilo.
2 Labour takes 50% longer to make each mould.
3 Royalties reduced by half.
4 Selling and administration costs are £40,000.
5 Productive hours increased to 1,100 per month.
6 Hourly labour rates reduced to £4.

These questions can literally be answered in split seconds! It is possible, therefore, to test 'what if?' questions with consummate ease, providing a valuable tool for decision making and planning.

20.5 TASK 3: PRICING ROOMS USING THE HUBBART FORMULA

The Palego Hotel has 16 rooms. The financial data is shown in Spreadsheet 3. Where percentages are to be displayed, the decimal should be typed in the cell, and then the cell may be formatted as a percentage by using the format command or selecting the % icon, if available. This has been done in cell B7 in Spreadsheet 3, with respect to the interest rate on debentures. Having completed this model, the price to charge per room is calculated. What is it?

This spreadsheet will quickly calculate the price to charge per room should some or all of these variables be changed. Try the following changes and observe the effect on the room price:

1 Change the required rate of return to 18%.
2 Change the profit margin on food, etc., to 50%.
3 Change the tax rate to 40%.
4 Change the debenture interest rate to 10% (in cell C7).
5 Change the occupancy rate to 80%.
6 Change the number of rooms available to 24.

Spreadsheet 3

		A	B	C	D	E
1	**Data table: (Hubbart formula)**					
2	---------------------					
3	**Net assets:**					**(£)**
4	Hotel net assets (assets - liabilities)					250000
5	Financed by:					
6	Shareholders' funds					200000
7	Debentures 0.08					50000
8						
9	Required rate of return for shareholders:					13%
10	Net profit required by shareholders					=E6*E9
11	Corporation tax rate					35%
12	Profit before tax					=(1/(1-E11)*E10)
13	Debenture interest					=E7*C7
14	All expenses except food					81500
15	Required income from rooms, food, etc.					=E12+E13+E14
16	Gross profit margin on food					40%
17	Food and drink costs					24000
18	Revenue from food and drink					=(1/(1-E16)*E17)
19	Revenue from room accommodation					=E15+E17-E18
20	Rooms available					16
21	Occupancy rate					75%
22	**Required room price:**					=E19/(365*E20*E21)

20.6 TASK 4: GRAPHING THE REVENUE AND COST FUNCTIONS OF A TRAVEL AGENCY

This task uses cost and revenue data to compile tables from which graphs may be produced. The initial data table is shown in Spreadsheet 4a. If a cell reference within another cell is preceded and succeeded by a $ sign, as in the formula originally entered in cell C9, this will fix absolutely the formula when copying the cell contents into another range of cells; it is needed in this example to multiply quantities by the marginal cost per unit in cells C10:C14. Formulae may be fixed absolutely by column or row only, by putting the $ sign either before or after the letter in the cell reference.

This example has been extracted from Chapter 14. The spreadsheet can be used to examine alternative variables and how they affect the table. For example, the variable cost per unit in cell D3 could be changed, or the fixed cost in cell B9, as could the quantities or the prices.

The table can be presented in graphical form by using the graphical function of the spreadsheet. This could be used to show the point of profit maximization and the average price to charge per holiday package. There are several different commands and functions for graphics, depending on the spreadsheet package.

The following columns of figures would need to be highlighted for inclusion as the series to use within a graphical representation.

Spreadsheet 4

	A	B	C	D	E	F	G	H
1	Cost and revenue functions of a travel agency:							
2	_____							
3	Marginal cost per holiday = £50.00							
4		FC	VC	TC	P	TR	MC	MR
5	Quantity	Fixed	Variable	Total	Price	Total	Marginal	Marginal
6	sold	cost	cost	cost		revenue	cost	revenue
7	(units)	(£)	(£)	(£)	(£)	(£)	(£)	(£)
8								
9	60	5000	=A9*$D$3	=B9+C9	180	=A9*E9		
10	=A9+20	=B9	=A10*$D$3	=B10+C10	160	=A10*E10	=D10-D9	=F10-F9
11	=A10+20	=B10	=A11*$D$3	=B11+C11	140	=A11*E11	=D11-D10	=F11-F10
12	=A11+20	=B11	=A12*$D$3	=B12+C12	120	=A12*E12	=D12-D11	=F12-F11
13	=A12+20	=B12	=A13*$D$3	=B13+C13	100	=A13*E13	=D13-D12	=F13-F12
14	=A13+20	=B13	=A14*$D$3	=B14+C14	80	=A14*E14	=D14-D13	=F14-F13

Total cost   (series D9:D14)
Total revenue   (series F9:F14)
Marginal cost   (series G9:G14)
Marginal revenue (series H9:H14)

Having highlighted or marked the four series for graphing, it is necessary to follow the chart/graph menus on the spreadsheet package being used, choosing the types of graph, specifying the ranges which contain the X series, and the function titles. The X series in this example contains the quantities of holidays provided and sold. To make the graph more informative and clearer, it will also be necessary to add legends (text labels) for the graph, including the graph name and the quantities plotted on the X and Y axes. Having created the graph, it is then possible to view it. With some spreadsheets it is possible to mark out the desired area of the worksheet to display the graph, and its size may be amended as required.

The four functions should be displayed on the screen, TC, TR, MC and MR. The point of profit maximization is identified as the point at which the MC and MR functions cross, or where the gap between the TC and TR functions is the widest. There will be some discrepancy as the MC and MR functions will be slightly offset to the TC and TR functions, but profit should be maximized just over 100 holidays.

In order to test the spreadsheet's versatility in showing the effect of changing certain variables, go back to the table, change the following items and observe the differences:

1 Change fixed costs to £8,000 in cell B9.
2 Change the variable cost per holiday to £40 in cell D3.
3 Change the demand levels at all prices by changing the quantity demanded at £180 to 50 in cell A9.

Note that the lines on the graph and their relative positions alter as the variables are changed. Note where the MC and MR functions cross, i.e. how the point of profit maximization is affected by each change.

Spreadsheet 5

	A	B	C	D	E	F
1	**Data table:**	Variable cost per meal:				£1.25
2	--------	Selling price per meal:				£2.75
3						
4	**Quantity**	**Fixed**	**Variable**	**Total**	**Total**	**Total**
5	**sold**	**costs**	**costs**	**costs**	**revenue**	**profit**
6	1000	10000	=A6*$F1	=B6+C6	=A6*$F2	=E6-D6
7	=A6+1,000	=B6	=A7*$F1	=B7+C7	=A7*$F2	=E7-D7
8	=A7+(A7-A6)	=B7	=A8*$F1	=B8+C8	=A8*$F2	=E8-D8
9	=A8+(A8-A7)	=B8	=A9*$F1	=B9+C9	=A9*$F2	=E9-D9
10	=A9+(A9-A8)	=B9	=A10*$F1	=B10+C10	=A10*$F2	=E10-D10
11	=A10+(A10-A9)	=B10	=A11*$F1	=B11+C11	=A11*$F2	=E11-D11
12	=A11+(A11-A10)	=B11	=A12*$F1	=B12+C12	=A12*$F2	=E12-D12
13	=A12+(A12-A11)	=B12	=A13*$F1	=B13+C13	=A13*$F2	=E13-D13
14	=A13+(A13-A12)	=B13	=A14*$F1	=B14+C14	=A14*$F2	=E14-D14
15	=A14+(A14-A13)	=B14	=A15*$F1	=B15+C15	=A15*$F2	=E15-D15

20.7 TASK 5: GRAPHING A BREAK-EVEN CHART

Easy Meals, a manufacturer of ready-packed meals, sells one product, a faggots and peas dinner. The basic facts for one month are in the data table of Spreadsheet 5. The next step is to graph the functions that comprise the break-even chart by selecting and highlighting (D6:D15), (E6:E15) and the X axis series (A6:A15), and following the necessary steps for creating graphs and labelling them. View the graph to see where TC crosses TR; this is the break-even point.

To test the flexibility of this spreadsheet model, take some 'what if?' situations and see how the break-even graph changes under each one. Here are some examples to investigate:

1 What if the variable cost of the meal were increased to £1.80?
   Test this by typing 1.80 in cell F1.
2 What if the price were increased to £2.95 per meal?
   Test this by typing 2.95 in cell F2.
3 What if the fixed costs were £8,000 per month?
   Test this by typing 8000 in cell B6.

After making each of these changes to the table, you should observe the effects it has on the break-even point. Read off the break-even point and check it by calculation.

20.8 TASK 6: PREPARING A CASH BUDGET

The exercise given in Chapter 16 is used as the basis for this spreadsheet model. The data table is shown in Spreadsheet 6a. The next stage is to select another working area, perhaps below the data table, and to prepare the cash budget. This is shown in Spreadsheet 6b. The spreadsheet model is now completed. What is the closing cash balance? Check it

Spreadsheet 6a

	A	B	C	D	E
1	Data table:				
2	--------	Credit	Cash	Credit	Cash
3		sales	sales	purchases	purchases
4		£	£	£	£
5	January	37500	35000	30000	5000
6	February	45000	12500	28750	2500
7	March	50000	30000	33750	2500
8	Debtors and creditors settle and are settled a month later				
9	Wages per month			2500	
10	Establishment expenses per month			3000	
11	Postage + packing			8.0% of credit sales	
12					
13	Shop fittings:		January	February	March
14	Purchases		5000	5000	5000
15	Disposals		1500		
16					
17	Proposed dividends:			3750	
18	Transfer to deposit account:				50000
19	Opening bank balance:		22484		
20	Opening debtors:		37500		
21	Opening creditors:		35000		

Spreadsheet 6b

	A	B	C	D	E
23	Cash budget				
24	(Leisure Books)		January	February	March
25			£	£	£
26	Cash sales		=C5	=C6	=C7
27	Receipts (debtors)		=C20	=B5	=B6
28	Disposals (fittings)		=C15		
29			----------	----------	----------
30			=sum(C26:C28)	=sum(D26:D28)	=sum(E26:E28)
31	Cash purchases		=E5	=E6	=E7
32	Payments (creditors)		=C21	=D5	=D6
33	Cash wages		=$C$9	=$C$9	=$C$9
34	Establishment exps		=$C$10	=$C$10	=$C$10
35	Post + packing		=(B5*$C$11)	=(B6*$C$11)	=(B7*$C$11)
36	Fixtures + fittings		=C14	=D14	=E14
37	Dividends			=D17	
38	Transfer to dep a/c				=E18
39			----------	----------	----------
40			=sum(C31:C38)	=sum(D31:D38)	=sum(E31:E38)
41	Opening bank balance		=C19	=C47	=D47
42	Add receipts		=C30	=D30	=E30
43			----------	----------	----------
44			=C41+C42	=D41+D42	=E41+E42
45	Less payments		=C40	=D40	=E40
46			----------	----------	----------
47	Closing balance		=C44-C45	=D44-D45	=E44-E45

against the answer to Exercise 2 in Chapter 16. Check the sensitivity of the cash flows by changing the following variables in the data table:

1 Change the opening bank balance to £10,500.
2 Change January's credit sales to £25,200.
3 Change the postage and packing percentage to 12%.
4 Change the monthly establishment expenses to £1,200.
5 Change the disposal value of the fittings to £3,800.

20.9 TASK 7: EXAMINING ALTERNATIVE PURCHASE OPTIONS

Chapter 18 examined alternative methods for appraising a capital investment decision. It concluded that the soundest method theoretically, if not in terms of simplicity and objectivity, was the net present value (NPV) method, so here is a spreadsheet model that quickly and easily assesses alternatives using NPV. Spreadsheet 13 shows three options for the Lapin Restaurant to purchase an industrial dishwasher.

The NPVs are calculated using the function =npv, which calculates the net present value of all cash flows in a range denoting a number of financial periods at a fixed percentage discount rate (here 12% per annum). If a monthly rate were required, the annual rate would be divided by 12.

This is a considerable time-saver where a great deal of data has to be converted to net present values. Its other advantage is that you can easily test the sensitivity of the decision by making changes to the cash flows and the interest rates. Try these changes:

1 Change the initial investment in option 1 to £–1,500 in cell C6.
2 Change the net cash flows in option 2 (C8:C11) to £3,500.
3 Change the annual discount rate to 10% in cell A4.

Spreadsheet 7

	A	B	C	D
1	Lapin Restaurant: Alternative investment projects			
2	-------------			
3	Discount rate:			
4	12%	Option 1	Option 2	Option 3
5		(£)	(£)	(£)
6	Investment at t0	-500	-4000	-5000
7	t0-t1 net c/flow	-2000	-2000	1000
8	t1-t2 net c/flow	-1000	3000	7000
9	t2-t3 net c/flow	2500	3000	2000
10	t3-t4 net c/flow	3000	3000	1000
11	t4-t5 net c/flow	5000	3000	-1000
12		----------	----------	----------
13	**NPV:**	=npv	=npv	=npv
14		($A$4,B6:B11)	($A$4,C6:C11)	($A$4,D6:D11)
15		==========	==========	==========

Spreadsheet 8a

	A	B	C	D
1	Lofty Heights and Auto Lodge: a comparative ratio analysis			
2	----------------------			
3			Lofty Heights	Auto Lodge
4	Capital employed		500000	200000
5	Number of rooms		50	100
6	Number of bed/places		75	200
7	Average price/room-night		100	30
8	Registered guests/night		30	90
9	Food and drink spend/night		1500	900
10	Cost of food and drink		900	600
11	Staff costs per month		10000	5000
12	Other overheads per month		20000	10000

20.10 TASK 8: COMPARING TWO HOTELS IN TWO DIFFERENT MARKET SECTORS

Two hotels are operating in two market sectors. Lofty Heights is a premium hotel catering for guests with a high disposable income and who want exclusivity and style. Auto Lodge is in the low-cost motel business, catering for travellers and holiday-makers. The basic data for each company is given in Spreadsheet 8a.

Having got this basic data from the internal records of the two hotels, it is now possible to calculate some useful ratios which may help to indicate the differences between them. The following ratios will be calculated on the next spreadsheet model:

- Net profit/sales
- Net profit/capital employed
- Sales/capital employed
- Gross profit margin on food and drink
- Occupancy rate (in room-night terms)
- Staff costs/sales
- Total overheads/turnover
- Food and drink spend per guest-night

Before these ratios are calculated in another part of the spreadsheet model, consider how the revenue per month is calculated, as the information available relates to spend per room and the number of guests registered. The best way to relate the number of guests registered per night, in terms of rooms occupied, is to calculate the proportion of rooms that will be occupied given a certain number of guests accommodated. In the two hotels, the proportion of rooms to bedplaces is as follows:

	Lofty Heights	Auto Lodge
Available rooms	50	100
Bedplaces	75	200
Bedplaces per available room	1.5	2.0

If the number of guests per night is divided by the number of bedplaces per available room, it is possible to calculate the average number of rooms occupied per night:

It is now possible to add this information and other relevant items to the data table. The eight ratios may then be calculated for each hotel. This is shown in Spreadsheet 8b. That completes the spreadsheet model. Note the differences in the ratios calculated. Can you determine the reasons why some of the ratios are so different for these two types of hotel? Try some changes to the original data table:

1 Reduce the average price/room-night at Lofty Heights to £75.00 in cell C7.
2 Increase the registered guests per night at Auto Lodge to 115 in cell D8.
3 Increase the average spend on food and drink at Lofty Heights to £1,750 in cell C9.
4 Increase the monthly staff costs of Auto Lodge to £8,000 in cell D11.

That completes the eight tasks. Some of them are more time-consuming than others, but if they are built up methodically, the real power, speed and flexibility of spreadsheet modelling may be appreciated. Used appropriately, spreadsheets can cut out repetitive calculations and act as an effective tool to test and evaluate the effects of alternative decisions.

Spreadsheet 8b

	A	B	C	D
13	Places per room		=C6/C5	=D6/D5
14	Rooms occupied per night		=C8/C13	=D8/D13
15	Room sales per month		=C7*C14*30	=D7*D14*30
16	Food + drink sales per month		=C9*30	=D9*30
17	Gross profit on food, etc.		=(C9-C10)*30	=(D9-D10)*30
18	Total overheads		=C11+C12	=D11+D12
19	Net profit		=C15+C17-C18	=D15+D17-D18
20				
21	**Ratio calculations:**			
22	--------------			
23			**Lofty Heights**	**Auto Lodge**
24	Net profit/sales ratio		=C19/(C15+C16)	=D19/(D15+D15)
25	Net profit/capital emp		=C19/C4	=D19/D4
26	Sales/capital employed		=C24/C25	=D24/D25
27	Gross margin on food, etc.		=C17/C16	=D17/D16
28	Occupancy rate		=C14/C5	=D14/D5
29	Staff costs/sales		=C11/(C15+C16)	=D11/(D15+D16)
30	Total overheads/sales		=C18/(C15+C16)	=D18/(D15+D16)
31	Food spend/guest-night		=C9/C8	=D9/D8

ANSWERS TO MULTIPLE-CHOICE QUESTIONS

CHAPTER 1

Question 1

B, because exchange involves a transaction between individuals from which they will both benefit, but not necessarily equally.

Question 2

B, because the capital in financial terms represents the owner's stake in the value of the total assets invested in the business.

Question 3

B, because assets equal all liabilities, including capital, therefore assets + capital is the same as total liabilities (including capital) + capital.

Question 4

C, because if you refer back to the balance sheet of Topaz International Travel, stocks are the only one of choices A to D included under current assets. Stocks are assets which are used or sold, and replaced on a regular basis, within a twelve-month timescale.

Question 5

A, because all the other items are current liabilities due for payment within twelve months, whereas a mortgage is a long-term liability, normally due for payment in more than twelve months.

CHAPTER 2

Question 1

D, as all transactions have the ultimate effect of leaving an equality between the two sides of the balance sheet. However, this can be arrived at by a fully compensating adjustment to one side of the balance sheet or the other, or a transaction that changes both sides by equal amounts.

Question 2

B, as expenditure on advertising is an example of non-compensating revenue expenditure, where there is no definable asset acquired which can be included

---

on the balance sheet to compensate for the original reduction in assets. This means that the balance sheet equality can only be maintained by making a compensating reduction to the owner's capital. Answers A, C, and D involve expenditure for which the business acquires a definable asset which can be included under the asset side of the balance sheet, in accordance with the money measurement concept.

Question 3

A, as all the other answers would be involved in a credit sale. Firstly, stock would be reduced. Secondly, there would be an increase in debtors, and thirdly, as the debtors would be increased by more than the stock would be reduced, it would be necessary to add the difference or profit to the capital in order to maintain the equality of the balance sheet.

Question 4

C, as an introduction of capital by the owner must cause an increase in the owner's capital. As the owner is paying off a business loan, the liabilities will be correspondingly reduced, causing no overall change to the total liabilities on the balance sheet.

Question 5

B, see the following working:

Effect on balance sheet total

	£	£	
Original total		70,000	
Insurances/capital		−3,500	(cash down, capital down)
Stock/creditors		+5,000	(stock up, creditors up)
		71,500	
Debtors	+3,150		(assets up)
Stock	−3,200		(assets down)
		−50	(loss, capital down)
Final total		71,450	

CHAPTER 3

Question 1

C, because the double-entry system is based on the fundamental principle that the balance sheet must always balance, and this is achieved by ensuring that assets always equal liabilities, as was demonstrated in Chapter 2.

Question 2

B, because if a business benefits from a reduction in a purchase invoice offered by a supplier for prompt payment, this is known as a discount received. The correct double entry for this is to reduce the creditor, debit (+) the account, and to increase the discount received account, credit (−) the account.

Question 3

D, because discounts allowed are always a positive or debit balance. The reason for this is that when a debtor is offered a discount on a sales invoice, the debt is being effectively reduced, and the asset debtor is therefore reduced by a credit (−) entry. The opposite entry in the discount allowed account logically must always be a debit (+) entry. Think through why answers A, B and C are correct in this way.

Question 4

B, as it is not true to say that a small discrepancy in the trial balance indicates only a few errors or that any errors are insignificant. It is possible to have very large or very important errors that almost cancel each other out, producing only a small discrepancy in the trial balance.

Question 5

A, because when returns are received from a customer, this requires that the asset account debtor should be reduced with a credit (−) entry, therefore a debit (+) entry in any other account will not create a discrepancy in the trial balance and will not form part of any suspense account. The actual error here is that the returns are in fact returns inwards not returns outwards, so the correction is made by crediting (−) the returns outwards account, cancelling the original debit (+) entry, and making a correct debit (+) in the returns inwards account.

CHAPTER 4

Question 1

B, because the net profit would be presented and calculated in the following way:

	£	£
Sales		13,000
Less returns inwards		45
		12,955
Cost of sales		6,500
Gross profit		6,455
Add rent received	560	
Add discounts received	80	
		640
		7,095
Discounts allowed	395	
Wages	2,700	
Insurance	1,100	
		4,195
Net profit		2,900

Question 2

C, because the existence of closing stocks means that this stock remains unsold at the end of the financial period. Under the accruals concept, where we match attributable expenditure against revenue generated, the value of this stock should be excluded from the cost of sales. Therefore, this will have the consequence of increasing gross profit and also the net profit by £400.

Question 3

A, because rent received in advance theoretically means that the business owes rent to the tenant at this moment, therefore this amount is described as an accrual.

Question 4

B, the calculation of the attributable expense is as follows:

Jan 1 to April 30 = 4 months	Rent = 4/6 × £2,400 = £1,600
May 1 to Oct 31 = 6 months	Rent = 6/6 × £3,200 = £3,200
Nov 1 to Dec 31 = 2 months	Rent = 2/6 × £3,600 = £1,200

Rent attributable for the period Jan 1 to Dec 31, 19x4   £6,000

Question 5

A, because the adjustments have the following effects on net profit:

	Effect on profit £
1 Wages accrued reduces profit	−120
2 Commission claimed back increases profit	+50
3 Rent received paid back reduces profit	−150
4 Closing stock overvalued decreases profit	−80
Overall effect of adjustments	−300

CHAPTER 5

Question 1

B, as a fixed asset is derived from business expenditure on an asset which is intended, within a going concern, to have a 'permanent' place within the business. Fixed assets were described in Chapter 1 as the 'bones' of a business, and essentially they help to generate revenues over a number of financial periods. Therefore, under the accruals concept, their original cost should be charged against those revenues which they help to generate.

Question 2

A, as the reducing-balance method is a mathematical formula which depicts the depreciation function as an expense that gradually reduces over the economic life of the asset. As each annual depreciation charge is based on a fixed percentage of the previous periods net book value (NBV), it is theoretically impossible for the asset value ever to reach zero. There is some logic in this, as very often fixed assets lose more value in their earlier years, and may always be worth something as scrap value even when they are very old and obsolete.

Question 3

C, as this statement refers to the need for businesses that continue trading to buy fixed assets and eventually to replace them, if continuity is to be maintained under the going-concern concept. The fixed asset has a finite economic life due to a number of factors, such as wear and tear, technological obsolescence, market trends and time itself. If a business does not recognize this loss in value or productive capability as an expense in the profit and loss account, there is a danger that fixed assets will be over-valued in the subsequent periods of their lives, and profits in those periods will be overstated.

Question 4

D, assuming as usual that depreciation is charged for a whole year in the year the asset is acquired and not at all in the year the asset is disposed. The annual depreciation charge under the straight-line method is

$$\frac{\text{Cost of asset} - \text{residual value}}{\text{Life in years}} = \frac{£10,000 - £2,500}{5} = £1,500 \text{ per annum}$$

Assuming that no depreciation is charged in the third year, the year of disposal, the net book value (NBV) of the asset at the time of disposal is as follows:

	£
Original cost	10,000
Depreciation (2 × 1,500)	3,000
NBV at time of disposal	7,000
Proceeds from disposal	8,000
Profit on disposal*	1,000

* Otherwise known as overprovision for depreciation.

Question 5

B, because under the prudence concept, most expenditure besides that on fixed assets, is considered to be revenue expenditure and is to be charged in the current year to the profit and loss account. However, a proportion of this expenditure will provide future economic benefits. Under the money measurement concept and the prudence concept, revenue expenditure that does not result in the acquisition of a verifiable tangible asset should not usually be included on the balance sheet. But if the value of a business as a whole has been verified as greater than the up-to-date value of its separable net assets, through the price that someone was willing to pay for it, then the difference attributable to such intangible assets as location, staff skills, competitive advantage and brand strength, is known as goodwill.

CHAPTER 6

Question 1

C, because businesses in the tourism, leisure and hospitality sector are mainly service-based businesses; they are not usually involved in buying and selling stocks. However, some retail businesses within this sector, such as food, snack, sport and leisure retailers, do carry stocks. Services offered by tourism, leisure and hospitality businesses often include the provision of food and drink, so any stock-in-trade will normally comprise drinks and perishable food.

Question 2

A, and the numerical explanation is as follows:

	£
Opening stock of fuel	200
Purchases of fuel	1,250
	1,450
Less fuel stock stolen	50
Fuel stock available to use	1,400
Less closing stock of fuel	120
Cost of fuel consumed	1,280

Any stocks which are not sold or consumed in the financial period concerned, are excluded from the cost of sales in the trading account. This means that the cost of stock lost to the business in a fire, stolen, damaged, or withdrawn by the owner should be excluded. The reason for this is that the trading account should show the normal gross profit earned by selling goods or services, recognizing only the difference between the revenue earned in the period and the normal cost of those sales. Furthermore, the accruals concept requires that stocks left unsold at the end of the period are also excluded in arriving at the calculation of gross profit for that period.

Question 3

B, because if items that were ordered by the business were neither delivered nor invoiced, no record of their being in stock would ever have been made either in physical or accounting terms. Hence no discrepancy would exist between the accounting record and the physical quantity. No business should operate its stock records simply on the basis of orders made, as it is common for orders not to be fulfilled or to be amended. For this reason a stock record should be based on the official delivery note or invoice received, as verified by a physical check at goods inwards.

Question 4

D, because a solvent business's prices should normally be higher than the costs of purchasing those items, However, the accounting concept of prudence requires that going concerns should not value their stocks at net realizable value, as this is tantamount to recognizing profit before it has been formally earned through making a sales contract. This concept requires businesses to value their stocks at cost or NRV, whichever is the lower. However, there are several bases for arriving at cost, and of these it is FIFO that produces the highest closing stock valuation. This is because FIFO requires issues to be made from the stock purchased earliest, usually valued at the lower prices, leaving the normally higher priced stocks at the end of the period.

Question 5

D, because the rule does recognize that for NRV to be used, a business must not be viewed as a going concern. It is highly unlikely that NRV would be used as the basis for valuing all stocks items held by a business, only for a one-off batch of obsolete or damaged stocks.

CHAPTER 7

Question 1

C, because when a cheque bounces, the entry in the bank account is a credit (−), therefore there must be an equal and opposite debit (+) in the other account, which in this case is the debtor account. The debit (+) in the debtor account effectively reinstates the debt, until such time as the debt is either cleared by a represented cheque, or is confirmed as bad. If a debt is confirmed as bad, the subsequent double entry is to credit (−) the debtor account, reducing the amount owed, and debit (+) the bad debts expense account.

Question 2

B, and the reconciliation is as follows. Correct the creditor balance in the customer books and the debtor balance in the supplier books. Following the corrections, the difference between them must logically equal the original discrepancy.

- To correct error 1, the creditor account should be reduced by £90.
- To correct error 2, the creditor account should be increased by £50.
- To correct error 3, the creditor account should be increased by £6.
- To correct error 4, the debtor account should be reduced by £25.

The overall discrepancy is £9, calculated as follows:

	Creditor £		Debtor £
(1)	−90		
(2)	+50		
(3)	+6	(4)	−25
	+34		−25

To correct the creditor account, the balance would need to be reduced by £34, but to correct the debtor account the balance would only need to be reduced by £25, proving that the original discrepancy must have been £9.

Question 3

D, and the explanation is as follows:

	Effect on profit £
Bad debts expense (+120)	−120
Reduction in provision (550 − 400)	+150
Income	+30

Balance sheet extract

	£	£
Current assets:		
Debtors	4,500	
Less provision for BD	400	
Net debtors		4,100

Question 4

C, and the working is as follows:

Debtor Control Account

Ref	£
Balance b/d	+3,200
Credit sales	+22,000
Bad debts	−880
Sales returns	−620
Discount all'd	−1,200
Bank (receipts)	−18,500
Balance b/d	+4,000

Therefore the provision for bad debts would need to have been increased by $0.05(£4,000 − £3,200) = £40$

Question 5

B, because all the other options would increase the proportion of cash sales, or would encourage existing debtors to pay more promptly. All other things being equal, A, C and D would reduce the total number of debtors within the business. But a bulk-buying discount would encourage a general increase in sales volume, both credit and cash. This would increase the number of debtors instead of reducing it, requiring the business to make greater provision against doubtful debtors, not less.

CHAPTER 8

Question 1

D, because if a cheque for £18 were sent to a supplier and the cash book were debited instead of credited, the cash book balance of the business would be £36 higher than the balance appearing on the bank statement.

Question 2

A, and the calculation is below:

Opening float − cash expenses + till roll total should equal the total contents of the till at the end. And £35 − £25 + £350 = £360, which was the total amount counted in the till at the end of the day.

Some staff paid hourly, such as highly skilled instructors or performers, can be as expensive or more expensive than staff on salaried contracts. Essentially there is no relationship between the type of contract offered to employees and the overall cost of those contracts to the employer. All the other factors will have a significant influence over the employment costs faced by a business.

If a business is highly automated, most of the costs involved will be based on the financing of loans and/or the depreciation on capital equipment rather than wages. If a business retails products which it buys in, it will have lower employee costs than a business which either makes that product or which provides a service itself. The reason for this is that the business which buys in its products or services includes those costs in the trading account as costs of sales, instead of in the profit and loss account as salaries. Finally, the economic, legal and commercial environment may significantly affect the employment costs of the business. Such influential factors may be direct taxation rates, minimum wage legislation, the strength of employee rights legislation, demand and supply of labour, the level and type of competition in the market.

Question 2

C, because the extent to which the capacity of the concert hall is filled reflects the level of demand for the performer. This will reflect the reputation and popularity of the performer and the repertoire. These factors will also influence the prices which may be charged for various types of tickets, and therefore will determine the total revenue and profit earned from the concert as a whole. The capacity of the concert hall itself is not a valid criterion for determining remuneration, as a large hall mostly empty will not be profitable. With this type of artist the length of performance would not be the critical factor determining remuneration, nor would the perceived difficulty of the pieces played or even the quality of the performance given.

However, past performances will determine the present reputation of the performer, so although the performance on the day will not determine the level of remuneration earned, it may affect future demand for that performer. Reward in most cases should be based on performance, even on past performance and reputation in a case such as this, but not on a factor which the performer cannot influence. Unlike the concert pianist, however, most staff in business would have their pay more closely linked to observable effort and performance, such as hours worked and productivity. This is usually easy to relate individual performance closely enough to revenue generated, particularly if the staff members are part of a team, or their work is remotely related to the revenue-earning activities of the business.

Question 3

D, because the petty cash imprest system (literally meaning money advanced for official or state business) is where a fixed float is advanced from the main cash book to the responsibility of a petty cashier for the purpose of undertaking certain minor transactions of the business. The float is maintained by a balancing transfer from the cash book at the end of a given period. The petty cash account avoids the need for a large number of minor items to appear in the main cash book, making it easier to undertake bank reconciliations and other checks.

Question 4

A, and the working is below:

$$\text{Commission} = 15 + 0.05(2{,}016/1.44 - 500)$$
$$= £60$$

$$\text{Profit} = (2{,}016/1.44) - (2{,}016/1.40)$$
$$= £40$$

$$\text{Total income} = 60 + 40$$
$$= £100$$

Question 5

B, the reconciliation of net profit to cash is as follows:

	£
Net profit after interest	20,000
Add depreciation	2,500
	22,500
Add loss on sale of fixed assets	2,000
	24,500
Increase in stocks (decrease cash)	(1,500)
Reduction in debtors (increase cash)	500
Increase in creditors (increase cash)	3,000
Net increase in cash	26,500

CHAPTER 9

Question 1

C, because whether the employees are hourly paid or paid on a salaried basis may not influence the total employment cost faced by the business.

Question 3

B, the calculation is as follows:

Free pay per week = £5,200/52 = £100

	£
Gross pay to date	1,200
Free pay to date	400
Taxable pay to date	800
Tax to date at 25%	200

Question 4

C, because the wages and salaries expense account should include gross wages along with employee's PAYE and employee's NI, but it should exclude employer's NI. Employer's NI should be shown in a separate expense account.

Question 5

D, as there is no requirement for companies to disclose the PAYE element of the gross pay of employees separately, although the gross staff costs should be disclosed. There is, however, a requirement that NI payments paid on behalf of the employee by the business should be separately disclosed in the annual report. This includes both employee's NI and employer's NI.

CHAPTER 10

Question 1

A, because although it is the final consumer who bears the tax as a specific percentage of the price of the good or service purchased, VAT is a tax, collected in stages as value is added to the product or service. It is based on the difference between the price of goods and services bought by a business, and what that business generates as revenue. The tax is collected at all the stages that a product or service may go through, either from its primary source or from when it was imported. The businesses that add value to the product act as collectors of VAT on goods and services sold to their customers, and reclaim VAT on goods and services supplied to them.

Question 2

B, because the difference between goods and services which are exempt and which are zero-rated is that when a business supplies zero-rated goods and services it can reclaim VAT on its bought-in goods and services charged at the standard rate. Such businesses don't collect VAT, but will be owed VAT from Customs and Excise. Businesses which deal in exempt goods and services cannot reclaim VAT on bought-in goods and services. These businesses must therefore include the VAT element in their bought-in items as part of the expenses on these items in their profit and loss accounts.

Question 3

D, and the calculation is as follows:

VAT including outputs at the standard rate

	£
Revenue from bedroom accommodation (assume short term)	23,500
Restaurant sales	8,225
Bar sales (4,000 × 47/40)	4,700
	36,425

Remember that room hire for conferences is exempt, so

$$VAT = £36,425 \times 7/47$$
$$= £5,425$$

VAT including inputs at the standard rate

	£
Fuel and power (8,000 × 47/40)	9,400
Alcoholic drinks (2,400 × 47/40)	2,820
Food costs (3,000 × 47/40)	3,525
	15,745

Wages and salaries are exempt, so

$$VAT = £15,745 \times 7/47$$
$$= £2,345$$

The net VAT payable to Customs and Excise is

$$£5,425 - £2,345 = £3,080$$

Question 4

A, because its suppliers are paid on credit, the purchases are infrequent, and cash is collected on a day-to-day basis. The best system is to pay over the VAT on the machine takings quarterly, as this is better from a cash flow perspective than operating a monthly scheme. Recording the VAT on a cash basis would not have any effect with regard to outputs, as they are all cash based. But there is a cash flow advantage in adopting an invoice basis for purchases of equipment, as the VAT reclaim can be recognised as soon as an invoice is received.

Question 5

B, and the workings are as follows:

Step 1: Calculate the sales of supplies (excluding exempt items)

	£
Turnover	56,000

Step 2: Add up the VAT-inclusive cost of standard-rated margin scheme supplies

	£
VAT exc cost = 35,000 × (0.12* + 0.40)	18,200
VAT (18,200 × 7/40)	3,185
	21,385

* This is 60% of 20% because only 60% of the cruising cost is treated as non-travel and taxed at the standard rate; the other 40% of the cruising cost is zero-rated.

Step 3: Add up the cost of the zero-rated margin scheme supplies

	£
VAT exc cost = 35,000 × 0.48	16,800
VAT	nil
	16,800

Step 4: Add together the results of steps 2 and 3

£21,385 + £16,800 = £38,185

Step 5: Calculate the total margin on the margin scheme supplies

step 1 – step 4 = £56,000 – £38,185
= £17,815

Step 6: Calculate the proportion of the margin represented by standard-rated margin scheme supplies

step 5 × (step 2/step 4) = £17,815 × (21,385/38,185)
= £9,977

Step 7: Calculate the standard-rated VAT element on the margin calculated in Step 6

£9,977 × 7/47 = £1,486

Therefore £1,486 is payable by the travel agent to Customs and Excise for the previous quarter.

CHAPTER 11

Question 1

B, because recreation and leisure clubs engage in many types of commercial transactions, like any other organization. The essential difference between so-called commercial organizations and recreation and leisure clubs is that their aims differ. Commercial organizations exist primarily to improve the financial position of their owners by as much as possible. The aims of a recreation and leisure club are much broader. Beyond financial survival, a club aims to provide a social framework, supported by adequate facilities, within pleasant surroundings, to the satisfaction of all its members.

Question 2

B, because if a club provides facilities which are central to its aims as an organization, it is not usual for the club to make additional charges for these facilities. The conventional wisdom is that members pay their annual subscriptions in order that such facilities are provided for no extra charge. However, if subsidiary facilities or equipment are provided that are incidental to the aims of the club, then they might be charged for. An example might be a pool table in a rugby club.

Question 3

B, and the calculation is as follows:

	£
Balances b/d	
Prepaid subs	-300
Accrued subs	+500
I+E account	+1,200
Bank	-1,800 (balancing item)
Balances c/d	
Prepaid subs	-600
Accrued subs	+200

Under the accruals concept the income that the club should recognize in the income and expenditure (I+E) account is $80 \times £15 = £1,200$.

Question 4

D, because under the accruals concept life membership income should be recognized over the life of the member. To ascertain the life of each member in advance is impossible, but the most prudent way to allocate this income to the income and expenditure account is to calculate the annual subscription as a percentage of the life membership fee, and allocate income on the basis of this percentage rate using the reducing-balance method. This method broadly adheres to the accruals concept as the income is gradually allocated to profit, and it is prudent because the life membership income is effectively never written off under the reducing-balance method. The method requires less record keeping than the other methods as there is no need to know who has died and when, or how many years have expired on any particular life membership.

Question 5

B, because all the other terms have an equivalent and more appropriate alternative meaning for use with recreation and leisure clubs. They also have a commercial or business meaning that is not applicable to this type of organization. The balance sheet, however, although clearly a financial term, has no exclusively commercial connotation. It merely recognizes that any organization has assets and liabilities which should balance against each other.

CHAPTER 12

Question 1

B, because although a partnership agreement may directly reward partners for the capital originally invested in the business, by making provision to pay interest at an agreed rate, no direct account is taken of the capital invested in their current accounts. However, account is taken of the current account balance indirectly, as interest may be charged on drawings; this penalizes partners for reducing their capital more than each other, or benefits them if their withdrawals are less than each other.

Question 2

A, because the new partner's capital invested is £50,000. This investment partly pays for the goodwill inherent in the business when the new partner is admitted. As the goodwill is valued at £12,000, and the new profit-sharing ratio is one-third each, the recognized balance on the capital account of the new partner is £50,000 − £4,000 = £46,000, where goodwill is not recognized in the accounts.

Question 3

C, because although preference shareholders have prior claims over profit and net assets as compared to the ordinary shareholder, it is the ordinary shareholder who carries most of the constitutional rights with regard to control over the business. It is ordinary shareholders who normally have voting rights, and who usually own the vast majority of the votes within a limited company. This control is to some extent delegated to the directors of the company as stewards of their interests, but on major constitutional issues such as on the rehiring of directors, or on take-over bids, or on matters such as extending the scope of the company's activities, the ordinary shareholder has a right to participate in the decision-making process whereas the preference shareholder would normally have no such powers.

Question 4

D, because the profits taken into account when calculating EPS for the ordinary shareholders is the net profit after tax before extraordinary items, less preference dividends paid and proposed, divided by the number of ordinary shares issued and paid up. In this example the EPS per ordinary share is

$$(£90,000 − £12,500)/1,000,000 = 7.75p$$

The reason for using net profit after tax and before extraordinary items is to give a more stable underlying performance measure, a measure that is not unduly distorted by commercial activities which are unusual or unrepresentative. Since FRS3 was issued, it is highly unlikely that any item could be classified as extraordinary, therefore the distinction is now less important.

Question 5

A, because the nominal or par value of the ordinary shares is 50p each; the premium on the share is 120p − 50p = 70p a share. As the company is issuing two shares for three, $2/3 \times 600,000 = 400,000$ shares are being issued to existing shareholders. The increase in the share premium will therefore amount to $400,000 \times £0.70 = £280,000$.

CHAPTER 13

Question 1

B, because a cost is the cause of an expense, or where an expense is consumed, by whom, when, how and why. The managers of a business need to know more than how much has been spent on a broad category of expense like total wages. This expenditure information is useless unless the exact cause of that expense is pinpointed. This involves holding people responsible for those expenditures over which they have control, and ensuring they can justify the level of cost consumption with respect to whether it is necessary in order to benefit the organization and its customers.

Question 2

C, as a hotel manager responsible to a regional director would have responsibility for most staff recruitment, for management and control of staff, for local purchasing of provisions and groceries, and for cash and stock management at the hotel. On the other hand, fixed-asset purchasing, particularly on items such as furniture and fittings would normally be a centralized function. This would be due to two main factors. Firstly, refurbishment would be less costly if furniture for all the hotels in the chain were purchased in bulk. Secondly, a distinctive chain of hotels would probably need to be furnished in the same way in order to create and maintain a particular style and ambience.

Question 3

D, because the rent of the factory would not be influenced by the main revenue-generating activity of the business. The test is to ask, if the scale of productive activity were to significantly change, would the consumption of this cost change accordingly? The answer would probably be no. Firstly, a change in the level of production would not influence the rent payable, but the productive capacity of the factory would be more greatly utilized. In the longer term, if production increased to such an extent that additional capacity were required, then a bigger factory might be needed. However, if you examine the other options, these would all be affected by a change in the level of production. The clay and glaze as a direct material cost would

be directly affected by the production level. The supervisor costs and the level of breakages would be more indirectly affected, although a correlation would certainly be observed over significant changes in productive activity.

Question 4

C, because the prime cost of a product or service includes all the direct costs which can be objectively embodied within the unit cost of an individual product or service. The prime cost includes the material costs, labour costs and expenses used directly in the process of making the product or providing the service. In the case of the slate quarry, the only costs that could be directly associated with each tour of the quarry would be the guide's wages, which is a standard rate per tour, and the cost of the consumables used each time a tour is made. Therefore the prime cost is £720 $+ £50 = £770$. The other costs are classified as overheads, although they can be subclassified into (1) overheads which partly depend on the number of visits and (2) overheads which in the short term are independent of the number of visits. Examples of type 1 are the power used in the cage and the activated laser lighting; examples of type 2 are the manager's salary, the royalties for the voice-over, the depreciation, the cashier's wages and the insurance premiums.

Question 5

B, the calculation is as follows. As the business is only making one product, there is no need to calculate departmental overhead recovery rates (ORRs). Therefore the productive hours given for each department are irrelevant to the calculation of the total cost of each chip. Aggregate the costs in both departments and divide the total by the number of chips produced.

		£
Direct materials (10,000 + 15,000)		25,000
Direct labour	(30,000 + 40,000)	70,000
Royalties		5,000
Prime cost		100,000
Overheads	(25,000 + 20,000)	45,000
Total cost of 200,000 chips		145,000

The cost per chip is $£145,000/200,000 = 72.5$p.

CHAPTER 14

Question 1

A, the calculation is as follows. The hotel follows a policy of full cost + 20%:

Total costs   £310,250
Desired revenue   £310,250 × 1.2 = £372,300

If the hotel has 30 singles and 20 doubles, and they are on average 60% occupied, there are

30 × 0.60 = 18 single rooms occupied per night

20 × 0.60 = 12 double rooms occupied per night

The revenue required per year in terms of single-room equivalents is

$$18P_s + (4/3 \times 12)P_s = £372,300$$

where P_s = price of a single room per year
P_d = price of a double room per year
$P_d = \frac{4}{3}P_s$

$$18P_s + 16P_s = £372,300$$

$$34P_s = £372,300$$

$$P_s = £10,950$$

So the price per night of a single room is £10,950/365 = £30.

Question 2

D, because a business such as a bus company or a golf club, which faces a cost structure that is predominantly fixed in the short term, should aim to maximize revenue. The reason for this is that if the business faces a downward-sloping demand curve, which is normal, there will be a price that maximizes the revenue to be obtained from selling the service, whether it is a bus journey or the use of a green. Where all costs are fixed, the maximization of profit exactly coincides with the maximization of revenue.

Question 3

D, because the first law of demand states that the quantity demanded should normally be inversely related to the price. However, demand elasticity is a measure of whether or not the total sales value is inversely related to a change in price. Demand inelasticity is observed when a change in price leads to a change in sales revenue of the same direction.

Question 4

C, and the calculation is as follows. Find out where the sales price is maximized, given that a £1 change in price leads to a change in demand of 50 units. Currently 100 green fees are sold at £5. The minimum price that can be charged to ensure that no one wants to play golf is £5 + (£100/50) = £7. The maximum price that can be charged to generate a given level of demand is

$$SP = 7 - (0.02 \times q)$$

$$SP = 7 - 0.02q$$

Multiply both sides by q to obtain TR:

$$TR = 7q - 0.02q^2$$

And MR = d(TR)/dq:

$$MR = 7 - 0.04q$$

Because all costs are fixed, MC = 0. Equate MC with MR to maximize profit:

$$0 = 7 - 0.04q$$

$$0.04q = 7$$

$$q = 7/0.04 = 175$$

Substituting into the original equation:

$$SP = 7 - (0.02 \times 175)$$
$$= 7 - 3.50$$
$$= 3.50$$

With a linear demand curve, and all costs fixed, the quickest way to arrive at the optimum price is to take the minimum price at which no demand for the product exists (i.e. £7) and halve it. This is because a linear demand curve results in a symmetrical curve, where the maximum revenue coincides with the mean price between 0 and the lowest price at which no demand for the product will exist.

Question 5

C, because where the demand for a product or service is inelastic over a particular range of prices, the relationship between price and total revenue is positive, therefore if revenue is to be maximized, the higher price should be set, not the lower price. Option A is true because, in the long term, all costs are variable and a business will lose money if its average price for all products or services does not exceed the average total costs. Option B is true because if a company sells product at lower than the marginal cost, the revenue obtained will be less than the additional cost of making them available for sale, reducing the overall profitability of the business. Option D is true because if the relationship between the demand for complementary or substitute goods and services is such, the consequent increase in profits may more than compensate for a loss incurred on selling one item at below its variable cost.

CHAPTER 15

Question 1

A, because an increase in price makes the total-revenue function steeper, increasing the rate at which contribution increases at all levels of output above zero. A decrease in unit variable costs would have the same overall effect, but the increased rate of contribution would be caused by the shallower angle on the total-cost function. A reduction in fixed costs would have no effect on contribution as contribution is only determined by the difference between price and variable cost.

Question 2

C, and the working is as follows. Total number of rooms available in a month is

$$40 \times 30 = 1,200$$

The contribution per room is £30 – £5 = £25. And the total contribution required to cover fixed costs and to achieve the required level of monthly profit is

$$£15,000 + £5,000 = £20,000$$

Therefore the monthly total of unit contributions, or rooms let, needs to be

$$20,000/25 = 800$$

which gives an overall required occupancy level of

$$800/1,200 = 2/3$$

Question 3

A, the calculations are as follows:

	Existing restaurant £	Quantity multiplier	Price multiplier	Proposal A £
Sales	100,000	0.90	1.20	108,000
VC	60,000	0.90	1.00	54,000
Cont	40,000			54,000
FC	20,000			20,000
Profit	20,000			34,000

	Existing restaurant £	Quantity multiplier	Price multiplier	Proposal C £
Sales	100,000	1.00	0.80	100,000
VC	60,000			48,000
Cont	40,000			52,000
FC	20,000		+10,000*	30,000
Profit	20,000			22,000

	Existing restaurant £	Quantity multiplier	Price multiplier	Proposal D £
Sales	100,000	1.20	0.90	108,000
VC	60,000	1.20	1.00	72,000
Cont	40,000			36,000
FC	20,000		+10,000*	30,000
Profit	20,000			6,000

* Increment, not multiplier

Proposal B means no change in profit.

Question 4

D, because if product A is discontinued, a negative contribution will be avoided, increasing overall profits by £500. If product B is discontinued, the business will lose contribution of £2,000, decreasing overall profits by £2,000. Therefore cutting one rather than another will make an overall difference to profits of £2,000 + £500 = £2,500.

Question 5

C, and the workings are as follows:

	Family	Double	Single
	£	£	£
Price per day	40	30	21
Variable cost per day	10	6	4
Contribution (price − VC)	30	24	17

The total number of hours required to clean all the rooms is (100×1) + (100×0.75) + (100×0.5) = 225. As only 200 hours are available, the hotel management must decide which types of room will have their availability limited.

To establish which types of room should not be cleaned, it is necessary to rank the rooms in terms of how much contribution each type earns for the hotel per hour of cleaning time used.

	Family	Double	Single
Contribution per room	£30.00	£24.00	£17
Cleaning time	1.00 h	0.75 h	0.50 h
Contribution per hour	£30.00	£32.00	£34.00

Therefore the most profitable rooms to make available are the doubles and the singles. The contribution earned from doubles and singles is

$$(100 \times £24) + (100 \times £17) = £2,400 + £1,700 = £4,100$$

These rooms require the following number of cleaning hours:

$$(100 \times 0.75) + (100 \times 0.5) = 75 + 50 = 125$$

So there are 75 hours left with which to clean any family rooms. As family rooms take an hour each to clean, only 75 may be made available. The contribution from family rooms is $75 \times £30 = £2,250$. So the total contribution is

$$£4,100 + £2,250 = £6,350$$

Therefore the maximum profit per night is

$$£6,350 - £4,250 = £2,100$$

CHAPTER 16

Question 1

A, because a business should first set overall financial objectives that meet the needs of the investors who have a stake in it. Next it should identify its own internal strengths and weaknesses to assess whether there are constraints on being able to pursue any particular alternative. Then it should select alternatives which can meet those objectives, by carrying out an environmental audit, identifying significant opportunities and threats. If constraints are violated, another alternative should be selected. If no feasible alternative exists, the original objectives may need to be reviewed.

Question 2

D, because this can best be described as a strategy to concentrate on the special needs of a small, highly specialized segment of a much wider market, where the segment of the market is probably small but highly defined. The low-cost fast-food outlet is an example of a cost leadership strategy. The no-smoking pub and licensed betting shop are probably both examples of a differentiation strategy, where the market is fairly large and broadly based, but where the business is merely gaining a competitive advantage over others in the same market. This is achieved by providing a better service in some fundamental way for a large proportion of the potential customers.

Question 3

A, because all the other alternatives meet the overall financial objective of achieving a 15% return on £200,000 invested. The hotel therefore needs to make a net profit of at least £30,000 per year. Option A fails to meet this objective:

	£
Revenue ($20 \times 0.75 \times 25 \times 360$)	135,000
Total annual costs ($100,000 + 10,000$)	110,000
Net profit	25,000

This achieves an annual rate of return of $25,000/200,000 = 12.50\%$, below the 30% requirement.

Question 4

B, and this is demonstrated by preparing a cash budget for the first three months of business:

	January £	February £	March £
Receipts			
Cash sales	12,000	15,000	19,500
Payments			
Cash purchases	10,000	10,000	12,500
Overheads	2,500	2,500	2,500
	12,500	12,500	15,000
Opening balance	5,000	4,500	7,000
Receipts	12,000	15,000	19,500
	17,000	19,500	26,500
Less payments	12,500	12,500	15,000
Closing balance	4,500	7,000	11,500

The purchases in February are 1.25 times the cost of sales in January:

£12,000 × 2/3 × 1.25 = £10,000

The purchases in March are 1.25 times the cost of sales in February:

£15,000 × 2/3 × 1.25 = £12,500

Question 5

C, because the laundry would be a department within which a range of costs would be consumed, many of which might be within the control of the departmental supervisor. Examples of these costs are the number of cleaning labour hours that are paid for, the price and amount of cleaning materials used, and the price and amount of other consumables used in room refreshment. It is possible that such a department might be set budgets for various categories of costs over which members within the department have direct control. The other options would not be best managed as a cost centre for the following reasons:

The **restaurant** is best run as a profit or contribution centre; the manager may well have the responsibility for the menu, including setting prices. The **reception** is unlikely to be designated a cost centre as it is doubtful whether members of this department have enough control over the consumption of costs, apart from stationery and minor consumables. The **bar** could be designated a profit centre, similar to the restaurant, because despite not having control over prices, its manager may have significant control over costs and revenue. The manager could control staff costs, leakages and the level of business, especially if the bar is open to the general public as well as hotel guests.

CHAPTER 17

Question 1

C, because a standard costing system is where attainable targets agreed between managers and subordinates are set at a level that is challenging and moves forward the overall performance of the business. The advantage is that, once agreed, the standards can be used to set regular budgets against which actual performance can be measured. As long as these standards are still seen as appropriate by all concerned, any meaningful differences between them can be investigated, and responsibility identified. Only significant differences are investigated, so the relevant approach is management by exception. If standards are consistently surpassed or underachieved, they may need to be reviewed.

Question 2

B, and the calculation is as follows. The flexible budget should compare actual costs and revenues with the standard budget. In this case the actual number of holidays sold is 175 rather than 200. If we compare revenues and costs at this level of sales, we obtain the following:

	Flexible budget £		Actual performance £
Sales (175 × 300)	52,500	(175 × 280)	49,000
Costs (175 × 260)	45,500	(175 × 250)	43,750
Contribution	7,000		5,250

The difference or flexible contribution variance is

£7,000 – £5,250 = £1,750(A)

Note that the fixed costs are not relevant to a flexible budget contribution variance, because as explained in Chapters 15, 16 and 17, fixed costs depend on time not output, so all other things being equal, they would not be expected to vary at different levels of productive output.

Question 3

C, the reason for this is that the only two main reasons for a material cost variance are (1) prices of materials vary from standard or (2) quantities used in a standard unit vary from standard. Where one of them is favourable and the other adverse, it is always possible that the adverse variance outweighs the favourable variance. So when the magnitudes of the variances are unknown, the only definite situation which cannot cause an overall adverse variance is when both variances are favourable, i.e. when prices and usage are lower than standard.

Question 4

A, and the calculation is below; see also the variance tree in Fig. 17.10.
The flexible budget contribution variance is

Sales price variance + material cost variance + labour cost variance
    + variable overhead cost variance

The question gives them as follows:

	£
Sales price variance	900(F)
Material cost variance	200(F)
Labour cost variance	800(A)
Variable overhead cost variance	400(F)
Flexible contribution variance	**700(F)**

The flexible budget profit variance is the flexible budget contribution variance + the fixed overhead expenditure variance:

	£
Flexible contribution variance	700(F)
Fixed o/head expenditure variance	800(A)
Flexible budget profit variance	**100(A)**

If the total profit variance is 400(F), the difference between the total profit variance and the flexible budget profit variance must be the sales volume contribution variance, i.e. the difference between the standard contribution per unit multiplied by the difference between the standard sales volume and the actual sales volume. This is the missing figure in our example, so the sales volume variance is as follows:

	£
Flexible budget profit variance	100(A)
Sales volume variance*	500(F)
Total profit variance	**400(F)**

* Balancing variance

Question 5

C, as a favourable labour efficiency variance is least likely to be consistent with a favourable labour wage rate variance. This is because a lower rate of pay than standard may result in inefficient staff being recruited in the first place and/or may cause demotivation and apathy. This situation is highly unlikely to result in an hourly production rate above the standard output. In fact, it is more likely that staff paid less than the standard rate may have a slow work rate, a disorganized working style and a propensity to take more unauthorized breaks.

The other variances could be deemed consistent with a favourable labour efficiency ratio:

Labour rate: an adverse labour rate variance can be seen as consistent, because often a more highly paid employee feels more highly regarded and may work more efficiently. They may have better qualifications, higher skill levels and greater experience.

Material usage: a more efficient employee in a kitchen will tend to be more efficient in all aspects of the job, and will tend to produce less waste with respect to food and other materials.

Sales volume: there will be a direct relationship between a member of the kitchen staff being more efficient and the sales of meals or covers being higher than standard. This is especially true for catering, where demand normally has an immediate effect on production. When a kitchen is operating with a favourable labour efficiency variance, it will almost inevitably operate with a favourable sales volume contribution variance.

CHAPTER 18

Question 1

C, because although the reward of investors and the satisfaction of customers often vie to be the paramount objective of business, they are both equally vital. A business that satisfies its customers by giving away its products or services at uneconomical prices will fail to reward investors adequately and will quickly become insolvent. A business that pursues only the maximum rewards for its investors through financial control, without taking adequate account of the satisfaction of customers, will lose custom and markets to competitors that provide better satisfaction. Essentially, therefore, the two objectives are of equal importance, and the achievement of both is a very tricky and highly critical balancing act.

Question 2

A, because the DCF method relies fundamentally for its decision rule on a discount factor or percentage rate of return in order to discriminate between projects that generate alternative patterns of cash flow. The cost of capital is often used, as it represents the weighted average minimum return acceptable to the financial investors in the business as a whole. It means that any capital investment undertaken using the investors' capital must yield at least this level of return, otherwise the investors will become poorer. The cost of capital can also be related to the opportunity cost of investing in the business. So any investment undertaken should yield a higher rate of return to the investors than they could get by investing their funds in the next best alternative.

Quite often the highest rate of return available in a safe investment over an equivalent period might be used. But this is probably not the most prudent discount factor, as it might well be lower than some equally risky alternative available to the business. The ARR method might well use the cost of capital as a 'hurdle' against which to reject or accept a project, but not in order to discriminate between projects.

None of the other methods of capital investment appraisal make any use of a discount factor or a target rate of return in order to evaluate the viability of a project.

Question 3

B, because the ARR and payback methods allow the hotel to break even or recover its costs in purely cash terms over the useful life of the project. Only where a discount factor is applied to the future cash flows does the project show a 'loss'. Therefore, using the DCF method, the hotel would reject the swimming-pool as its DCF is bound to be negative.

Question 4

B, because all the other methods are based on measuring or timing cash flows to and from the project. But because the ARR method relies heavily on accounting concepts, particularly the accruals concept, it will ignore the timing of cash flows where this accords with accounting convention. This is particularly significant with regard to capital expenditure, where the profits recognized each year depend on the depreciation policy of the business. It is also the case with credit purchases and sales, where there may be significant timing differences between the issue of the invoice and the final settlement of the account.

Question 5

D, because, under most objective short-term financial appraisals, all the other types of investment would produce a recommendation to reject. This is because these types of investment are much longer-term, where net cash flows may occur very far into the future, and more significant, they may be very hard to associate and identify with the original investment. On the other hand, investment in NIT would be much easier to appraise financially, as the cost benefits in labour savings and other efficiencies would be clearly identified and measurable in obvious financial terms.

The main point is the inability of capital investment appraisal to take a wider view of business investment and strategic direction. Investing in social facilities, training programmes, environmental improvement schemes, even in research and development, would be rejected from the short-term financial perspective. However, taking the longer-term view, it is clear that most of these types of expenditure would be desirable, and overall financially beneficial, yet very hard to quantify.

CHAPTER 19

Question 1

C, because the net profit for this business is 50%; this is higher than for A, B and D, which show profits of 10%, 20% and 5% respectively. C's profit is calculated by subtracting from sales the cost of sales and the expenses, dividing the result by the sales then multiplying by 100:

$$\frac{80,000 - 30,000 - 10,000}{80,000} \times 100\% = 50\%$$

Question 2

D, because financing the acquisition of fixed assets by increasing current liabilities has no overall effect on long-term capital employed, nor does the transaction itself have any impact on profit as this is an example of capital expenditure. However, the subsequent effect of this transaction would be to reduce net profit, as the depreciation charge associated with the acquisition is charged against profits. All of the other transactions would have a direct effect on net profit, capital employed or both:

- Increasing price would increase gross profit and net profit.
- Paying off a long-term loan with current assets would reduce the long-term capital employed within the business.
- A fixed-cost reduction programme would increase the net profit of the business.

Question 3

B is more likely to be the boxing promoter as it has an exceptionally high asset turnover ratio and its net profit margin is low, as would be expected when profit is effectively the 'cut' made on very large financial deals. This is indicative of a type of business which relies heavily for its success on the productive or creative capabilities of people rather than on fixed assets or capital equipment. Many businesses in the tourism, leisure and hospitality sectors fall into this category, particularly in areas such as crafts and the performing arts.

Business C is most likely to be a hotel as it would rely quite heavily for its revenue-generating capability on land and buildings, fixtures and fittings. Such a business is likely to have a reasonably low asset turnover ratio, such as 1:1, and its profit per pound of sales and capital employed is also likely to be more moderate due to having to meet a considerable amount of overheads, such as staff costs. Business D is probably the fitness centre, very highly capital intensive but much more profitable per pound of takings, due to low overheads and operating costs.

Question 4

B, because all the other options would either reduce the cash operating cycle or not affect it directly. The cash operating cycle is governed by three factors: the length of the stock turnover period, the length of credit extended to customers, and the length of credit obtained from suppliers. The policy of extending credit to customers would on average lengthen the cash operating cycle not reduce it. Ordering more frequently would reduce it, as would delaying further payments to creditors. Increasing the advertising and promotional spending budget would probably increase future sales volumes, and may help to increase the amount and rate of cash flow, but the actual length of the cash operating cycle would not necessarily change as a result, unless it led to an increase in cash sales as a proportion of total sales.

Question 5

B, and the calculation is as follows. The number of occupied room-nights is

$$(50 \times 0.60) \times 365 = 10,950$$

The total food and drinks costs were £137,970, which represents 60/100 the price of food and drink charged to guests. The gross sales invoice value of the food and drink was therefore £137,970 × 100/60 = £229,950 for the whole year, which gives an average food and drink bill per room-night of £229,950/10,950 = £21.

Question 6

A, the calculation is as follows:

	Chain A £	Chain B £
Profit available to shareholders (share capital × 0.20)	300,000	600,000
Interest (debt × 0.10)	300,000	150,000
Net profit before interest	600,000	750,000
Doubled up	600,000	750,000
	1,200,000	1,500,000
Less interest (same)	300,000	150,000
Profit for shareholders	900,000	1,350,000
Percentage rate of return (net profit/shareholder funds)	60%	45%

Therefore the difference would now be 15%.

Question 7

B, and the calculation is as follows. The contribution per cover of the Santos restaurant is £15 × 40% = £6. The break-even point is

$$\frac{\text{Fixed costs}}{\text{Contribution per cover}} = \frac{£120,000 \text{ per year}}{£6 \text{ per cover}}$$

$$= 20,000 \text{ covers per year}$$

The capacity of the restaurant is

250 nights per year × 30 tables per sitting × 4 sittings per night × 2 covers per table = 60,000 covers per year

Therefore the break-even operating capacity of the restaurant is 20,000/60,000 = 1/3.

Question 8

A, and the calculation is as follows:

$$\text{Margin of safety} = \frac{\text{Sales value} - \text{B/E value}}{\text{Sales value}}$$

$$\text{Current sales value} = \frac{\text{B/E value}}{1 - \text{margin of safety}}$$

The current sales values of the respective hotels are therefore as follows:

	Hotel A £	Hotel B £	Hotel C £	Hotel D £
	50,000	45,000	50,000	56,000
Multiply by C/S ratio	0.30	0.25	0.20	0.25
	15,000	11,250	10,000	14,000

Therefore hotel A contributes most to its overall fixed costs.

Question 9

B, and the explanation is as follows. The value added by an organization is defined as

Sales – bought-in goods and services

The bought-in goods and services are the food and the power; all other items are applications of added value. Food costs are marked up by 50%, so the profit as a proportion of sales revenue is $50/(100 + 50) = 1/3$, hence the value added is

$$£120,000 - (£80,000 + £4,000) = £36,000$$

The distributed amounts (excluding drawings) are as follows:

	£
Staff costs	11,000
Interest	2,000
Rent	5,000
	18,000

Therefore $£36,000 - £18,000 = £18,000$ was available to the owner, of which 50% was taken as drawings. The distributed proportion of the value added by the sandwich bar is

$$(18,000 + 9,000)/36,000 = 0.75$$

Question 10

B, because it is the only option which would not affect the VA/sales ratio. The only transactions which affect this ratio are those which (1) change the sales value, e.g. C, or (2) change the value of the bought-in goods and services, e.g. A and D. Increasing or reducing the staff costs in an organization has no effect on the total value added, it merely redistributes it between staff and owners.

GLOSSARY

absorption cost the total cost of producing a unit of product or providing a unit of service. This includes direct costs, allocated costs and apportioned indirect and remote costs.

accounting rate of return the percentage rate of return earned by a capital investment project, based on accounting concepts and conventions.

accruals expenditure incurred by a business in a financial period which remains owing to third parties outside the business at the end of that financial period.

accruals concept one of the fundamental concepts of accounting. It determines that accounting profit should be based on charging attributable costs against the attributable revenue for an accounting period, not necessarily on cash receipts less cash payments made in that accounting period.

accumulated fund the equivalent of capital in a 'not for profit' organization.

ageing debtor schedule this is a breakdown of debts owing to the business classified by the length of time that the debts have been outstanding.

allocation an objective method by which indirect or overhead costs can be assigned to a productive department in order that these overheads may be recovered in the cost of the product or service.

amortization *see* depreciation

apportionment a subjective method by which indirect or overhead costs can be assigned to a productive department in order that these overheads may be recovered in the absorption cost of the product or service.

assets possessions of a business, which can be tangible or intangible.

avoidable costs costs which can be saved as a consequence of discontinuing an activity, service or product.

bad debts outstanding amounts due from debtors which are known to be uncollectable, or where there is reasonable doubt about their eventual collection.

balance sheet a schedule of possessions and obligations of a business, arranged in a format that demonstrates equality between them.

bank reconciliation statement a statement that reconciles the balance on a business's bank statement and the balance on its cash book. The reconciliation accounts for timing differences, unilateral entries and errors.

break-even point the point at which the sales revenue of a business exactly covers all its costs.

budgets monetary or quantitative tabulations of the planned future business activities and transactions to be undertaken by the organization. These tables are based on programmes determined in the first place by the strategic objectives of the organization.

capital capital in accounting terms represents the proportion of the total business assets financed by the owner or owners.

capital reserve a proportion of owner's capital which is represented by unrealized gains or profits from commercial transactions undertaken.

capital/revenue distinction this is the distinction made between business expenditure that leads to the acquisition of an asset expected to have value lasting for more than one accounting period, and expenditure that provides economic benefits for less than one financial period.

carriage incidental expenditure associated with the delivery of goods. Carriage costs associated with purchases are known as carriage inwards. Carriage costs associated with sales are known as carriage outwards. Carriage inwards is a trading account expense, whereas carriage outwards is a profit and loss account expense.

cash flow statement a statement which reconciles the net profit recognized by a business in a period and the net cash flow generated by that business over the same period of time. It also shows the sources of cash inflows and where and upon what the cash has been applied.

cash operating cycle the length of time that cash takes to be recycled through trading. This is normally calculated as debtor turnover and stock turnover less creditor turnover.

cashing-off slip a reconciliation of the till-roll total with actual cash takings for a given period.

cell the cell is a coordinate of the rows and columns of a spreadsheet. For example the top left hand cell in a spreadsheet is known as A1.

column width this function allows the spreadsheet user to widen or narrow the width of the column. On later spreadsheet versions this is achieved by clicking on the column border of the desired column with the mouse, and dragging the border out or into the required width.

compounded cash fund the terminal value of cash invested now at a fixed rate of return, and for a given number of equal periods.

consistency concept one of the fundamental concepts of accounting. It determines that acounting methods and policies should be applied consistently between different businesses and over different accounting periods.

contribution the difference between total or unit revenue and total or unit variable costs.

contribution-to-sales ratio contribution as a proportion of sales.

copy function this function allows the spreadsheet user to copy the contents of a cell or cell to another location within the spreadsheet. This function is particularly useful as it allows the user to copy formulae across from one cell or cells to another area, and the formulae will automatically be adjusted to take into account the relative change of location.

cost expenditure classified by specific activities within the business. Costs are categorized in terms of who consumed them, why and where they were consumed.

cost centre a part of the business or department to which costs can be attributed, and over which individuals within that department have a significant level of influence or control.

cost of capital the overall rate of return required by investors in the business, both lenders and owners, which must be exceeded if a capital investment programme is to be undertaken to increase the economic wealth of those investors.

cost-plus pricing pricing policies which focus on covering the costs of the business rather than with reference to market conditions and competitive position.

cost–volume–profit chart a restatement of a break-even chart which shows profitability against sales and output rather than showing revenues and costs as separate functions.

creditor financial obligations to third parties of a business.

creditor turnover ratio average creditor balances divided by credit purchases or cost of sales.

current accounts the proportion of the capital of partners that has been accumulated through profitable trading, net of drawings.

current assets possessions of the business that can in theory be converted to cash within a period of one year.

current liabilities financial obligations which must in theory be met within a period of one year.

current ratio current assets divided by current liabilities.

debentures fixed-interest long-term loans. The debenture certificate stipulates the outstanding loan, when it is redeemable, the annual percentage rate of interest and when it is payable.

debtors debts owing to the business from third parties.

debtor turnover ratio average debtor balances divided by credit sales.

demand curve a function expressing the average price charged for a product or service as a function of the total quantity demanded of that product or service.

depreciation the proportion of the cost or value of a fixed asset which has been charged against the gross profit of the business, either in the current financial period or cumulatively.

direct expenses the part of the prime cost of a product which is not made up of either direct labour costs or direct material costs.

direct labour the proportion of the prime cost taken up by remunerating employees that are directly involved in the production of products or provision of services.

direct materials the proportion of the prime cost taken up by expenditure on materials directly used in the production process or in the provision of a service.

discount the proportion of the invoice price foregone by the seller in order to sell greater numbers of products or services per invoice, or to be paid immediately or promptly.

discounted cash fund future monetary receipts expressed in present value terms after taking into account an appropriate rate of return.

discount factor the percentage rate of return which most closely represents the opportunity cost of using financial resources in one way rather than in the next best available alternative.

disposal account the assessment of how accurate the business has been in allocating the cost or value of a fixed asset over its useful economic life. If a profit is made on disposal, the business has overprovided for depreciation and the overprovision must be added to profit in the current period. If the business has made a loss, it has underprovided for depreciation and the underprovision must be charged as additional depreciation in the current period.

DOS disk operating system. This is the system which allows the user to interface with the computer and its capabilities. Before the Windows environment was developed, it was necessary for computer users to have at least a basic knowledge of the main commands of DOS, in order to access, run, or organise files. Windows allows DOS commands to be used much more easily and quickly, via mouse based control systems.

double entry the system of recording the financial effects of transactions undertaken by the business based on a mathematical system devised by Pacioli, a Venetian mathematician.

The system is based around recording a transaction as two equal but opposite monetary amounts.

drawings the monetary amount of the net assets withdrawn from the business for the owner's consumption.

dual aspect *see* double entry.

earnings per share a measure of the net profit per issued share available to ordinary shareholders after tax and extraordinary items. Normally expressed in pence.

economic order quantity a formula which calculates the optimum level of stocks to carry within a business. The formula takes into account the countervailing effects of decreasing ordering costs and increasing holding costs.

economic value the valuation placed on an asset, combination of assets or a business; it is determined by the present value of the future net cash flows that are expected to be generated.

elastic demand the range of quantity demanded over which price charged and revenue generated moves in the opposite direction.

employee's NI this is a tax on employees which is charged in bands on the pay of employees. As with PAYE the employer is responsible for paying this liability to the Inland Revenue monthly.

employer's NI this is an employer's tax liability on employment paid at various rates, in bands, on the employee pay and payable monthly to the Inland Revenue.

error errors in the recording of financial transactions may or may not violate the double-entry rules. Where recording errors violate the double-entry convention, the discrepancy will be revealed in the trial balance. Errors which do not contravene the double-entry convention may not be so revealed. These errors include errors of commission, errors of principle, errors of ommission and compensating errors.

exchange an economic interaction between two parties where both give up a possession or right they value less in order to acquire a possession or right they value more highly.

expenditure under the accruals concept, expenditure is the sum of all attributable charges made against the revenue an organization generates in a given financial period.

expenses financial accounting expenses are broad subclassifications of total expenditure made by the business in a given financial period.

extended trial balance a development of the trial balance used as a working paper, which is most effectively used on a spreadsheet. The extended trial balance allows the user to post adjustments in columns to the right of the original trial balance, which when summed across give a final adjusted trial balance, from which final accounts may be prepared.

FIFO first in, first out stock valuation system is a cost-based valuation system that assumes the earliest less costly stock should be matched against sales revenue. When prices are rising the system tends to overstate profit and stock valuations.

financial gearing this is a measure of the extent to which a business is financed by long-term fixed-interest debt finance as against shareholders' funds.

fixed assets these are the possessions of the business which form the infrastructural environment within which trading activities take place. Fixed assets are generally defined as having a value which can be attributed to more than one accounting period.

fixed costs these are costs which are consumed with respect to the passage of time as opposed to being consumed with respect to the volume of activity. These costs are sometimes called period costs for that reason.

flexible budget this is a budget that tabulates planned revenues and costs based on the actual volume of activity achieved. The flexible budget is therefore more meaningful when comparing budgeted revenues and costs with actual revenues and costs at the achieved level of activity.

formula a formula enables the relationship between the contents of other cell references to be processed and displayed in a current cell. Example +(A4+A6) displays the sum of the contents of cells A4 and A6 at the current cell location.

gearing ratio this is normally calculated as long-term debt divided by total long-term capital employed.

going-concern concept a fundamental accounting concept which determines that income recognition and balance sheet valuations should be made under the assumption that the business will continue to trade into the foreseeable future.

goodwill goodwill is the monetary value of the difference between what a buyer is prepared to pay for a business as a going concern and the fair value of the net assets as disclosed on that business's balance sheet. There are several reasons why the buyer of a going concern is willing to pay more for a business than the fair value of its net assets: reputation, customer loyalty, location, staff capabilities, etc. Essentially though, goodwill represents the difference between accounting 'valuation' and economic value.

gross profit margin a primary ratio which indicates the basic profitability of a business, gross profit margin is gross profit divided by sales. It is a ratio that should remain reasonably stable over time, but is affected by changes in pricing policy, by purchasing costs, or in the case of a manufacturer, by changes in production costs.

help function most if not all software include help facilities. The help facility may be accessed quickly and easily while working. It contains step by step instructions, and has comprehensive menus, sub menus, and indexes.

Hubbart formula this is a formula used by the hotel industry in order to determine pricing policy. It is a cost-plus system that works back from a required rate of return on capital employed to the required revenue from accommodation or from restaurants and bars.

icon this is a visual representation of a function, command or feature. Within a spreadsheet these are usually arranged in rows along the top of the screen known as tool bars.

income and expenditure account this is the equivalent financial report of a 'not for profit' organization to the profit and loss account of a commercial organization. The report discloses income and expenditure from various sources calculated using accounting concepts and conventions. The final figure is known as an excess of income over expenditure or as an excess of expenditure over income.

indirect costs these are the costs of an organization which are not consumed directly in the primary production or service provision. They are consumed in functions which support the primary activity of the business, and may be very difficult to associate with that activity in any meaningful or objective way if the association is remote.

inelastic demand the range of quantity demanded over which price charged and revenue generated moves in the same direction.

intangible assets these are classified as the fixed assets of a business; they are based on valuations to do with rights as opposed to physical possession. The main example is goodwill, which could be described as the owner's right to benefit from future net cash inflows. Other examples are legal rights, patents, licences, and ownership of brands.

input tax VAT on the cost of goods and services paid for by the business; it is normally reclaimable against the VAT collected from customers.

investment centre this is the most sophisticated and devolved type of performance measure, where responsible individuals are held accountable for revenues generated, costs incurred and capital invested.

journal the journal is a type of daybook. Specifically the journal in financial accounting is a record of certain financial transactions which are not recorded in other books of original entry. These transactions comprise the least prolific types, such as the purchasing and disposal of fixed assets, the raising and redemption of financial capital, and the correction of errors.

liabilities the separate classification of a business's obligations to outside parties that have financed its possessions.

lifetime cash surplus the aggregate net cash flow associated with a capital investment project over its economic lifetime.

LIFO a last in, first out stock valuation system is a cost-based valuation system that assumes the latest more costly stock should be matched against sales revenue. When prices are rising the system tends to understate profit and stock valuations.

limiting factor normally the potential output and sales volume of a product or service is restricted by some limiting factor, either demand related or resource related. The effective demand for a product or service is finite, as are the available resources required to make it available. Where one factor is so limited that a decision has to be made about which product or service should take priority, the unit contribution per unit of the limiting factor should be used as a basis for that decision.

linear programming a mathematical technique to find the optimum combination of products and services under multiple constraints. For two products or services, the optimum combination can be found graphically or solved by simultaneous equations. For three or more products or services, the optimum may be found using a technique called simplex.

liquidity a measure of a business's ability or potential ability to meet obligations to its third-party investors.

make-or-buy decisions where a business has to decide between producing in-house or purchasing from third parties. In financial terms the business should compare the variable or avoidable costs of producing in-house with the buying-in price from outside suppliers, and choose the option with the lowest cost. Qualitative judgements may override the purely financial considerations.

management efficiency ratio this measures how well the business is providing financial reward to all long-term investors. It is calculated by dividing net profit before interest and tax by the long-term capital employed.

marginal cost the marginal cost of producing or providing a product or service is defined as the change in total costs caused by producing or providing one additional unit of product or service.

marginal revenue the marginal revenue of selling a product or service is defined as the change in total revenue caused by selling one additional unit of product or service. It is not the same as the price.

margin of opportunity this measures the scope of a business to increase its productive output within the short term. It is calculated by dividing short-run capacity less current sales volume by the current sales volume.

margin of safety this measures the vulnerability of the business to a downturn in sales volume. It is calculated by taking the current sales volume less the break-even units divided by the current sales volume. It measures the extent to which sales volume may fall before the business moves into losses.

money measurement concept a fundamental accounting concept which determines that financial records and reports are objective. It requires that where a definite and verifiable monetary value cannot be placed upon a transaction, this transaction cannot be formally recognized.

net present value *see* economic value, discounted cash flow.

net profit margin this measures the extent to which attributable revenue within a financial period has exceeded total attributable expenditure charged against that revenue in the same financial period. As a ratio it is net profit divided by sales.

net realizable value this is the value placed on an asset assuming that asset's imminent disposal. With stocks it is defined as the proceeds from sale net of additional costs incurred in making it available for sale. The prudence concept determines that stocks should be valued at the lower of cost or net realizable value. This valuation can only be placed generally on assets if the going-concern assumption is abandoned.

occupancy ratios efficiency ratios that indicate the utilization of assets in hotels and similar businesses. Examples are room-nights occupied as a proportion of available room-nights in a given period.

operational gearing the extent to which a company's costs are fixed as against variable. Operational gearing is related to financial gearing in that it indicates the vulnerability of a company to a downturn in business.

opportunity cost this measures what has been given up in order to engage in a particular transaction. It springs from the notion of exchange. Exchange takes place where both parties become better off as a result of that transaction, i.e. where the benefits derived from the acquisition of a product or service exceed the cost of giving up the exchanged product or service. Opportunity cost is strictly defined as the cost of doing something measured in terms of the value of the lost opportunity to pursue the best alternative activity with the same resources.

ordinary shareholders the owners of a limited company who have democratic control over that company by exercising their voting rights, and who have the final claim on the net assets and profits of the business. Although ordinary shares are comparatively risky investments, they tend to produce commensurate levels of return.

output tax payable to Customs and Excise, it is the VAT charged in the prices of goods that are sold to consumers. The liability to output tax can be reduced by the total of input tax paid during the same period.

overhead costs *see* indirect costs.

overhead recovery rate this is the rate at which indirect costs incurred by a business are to be charged to the production or provision of physical units of product or service per hour spent on them. The overhead recovery rate is calculated by taking the total allocated and apportioned costs to a productive department and dividing this by the normal productive capacity of the department in a given period of time, as measured in labour or machine hours.

partnership a partnership is a business with unlimited liability in multiple ownership which has between two and twenty owners. How partnerships are defined and how they are to operate in financial terms in the absence of explicit or implicit agreement between partners is governed by the 1890 Partnership Act.

partnership agreement partnership agreements may be expressly documented or implied by past behaviour and actions. They can involve such matters as the respective rewards that partners should receive in compensation for financial, physical or mental investment in the partnership business. These rewards can include an agreed rate of return on capital originally invested, agreed salaries for working partners, and an agreed profit-sharing ratio for appropriating residual profits. The agreement can include provisions to charge partners interest on drawings made on the business, and agreed rates of interest for loans advanced.

payback method a popular and intuitively acceptable method for discriminating between alternative projects competing for scarce resources. The method discriminates between projects on the basis of how quickly the original cash investment is repaid by way of future net cash inflows. The method is prudent but somewhat crude as it ignores net cash flows beyond the payback period, and ignores the timings of the cash flows within the payback period.

PAYE a system whereby an employee's liabilities to tax are deducted by their employer from their gross wages. Employers are then held responsible for making payments of these liabilities on behalf of their employees to the Inland Revenue.

petty cash imprest system a subordinate cash book which deals predominantly with frequent and minor cash transactions; it is funded by a single debit topping up the fund to a predetermined fixed amount every period.

preference shareholder the preferential shareholder, unlike the ordinary shareholder, does not usually have voting rights. The preference share has a prior claim over ordinary shares on the profits and net assets of the business. These shares carry a fixed percentage rate of dividend, which must be paid if profits suffice.

prepayments payments made by a business in the current financial period which relate to expenditure due in a future accounting period.

prime cost the total direct cost of producing or providing a product or service. This comprises direct material costs, direct labour costs and direct expenses.

product cost structure this is a statement which breaks down the cost of producing or providing one unit of product or service. It subclassifies the unit cost of a product into direct costs (prime cost), and indirect costs. These costs are itemized by productive department or cost centre.

profit and loss reserve *see* retained profits.

profit centre a department or activity centre whose management is responsible for both revenues generated and costs incurred.

profit reconciliation statement this is a statement that begins with the budgeted profit at the standard volume of activity, and via a series of adverse or favourable variances, works out the actual profit earned at the actual volume of activity.

provision for bad debts the concept of prudence requires that recognized profits and balance sheet values should be conservatively reported and should not be overstated. Unrealized profits should not be recognized, whereas probable losses should be recognized as soon as they are anticipated. The provision for bad debts requires the business to recognize that a proportion of

the balances on the debtors ledger should be provided against as doubtful. This is achieved by making a provision against net profits and reviewing this provision periodically.

provision for taxation since 1990 all UK companies have had to pay corporation tax liabilities nine months after the last day of their financial accounting period. At the end of each period a provision is therefore recognized in the profit and loss account, which appears in the balance sheet as a current liability.

prudence concept a fundamental accounting concept which requires that profits should not be recognized until realized, and that all losses should be anticipated and provided against at the earliest possible opportunity.

quick ratio a variant on the current ratio which measures the liquidity of a business; it is more conservative because it excludes stock valuations from the current asset figure on the grounds they are the least liquid of the current assets within the trading cycle.

rates of VAT VAT rates depend on the nature of the goods or services. The current VAT rates are 0%, 5% and 17.5%.

ratio analysis a method for systematically comparing the financial performance and status of a business over time and between organizations. Based on two-dimensional comparisons, ratio analysis is useful in making relative assessments of aspects of performance, but its conclusions are only as good as the underlying financial data upon which they are based.

realization account this is a ledger account used to transfer the assets and liabilities of a business that is about to be dissolved or taken over. Any proceeds from the disposal of these net assets, any expenses incurred, or the total consideration made for the going concern as a whole are also posted to the account. The final balance on the account represents a profit or loss on realization, which is credited to the capital account of the owner(s).

recreation and leisure clubs these are organizations which have non-commercial objectives but which like all organizations need to be properly controlled in financial terms and need to be accountable to their members.

reducing-balance method one of the main methods of depreciating fixed assets. The method is based on the premise that periodic depreciation charges against profits are higher in the earlier years of an asset's economic life than in the later years. The method is based on a mathematical formula which inevitably means the asset will never be fully depreciated; this accords with the view that all fixed assets will always have some value, however old, worn or obsolete. The charge is normally calculated as $x\%$ of the last known net book value of the fixed asset.

remote costs indirect costs which cannot be identified objectively with the productive activities of a business. Remote costs may include certain administrative, establishment, and sales and marketing costs.

retail schemes these are accounting schemes set up by Customs and Excise to allow certain businesses to make standing order payments of VAT, which are then adjusted at the end of the financial year.

retained profits the net profits of a business which are not immediately consumed by the owners by way of drawings or dividends. These retained profits are added to the capital of the owners at the end of the financial period and form part of the owners' funds within the 'financed by' section of the balance sheet.

return periods there are four three-monthly periods for which liability to VAT is recognized. Businesses are allocated particular return periods depending upon the month of their year-end.

returns sales or purchases which have been cancelled for some reason. They are either returns or allowances related to customers or suppliers, caused by faulty goods, damaged goods or wrongly processed orders. Returns and allowances are recognized using credit notes. Sales returns are deducted from sales in the trading account. Purchase returns are deducted from purchases in the trading account.

revaluation reserve this is the part of owners' capital which is represented by the subsequent revaluation of fixed assets. Where the market value of a fixed asset or investment materially increases beyond its purchase cost, it is permissible to revalue this asset. Then both the asset value and a revaluation reserve are increased. A revaluation reserve represents an unrealized gain as far as shareholders are concerned, so it is classified as non-distributable.

revenue reserves *see* retained profits.

ROCE return on capital employed. ROCE expresses income as a proportion of the capital invested by those concerned.

scope of VAT this is a term describing the extent to which VAT is chargeable upon goods and services. There are still several categories of goods and services which are exempt from VAT.

separate entity concept a fundamental concept which requires that the financial transactions of a business are treated entirely separately from those of its owners.

share premium that proportion of the capital of ordinary shareholders which is represented by

the difference between the issue price and the par or nominal value of shares issued.

SMP statutory maternity pay. This is a capped benefit paid by employers to female employees when they are absent due to childbirth, and is effectively recoverable from the Inland Revenue.

spreadsheet a software package which enables the user to enter, sort, process, manipulate, analyse, and present numerical and other data easily, quickly, accurately, and professionally. The spreadsheet is divided up into labelled columns along the top and numbered rows down the side. The coordinates of the rows and columns are known as cells.

S-shaped curve the shape of the variable-cost function as determined by economic theory. It is based on the argument that, up to a point within the short-run capacity of a business, there are several reasons why average unit variable costs will fall, until the law of diminishing returns causes them to increase as far as the short-term capacity of the business.

SSP statutory sick pay. This is a capped benefit paid by employers to employees when they are sick and is effectively recoverable from the Inland Revenue.

standard costing a system based on agreeing and setting monetary and physical targets for activities and functions based on figures which are both challenging for and achievable by those working with them. These standard values or quantities must be set at an appropriate level which takes into account the motivation of the individuals ultimately held responsible for their achievement.

stocks these are the least liquid of the current assets. Stocks can come in a variety of forms. A manufacturer can carry raw materials, work-in-progress and finished goods. A trading or service organization may carry finished goods such as food or beverages, but may also carry consumables necessary for the proper operation of the business. Stocks can be valued in several ways (*see* FIFO, LIFO, WAVCO).

stock turnover ratio this is a measure which takes into account the levels of stocks held and how quickly they are rotated. Stock turnover ratio can be calculated by taking the average stock level and dividing it by the periodic cost of sales.

straight-line method the simplest and most common method for depreciating fixed assets. It is based on the notion that depreciation is largely a function of time. The periodic depreciation charge is calculated by taking the cost of the asset less its expected residual value and dividing this by the anticipated economic life in accounting periods. The charge is normally described as $x\%$ of the cost of the asset.

strategic planning the starting-point for planning based on broad objectives set for an organization following the audit of environmental influences and internal resource constraints. The strategic plan is usually framed over a period of three to seven years and is underpinned by an annual planning cycle based on a programme of budgets.

subscriptions the predominant source of income for recreation and leisure clubs. Subscription income is credited to the income and expenditure account as determined by the accruals concept. Subscription income can arrive in the form of annual or life memberships.

sum function this function allows the user to quickly add together the sum of a row, column, or block of cells at the current cell location. Example: =SUM(A1.Z100). This formula sums the contents of all cells 26 columns across the screen and 100 rows down the screen in the current cell location.

sum-of-digits method a simpler method for calculating depreciation than the reducing-balance method, which allocates depreciation in a similar fashion.

sunk costs costs which have already been incurred and which by definition are unavoidable. Decisions concerning the efficient allocation of scarce resources require that incurred expenditure is ignored; only future alternatives should be taken into consideration.

suspense account this is a temporary ledger account which contains the aggregate balances of double-entry errors resulting from the recording of financial transactions.

SWOT analysis a technique for strategic planning that involves an internal audit and an external audit. SWOT is an acronym for strengths, weaknesses, opportunities and threats.

tax code a letter denoting employee status followed by the total annual free pay taking into account any entitlements and allowances.

tickets sales invoices for businesses predominantly used within the hospitality, tourism and leisure sector. Tickets represent negative credit, where the service is paid for before it is enjoyed by the customer.

tool bar a tool bar is a row of icons representing functions, commands, or features of the software being used. These may be activated by clicking with the mouse pointer.

transaction the financial consequence of an agreement to exchange goods or services between two parties. A transaction can involve the actual transfer of goods and monetary value, or a promise to make such a transfer at some time in the future.

trial balance this is a list of balances for financial ledger accounts which, if double-entry principles have been followed properly, will lead to a zero sum total.

unappropriated profits *see* retained profits.

utility the quantification of the satisfaction to be derived from the consumption of economic goods and services. Exchange is the process which results from individuals seeking to increase the satisfaction they derive from their possessions or rights.

value added an economic term representing the wealth created by a nation, a business or even an individual. Value added is defined as sales less bought-in goods and services. What is defined as bought-in and what is defined as added value is a source of debate and controversy.

variance the differences between standard values and quantities budgeted for, and those actually achieved.

variance analysis report a report which explains the significant variances as identified in the profit reconciliation statement. (*see* profit reconcilitaion statement). The variance analysis report should attempt to look behind the figures and identify real business problems and opportunities, and make valid recommendations to management. The report should also attempt to relate and link codependent variances.

VAT value added tax. A tax introduced in 1973 which effectively taxes the consumption of goods and is collected in stages throughout the commercial value chain.

VAT return a form called VAT 100 to be completed by all business liable to VAT. It summarizes output and input tax, and it identifies liabilities to or claims from Customs and Excise.

VAT tax point this is the point at which a VAT transaction is recognized. Businesses may elect for VAT to be payable on a cash or credit basis.

WAVCO one of the three main methods of valuing stocks based on historical costs. The method has a number of variants, but the most popular and useful is to aggregate the values of stocks after each receipt of goods then divide them by the number of units held in store. The method will result in the profit and stock valuation being somewhere between FIFO and LIFO valuations.

Windows an operating system environment that allows the user to access, run, and organise files by using the mouse. A Windows system avoids the need for users to understand the underlying disk operating system language which drives it.

INDEX

UNIVERSITY OF GLAMORGAN
PRIFYSGOL MORGANNWG

Learning Resources
Centre